The Topical Bible
Concordance

The Topical Bible Concordance

Edited with additional material
by

D. M. Miller

"Search the Scriptures." John 5:39

Abingdon
Nashville

The Topical Bible Concordance

A FESTIVAL BOOK

Copyright Lutterworth Press
All rights reserved

Festival edition published by Abingdon October, 1977

ISBN 0-687-42390-2
Printed in the United States of America

Introduction

by

The Rev. W. GRAHAM SCROGGIE, D.D. *(Edin.)*

THIS is not just another ordinary Bible Concordance, for with such works we are well supplied, including Cruden's, Young's and Strong's. *The Topical Bible Concordance* omits the most of what they supply, and supplies, by reason of its form, what they do not. The standard concordances do not present subjects, but only the occurrences of words, but in this book words are classified in subjects, so that the preacher and teacher may have ready access to what the Bible says on some 313 themes which he may wish to use.

The difference between Scripture and theology is one of arrangement. Scripture supplies theology with its materials, and theology collects, classifies, and correlates them. A florist will supply you with many kinds of seed, but it is for you so to arrange the seeds in your soil as to make beds of flowers. All that we need to know about God, Christ, the Holy Spirit, Man, Sin, Salvation, and many another theme is in the Bible, but the doctrines of these subjects can be known only by the mobilizing and systematizing of them, for God will not do for us what He has given us the power to do for ourselves.

The subjects in this book are set out in alphabetical order. There is a list of these topics given in the back of the book. He who will carefully study these subjects with an open Bible will find himself personally enriched, and better equipped to lead others into the truth. Of course this publication is very far from being complete, but it is a most useful addition to the busy worker's library. It has long been out of print, and so its reissue should be widely welcomed, and its portable form is an additional advantage.

Editor's Preface

THE plan of this book is to provide topical outlines of a variety of major themes for the guidance of students and workers engaged in Christian service at home and in all parts of the world.

The study of the Bible topically is one of the most interesting and perhaps one of the most fruitful methods. The value of these outlines to the busy Christian worker and missionary overseas is incalculable.

The outlines provide the basic material for specific subjects or for a series of studies under such subjects as The Gospel, The Holy Spirit, Christian Life and Service—and a host of other matters. The value of *The Topical Bible Concordance* to Christian workers cannot be overstressed, providing as it does a balanced framework, skilfully prepared by master builders of the Christian faith.

In many foreign countries, nationals are often without either a concordance or a Bible containing references, and here is a compilation of vital subjects which cannot but give direction and inspiration and provide sure foundations for a healthy and useful Christian up-building.

The original MSS. of this volume made its appearance over one hundred years ago, dispensing blessing and giving spiritual direction to multitudes. This up-to-date issue, slightly revised and edited to meet present-day requirements, is sent forth with the prayer, that under God it may fulfil its mission of goodwill and sound teaching to the Christians of this generation.

D.M.M.

The Topical Bible Concordance

NOTE. In order to save space, reference is often made to a *single verse*, although the matter referred to may be contained in several verses in connexion with it; therefore, *let reference be made to the context.*

ACCESS TO GOD

Is of God. *Ps.* 65: 4.

Is by Christ. *John* 10: 7, 9. *John* 14: 6. *Rom.* 5: 2. *Eph.* 2: 13. *Eph.* 3: 12. *Heb.* 7: 19, 25. *Heb.* 10: 19. 1 *Pet.* 3: 18. 1 *Tim.* 2: 5.

Is by the Holy Ghost. *Eph.* 2: 18.

Obtained through faith. *Acts* 14: 27. *Rom.* 5: 2. *Eph.* 3: 12. *Heb.* 11: 6.

Follows upon reconciliation to God. *Col.* 1: 21, 22.

In prayer. *Deut.* 4: 7. *Matt.* 6: 6. 1 *Pet.* 1: 17. (See Prayer)

In his temple. *Ps.* 15: 1. *Ps.* 27: 4. *Ps.* 43: 3. *Ps.* 65: 4.

To obtain mercy and grace. *Heb.* 4: 16.

A privilege of saints. *Deut.* 4: 7. *Ps.* 15: 2–5. *Ps.* 23: 6. *Ps.* 24: 3, 4.

Saints have, with confidence. *Eph.* 3: 12. *Heb.* 4: 16. *Heb.* 10: 19, 22.

Vouchsafed to repenting sinners. *Hos.* 14: 2. *Joel* 2: 12. (See Repentance)

Saints earnestly seek. *Ps.* 27: 4. *Ps.* 42: 1, 2. *Ps.* 43: 3. *Ps.* 84: 1, 2.

The wicked commanded to seek. *Isa.* 55: 6, 7. *Jas.* 4: 8.

Urge others to seek. *Isa.* 2: 3. *Jer.* 31: 6.

Promises connected with. *Ps.* 145: 18. *Isa.* 55: 3. *Matt.* 6: 6. *Jas.* 4: 8.

Blessedness of. *Ps.* 16: 11. *Ps.* 65: 4. *Ps.* 73: 28.

Typified. *Lev.* 16: 12–15, with *Heb.* 10: 19–22.

Exemplified. MOSES, *Exod.* 24: 2. *Exod.* 34: 4–7. *Deut.* 5: 5.

ADOPTION

Explained. 2 *Cor.* 6: 18.

Is according to promise. *Rom.* 9: 8. *Gal.* 3: 29.

Is by faith. *Gal.* 3: 7, 26.

Is of God's grace. *Ezek.* 16: 3–6. *Rom.* 4: 16, 17. *Eph.* 1: 5, 6, 11.

Is through Christ. *John* 1: 12. *Gal.* 4: 4, 5. *Eph.* 1: 5. *Heb.* 2: 10, 13.

Saints predestinated unto. *Rom.* 8: 29. *Eph.* 1: 5, 11.

Of Gentiles, predicted. *Hos.* 2: 23. *Rom.* 9: 24–26. *Eph.* 3: 6.

The Adopted are gathered together in one by Christ. *John* 11: 52.

New birth connected with. *John* 1: 12, 13.

The Holy Spirit is a Witness of. *Rom.* 8: 16.

Being led by the Spirit is an evidence of. *Rom.* 8: 14.

Saints receive the Spirit of. *Rom.* 8: 15. *Gal.* 4: 6.

A privilege of saints. *John* 1: 12. 1 *John* 3: 1.

Saints become brethren of Christ by. *John* 20: 17. *Heb.* 2: 11, 12.

Saints wait for the final consummation of. *Rom.* 8: 19, 23. 1 *John* 3: 2.

Subjects saints to the fatherly discipline of God. *Deut.* 8: 5. 2 *Sam.* 7: 14. *Prov.* 3: 11, 12. *Heb.* 12: 5–11.

God is long-suffering and merciful towards the partakers of. *Jer.* 31: 1, 9, 20.

Should lead to holiness. 2 *Cor.* 6: 17, 18, with 2 *Cor.* 7: 1. *Phil.* 2: 15. 1 *John* 3: 2, 3.

Should Produce

Likeness to God. *Matt.* 5: 44, 45, 48. *Eph.* 5: 1.

Child-like confidence in God. *Matt.* 6: 25–34.

A desire for God's glory. *Matt.* 5: 16.

A spirit of prayer. *Matt.* 7: 7–11.

A love of peace. *Matt.* 5: 9.

A forgiving spirit. *Matt.* 6: 14.

A merciful spirit. *Luke* 6: 35, 36.

An avoidance of ostentation. *Matt.* 6: 1–4, 6, 18.

Safety of those who receive. *Prov.* 14: 26.

Confers a new name. *Num.* 6: 27. *Isa.* 62: 2. *Acts* 15: 17. (See Titles of Saints)

Entitles to an inheritance. *Matt.* 13: 43. *Rom.* 8: 17. *Gal.* 3: 29. *Gal.* 4: 7. *Eph.* 3: 6.

Is to be pleaded in prayer. *Isa.* 63: 16. *Matt.* 6: 9.

Illustrated. JOSEPH'S SONS, *Gen.* 48: 5, 14, 16, 22. MOSES, *Exod.* 2: 10. ESTHER, *Esther* 2: 7.

Typified. ISRAEL, *Exod.* 4: 22. *Hos.* 11: 1. *Rom.* 9: 4.

Exemplified. SOLOMON, 1 *Chron.* 28: 6.

AFFECTIONS, THE

Should be supremely set upon God. *Deut.* 6: 5. *Mark* 12: 30.

Should be set

Upon the commandments of God. *Ps.* 19: 8–10. *Ps.* 119: 20, 97, 103, 167.

Upon the house and worship of God. 1 *Chron.* 29: 3. *Ps.* 26: 8. *Ps.* 27: 4. *Ps.* 84: 1, 2.

Upon the people of God. *Ps.* 16: 3. *Rom.* 12: 10. 2 *Cor.* 7: 13–15. 1 *Thess.* 2: 8.

Upon heavenly things. *Col.* 3: 1, 2.

Should be zealously engaged for God. *Ps.* 69: 9. *Ps.* 119: 139. *Gal.* 4: 18.

Christ claims the first place in. *Matt.* 10: 37. *Luke* 14: 26.

Enkindled by communion with Christ. *Luke* 24: 32.

Blessedness of making God the object of. *Ps.* 9: 114.

Should not grow cold. *Ps.* 106: 12, 13. *Matt.* 24: 12. *Gal.* 4: 15. *Rev.* 2: 4.

Of saints, supremely set on God. *Ps.* 42: 1. *Ps.* 73: 25. *Ps.* 119: 10.

Of the wicked, not sincerely set on God. *Isa.* 58: 1, 2. *Ezek.* 33: 31, 32. *Luke* 8: 13.

Carnal affections should be mortified. *Rom.* 8: 13. *Rom.* 13: 14. 1 *Cor.* 9: 27. *Col.* 3: 5. 1 *Thess.* 4: 5.

Carnal affections crucified in saints. *Rom.* 6: 6. *Gal.* 5: 24.

False teachers seek to captivate. *Gal.* 1: 10. *Gal.* 4: 17. 2 *Tim.* 3: 6. 2 *Pet.* 2: 3, 18. *Rev.* 2: 14, 20.

Of the wicked, are unnatural and perverted. *Rom.* 1: 31. 2 *Tim.* 3: 3. 2 *Pet.* 2: 10.

AFFLICTIONS

God appoints. 1 *Kings* 22: 19–23. 2 *Kings* 6: 33. *Job* 1: 6, 12. *Ps.* 66: 11. *Amos* 3: 6. *Mic.* 6: 9.

God dispenses, as He will. *Job* 11: 10. *Isa.* 10: 15. *Isa.* 45: 7.

God regulates the measure of. *Ps.* 80: 5. *Isa.* 9: 1. *Jer.* 46: 28.

God determines the continuance of. *Gen.* 15: 13, 14.

Num. 14: 33. *Isa.* 10: 25. *Jer.* 29: 10.

God does not willingly send. *Lam.* 3: 33.

Man is born to. *Job* 5: 6, 7. *Job* 14: 1.

Saints appointed to. 1 *Thess.* 3: 3.

Consequent upon the fall. *Gen.* 3: 16–19.

Sin produces. *Job* 4: 8. *Job* 20: 11. *Prov.* 1: 31.

Sin visited with. 2 *Sam.* 12: 14. *Ps.* 89: 30–32. *Isa.* 57: 17. *Acts* 13: 10, 11.

Often severe. *Job* 16: 7–16. *Ps.* 42: 7. *Ps.* 66: 12. *Jonah* 2: 3. *Rev.* 7: 14.

Always less than we deserve. *Ezra* 9: 13. *Ps.* 103: 10.

Frequently terminate in good. *Gen.* 50: 20. *Exod.* 1: 11, 12. *Deut.* 8: 15, 16. *Jer.* 24: 5, 6. *Ezek.* 20: 37.

Tempered with mercy. *Ps.* 78: 38, 39. *Ps.* 106: 43–46. *Isa.* 30: 18–21. *Lam.* 3: 32. *Mic.* 7: 6–9. *Nahum* 1: 12.

Saints are to expect. *John* 16: 33. *Acts* 14: 22.

Of saints, are comparatively light. *Acts* 20: 23, 24. *Rom.* 8: 18. 2 *Cor.* 4: 17.

Of saints, are but temporary. *Ps.* 30: 5. *Ps.* 103: 9. *Isa.* 54: 7, 8. *John* 16: 20. 1 *Pet.* 1: 6. 1 *Pet.* 5: 10.

Saints have joy under. *Job* 5: 17. *Jas.* 5: 11.

Of saints, end in joy and blessedness. *Ps.* 126: 5, 6. *Isa.* 61: 2, 3. *Matt.* 5: 4. 1 *Pet.* 4: 13, 14.

Often arise from the profession of the gospel. *Matt.* 24: 9. *John* 15: 21. 2 *Tim.* 3: 11, 12.

Exhibit the love and faithfulness of God. *Deut.* 8: 5. *Ps.*

119: 75. *Prov.* 3: 12. 1 *Cor.*
11: 32. *Heb.* 12: 6, 7. *Rev.*
3: 19.

AFFLICTED, SAINTS

God is with. *Ps.* 46: 5, 7. *Isa.*
43: 2.

God is a refuge and strength to.
Ps. 27: 5, 6. *Isa.* 25: 4. *Jer.*
16: 19. *Nahum* 1: 7.

God comforts. *Isa.* 49: 13.
Jer. 31: 13. *Matt.* 5: 4. 2 *Cor.*
1: 4, 5. 2 *Cor.* 7: 6.

God preserves. *Ps.* 34: 20.

God delivers. *Ps.* 34: 4, 19.
Prov. 12: 13. *Jer.* 39: 17, 18.

Christ is with. *John* 14: 18.

Christ supports. 2 *Tim.* 4: 17.
Heb. 2: 18.

Christ comforts. *Isa.* 61: 2.
Matt. 11: 28–30. *Luke* 7: 13.
John 14: 1. *John* 16: 33.

Christ preserves. *Isa.* 63: 9.
Luke 21: 18.

Christ delivers. *Rev.* 3: 10.

Should praise God. *Ps.* 13:
5, 6. *Ps.* 56: 8–10. *Ps.* 57: 6,
7. *Ps.* 7´: 20–23.

Should imitate Christ. *Heb.*
12: 1–3. 1 *Pet.* 2: 21–23.

Should imitate the prophets.
Jas. 5: 10.

Should be patient. *Luke* 21:
19. *Rom.* 12: 12. 2 *Thess.* 1:
4. *Jas.* 1: 4. 1 *Pet.* 2: 20.

Should be resigned. 1 *Sam.*
3: 18. 2 *Kings* 20: 19. *Job* 1:
21. *Ps.* 39: 9.

Should not despise chastening.
Job 5: 17. *Prov.* 3: 11. *Heb.*
12: 5.

Should acknowledge the justice of their chastisements.
Neh. 9: 33. *Job* 2: 10. *Isa.*
64: 5–7. *Lam.* 3: 39. *Mic.*
7: 9.

Should avoid sin. *Job* 34: 31,
32. *John* 5: 14.

Should trust in the goodness of
God. *Job* 13: 15. *Ps.* 71: 20.
2 *Cor.* 1: 9.

Should turn and devote themselves to God. *Ps.* 116: 7–9.
Jer. 50: 3, 4. *Hos.* 6: 1.

Should keep the pious resolu-
tions made during affliction.
Ps. 66: 13–15

Should be frequent in prayer.
Ps. 50: 15. *Ps.* 55: 16, 17.
(See Affliction, Prayer under)

Should take encouragement
from former mercies. *Ps.* 27:
9. 2 *Cor.* 1: 10.

Examples of afflicted saints.
JOSEPH, *Gen.* 39: 20–23. *Ps.*
105: 17–19. MOSES, *Heb.* 11:
25. ELI, 1 *Sam.* 3: 18. NEHE-
MIAH, *Neh.* 1: 4. JOB, *Job* 1:
20–22. DAVID, 2 *Sam.* 12: 15–
23. PAUL, *Acts* 20: 22–24.
Acts 21: 13. APOSTLES, 1 *Cor.*
4: 13. 2 *Cor.* 6: 4–10.

AFFLICTION, PRAYER UNDER

Exhortation to. *Jas.* 5: 13.

That God would consider our
trouble. 2 *Kings* 19: 16.
Neh. 9: 32. *Ps.* 9: 13. *Lam.*
5: 1.

For the presence and support of
God. *Ps.* 10: 1. *Ps.* 102: 2.

That the Holy Spirit may not
be withdrawn. *Ps.* 51: 11.

For divine comfort. *Ps.* 4: 6.
Ps. 119: 76.

For mitigation of troubles.
Ps. 39: 12, 13.

For deliverance. *Ps.* 25: 17,
22. *Ps.* 39: 10. *Isa.* 64: 9–12.
Jer. 17: 14.

For pardon and deliverance
from sin. *Ps.* 39: 8. *Ps.* 51:
1. *Ps.* 79: 8.

That we may be turned to God.

Ps. 80: 7. *Ps.* 85: 4–6. *Jer.* 31: 18.

For divine teaching and direction. *Job* 34: 32. *Ps.* 27: 11. *Ps.* 143: 10.

For increase of faith. *Mark* 9: 24.

For mercy. *Ps.* 6: 2. *Hab.* 3: 2.

For restoration to joy. *Ps.* 51: 8, 12. *Ps.* 69: 29. *Ps.* 90: 14, 15.

For protection and preservation from enemies. 2 *Kings* 19: 19. 2 *Chron.* 20: 12. *Ps.* 17: 8, 9.

That we may know the causes of our trouble. *Job* 6: 24. *Job* 13: 23, 24.

That we may be taught the uncertainty of life. *Ps.* 39: 4.

That we may be quickened. *Ps.* 143: 11.

AFFLICTION, CONSOLATION UNDER

God is the Author and Giver of. *Ps.* 23: 4. *Rom.* 15: 5. 2 *Cor.* 1: 3. 2 *Cor.* 7: 6. *Col.* 1: 11. 2 *Thess.* 2: 16, 17.

Christ is the Author and Giver of. *Isa.* 61: 2. *John* 14: 18. 2 *Cor.* 1: 5.

The Holy Ghost is the Author and Giver of. *John* 14: 16, 17. *John* 15: 26. *John* 16: 7. *Acts* 9: 31.

Promised. *Isa.* 51: 3, 12. *Isa.* 66: 13. *Ezek.* 14: 22, 23. *Hos.* 2: 14. *Zech.* 1: 17.

Through the Holy Scriptures. *Ps.* 119: 50, 76. *Rom.* 15: 4.

By ministers of the gospel. *Isa.* 40: 1, 2. 1 *Cor.* 14: 3. 2 *Cor.* 1: 4, 6.

Is abundant. *Ps.* 71: 21. *Isa.* 66: 11.

Is strong. *Heb.* 6: 18.

Is everlasting. 2 *Thess.* 2: 16.

Is a cause of praise. *Isa.* 12: 1. *Isa.* 49: 13.

Pray for. *Ps.* 119: 82.

Saints should administer to each other. 1 *Thess.* 4: 18. 1 *Thess.* 5: 11, 14.

Is sought in vain from the world. *Ps.* 69: 20. *Eccles.* 4: 1. *Lam.* 1: 2.

To those who mourn for sin. *Ps.* 51: 17. *Isa.* 1: 18. *Isa.* 40: 1, 2. *Isa.* 61: 1. *Mic.* 7: 18, 19. *Luke* 4: 18.

To the troubled in mind. *Ps.* 42: 5. *Ps.* 94: 19. *John* 14: 1, 27. *John* 16: 20, 22.

To those deserted by friends. *Ps.* 27: 10. *Ps.* 41: 9–12. *John* 14: 18. *John* 15: 18, 19.

To the persecuted. *Deut.* 33: 27.

To the poor. *Ps.* 10: 14. *Ps.* 34: 6, 9, 10.

To the sick. *Ps.* 41: 3.

To the tempted. *Rom.* 16: 20. 1 *Cor.* 10: 13. 2 *Cor.* 12: 9. *Jas.* 1: 12. *Jas.* 4: 7. 2 *Pet.* 2: 9. *Rev.* 2: 10.

In prospect of death. *Job* 19: 25, 26. *Ps.* 23: 4. *John* 14: 2. 2 *Cor.* 5: 1. 1 *Thess.* 4: 14. *Heb.* 4: 9. *Rev.* 7: 14–17. *Rev.* 14: 13.

Under the infirmities of age. *Ps.* 71: 9, 18.

AFFLICTIONS MADE BENEFICIAL

In promoting the glory of God. *John* 9: 1–3. *John* 11: 3, 4. *John* 21: 18, 19.

In exhibiting the power and faithfulness of God. *Ps.* 34: 19, 20. 2 *Cor.* 4: 8–11.

In teaching us the will of God.

Ps. 119: 71. *Isa.* 26: 9. *Mic.* 6: 9.

In turning us to God. *Deut.* 4: 30, 31. *Neh.* 1: 8, 9. *Ps.* 78: 34. *Isa.* 10: 20, 21. *Hos.* 2: 6, 7.

In keeping us from again departing from God. *Job* 34: 31, 32. *Isa.* 10: 20. *Ezek.* 14: 10, 11.

In leading us to seek God in prayer. *Judges* 4: 3. *Jer.* 31: 18. *Lam.* 2: 17–19. *Hos.* 5: 14, 15. *Jonah* 2: 1.

In convincing us of sin. *Job* 36: 8, 9. *Ps.* 119: 67. *Luke* 15: 16–18.

In leading us to confession of sin. *Num.* 21: 7. *Ps.* 32: 5. *Ps.* 51: 3–5.

In testing and exhibiting our sincerity. *Job* 23: 10. *Ps.* 66: 10. *Prov.* 17: 3.

In trying our faith and obedience. *Gen.* 22: 1, 2, with *Heb.* 11: 17. *Exod.* 15: 23–25. *Deut.* 8: 2, 16. 1 *Pet.* 1: 7. *Rev.* 2: 10.

In humbling us. *Deut.* 8: 3, 16. 2 *Chron.* 7: 13, 14. *Lam.* 3: 19, 20. 2 *Cor.* 12: 7.

In purifying us. *Eccles.* 7: 2, 3. *Isa.* 1: 25, 26. *Isa.* 48: 10. *Jer.* 9: 6, 7. *Zech.* 13: 9. *Mal.* 3: 2, 3.

In exercising our patience. *Ps.* 40: 1. *Rom.* 5: 3. *Jas.* 1: 3. 1 *Pet.* 2: 20.

In rendering us fruitful in good works. *John* 15: 2. *Heb.* 12: 10, 11.

In furthering the gospel. *Acts* 8: 3, 4. *Acts* 11: 19–21. *Phil.* 1: 12. 2 *Tim.* 2: 9, 10. 2 *Tim.* 4: 16, 17.

Exemplified. JOSEPH'S BRETHREN, *Gen.* 42: 21. JOSEPH, *Gen.* 45: 5, 7, 8. ISRAEL, *Deut.* 8: 3, 5. JOSIAH, 2 *Kings* 22: 19. HEZEKIAH, 2 *Chron.* 32: 25, 26. MANASSEH, 2 *Chron.* 33: 12. JONAH. *Jonah* 2: 7. PRODIGAL SON, *Luke* 15: 21.

AFFLICTED, DUTY TOWARD THE

To pray for them. *Acts* 12: 5. *Phil.* 1: 16, 19. *Jas.* 5: 14–16.

To sympathize with them. *Rom.* 12: 15. *Gal.* 6: 2.

To pity them. *Job* 6: 14.

To bear them in mind. *Heb.* 13: 3.

To visit them. *Jas.* 1: 27.

To comfort them. *Job* 16: 5. *Job* 29: 25. 2 *Cor.* 1: 4. 1 *Thess.* 4: 18.

To relieve them. *Job* 31: 19, 20. *Isa.* 58: 10. *Phil.* 4: 14. 1 *Tim.* 5: 10.

To protect them. *Ps.* 82: 3. *Prov.* 22: 22. *Prov.* 31: 5.

AFFLICTIONS OF THE WICKED, THE

God is glorified in. *Exod.* 14: 4. *Ezek.* 38: 22, 23.

God holds in derision. *Ps.* 37: 13. *Prov.* 1: 26, 27.

Are multiplied. *Deut.* 31: 17. *Job* 20: 12–18. *Ps.* 32: 10.

Are continual. *Job* 15: 20. *Eccles.* 2: 23. *Isa.* 32: 10.

Are often sudden. *Ps.* 73: 19. *Prov.* 6: 15. *Isa.* 30: 13. *Rev.* 18: 10.

Are often judicially sent. *Job* 21: 17. *Ps.* 107: 17. *Jer.* 30: 15.

Are for examples to others. *Ps.* 64: 7–9. *Zeph.* 3: 6, 7. 1 *Cor.* 10: 5–11. 2 *Pet.* 2: 6.

Are ineffectual of themselves, for their conversion. *Exod.*

9: 30. *Isa.* 9: 13. *Jer.* 2: 30. *Hag.* 2: 17.

Their persecution of saints, a cause of. *Deut.* 30: 7. *Ps.* 55: 19. *Zech.* 2: 9. 2 *Thess.* 1: 6.

Impenitence is a cause of. *Prov.* 1: 30, 31, *Ezek.* 24: 13. *Amos* 4: 6–12. *Zech.* 7: 11, 12. *Rev.* 2: 21, 22.

Sometimes humble them. 1 *Kings* 21: 27.

Frequently harden. *Neh.* 9: 28, 29. *Jer.* 5: 3.

Produce slavish fear. *Job* 15: 24. *Ps.* 73: 19. *Jer.* 49: 3, 5.

Saints should not be alarmed at. *Prov.* 3: 25, 26.

Exemplified. PHARAOH AND THE EGYPTIANS, *Exod.* 9: 14, 15. *Exod.* 14: 24, 25. AHAZIAH 2 *Kings* 1: 1–4. GEHAZI, 2 *Kings* 5: 27. JEHORAM, 2 *Chron.* 21: 12–19. UZZIAH, 2 *Chron.* 26: 19–21, AHAZ, etc., 2 *Chron.* 28: 5–8, 22.

ALLIANCE AND SOCIETY WITH THE ENEMIES OF GOD

Forbidden. *Exod.* 23: 32. *Exod.* 34: 12. *Deut.* 7: 2, 3. *Deut.* 13: 6, 8. *Joshua* 23: 6, 7. *Judges* 2: 2. *Ezra* 9: 12. *Prov.* 1: 10, 15. 2 *Cor.* 6: 14–17. *Eph.* 5: 11.

Lead to idolatry. *Exod.* 34: 15, 16. *Num.* 25: 1–8. *Deut.* 7: 4. *Judges* 3: 5–7. *Rev.* 2: 20.

Have led to murder and human sacrifice. *Ps.* 106: 37, 38.

Provoke the anger of God. *Deut.* 7: 4. *Deut.* 31: 16, 17. 2 *Chron.* 19: 2. *Ezra* 9: 13, 14. *Ps.* 106: 29, 40. *Isa.* 2: 6.

Provoke God to leave men to reap the fruits of them. *Joshua* 23: 12, 13. *Judges* 2: 1–3.

Are ensnaring. *Exod.* 23: 33. *Num.* 25: 18. *Deut.* 12: 30. *Deut.* 13: 6. *Ps.* 106: 36.

Are enslaving. 2 *Pet.* 2: 18, 19.

Are defiling. *Ezra* 9: 1, 2.

Are degrading. *Is.* 1: 23.

Are ruinous to spiritual interests. *Prov.* 29: 24. *Heb.* 12: 14, 15. 2 *Pet.* 3: 17.

Are ruinous to moral character. 1 *Cor.* 15: 33.

Are a proof of folly. *Prov.* 12: 11.

Children who enter into, bring shame upon their parents. *Prov.* 28: 7.

Evil consequences of. *Prov.* 28: 19. *Jer.* 51: 7.

The wicked are prone to. *Ps.* 50: 18. *Jer.* 2: 25.

The wicked tempt saints to. *Neh.* 6: 2–4.

Sin of, to be confessed, deeply repented of, and forsaken. *Ezra* 10th chap.

Involve saints in their guiltiness. 2 *John* 9–11. *Rev.* 18: 4.

Involve saints in their punishment. *Num.* 16: 26. *Jer.* 51: 6. *Rev.* 18: 4.

Unbecoming in those called saints. 2 *Chron.* 19: 2. 2 *Cor.* 6: 14–16. *Phil.* 2: 15.

Exhortations to shun all inducements to. *Prov.* 1: 10–15. *Prov.* 4: 14, 15. 2 *Pet.* 3: 17.

Exhortations to hate and avoid. *Prov.* 14: 7. *Rom.* 16: 17. 1 *Cor.* 5: 9–11. *Eph.* 5: 6, 7. 1 *Tim.* 6: 5. 2 *Tim.* 3: 5.

A call to come out from. *Num.* 16: 26. *Ezra* 10: 11.

Jer. 51: 6, 45. 2 *Cor.* 6: 17. 2 *Thess.* 3: 6. *Rev.* 18: 4.

Means of preservation from. *Prov.* 2: 10–20. *Prov.* 19: 27.

Blessedness of avoiding. *Ps.* 1: 1.

Blessedness of forsaking. *Ezra* 9: 12. *Prov.* 9: 6. 2 *Cor.* 6: 17, 18.

Saints grieve to meet with, in their intercourse with the world. *Ps.* 57: 4. *Ps.* 120: 5, 6. 2 *Pet.* 2: 7, 8.

Saints grieve to witness in their brethren. *Gen.* 26: 35. *Ezra* 9: 3. *Ezra* 10: 6.

Saints hate and avoid. *Ps.* 26: 4, 5. *Ps.* 31: 6. *Ps.* 101: 7. *Rev.* 2: 2.

Saints deprecate. *Gen.* 49: 6. *Ps.* 6: 8. *Ps.* 15: 4. *Ps.* 101: 4, 7. *Ps.* 119: 115. *Ps.* 139: 19.

Saints are separate from. *Exod.* 33: 16. *Ezra* 6: 21.

Saints should be circumspect when undesignedly thrown into. *Matt.* 10: 16. *Col.* 4: 5. 1 *Pet.* 2: 12.

Pious parents prohibit, to their children. *Gen.* 28: 1.

Persons in authority should denounce. *Ezra* 10: 9–11. *Neh.* 13: 23–27.

Punishment of. *Num.* 33: 56. *Deut.* 7: 4. *Joshua* 23: 13. *Judges* 2: 3. *Judges* 3: 5–8. *Ezra* 9: 7, 14. *Ps.* 106: 41, 42. *Rev.* 2: 16, 22, 23.

Exemplified. SOLOMON, 1 *Kings* 11: 1–8. REHOBOAM, 1 *Kings* 12: 8, 9. JEHOSHAPHAT, 2 *Chron.* 18: 3. 2 *Chron.* 19: 2. 2 *Chron.* 20: 35–38. JEHORAM, 2 *Chron.* 21: 6. AHAZIAH, 2 *Chron.* 22: 3–5. ISRAELITES, *Ezra* 9: 1, 2. ISRAEL, *Ezra* 44: 7. JUDAS ISCARIOT, *Matt.* 26: 14–16.

Examples of avoiding. MAN OF GOD, 1 *Kings* 13: 7–10. NEHEMIAH, etc., *Neh.* 6: 2–4. *Neh.* 10: 29–31. DAVID, *Ps.* 101: 4–7. *Ps.* 119: 115. JEREMIAH, *Jer.* 15: 17. JOSEPH OF ARIMATHEA, *Luke* 23: 51. CHURCH OF EPHESUS, *Rev.* 2: 6.

Examples of forsaking. ISRAELITES, *Num.* 16: 27. *Ezra* 6: 21, 22. *Ezra* 10: 3, 4, 16, 17. SONS OF THE PRIESTS, *Ezra* 10: 18, 19.

Examples of the judgments of God against. KORAH, etc., *Num.* 16: 32. AHAZIAH, 2 *Chron.* 22: 7, 8. JUDAS ISCARIOT, *Acts* 1: 18.

AMBITION

God condemns. *Gen.* 11: 7. *Isa.* 5: 8.

Christ condemns. *Matt.* 18: 1, 3, 4. *Matt.* 20: 25, 26. *Matt.* 23: 11, 12.

Saints avoid. *Ps.* 131: 1, 2.

Vanity of. *Job* 20: 5–9. *Job* 24: 24. *Ps.* 49: 11–20.

Leads to strife and contention. *Jas.* 4: 1, 2.

Punishment of. *Prov.* 17: 19. *Isa.* 14: 12–15. *Ezek.* 31: 10, 11. *Obad.* 3, 4.

Connected with

Pride. *Hab.* 2: 5.

Covetousness. *Hab.* 2: 8, 9.

Cruelty. *Hab.* 2: 12.

Exemplified. ADAM AND EVE, *Gen.* 3: 5, 6. BUILDERS OF BABEL, *Gen.* 11: 4. MIRIAM AND AARON, *Num.* 12: 2. KORAH, etc., *Num.* 16: 3. ABSALOM, 2 *Sam.* 15: 4. 2 *Sam.* 18: 18. ADONIJAH, 1 *Kings* 1: 5. SENNACHERIB, 2 *Kings* 19: 23. SHEBNA, *Isa.* 22: 16. SONS OF ZEBEDEE,

Matt. 20: 21. ANTICHRIST, 2 *Thess.* 2: 4. DIOTREPHES, 3 *John* 9.

AMUSEMENTS AND PLEASURES, WORLDLY

Belong to the works of the flesh. *Gal.* 5: 19, 21.

Are transitory. *Job* 21: 12, 13. *Heb.* 11: 25.

Are all vanity. *Eccles.* 2: 11.

Choke the word of God in the heart. *Luke* 8: 14.

Formed a part of idolatrous worship. *Exod.* 32: 4, 6, 19, with 1 *Cor.* 10: 7. *Judges* 16: 23–25.

Lead to
Rejection of God. *Job* 21: 14, 15.

Poverty. *Prov.* 21: 17.

Disregard of the judgments and works of God. *Isa.* 5: 12. *Amos* 6: 1–6.

Terminate in sorrow. *Prov.* 14: 13.

Are likely to lead to greater evil. *Job* 1: 5. *Matt.* 14: 6–8.

The wicked seek for happiness in. *Eccles.* 2: 1, 8.

Indulgence in
A proof of folly. *Eccles.* 7: 4.

A characteristic of the wicked. *Isa.* 47: 8. *Eph.* 4: 17, 19. 2 *Tim.* 3: 4. *Titus* 3: 3. 1 *Pet.* 4: 3.

A proof of spiritual death. 1 *Tim.* 5: 6.

An abuse of riches. *Jas.* 5: 1, 5.

Wisdom of abstaining from. *Eccles.* 7: 2, 3.

Shunned by the primitive saints. 1 *Pet.* 4: 3.

Abstinence from, seems strange to the wicked. 1 *Pet.* 4: 4.

Denounced by God. *Isa.* 5: 11, 12.

Exclude from the kingdom of God. *Gal.* 5: 21.

Punishment of. *Eccles.* 11: 9. 2 *Pet.* 2: 13.

Renunciation of, Exemplified. MOSES, *Heb.* 11: 25.

ANGELS

Created by God and Christ. *Neh.* 9: 6. *Col.* 1: 16.

Worship God and Christ. *Neh.* 9: 6. *Phil.* 2: 9–11. *Heb.* 1: 6.

Are ministering Spirits. 1 *Kings* 19: 5. *Ps.* 68: 17. *Ps.* 104: 4. *Luke* 16: 22. *Acts* 12: 7–11. *Acts* 27: 23. *Heb.* 1: 7, 14.

Communicate the will of God and Christ. *Dan.* 8: 16, 17. *Dan.* 9: 21–23. *Dan.* 10: 11. *Dan.* 12: 6, 7. *Matt.* 2: 13, 20. *Luke* 1: 19, 28. *Acts* 5: 20. *Acts* 8: 26. *Acts* 10: 5. *Acts* 27: 23. *Rev.* 1: 1.

Obey the will of God. *Ps.* 103: 20. *Matt.* 6: 10.

Execute the purposes of God. *Num.* 22: 22. *Ps.* 103: 21. *Matt.* 13: 39–42. *Matt.* 28: 2. *John* 5: 4. *Rev.* 5: 2.

Execute the judgments of God. 2 *Sam.* 24: 16. 2 *Kings* 19: 35. *Ps.* 35: 5, 6. *Acts* 12: 23. *Rev.* 16: 1.

Celebrate the praises of God. *Job* 38: 7. *Ps.* 148: 2. *Isa.* 6: 3. *Luke* 2: 12, 14. *Rev.* 5: 11, 12. *Rev.* 7: 11, 12.

The law given by the ministration of. *Ps.* 68: 17. *Acts* 7: 53. *Heb.* 2: 2.

Announced

The conception of Christ. *Matt.* 1: 20, 21. *Luke* 1: 31.

The birth of Christ. *Luke* 2: 10–12.

The resurrection of Christ. *Matt.* 28: 5–7. *Luke* 24: 23.

The ascension and second coming of Christ. *Acts* 1: 11.

The conception of John the Baptist. *Luke* 1: 13, 36.

Minister to Christ. *Matt.* 4: 11. *Luke* 22: 43. *John* 1: 51.

Are subject to Christ. *Eph.* 1: 21. *Col.* 1: 16. *Col.* 2: 10. 1 *Pet.* 3: 22.

Shall execute the purposes of Christ. *Matt.* 13: 41. *Matt.* 24: 31.

Shall attend Christ at his second coming. *Matt.* 16: 27. *Matt.* 25: 31. *Mark* 8: 38. 2 *Thess.* 1: 7.

Know and delight in the gospel of Christ. *Eph.* 3: 9, 10. 1 *Tim.* 3: 16. 1 *Pet.* 1: 12.

Ministration of, obtained by prayer. *Matt.* 26: 53. *Acts* 12: 5, 7.

Rejoice over every repentant sinner. *Luke* 15: 7, 10.

Have charge over the children of God. *Ps.* 34: 7. *Ps.* 91: 11, 12. *Dan.* 6: 22. *Matt.* 18: 10.

Are of different orders. *Isa.* 6: 2. 1 *Thess.* 4: 16. 1 *Pet.* 3: 22. *Jude* 9. *Rev.* 12: 7.

Not to be worshipped. *Col.* 2: 18. *Rev.* 19: 10. *Rev.* 22: 9.

Are examples of meekness. 2 *Pet.* 2: 11. *Jude* 9.

Are wise. 2 *Sam.* 14: 20.

Are mighty. *Ps.* 103: 20.

Are holy. *Matt.* 25: 31.

Are elect. 1 *Tim.* 5: 21.

Are innumerable. *Job* 25: 3. *Heb.* 12: 22.

ANGER

Forbidden. *Eccles.* 7: 9. *Matt.* 5: 22. *Rom.* 12: 19.

A work of the flesh. *Gal.* 5: 20.

A characteristic of fools. *Prov.* 12: 16. *Prov.* 14: 29. *Prov.* 27: 3. *Eccles.* 7: 9.

Connected with

Pride. *Prov.* 21: 24.

Cruelty. *Gen.* 49: 7. *Prov.* 27: 4.

Clamour and evil-speaking. *Eph.* 4: 31.

Malice and blasphemy. *Col.* 3: 8.

Strife and contention. *Prov.* 21: 19. *Prov.* 29: 22. *Prov.* 30: 33.

Brings its own punishment. *Job* 5: 2. *Prov.* 19: 19. *Prov.* 25: 28.

Grievous words stir up. *Judges* 12: 4. 2 *Sam.* 19: 43. *Prov.* 15: 1.

Should not betray us into sin. *Ps.* 37: 8. *Eph.* 4: 26.

In prayer be free from. 1 *Tim.* 2: 8.

May be averted by wisdom. *Prov.* 29: 8.

Meekness pacifies. *Prov.* 15: 1. *Eccles.* 10: 4.

Children should not be provoked to. *Eph.* 6: 4. *Col.* 3: 21.

Be slow to. *Prov.* 15: 18. *Prov.* 16: 32. *Prov.* 19: 11. *Titus* 1: 7. *Jas.* 16: 32.

Avoid those given to. *Gen.* 49: 6. *Prov.* 22: 24.

Justifiable, Exemplified. OUR LORD, *Mark* 3: 5. JACOB, *Gen.* 31: 36. MOSES, *Exod.* 11: 8.

Exod. 32: 19. *Lev.* 10: 16. *Num.* 16: 15. NEHEMIAH, *Neh.* 5: 6. *Neh.* 13: 17, 25.

Sinful, Exemplified. CAIN, *Gen.* 4: 5, 6. ESAU, *Gen.* 27: 45. SIMEON AND LEVI, *Gen.* 49: 5–7. MOSES, *Num.* 20: 10, 11. BALAAM, *Num.* 22: 27. SAUL, 1 *Sam.* 20: 30. AHAB, 1 *Kings* 21: 4. NAAMAN, 2 *Kings* 5: 11. ASA, 2 *Chron.* 16: 10. UZZIAH, 2 *Chron.* 26: 19. HAMAN, *Esther* 3: 5. NEBUCHADNEZZAR, *Dan.* 3: 13. JONAH, *Jonah* 4: 4. HEROD, *Matt.* 2: 16. JEWS, *Luke* 4: 28. HIGH PRIEST, etc., *Acts* 5: 17. *Acts* 7: 54.

ANGER OF GOD, THE

Averted by Christ. *Luke* 2: 11, 14. *Rom.* 5: 9. 2 *Cor.* 5: 18, 19. *Eph.* 2: 14, 17. *Col.* 1: 20. 1 *Thess.* 1: 10.

Is averted from them that believe. *John* 3: 14–18. *Rom.* 3: 25. *Rom.* 5: 1.

Is averted upon confession of sin and repentance. *Job* 33: 27, 28. *Ps.* 106: 43–45. *Jer.* 3: 12, 13. *Jer.* 18: 7, 8. *Jer.* 31: 18–20. *Joel* 2: 12–14. *Luke* 15: 18–20.

Is slow. *Ps.* 103: 8. *Isa.* 48: 9. *Jonah* 4: 2. *Nahum* 1: 3.

Is righteous. *Ps.* 58: 10, 11. *Lam.* 1: 18. *Rom.* 2: 6, 8. *Rom.* 3: 5, 6. *Rev.* 16: 6, 7.

The justice of, not to be questioned. *Rom.* 9: 18, 20, 22.

Manifested in terrors. *Exod.* 14: 24. *Ps.* 76: 6–8. *Jer.* 10: 10. *Lam.* 2: 20–22.

Manifested in judgments and afflictions. *Job* 21: 17. *Ps.* 78: 49–51. *Ps.* 90: 7. *Isa.* 9: 19. *Jer.* 7: 20. *Ezek.* 7: 19. *Heb.* 3: 17.

Cannot be resisted. *Job* 9: 13. *Job* 14: 13. *Ps.* 76: 7. *Nahum* 1: 6.

Aggravated by continual provocation. *Num.* 32: 14.

Specially reserved for the day of wrath. *Zeph.* 1: 14–18. *Matt.* 25: 41. *Rom.* 2: 5, 8. 2 *Thess.* 1: 8. *Rev.* 6: 17. *Rev.* 11: 18. *Rev.* 19: 15.

Against

The wicked. *Ps.* 7: 11. *Ps.* 21: 8, 9. *Isa.* 3: 8. *Isa.* 13: 9. *Nahum* 1: 2, 3. *Rom.* 1: 18. *Rom.* 2: 8. *Eph.* 5: 6. *Col.* 3: 6.

Those who forsake him. *Ezra* 8: 22. *Isa.* 1: 4.

Unbelief. *Ps.* 78: 21, 22. *Heb.* 3: 18, 19. *John* 3: 36.

Impenitence. *Ps.* 7: 12. *Prov.* 1: 30, 31. *Isa.* 5: 13, 14. *Rom.* 2: 5.

Apostacy. *Heb.* 10: 26, 27.

Idolatry. *Deut.* 29: 20, 27, 28. *Deut.* 32: 19, 20, 22. *Joshua* 23: 16. 2 *Kings* 22: 17. *Ps.* 78: 58, 59. *Jer.* 44: 3.

Sin, in saints. *Ps.* 89: 30–32. *Ps.* 90: 7–9. *Ps.* 99: 8. *Ps.* 102: 9, 10. *Isa.* 47: 6.

Extreme, against those who oppose the gospel. *Ps.* 2: 2, 3, 5. 1 *Thess.* 2: 16.

Folly of provoking. *Jer.* 7: 19. 1 *Cor.* 10: 22.

To be dreaded. *Ps.* 2: 12. *Ps.* 76: 7. *Ps.* 90: 11. *Matt.* 10: 28.

To be deprecated. *Exod.* 32: 11. *Ps.* 6: 1. *Ps.* 38: 1. *Ps.* 74: 1, 2. *Isa.* 64: 9.

Removal of, should be prayed for. *Ps.* 39: 10. *Ps.* 79: 5. *Ps.* 80: 4. *Dan.* 9: 16. *Hab.* 3: 2.

Tempered with mercy to saints. *Ps.* 30: 5. *Isa.* 26: 20. *Isa.* 54: 8. *Isa.* 57: 15, 16. *Jer.* 30: 11. *Mic.* 7: 11.

To be borne with submission. 2 *Sam.* 24: 17. *Lam.* 3: 39, 43. *Mic.* 7: 9.

Should lead to repentance. *Isa.* 42: 24, 25. *Jer.* 4: 8.

Exemplified against, THE OLD WORLD, *Gen.* 7: 21–23. BUILDERS OF BABEL, *Gen.* 11: 8. CITIES OF THE PLAIN, *Gen.* 19: 24, 25. EGYPTIANS, *Exod.* 7: 20. *Exod.* 8: 6, 16, 24. *Exod.* 9: 3, 9, 23. *Exod.* 10: 13, 22. *Exod.* 12: 29. *Exod.* 14: 27. ISRAELITES, *Exod.* 32: 35. *Num.* 11: 1, 33. *Num.* 14: 40–45. *Num.* 21: 6. *Num.* 25: 9. 2 *Sam.* 24: 1, 15. ENEMIES OF ISRAEL, 1 *Sam.* 5: 6. 1 *Sam.* 7: 10. NADAB, etc., *Lev.* 10: 2. THE SPIES, *Num.* 14: 37. KORAH, etc., *Num.* 16: 31, 35. AARON AND MIRIAM, *Num.* 12: 9, 10. FIVE KINGS, *Joshua* 10: 25. ABIMELECH, *Judges* 9: 56. MEN OF BETH-SHEMESH, 1 *Sam.* 6: 19. SAUL, 1 *Sam.* 31: 6. UZZAH, 2 *Sam.* 6: 7. SAUL'S FAMILY, 2 *Sam.* 21: 1. SENNACHERIB, 2 *Kings* 19: 28, 35, 37.

ANOINTING OF THE HOLY SPIRIT

Is from God. 2 *Cor.* 1: 21.

That Christ should receive
  Foretold. *Ps.* 45: 7. *Isa.* 61: 1. *Dan.* 9: 24.
  Fulfilled. *Luke* 4: 18, 21. *Acts* 4: 27. *Acts* 10: 38. *Heb.* 1: 9.
God preserves those who re-ceive. *Ps.* 18: 50. *Ps.* 20: 6. *Ps.* 89: 20–23.

Saints receive. *Isa.* 61: 3. 1 *John* 2: 20.

Is abiding in saints. 1 *John* 2: 27.

Guides into all truth. 1 *John* 2: 27.

Typified. *Exod.* 40: 13–15. *Lev.* 8: 12. 1 *Sam.* 16: 13. 1 *Kings* 19: 16.

ANTICHRIST

Denies the Father and the Son. 1 *John* 2: 22.

Denies the incarnation of Christ. 1 *John* 4: 3. 2 *John* 7.

Spirit of, prevalent in the Apostolic times. 1 *John* 2: 18.

Deceit, a characteristic of. 2 *John* 7.

Described. *Dan.* 7: 8. 2 *Thess.* 2: 8, 9.

APOSTATES

Described. *Deut.* 13: 13. *Heb.* 3: 12.

Persecution tends to make. *Matt.* 24: 9, 10. *Luke* 8: 13.

A worldly spirit tends to make. 2 *Tim.* 4: 10.

Never belonged to Christ. 1 *John* 2: 19.

Saints do not become. *Ps.* 44: 18, 19. *Heb.* 6: 9. *Heb.* 10: 39.

It is impossible to restore. *Heb.* 6: 4–6.

Guilt and punishment of. *Zeph.* 1: 4–6. *Heb.* 10: 25–31, 39. 2 *Pet.* 2: 17, 20–22.

Cautions against becoming. *Heb.* 3: 12. 2 *Pet.* 3: 17.

Shall abound in the latter days. *Matt.* 24: 12. 2 *Thess.* 2: 3. 1 *Tim.* 4: 1–3.

Exemplified. AMAZIAH, 2 *Chron.*

25: 14, 27. PROFESSED DISCIPLES, *John* 6: 66. HYMENEUS AND ALEXANDER, 1 *Tim.* 1: 19, 20.

APOSTLES, THE

Christ pre-eminently called "The Apostle" *Heb.* 3: 1.

Ordained by Christ. *Mark* 3: 14. *John* 15: 16.

Received their title from Christ. *Luke* 6: 13.

Called by

God. 1 *Cor.* 1: 1. 1 *Cor.* 12: 28. *Gal.* 1: 1, 15, 16.

Christ. *Matt.* 10: 1. *Mark* 3: 13. *Acts* 20: 24. *Rom.* 1: 5.

The Holy Ghost. *Acts* 13: 2, 4.

Were unlearned men. *Acts* 4: 13.

Selected from obscure stations. *Matt.* 4: 18.

Sent first to the house of Israel. *Matt.* 10: 5, 6. *Luke* 24: 47. *Acts* 13: 46.

Sent to preach the gospel to all nations. *Matt.* 28: 19, 20. *Mark* 16: 15. 2 *Tim.* 1: 11.

Christ always present with. *Matt.* 28: 20.

Warned against a timid profession of Christ. *Matt.* 10: 27–33.

The Holy Ghost given to. *John* 20: 22. *Acts* 2: 1–4. *Acts* 9: 17.

Guided by the Spirit into all truth. *John* 14: 26. *John* 15: 26. *John* 16: 13.

Instructed by the Spirit to answer adversaries. *Matt.* 10: 19, 20. *Luke* 12: 11, 12.

Specially devoted to the office of the ministry. *Acts* 6: 4. *Acts* 20: 27.

Humility urged upon. *Matt.* 20: 26, 27. *Mark* 9: 33–37. *Luke* 22: 24–30.

Self-denial urged upon. *Matt.* 10: 37–39.

Mutual love urged upon. *John* 15: 17.

Equal authority given to each of. *Matt.* 16: 19, with *Matt.* 18: 18. 2 *Cor.* 11: 5.

Were not of the world. *John* 15: 19. *John* 17: 16.

Were hated by the world. *Matt.* 10: 22. *Matt.* 24: 9. *John* 15: 18.

Persecutions and sufferings of. *Matt.* 10: 16, 18. *Luke* 21: 16. *John* 15: 20. *John* 16: 2.

Saw Christ in the flesh. *Luke* 1: 2. *Acts* 1: 22. 1 *Cor.* 9: 1. 1 *John* 1: 1. 1 *Cor.* 15: 8, 9.

Witnesses of the resurrection and ascension of Christ. *Luke* 24: 33–41, 51. *Acts* 1: 2–9. *Acts* 10: 40, 41. 1 *Cor.* 15: 8.

Empowered to work miracles. *Matt.* 10: 1, 8. *Mark* 16: 20. *Luke* 9: 1. *Acts* 2: 43.

ASCENSION OF CHRIST, THE

Prophecies respecting. *Ps.* 24: 7. *Ps.* 68: 18, with *Eph.* 4: 7, 8.

Foretold by himself. *John* 6: 62. *John* 7: 33. *John* 14: 28. *John* 16: 5. *John* 20: 17.

Forty days after his resurrection. *Acts* 1: 3.

Described. *Acts* 1: 9.

From Mount Olivet. *Luke* 24: 50, with *Mark* 11: 1. *Acts* 1: 12.

While blessing his disciples. *Luke* 24: 50.

When he had atoned for sin.
Heb. 9: 12. *Heb.* 10: 12.

Was triumphant. *Ps.* 68: 18.

Was to supreme power and
dignity. *Luke* 24: 26. *Eph.*
1: 20, 21. 1 *Pet.* 3: 22.

As the Forerunner of his people. *Heb.* 6: 20.

To intercede. *Rom.* 8: 34.
Heb. 9: 24.

To send the Holy Ghost. *John*
16: 7. *Acts* 2: 33.

To receive gifts for men. *Ps.*
68: 18, with *Eph.* 4: 8, 11.

To prepare a place for his
people. *John* 14: 2.

His second coming shall be in
like manner as. *Acts* 1: 10,
11.

Typified. *Lev.* 16: 15. *Lev.*
23: 13, with *Heb.* 6: 20.
Heb. 9: 7, 9, 12.

ASSURANCE

Produced by faith. *Eph.* 3: 12.
2 *Tim.* 1: 12. *Heb.* 10: 22.

Made full by hope. *Heb.* 6:
11, 19.

Confirmed by love. 1 *John* 3:
14, 19. 1 *John* 4: 18.

Is the effect of righteousness.
Isa. 32: 17.

Is abundant in the understanding of the gospel. *Col.* 2: 2.
1 *Thess.* 1: 5.

Saints privileged to have, of

Their election. *Ps.* 4: 3.
1 *Thess.* 1: 4.

Their redemption. *Job* 19:
25.

Their adoption. *Rom.* 8: 16.
1 *John* 3: 2.

Their salvation. *Isa.* 12: 2.

Eternal life. 1 *John* 5: 13.

The unalienable love of God.
Rom. 8: 38, 39.

Union with God and Christ.
1 *Cor.* 6: 15. 2 *Cor.* 13: 5.

Eph. 5: 30. 1 *John* 2: 5.
1 *John* 4: 13.

Peace with God by Christ.
Rom. 5: 1.

Preservation. *Ps.* 3: 6, 8.
Ps. 27: 3–5. *Ps.* 46: 1–3.

Answers to prayer. 1 *John*
3: 22. 1 *John* 5: 14, 15.

Continuance in grace.
Phil. 1: 6.

Comfort in affliction. *Ps.*
73: 26. *Luke* 4: 18, 19.
2 *Cor.* 4: 8–10, 16–18.

Support in death. *Ps.* 23: 4.

A glorious resurrection.
Job 19: 26. *Ps.* 17: 15.
Phil. 3: 21. 1 *John* 3: 2.

A kingdom. *Heb.* 12: 28.
Rev. 5: 10.

A crown. 2 *Tim.* 4: 7, 8.
Jas. 1: 12.

Give diligence to attain to.
2 *Pet.* 1: 10, 11.

Strive to maintain. *Heb.* 3: 14,
18.

Confident hope in God restores.
Ps. 42: 11.

Exemplified. DAVID, *Ps.* 23: 4.
Ps. 73: 24–26. PAUL, 2 *Tim.* 1:
12. 2 *Tim.* 4: 18.

ATONEMENT, THE

Explained. *Rom.* 5: 8–11.
2 *Cor.* 5: 18, 19. *Gal.* 1: 4.
1 *John* 2: 2. 1 *John* 4: 10.

Foreordained. *Rom.* 3: 25.
(Margin) 1 *Pet.* 1: 11, 20.
Rev. 13: 8.

Foretold. *Isa.* 53: 4–6, 8–12.
Dan. 9: 24–27. *Zech.* 13: 1, 7.
John 11: 50, 51.

Effected by Christ alone. *John*
1: 29, 36. *Acts* 4: 10, 12.
1 *Thess.* 1: 10. 1 *Tim.* 2: 5, 6.
Heb. 2: 9. 1 *Pet.* 2: 24.

Was voluntary. *Ps.* 40: 6–8.
with *Heb.* 10: 5–9. *John* 10: 11.
15, 17, 18.

Exhibits the

Grace and mercy of God. *Rom.* 8: 32. *Eph.* 2: 4, 5, 7. 1 *Tim.* 2: 4. *Heb.* 2: 9.

Love of God. *Rom.* 5: 8. 1 *John 4: 9, 10.*

Love of Christ. *John* 15:13. *Gal.* 2: 20. *Eph.* 5: 2, 25. *Rev.* 1: 5.

Reconciles the justice and mercy of God. *Isa.* 45: 21. *Rom.* 3: 25, 26.

Necessity for. *Luke* 19: 10. *Heb.* 9: 22.

Made but once. *Heb.* 7: 27. *Heb.* 9: 24–28. *Heb.* 10: 10, 12, 14. 1 *Pet.* 3: 18.

Acceptable to God. *Eph.* 5: 2.

Reconciliation to God effected by. *Rom.* 5: 10. 2 *Cor.* 5: 18–20. *Eph.* 2: 13–16. *Col.* 1: 20–22. *Heb.* 2: 17. 1 *Pet.* 3: 18.

Access to God by. *Heb.* 10: 19, 20.

Remission of sins by. *John* 1: 29. *Rom.* 3: 25. *Eph.* 1: 7. 1 *John* 1: 7. *Rev.* 1: 5.

Justification by. *Rom.* 5: 9. 2 *Cor.* 5: 21.

Sanctification by. 2 *Cor.* 5: 15. *Eph.* 5: 26, 27. *Titus* 2: 14. *Heb.* 10: 10. *Heb.* 13: 12.

Redemption by. *Matt.* 20: 28. 1 *Tim.* 2: 6. *Heb.* 9: 12. *Rev.* 5: 9.

Has delivered saints from the

Power of sin. *Rom.* 8: 3. 1 *Pet.* 1: 18, 19.

Power of the World. *Gal.* 1: 4. *Gal.* 6: 14.

Power of the devil. *Col.* 2: 15. *Heb.* 2: 14, 15.

Saints glorify God for. 1 *Cor.* 6: 20. *Gal.* 2: 20. *Phil.* 1: 20, 21.

Saints rejoice in God for. *Rom.* 5: 11.

Saints praise God for. *Rev.* 5: 9–13.

Faith in, indispensable. *Rom.* 3: 25. *Gal.* 3: 13, 14.

Commemorated in the Lord's Supper. *Matt.* 26: 26–28. 1 *Cor.* 11: 23–26.

Ministers should fully set forth. *Acts* 5: 29–31, 42. 1 *Cor.* 15: 3. 2 *Cor.* 5: 18–21.

Typified. *Gen.* 4: 4, with *Heb.* 11: 4. *Gen.* 22: 2, with *Heb.* 11: 17, 19. *Exod.* 12: 5, 11, 14, with 1 *Cor.* 5: 7. *Exod.* 24: 8, with *Heb.* 9: 20. *Lev.* 16: 30, 34, with *Heb.* 9: 7, 12, 28. *Lev.* 17: 11, with *Heb.* 9: 22.

BACKSLIDING

Is turning from God. 1 *Kings* 11: 9.

Is leaving the first love. *Rev.* 2: 4.

Is departing from the simplicity of the gospel. 2 *Cor.* 11: 3. *Gal.* 3: 1–3. *Gal.* 5: 4, 7.

God is displeased at. *Ps.* 78: 57, 59.

Warnings against. *Ps.* 85: 8. 1 *Cor.* 10: 12.

Guilt and consequences of. *Num.* 14: 43. *Ps.* 125: 5. *Isa.* 59: 2, 9–11. *Jer.* 5: 6. *Jer.* 8: 5, 13. *Jer.* 15: 6. *Luke* 9: 62.

Brings its own punishment. *Prov.* 14: 14. *Jer.* 2: 19.

A haughty spirit leads to. *Prov.* 16: 18.

Proneness to. *Prov.* 24: 16. *Hos.* 11: 7.

Liable to continue and increase. *Jer.* 8: 5. *Jer.* 14: 7.

Exhortations to return from. 2 *Chron.* 30: 6. *Isa.* 31: 6. *Jer.* 3: 12, 14, 22. *Hos.* 6: 1.

Pray to be restored from. *Ps.* 80: 3. *Ps.* 85: 4. *Lam.* 5: 21.

Punishment of tempting others to the sin of. *Prov.* 28: 10. *Matt.* 18: 6.

Not hopeless. *Ps.* 37: 24. *Prov.* 24: 16.

Endeavour to bring back those guilty of. *Gal.* 6: 1. *Jas.* 5: 19, 20.

Sin of, to be confessed. *Is.* 59: 12–14. *Jer.* 3: 13, 14. *Jer.* 14: 7–9.

Pardon of, promised. *2 Chron.* 7: 14. *Jer.* 3: 12. *Jer.* 31: 20. *Jer.* 36: 3.

Healing of, promised. *Jer.* 3: 22. *Hos.* 14: 4.

Afflictions sent to heal. *Hos.* 5: 15.

Blessedness of those who keep from. *Prov.* 28: 14. *Isa.* 26: 3, 4. *Col.* 1: 21–23.

Hateful to saints. *Ps.* 101: 3.

Exemplified. ISRAEL, *Exod.* 32: 8. *Neh.* 9: 26. *Jer.* 3: 11. *Hos.* 4: 16. SAUL, 1 *Sam.* 15: 11. SOLOMON, 1 *Kings* 11: 3, 4. PETER, *Matt.* 26: 70–74.

BAPTISM

As administered by John. *Matt.* 3: 5–12. *John* 3: 23. *Acts* 13: 24. *Acts* 19: 4.

Sanctioned, by Christ's submission to it. *Matt.* 3: 13–15. *Luke* 3: 21.

Adopted by Christ. *John* 3: 22. *John* 4: 1, 2.

Appointed an ordinance of the Christian Church. *Matt.* 28: 19, 20. *Mark* 16: 15, 16.

To be administered in the name of the Father, the Son, and the Holy Spirit. *Matt.* 28: 19.

Water, the outward and visible sign in. *Acts* 8: 36. *Acts* 10: 47.

Regeneration, the inward and spiritual grace of. *John* 3: 3, 5, 6. *Rom.* 6: 3, 4, 11.

Remission of sins, signified by. *Acts* 2: 38. *Acts* 22: 16.

Unity of the Church effected by. 1 *Cor.* 12: 13. *Gal.* 3: 27, 28.

Confession of sin necessary to. *Matt.* 3: 6.

Repentance necessary to. *Acts* 2: 38.

Faith necessary to. *Acts* 8: 37. *Acts* 18: 8.

There is but one. *Eph.* 4: 5.

Administered to

Individuals. *Acts* 8: 38. *Acts* 9: 18.

Households. *Acts* 16: 15. 1 *Cor.* 1: 16.

Emblematic of the influence of the Holy Spirit. *Matt.* 3: 11. *Titus* 3: 5.

Typified. 1 *Cor.* 10: 2. 1 *Pet.* 3: 20, 21.

BAPTISM WITH THE HOLY SPIRIT

Foretold. *Ezek.* 36: 25.

Is through Christ. *Titus* 3: 6.

Christ administered. *Matt.* 3: 11. *John* 1: 33.

Promised to saints. *Acts* 1: 5. *Acts* 2: 38, 39. *Acts* 11: 16.

All saints partake of. 1 *Cor.* 12: 13.

Necessity for. *John* 3: 5. *Acts* 19: 2–6.

Renews and cleanses the soul. *Titus* 3: 5. 1 *Pet.* 3: 20, 21.

The word of God instrumental to. *Acts* 10: 44. *Eph.* 5: 26.

Typified. *Acts* 2: 1–4.

BLASPHEMY

Christ assailed with. *Matt.* 10: 25. *Luke* 22: 64, 65. 1 *Pet.* 4: 14.

Charged upon Christ. *Matt.* 9: 2, 3. *Matt.* 26: 64, 65. *John* 10: 33, 36.

Charged upon saints. *Acts* 6: 11, 13.

Proceeds from the heart. *Matt.* 15: 19.

Forbidden. *Exod.* 20: 7. *Col.* 3: 8.

The wicked addicted to. *Ps.* 74: 18. *Isa.* 52: 5. 2 *Tim.* 3: 2. *Rev.* 16: 11, 21.

Idolatry counted as. *Isa.* 65: 7. *Ezek.* 20: 27, 28.

Hypocrisy counted as. *Rev.* 2: 9.

Saints grieved to hear. *Ps.* 44: 15, 16. *Ps.* 74: 10, 18, 22.

Give no occasion for. 2 *Sam.* 12: 14. 1 *Tim.* 6: 1.

Against the Holy Ghost, unpardonable. *Matt.* 12: 31, 32. *Mark* 3: 28–30. *Luke* 12: 10.

Connected with folly and pride. 2 *Kings* 19: 22. *Ps.* 74: 18.

Punishment of. *Lev.* 24: 16. *Isa.* 65: 7. *Ezek.* 20: 27–33. *Ezek.* 35: 11, 12.

Exemplified. THE DANITE, *Lev.* 24: 11. SENNACHERIB, 2 *Kings* 19: 4, 10, 22. THE JEWS, *Luke* 22: 65. HYMENEUS, 1 *Tim.* 1: 20.

BLESSED, THE

Whom God chooses. *Ps.* 65: 4. *Eph.* 1: 3, 4.

Whom God calls. *Isa.* 51: 2. *Rev.* 19: 9.

Who know Christ. *Matt.* 16: 16, 17.

Who know the gospel. *Ps.* 89: 15.

Who are not offended at Christ. *Matt.* 11: 6.

Who believe. *Luke* 1: 45. *Gal.* 3: 9.

Whose sins are forgiven. *Ps.* 32: 1. *Rom.* 4: 7.

To whom God imputes righteousness without works. *Rom.* 4: 6–9.

Whom God chastens *Job* 5: 17. *Ps.* 94: 12.

Who suffer for Christ. *Luke* 6: 22.

Who have the Lord for their God. *Ps.* 144: 15.

Who trust in God. *Ps.* 2: 12. *Ps.* 34: 8. *Ps.* 40: 4. *Ps.* 84: 12. *Jer.* 17: 7.

Who fear God. *Ps.* 112: 1. *Ps.* 128: 1, 4.

Who hear and keep the word of God. *Ps.* 119: 2. *Jas.* 1: 25. *Matt.* 13: 16. *Luke* 11: 28. *Rev.* 1: 3. *Rev.* 22: 7.

Who delight in the commandments of God. *Ps.* 112: 1.

Who keep the commandments of God. *Rev.* 22: 14.

Who wait for the Lord. *Isa.* 30: 18.

Whose strength is in the Lord. *Ps.* 84: 5.

Who hunger and thirst after righteousness. *Matt.* 5: 6.

Who frequent the house of God. *Ps.* 65: 4. *Ps.* 84: 4.

Who avoid the wicked. *Ps.* 1: 1.

Who endure temptation. *Jas.* 1: 12.

Who watch against sin. *Rev.* 16: 15.

Who rebuke sinners. *Prov.* 24: 25.

Who watch for the Lord. *Luke* 12: 37.

Who die in the Lord. *Rev.* 14: 13.

Who have part in the first resurrection. *Rev.* 20: 6.

Who favour saints. *Gen.* 12: 3. *Ruth* 2: 19.

The undefiled. *Ps.* 119: 1.

The pure in heart. *Matt.* 5: 8.

The just. *Ps.* 106: 3. *Prov.* 10: 6.

The children of the just. *Prov.* 20: 7.

The righteous. *Ps.* 5: 12.

The generation of the upright. *Ps.* 112: 2.

The faithful. *Prov.* 28: 20.

The poor in spirit. *Matt.* 5: 3.

The meek. *Matt.* 5: 5.

The merciful. *Matt.* 5: 7.

The bountiful. *Deut.* 15: 10. *Ps.* 41: 1. *Prov.* 22: 9. *Luke* 14: 13, 14.

The peace-makers. *Matt.* 5: 9.

Holy mourners. *Matt.* 5: 4. *Luke* 6: 21.

Saints at the judgment-day. *Matt.* 25: 34.

Who shall eat bread in the kingdom of God. *Luke* 14: 15. *Rev.* 19: 9.

BLINDNESS, SPIRITUAL

Explained. *John* 1: 5. 1 *Cor.* 2: 14.

The effect of sin. *Matt.* 6: 23. *John* 3: 19, 20.

Unbelief the effect of. 2 *Cor.* 4: 3, 4.

Uncharitableness, a proof of. 1 *John* 2: 9, 11.

A work of the devil. 2 *Cor.* 4: 4.

Leads to all evil. *Eph.* 4: 17–19.

Is inconsistent with communion with God. 1 *John* 1: 6, 7.

Of ministers, fatal to themselves and to the people. *Matt.* 15: 14.

The wicked are in. *Ps.* 82: 5. *Jer.* 5: 21.

The self-righteous are in. *Matt.* 23: 19, 26. *Rev.* 3: 17.

The wicked wilfully guilty of. *Isa.* 26: 11. *Rom.* 1: 19–21.

Judicially inflicted. *Ps.* 69: 23. *Isa.* 29: 10. *Isa.* 44: 18. *Matt.* 13: 13, 14. *John* 12: 40.

Pray for the removal of. *Ps.* 13: 3. *Ps.* 119: 18.

Christ appointed to remove. *Isa.* 42: 7. *Luke* 4: 18. *John* 8: 12. *John* 9: 39. 2 *Cor.* 3: 14. 2 *Cor.* 4: 6.

Christ appoints his ministers to remove. *Matt.* 5: 14. *Acts* 26: 18.

Saints are delivered from. *John* 8: 12. *Eph.* 5: 8. *Col.* 1: 13. 1 *Thess.* 5: 4, 5. 1 *Pet.* 2: 9.

Removal of, illustrated. *Matt.* 11: 5. *John* 9: 7, 11, 25. *Acts* 9: 18. *Rev.* 3: 18.

Exemplified. ISRAEL, *Rom.* 11: 25. 2 *Cor.* 3: 15. SCRIBES AND PHARISEES, *Matt.* 23: 16, 24. CHURCH OF LAODICEA, *Rev.* 3: 17.

BOLDNESS, HOLY

Christ set an example of. *John* 7: 26.

Is through faith in Christ. *Eph.* 3: 12. *Heb.* 10: 19.

A characteristic of saints. *Prov.* 28: 1.

Produced by

Trust in God. *Isa.* 50: 7.

The fear of God. *Acts* 5: 29.

Faithfulness to God. 1 *Tim.* 3: 13.

Express your trust in God with. *Heb.* 13: 6.

Have, in prayer. *Eph.* 3: 12. *Heb.* 4: 16.

Saints shall have, in judgment. 1 *John* 4: 17.

Exhortations to. *Joshua* 1: 7. 2 *Chron.* 19: 11. *Jer.* 1: 8. *Ezek.* 3: 9.

Pray for. *Acts* 4: 29. *Eph.* 6: 19, 20.

Ministers should exhibit, in

Faithfulness to their people. 2 Cor. 7: 4. 2 Cor. 10: 1.

Preaching. Acts 4: 31. Phil. 1: 14.

Reproving sin. Isa. 58: 1. Mic. 3: 8.

The face of opposition. Acts 13: 46. 1 Thess. 2: 2.

Exemplified. ABRAHAM, Gen. 18: 22–32. JACOB, Gen. 32: 24–29. MOSES, Exod. 32: 31, 32. Exod. 33: 18. AARON, Num. 16: 47, 48. DAVID, 1 Sam. 17: 45. ELIJAH, 1 Kings 18: 15, 18. NEHEMIAH, Neh. 6: 11. SHADRACH, Dan. 3: 17, 18. DANIEL, Dan. 6: 10. JOSEPH, Mark 15: 43. PETER AND JOHN, Acts 4: 8–13. STEPHEN, Acts 7: 51. PAUL, Acts 9: 27, 29. Acts 19: 8. BARNABAS, Acts 14: 3. APOLLOS, Acts 18: 26.

BONDAGE, SPIRITUAL

Is to the devil. 1 Tim. 3: 7. 2 Tim. 2: 25.

Is to the fear of death. Heb. 2: 14, 15.

Is to sin. John 8: 34. Acts 8: 23. Rom. 6: 16. Rom. 7: 23. 2 Pet. 2: 19.

Deliverance from, promised. Isa. 61: 1, 2. Isa. 42: 6, 7. Luke 4: 18.

Christ delivers from. Luke 4: 18, 21. John 8: 36. Rom. 7: 24, 25. Eph. 4: 8.

The gospel, the instrument of deliverance from. John 8: 32. Rom. 8: 2.

Saints are delivered from. Rom. 6: 18, 22.

Deliverance from, illustrated. Deut. 4: 20.

Typified. ISRAEL IN EGYPT, Exod. 1: 13, 14.

BUSY-BODIES

Fools are. Prov. 20: 3.

The idle are. 2 Thess. 3: 11. 1 Tim. 5: 13.

Are mischievous tale-bearers. 1 Tim. 5: 13.

Bring mischief upon themselves. 2 Kings 14: 10. Prov. 26: 17.

Christians must not be. 1 Pet. 4: 15.

CALL OF GOD, THE

By Christ. Isa. 55: 5. Rom. 1: 6.

By his Spirit. Rev. 22: 17.

By his works. Ps. 19: 2, 3. Rom. 1: 20.

By his ministers. Jer. 35: 15. 2 Cor. 5: 20.

By his gospel. 2 Thess. 2: 14.

Is from darkness. 1 Pet. 2: 9.

Addressed to all. Isa. 45: 22. Matt. 20: 16.

Most reject. Prov. 1: 24. Matt. 20: 16.

Effectual to saints. Ps. 110: 3. Acts 13: 48. 1 Cor. 1: 24.

To saints, is

Of grace. Gal. 1: 15. 2 Tim. 1: 9.

According to the purpose of God. Rom. 8: 28. Rom. 9: 11, 23, 24.

High. Phil. 3: 14.

Holy. 2 Tim. 1: 9.

Heavenly. Heb. 3: 1.

To fellowship with Christ. 1 Cor. 1: 9.

To holiness. 1 Thess. 4: 7.

To liberty. Gal. 5: 13.

To peace. 1 Cor. 7: 15. Col. 3: 15.

To glory and virtue. 2 Pet. 1: 3.

To the eternal glory of Christ. 2 Thess. 2: 14. 1 Pet. 5: 10.

To eternal life. 1 Tim. 6: 12.

Partakers of, justified. *Rom.* 8: 30.

Walk worthy of. *Eph.* 4: 1.

Blessedness of receiving. *Rev.* 19: 9.

Praise God for. 1 *Pet.* 2: 9.

Illustrated. *Prov.* 9: 3, 4. *Matt.* 23: 3–9.

Rejection of, leads to

Judicial blindness. *Isa.* 6: 9, with *Acts* 28: 24–27. *Rom.* 11: 8–10.

Delusion. *Isa.* 66: 4. 2 *Thess.* 2: 10, 11.

Withdrawal of the means of grace. *Jer.* 26: 4–6. *Acts* 13: 46. *Acts* 18: 6. *Rev.* 2: 5.

Temporal judgments. *Isa.* 28: 12. *Jer.* 6: 16, 19. *Jer.* 35: 17. *Zech.* 7: 12–14.

Exclusion from the benefits of the gospel. *Luke* 12: 24.

Rejection by God. *Prov.* 1: 24–32. *Jer.* 6: 19, 30.

Condemnation. *John* 12: 48. *Heb.* 2: 1–3. *Heb.* 12: 25.

Destruction. *Prov.* 29: 1. *Matt.* 22: 3–7.

CARE, OVERMUCH

About earthly things forbidden. *Matt.* 6: 25. *Luke* 12: 22, 29. *John* 6: 27.

God's providential goodness should keep us from. *Matt.* 6: 26, 28, 30. *Luke* 22: 35.

God's promises should keep us from. *Heb.* 13: 5.

Trust in God should free us from. *Jer.* 17: 7, 8. *Dan.* 3: 16.

Should be cast on God. *Ps.* 37: 5. *Ps.* 55: 22. *Prov.* 16: 3. 1 *Pet.* 5: 7.

An obstruction to the gospel. *Matt.* 12: 22. *Luke* 8: 14. *Luke* 14: 18–20.

Be without. 1 *Cor.* 7: 32. *Phil.* 4: 6.

Unbecoming in saints. 2 *Tim.* 2: 4.

Inutility of. *Matt.* 6: 27. *Luke* 12: 25, 26.

Vanity of. *Ps.* 39: 6. *Eccles.* 4: 8.

Warning against. *Luke* 21: 34.

Sent as a punishment to the wicked. *Ezek.* 4: 16. *Ezek.* 12: 19.

Exemplified. MARTHA, *Luke* 10: 41. PERSONS WHO OFFERED TO FOLLOW CHRIST, *Luke* 9: 57, etc.

CHARACTER OF SAINTS

Attentive to Christ's voice. *John* 10: 3, 4.

Blameless and harmless. *Phil.* 2: 15.

Bold. *Prov.* 28: 1.

Contrite. *Isa.* 57: 15. *Isa.* 66: 2.

Devout. *Acts* 8: 2. *Acts* 22: 12.

Faithful. *Rev.* 17: 14.

Fearing God. *Mal.* 3: 16. *Acts* 10: 2.

Following Christ. *John* 10: 4, 27.

Godly. *Ps.* 4: 3. 2 *Pet.* 2: 9.

Guileless. *John* 1: 47.

Holy. *Deut.* 7: 6. *Deut.* 14: 2. 2 *Col.* 3: 12.

Humble. *Ps.* 34: 2. 1 *Pet.* 5: 5.

Hungering after righteousness. *Matt.* 5: 6.

Just. *Gen.* 6: 9. *Hab.* 2: 4. *Luke* 2: 25.

Led by the Spirit. *Rom.* 8: 14.

Liberal. *Isa.* 32: 8. 2 *Cor.* 9: 13.

Loving. *Col.* 1: 4. 1 *Thess.* 4: 9.

Lowly. *Prov.* 16: 19.

Loathing themselves. *Ezek.* 20: 43.

Meek. *Isa.* 29: 19. *Matt.* 5: 5.

Merciful. *Ps.* 37: 26. *Matt.* 5: 7.

New creatures. 2 *Cor.* 5: 17. *Eph.* 2: 10.

Obedient. *Rom.* 16: 19. 1 *Pet.* 1: 14.

Poor in spirit. *Matt.* 5: 3.

Prudent. *Prov.* 16: 21.

Pure in heart. *Matt.* 5: 8. 1 *John* 3: 3.

Righteous. *Isa.* 60: 21. *Luke* 1: 6.

Sincere. 2 *Cor.* 1: 12. 2 *Cor.* 2: 17.

Stedfast. *Acts* 2: 42. *Col.* 2: 5.

Taught of God. *Isa.* 54: 13. 1 *John* 2: 27.

True. 2 *Cor.* 6: 8.

Undefiled. *Ps.* 119: 1.

Upright. 1 *Kings* 3: 6. *Ps.* 15: 2.

Watchful. *Luke* 12: 37.

Zealous of good works. *Titus* 2: 14.

CHARACTER OF THE WICKED

Abominable. *Rev.* 21: 8.

Alienated from God. *Eph.* 4: 18. *Col.* 1: 21.

Blasphemous. *Luke* 22: 65. *Rev.* 16: 9.

Blinded. 2 *Cor.* 4: 4. *Eph.* 4: 18.

Boastful. *Ps.* 10: 3. *Ps.* 49: 6.

Conspiring against saints. *Neh.* 4: 8. *Neh.* 6: 2. *Ps.* 38: 12.

Covetous. *Mic.* 2: 2. *Rom.* 1: 29.

Deceitful. *Ps.* 5: 6. *Rom.* 3: 13.

Delighting in the iniquity of others. *Prov.* 2: 14. *Rom.* 1: 32.

Despising saints. *Neh.* 2: 19. *Neh.* 4: 2. 2 *Tim.* 3: 3, 4.

Destructive. *Isa.* 59: 7.

Disobedient. *Neh.* 9: 26. *Titus* 3: 3. 1 *Pet.* 2: 7.

Enticing to evil. *Prov.* 1: 10–14. 2 *Tim.* 3: 6.

Envious. *Neh.* 2: 10. *Titus* 3: 3.

Fearful. *Prov.* 28: 1. *Rev.* 21: 8.

Fierce. *Prov.* 16: 29. 2 *Tim.* 3: 3.

Foolish. *Deut.* 32: 6. *Ps.* 5: 5.

Forgetting God. *Job* 8: 13.

Fraudulent. *Ps.* 37: 21. *Mic.* 6: 11.

Froward. *Prov.* 21: 8. *Isa.* 57: 17.

Glorying in their shame. *Phil.* 3: 19.

Hard-hearted. *Ezek.* 3: 7.

Hating the light. *Job* 24: 13. *John* 3: 20.

Heady and high-minded. 2 *Tim.* 3: 4.

Hostile to God. *Rom.* 8: 7. *Col.* 1: 21.

Hypocritical. *Isa.* 29: 13. 2 *Tim.* 3: 5.

Ignorant of God. *Hos.* 4: 1. 2 *Thess.* 1: 8.

Impudent. *Ezek.* 2: 4.

Incontinent. 2 *Tim.* 3: 3.

Infidel. *Ps.* 10: 4. *Ps.* 14: 1.

Loathsome. *Prov.* 13: 5.

Lovers of pleasure more than of God. 2 *Tim.* 3: 4.

Lying. *Ps.* 58: 3. *Ps.* 62: 4. *Isa.* 59: 4.

Mischievous. *Prov.* 24: 8. *Mic.* 7: 3.

Murderous. *Ps.* 10: 8. *Ps.* 94: 6. *Rom.* 1: 29.

Prayerless. *Job* 21: 15. *Ps.* 53: 4.

Persecuting. *Ps.* 69: 26. *Ps.* 109: 16.

Perverse. *Deut.* 32: 5.

Proud. *Ps.* 59: 12. *Obad.* 3. 2 *Tim.* 3: 2.

Rejoicing in the affliction of saints. *Ps.* 35: 15.

Reprobate. 2 *Cor.* 13: 5. 2 *Tim.* 3: 8. *Titus* 1: 16.

Selfish. 2 *Tim.* 3: 2.

Sensual. *Phil.* 3: 19. *Jude* 19.

Sold under sin. 1 *Kings* 21: 20. 2 *Kings* 17: 17.

Stiff-hearted. *Ezek.* 2: 4.

Stiff-necked. *Exod.* 33: 5. *Acts* 7: 51.

Uncircumcised in heart. *Jer.* 9: 26. *Acts* 7: 51.

Unjust. *Prov.* 11: 7. *Isa.* 26: 10.

Unmerciful. *Rom.* 1: 31.

Ungodly. *Prov.* 16: 27.

Unholy. 2 *Tim.* 3: 2.

Unprofitable. *Matt.* 25: 30. *Rom.* 3: 12.

Unruly. *Titus* 1: 10.

Unthankful. *Luke* 6: 35. 2 *Tim.* 3: 2.

Untoward. *Acts* 2: 40.

Unwise. *Deut.* 32: 6.

CHARITY

Explained. 1 *Cor.* 13: 4–7.

Enjoined. *Col.* 3: 14. (See Love to Man)

CHASTITY

Commanded. *Exod.* 20: 14. *Prov.* 31: 3. *Acts* 15: 20. *Rom.* 13: 13. *Col.* 3: 5. 1 *Thess.* 4: 3.

Required in look. *Job* 31: 1. *Matt.* 5: 28.

Required in heart. *Prov.* 6: 25.

Required in speech. *Eph.* 5: 3.

Keep the body in. 1 *Cor.* 6: 13, 15–18.

Preserved by wisdom. *Prov.* 2: 10, 11, 16. *Prov.* 7: 1–5.

Saints are kept in. *Eccles.* 7: 26.

Advantages of. 1 *Pet.* 3: 1, 2.

Shun those devoid of. 1 *Cor.* 5: 11. 1 *Pet.* 4: 3.

The wicked are devoid of. *Rom.* 1: 29. *Eph.* 4: 19. 2 *Pet.* 2: 14. *Jude* 8.

Temptation to deviate from, dangerous. 2 *Sam.* 11: 2–4.

Consequences of associating with those devoid of. *Prov.* 5: 3–11. *Prov.* 7: 25–27. *Prov.* 22: 14.

Want of, excludes from heaven. *Gal.* 5: 19–21.

Drunkenness destructive to. *Prov.* 23: 31–33.

Breach of, punished. 1 *Cor.* 3: 16, 17. *Eph.* 5: 5, 6. *Heb.* 13: 4. *Rev.* 22: 15.

Motives for. 1 *Cor.* 6: 19. 1 *Thess.* 4: 7.

Exemplified. ABIMELECH, *Gen.* 20: 4, 5. *Gen.* 26: 10, 11. JOSEPH, *Gen.* 39: 7–10. RUTH, 3: 10, 11. BOAZ, *Ruth* 3: 13.

CHILDREN

Christ was an example to. *Luke* 2: 51. *John* 19: 26, 27.

Are a gift from God. *Gen.* 33: 5. *Ps.* 127: 3.

Are capable of glorifying God. *Ps.* 8: 2. *Ps.* 148: 12, 13. *Matt.* 21: 15, 16.

Should be

Brought to Christ. *Mark* 10: 13–16.

Brought early to the house of God. 1 *Sam.* 1: 24.

Instructed in the ways of God. *Deut.* 31: 12, 13. *Prov.* 22: 6.

Judiciously corrected. *Prov.* 22: 15. *Prov.* 29: 17.

Should

Obey God. *Deut.* 30: 2.

Fear God. *Prov.* 24: 21.

Remember God. *Eccles.* 12: 1.

Attend to parental teaching. *Prov.* 1: 8, 9.

Honour parents. *Exod.* 20: 12. *Heb.* 12: 9.

Fear parents. *Lev.* 19: 3.

Obey parents. *Prov.* 6: 20. *Eph.* 6: 1.

Take care of parents. 1 *Tim.* 5: 4.

Honour the aged. *Lev.* 19: 32. 1 *Pet.* 5: 5.

Not imitate bad parents. *Ezek.* 20: 18.

CHILDREN, GOOD

The Lord is with. 1 *Sam.* 3: 19.

Know the scriptures. 2 *Tim.* 3: 15.

Observe the law of God. *Prov.* 28: 7.

Their obedience to parents is well pleasing to God. *Col.* 3: 20.

Partake of the promises of God. *Acts* 2: 39.

Shall be blessed. *Prov.* 3: 1–4. *Eph.* 6: 2, 3.

Show love to parents. *Gen.* 46: 29.

Obey parents. *Gen.* 28: 7. *Gen.* 47: 30.

Attend to parental teaching. *Prov.* 13: 1.

Take care of parents. *Gen.* 45: 9–11. *Gen.* 47: 12.

Make their parents' hearts glad. *Prov.* 10: 1. *Prov.* 29: 17.

Honour the aged. *Job* 32: 6, 7.

Adduced as a motive for submission to God. *Heb.* 12: 9.

Character of, illustrative of conversion. *Matt.* 18: 3.

Illustrative of a teachable spirit. *Matt.* 18: 4.

Exemplified. ISAAC, *Gen.* 22: 6–10. JOSEPH, *Gen.* 45: 9. *Gen.* 46: 29. JEPHTHAH'S DAUGHTER, *Judges* 11: 34, 36. SAMSON, *Judges* 13: 24. SAMUEL, 1 *Sam.* 3: 19. OBADIAH, 1 *Kings* 18: 12. JOSIAH, 2 *Chron.* 34: 3. ESTHER, *Esther* 2: 20. JOB, *Job* 29: 4. DAVID, 1 *Sam.* 17: 20. *Ps.* 71: 5. DANIEL, *Dan.* 1: 6. JOHN THE BAPTIST, *Luke* 1: 80. CHILDREN IN THE TEMPLE, *Matt.* 21: 15, 16. TIMOTHY, 2 *Tim.* 3: 15.

CHILDREN, WICKED

Know not God. 1 *Sam.* 2: 12.

Are void of understanding. *Prov.* 7: 7.

Are proud. *Isa.* 3: 5.

With regard to parents

Hearken not to them. 1 *Sam.* 2: 25.

Despise them. *Prov.* 15: 5, 20. *Ezek.* 22: 7.

Curse them. *Prov.* 30: 11.

Bring reproach on them. *Prov.* 19: 26.

Are a calamity to them. *Prov.* 19: 13.

Are a grief to them. *Prov.* 17: 25.

Despise their elders. *Job* 19: 18.

Punishment of, for

Setting light by parents. *Deut.* 27: 16.

Disobeying parents. *Deut.* 21: 21.

Mocking parents. *Prov.* 30: 17.

Cursing parents. *Exod.* 21: 17, with *Mark* 7: 10.

Smiting parents. *Exod.* 21: 15.

Mocking saints. 2 *Kings* 2: 23, 24.

Gluttony and drunkenness. *Deut.* 21: 20, 21.

Their guilt in robbing parents. *Prov.* 28, 24.

Exemplified. ESAU, *Gen.* 26: 34, 35. SONS OF ELI, 1 *Sam.* 2: 12, 17. SONS OF SAMUEL, 1 *Sam.* 8: 3. ABSALOM, 2 *Sam.* 15: 10. ADONIJAH, 1 *Kings* 1: 5, 6. CHILDREN AT BETHEL, 2 *Kings*

2: 23. ADRAMMELECH AND SHAREZER, 2 *Kings* 19: 37.

CHRIST IS GOD

As Jehovah. *Isa.* 40: 3, with *Matt.* 3: 3.

As Jehovah of glory. *Ps.* 24: 7, 10, with 1 *Cor.* 2: 8. *Jas.* 2: 1.

As Jehovah, our RIGHTEOUSNESS. *Jer.* 23: 5, 6, with 1 *Cor.* 1: 30.

As Jehovah, above all. *Ps.* 97: 9, with *John* 3: 31.

As Jehovah, the First and the Last. *Isa.* 44: 6, with *Rev.* 1: 17. *Isa.* 48: 12–16, with *Rev.* 22: 13.

As Jehovah's Fellow and Equal. *Zech.* 13: 7. *Phil.* 2: 6.

As Jehovah of hosts. *Isa.* 6: 1–3, with *John* 12: 41. *Isa.* 8: 13, 14, with 1 *Pet.* 2: 8.

As Jehovah of David. *Ps.* 110: 1, with *Matt.* 22: 42–45.

As Jehovah, the Shepherd. *Isa.* 40: 10, 11. *Heb.* 13: 20.

As Jehovah, for whose glory all things were created. *Prov.* 16: 4, with *Col.* 1: 16.

As Jehovah, the Messenger of the covenant. *Mal.* 3: 1, with *Luke* 2: 27.

Invoked as Jehovah. *Joel* 2: 32, with 1 *Cor.* 1: 2.

As the Eternal God and Creator. *Ps.* 102: 24–27, with *Heb.* 1: 8, 10–12.

As the Mighty God. *Isa.* 9: 6.

As the Great God and Saviour. *Hos.* 1: 7, with *Titus* 2: 13.

As God over all. *Rom.* 9: 5.

As the true God. *Jer.* 10: 10, with 1 *John* 5: 20.

As God the Word. *John* 1: 1.

As God, the Judge. *Eccles.* 12: 14, with 1 *Cor.* 4: 5. 2 *Cor.* 5: 10. 2 *Tim.* 4: 1.

As Emmanuel. *Isa.* 7: 14, with *Matt.* 1: 23.

As King of kings and Lord of lords. *Dan.* 10: 17, with *Rev.* 1: 5. *Rev.* 17: 14.

As the Holy One. 1 *Sam.* 2: 2, with *Acts* 3: 14.

As the Lord from heaven. 1 *Cor.* 15: 47.

As Lord of the sabbath. *Gen.* 2: 3, with *Matt.* 12: 8.

As Lord of all. *Acts* 10: 36. *Rom.* 10: 11–13.

As Son of God. *Matt.* 26: 63–67.

As the Only-begotten Son of the Father. *John* 1: 14, 18. *John* 3: 16, 18. 1 *John* 4: 9.

His blood is called the blood of God. *Acts* 20: 28.

As One with the Father. *John* 10: 30, 38. *John* 12: 45. *John* 14: 7–10. *John* 17: 10.

As sending the Spirit, equally with the Father. *John* 14: 16, with *John* 15: 26.

As entitled to equal honour with the Father. *John* 5: 23.

As Owner of all things, equally with the Father. *John* 16: 15.

As unrestricted by the law of the sabbath, equally with the Father. *John* 5: 17.

As the Source of grace, equally with the Father. 1 *Thess.* 3: 11. 2 *Thess.* 2: 16, 17.

As unsearchable, equally with the Father. *Prov.* 30: 4. *Matt.* 11: 27.

As Creator of all things. *Isa.* 40: 28. *John* 1: 3. *Col.* 1: 16.

As Supporter and Preserver of all things. *Neh.* 9: 6, with *Col.* 1: 17. *Heb.* 1: 3.

As possessed of the fulness of the Godhead. *Col.* 2: 9.

As raising the dead. *John* 5: 21. *John* 6: 40, 54.

As raising himself from the dead. *John* 2: 19, 21. *John* 10: 18.

As Eternal. *Isa.* 9: 6. *Mic.* 5: 2. *John* 1: 1. *Col.* 1: 17. *Heb.* 1: 8–10. *Rev.* 1: 8.

As Omnipresent. *Matt.* 18: 20. *Matt.* 28: 20. *John* 3: 13.

As Omnipotent. *Ps.* 45: 3. *Phil.* 3: 21. *Rev.* 1: 8.

As Omniscient. *John* 16: 30. *John* 21: 17.

As discerning the thoughts of the heart. 1 *Kings* 8: 39, with *Luke* 5: 22. *Ezek.* 11: 5, with *John* 2: 24, 25. *Rev.* 2: 23.

As unchangeable. *Mal.* 3: 6, with *Heb.* 1: 12. *Heb.* 13: 8.

As having power to forgive sins. *Col.* 3: 13, with *Mark* 2: 7, 10.

As Giver of pastors to the Church. *Jer.* 3: 15, with *Eph.* 4:11–13.

As Husband of the Church. *Isa.* 54: 5, with *Eph.* 5: 25–32. *Isa.* 62: 5, with *Rev.* 21: 2, 9.

As the object of divine worship. *Acts* 7: 59. 2 *Cor.* 12: 8, 9. *Heb.* 1: 6. *Rev.* 5: 12.

As the object of faith. *Ps.* 2: 12, with 1 *Pet.* 2: 6. *Jer.* 17: 5, 7, with *John* 14: 1.

As God, He redeems and purifies the Church unto himself. *Rev.* 5: 9, with *Titus* 2: 14.

As God, He presents the Church to himself. *Eph.* 5: 27, with *Jude* 24: 25.

Saints live unto him, as God. *Rom.* 6: 11, and *Gal.* 2: 19, with 2 *Cor.* 5: 15.

Acknowledged by his Apostles. *John* 20: 28.

Acknowledged by Old Testament saints. *Gen.* 17: 1, with *Gen.* 48: 15, 16. *Gen.* 32: 24–30, with *Hos.* 12: 3–5. *Judges* 6: 22–24. *Judges* 12: 31, 22. *Job* 19: 25–27.

CHRIST, THE MEDIATOR

In virtue of his atonement. *Eph.* 2: 13–18. *Heb.* 9: 15. *Heb.* 12: 24.

The only One between God and man. 1 *Tim.* 2: 5.

Of the gospel-covenant. *Heb.* 8: 6. *Heb.* 12: 24.

Typified. MOSES, *Deut.* 5: 5. *Gal.* 3: 19. AARON, *Num.* 16: 48. MELCHIZEDEK, *Heb.* 7: 1–6.

CHRIST, THE HIGH PRIEST

Appointed and called by God. *Heb.* 3: 1, 2. *Heb.* 5: 4, 5.

After the order of Melchizedek. *Ps.* 110: 4, with *Heb.* 5: 6. *Heb.* 6: 20, *Heb.* 7: 15, 17.

Superior to Aaron and the Levitical priests. *Heb.* 7: 11, 16, 22. *Heb.* 8: 1, 2, 6.

Consecrated with an oath. *Heb.* 7: 20, 21.

Has an unchangeable priesthood. *Heb.* 7: 23, 28.

Is of unblemished purity. *Heb.* 7: 26, 28.

Faithful. *Heb.* 3: 2.

Needed no sacrifice for himself. *Heb.* 7: 27.

Offered himself a sacrifice. *Heb.* 9: 14, 26.

His sacrifice superior to all others. *Heb.* 9: 13, 14, 23.

Offered sacrifice but once. *Heb.* 7: 27.

Made reconciliation. *Heb.* 2: 17.

Obtained redemption for us. *Heb.* 9: 12.

Entered into heaven. *Heb.* 4: 14. *Heb.* 10: 12.

Sympathizes with saints. *Heb.* 2: 18. *Heb.* 4: 15.

Intercedes. *Heb.* 7: 25. *Heb.* 9: 24.

Blesses. *Num.* 6: 23–26, with *Acts* 3: 26.

On his throne. *Zech.* 6: 13.

Appointment of, an encouragement to stedfastness. *Heb.* 4: 14.

Typified. MELCHIZEDEK, *Gen.* 14: 18–20. AARON, etc., *Exod.* 40: 12–15.

CHRIST, THE PROPHET

Foretold. *Deut.* 18: 15, 18. *Isa.* 52: 7. *Nahum* 1: 15.

Anointed with the Holy Ghost. *Isa.* 42: 1. *Isa.* 61: 1, with *Luke* 4: 18. *John* 3: 34.

Alone knows and reveals God. *Matt.* 11: 27. *John* 3: 2, 13, 14. *John* 17: 6, 14, 26. *Heb.* 1: 1, 2.

Declared his doctrine to be that of the Father. *John* 8: 26, 28. *John* 12: 49, 50. *John* 14: 10, 24. *John* 15: 15. *John* 17: 8, 16.

Preached the gospel, and worked miracles. *Matt.* 4: 23. *Matt.* 11: 5. *Luke* 4: 43.

Foretold things to come. *Matt.* 24: 3–35. *Luke* 19: 41–44.

Faithful to his trust. *Luke* 4: 43. *John* 17: 8. *Heb.* 3: 2. *Rev.* 1: 5. *Rev.* 3: 14.

Abounded in wisdom. *Luke* 2: 40, 47, 52. *Col.* 2: 3.

Mighty in deed and word. *Matt.* 13: 54. *Mark* 1: 27. *Luke* 4: 32. *John* 7: 46.

Meek and unostentatious in his teaching. *Isa.* 42: 2. *Matt.* 12: 17–20.

God commands us to hear. *Deut.* 18: 15. *Acts* 3: 22.

God will severely visit our neglect of. *Deut.* 18: 19. *Acts* 3: 23. *Heb.* 2: 3.

Typified. MOSES, *Deut.* 18: 15. JONAH, *Matt.* 12: 40.

CHRIST, THE KING

Foretold. *Num.* 24: 17. *Ps.* 2: 6. *Ps.* 45. *Isa.* 9: 7. *Jer.* 23: 5. *Mic.* 5: 2.

Glorious. *Ps.* 24: 7–10. 1 *Cor.* 2: 8. *Jas.* 2: 1.

Supreme. *Ps.* 89: 27. *Ps.* 2: 9. *Rev.* 1: 5. *Rev.* 19: 16.

Sits in the throne of God. *Rev.* 3: 21.

Sits on the throne of David. *Isa.* 9: 7. *Ezek.* 37: 24, 25. *Luke* 1: 32. *Acts* 2: 30.

Is King of Zion. *Ps.* 2: 6. *Isa.* 52: 7. *Zech.* 9: 9. *Matt.* 21: 5. *John* 12: 12–15.

Has a righteous kingdom. *Ps.* 45: 6, with *Heb.* 1: 9, 9. *Isa.* 32: 1. *Jer.* 23: 5.

Has an everlasting kingdom. *Dan.* 2: 44. *Dan.* 7: 14. *Luke* 1: 33.

Has a universal kingdom. *Ps.* 2: 8. *Ps.* 72: 8. *Zech.* 14: 9. *Rev.* 11: 15.

His kingdom, not of this world. *John* 18: 36.

Saints, the subjects of. *Col.* 1: 13. *Rev.* 15: 3.

Saints receive a kingdom from. *Luke* 22: 29, 30. *Heb.* 12: 28.

Acknowledged by

The wise men from the East. *Matt.* 2: 2.

Nathanael. *John* 1: 49.

His followers. *Luke* 19: 38. *John* 12: 13.

Declared by himself. *Matt.* 25: 34. *John* 18: 37.

Written on his cross. *John* 19: 19.

The Jews shall seek unto. *Hos.* 3: 5.

Saints shall behold. *Isa.* 33: 17. *Rev.* 22: 3, 4.

Kings shall do homage to. *Ps.* 72: 10. *Isa.* 49: 7.

Shall overcome all his enemies. *Ps.* 110: 1. *Mark* 12: 36. 1 *Cor.* 15: 25. *Rev.* 17: 14.

Typified. MELCHIZEDEK, *Gen.* 14: 18. DAVID, 1 *Sam.* 16: 1, 12, 13, with *Luke* 1: 32. SOLOMON, 1 *Chron.* 28: 6, 7.

CHRIST, THE SHEPHERD

Foretold. *Gen.* 49: 24. *Isa.* 40: 11. *Ezek.* 34: 23. *Ezek.* 37: 24.

The Chief. 1 *Pet.* 5: 4.

The good. *John* 10: 11, 14.

The great. *Mic.* 5: 4. *Heb.* 13: 20.

His sheep

He knows. *John* 10: 14, 27.

He calls. *John* 10: 3.

He gathers. *Isa.* 40: 11. *John* 10: 16.

He guides. *Ps.* 23: 3. *John* 10: 3, 4.

He feeds. *Ps.* 23: 1, 2. *John* 10: 9.

He cherishes tenderly. *Isa.* 40: 11.

He protects and preserves. *Jer.* 31: 10. *Ezek.* 34: 10. *Zech.* 9: 16. *John* 10: 28.

He laid down his life for. *Zech.* 13: 7, *Matt.* 26: 31. *John* 10: 11, 15. *Acts* 20: 28.

He gives eternal life to. *John* 10: 28.

Typified. DAVID, 1 *Sam.* 16: 11. JOSEPH, *Gen.* 41: 47.

CHRIST, THE HEAD OF THE CHURCH

Predicted. *Ps.* 118: 22, with *Matt.* 21: 42.

Appointed by God. *Eph.* 1: 22.

Declared by himself. *Matt.* 21: 42.

As his mystical body. *Eph.* 4: 12, 15. *Eph.* 5: 23.

Has the pre-eminence in all things. 1 *Cor.* 11: 3. *Eph.* 1: 22. *Col.* 1: 18.

Commissioned his Apostles. *Matt.* 10: 1, 7. *Matt.* 28: 19.

Instituted the sacraments. *Matt.* 28: 19. *Luke* 22: 19, 20.

Imparts gifts. *Ps.* 68: 18, with *Eph.* 4: 8.

Saints are complete in. *Col.* 2: 10.

Perverters of the truth do not hold. *Col.* 2: 18, 19.

CHRIST, CHARACTER OF

Altogether lovely. *Song of Sol.* 5: 16.

Holy. *Luke* 1: 35. *Acts* 4: 27. *Rev.* 3: 7.

Righteous. *Isa.* 53: 11. *Heb.* 1: 9.

Good. *Matt.* 19: 33.

Faithful. *Isa.* 11: 5. 1 *Thess.* 5: 24.

True. *John* 1: 14. *John* 7: 18. 1 *John* 5: 20.

Just. *Zech.* 9: 9. *John* 5: 30. *Acts* 22: 14.

Guileless. *Isa.* 53: 9. 1 *Pet.* 2: 22.

Sinless. *John* 8: 46. 2 *Cor.* 5: 21.

Spotless. 1 *Pet.* 1: 19.

Innocent. *Matt.* 27: 4.

Harmless. *Heb.* 7: 26.

Resisting temptation. *Matt.* 4: 1–10.

Obedient to God the Father. *Ps.* 40: 8. *John* 4: 34. *John* 15: 10.

Zealous. *Luke* 2: 49. *John* 2: 17. *John* 8: 29.

Meek. *Isa.* 53: 7. *Zech.* 9: 9. *Matt.* 11: 29.

Lowly in heart. *Matt.* 11: 29.

Merciful. *Heb.* 2: 17.

Patient. *Isa.* 53: 7. *Matt.* 27: 14.

Long-suffering. 1 *Tim.* 1: 16.

Compassionate. *Isa.* 40: 11. *Luke* 19: 41.

Benevolent. *Matt.* 4: 23, 24. *Acts* 10: 38.

Loving. *John* 13: 1. *John* 15: 13.

Self-denying. *Matt.* 8: 20. 2 *Cor.* 8: 9.

Humble. *Luke* 22: 27. *Phil.* 2: 8.

Resigned. *Luke* 22: 42.

Forgiving. *Luke* 23: 34.

Subject to his parents. *Luke* 2: 51.

Saints are conformed to. *Rom.* 8: 29.

CHURCH, THE

Belongs to God 1 *Tim.* 3: 15.

The body of Christ. *Eph.* 1: 23. *Col.* 1: 24.

Christ, the foundation-stone of. 1 *Cor.* 3: 11. *Eph.* 2: 20. 1 *Pet.* 2: 4, 6.

Christ, the head of. *Eph.* 1: 22. *Eph.* 5: 23.

Loved by Christ. *Song of Sol.* 7: 10. *Eph.* 5: 25.

Purchased by the blood of Christ. *Acts* 20: 28. *Eph.* 5: 25. *Heb.* 9: 12.

Sanctified and cleansed by Christ. 1 *Cor.* 6: 11. *Eph.* 5: 26, 27.

Subject to Christ. *Rom.* 7: 4. *Eph.* 5: 24.

The object of the grace of God. *Isa.* 27: 3. 2 *Cor.* 8: 1.

Displays the wisdom of God. *Eph.* 3: 10.

Shews forth the praises of God. *Isa.* 60: 6.

God defends. *Ps.* 89: 18. *Isa.* 4: 5. *Isa.* 49: 25. *Matt.* 16: 18.

God provides ministers for. *Jer.* 3: 15. *Eph.* 4: 11, 12.

Glory to be ascribed to God by. *Eph.* 3: 21.

Elect. 1 *Pet.* 5: 13.

Glorious. *Ps.* 35: 13. *Eph.* 5: 27.

Clothed in righteousness. *Rev.* 19: 8.

Believers continually added to, by the Lord. *Acts* 2: 47. *Acts* 5: 14. *Acts* 11: 24.

Unity of. *Rom.* 12: 5. 1 *Cor.* 10: 17. 1 *Cor.* 12: 12. *Gal.* 3: 28.

Saints baptised into, by one Spirit. 1 *Cor.* 12: 13.

Ministers commanded to feed. *Acts* 20: 28.

Is edified by the word. 1 *Cor.* 14: 4, 13. *Eph.* 4: 15, 16.

The wicked persecute. *Acts* 8: 1–3. 1 *Thess.* 2: 14, 15.

Not to be despised. 1 *Cor.* 11: 22.

Defiling of, will be punished. 1 *Cor.* 3: 17.

Extent of, predicted. *Isa.* 2: 2. *Ezek.* 17: 22–24. *Dan.* 2: 34, 35.

COMMANDMENTS, THE TEN

Spoken by God. *Exod.* 20: 1. *Deut.* 5: 4, 22.

Written by God. *Exod.* 32: 16. *Exod.* 34: 1, 28. *Deut.* 4: 13. *Deut.* 10: 4.

Enumerated. *Exod.* 20: 3–17.

Summed up by Christ. *Matt.* 22: 35–40.

Law of, is spiritual. *Matt.* 5: 28. *Rom.* 7: 14. (See Law of God)

COMMUNION WITH GOD

Is communion with the Father. 1 *John* 1: 3.

Is communion with the Son. 1 *Cor.* 1: 9. 1 *John* 1: 3. *Rev.* 3: 20.

Is communion with the Holy Ghost. 1 *Cor.* 12: 13. 2 *Cor.* 13: 14. *Phil.* 2: 1.

Reconciliation must precede. *Amos* 3: 3.

Holiness essential to. 2 *Cor.* 6: 14–16.

Promised to the obedient. *John* 14: 23.

Saints

Desire. *Ps.* 42: 1. *Phil.* 1: 23.

Have, in meditation. *Ps.* 63: 5, 6.

Have, in prayer. *Phil.* 4: 6. *Heb.* 4: 16.

Have, in the Lord's Supper. 1 *Cor.* 10: 16.

Should always enjoy. *Ps.* 16: 8. *John* 14: 16–18.

Exemplified. ENOCH, *Gen.* 5: 24. NOAH, *Gen.* 6: 9. ABRAHAM, *Gen.* 18: 33. JACOB, *Gen.* 32: 24–29. MOSES, *Exod.* 33: 11: 23.

COMMUNION OF SAINTS

According to the prayer of Christ. *John* 17: 20, 21.

Is with

God. 1 *John* 1: 3.

Saints in heaven. *Heb.* 12: 22–24.

Each other. *Gal.* 2: 9. 1 *John* 1: 3, 7.

God marks, with his approval. *Mal.* 3: 16.

Christ is present in. *Matt.* 18: 20.

In public and social worship. *Ps.* 34: 3. *Ps.* 55: 14. *Acts* 1: 14. *Heb.* 10: 25.

In the Lord's Supper. 1 *Cor.* 10: 17.

In holy conversation. *Mal.* 3: 16.

In prayer for each other. 2 *Cor.* 1: 11. *Eph.* 6: 18.

In exhortation. *Col.* 3: 16. *Heb.* 10: 25.

In mutual comfort and edification. 1 *Thess.* 4: 18. 1 *Thess.* 5: 11.

In mutual sympathy and kindness. *Rom.* 12: 15. *Eph.* 4: 32.

Delight of. *Ps.* 16: 3. *Ps.* 42: 4. *Ps.* 133: 1–3. *Rom.* 15: 32.

Exhortation to. *Eph.* 4: 1–3.

Opposed to communion with the wicked. 2 *Cor.* 6: 14–17. *Eph.* 5: 11.

Exemplified. JONATHAN, 1 *Sam.* 23: 16. DAVID, *Ps.* 119: 63. DANIEL, *Dan.* 2: 17, 18. APOSTLES, *Acts* 1: 14. THE PRIMITIVE CHURCH, *Acts* 2: 42. *Acts* 5: 12. PAUL, *Acts* 20: 36–38.

COMMUNION OF THE LORD'S SUPPER

Prefigured. *Exod.* 12: 21–28. 1 *Cor.* 5: 7, 8.

Instituted. *Matt.* 26: 26. 1 *Cor.* 11: 23.

Object of. *Luke* 22: 19. 1 *Cor.* 11: 24, 26.

Is the communion of the body and blood of Christ. 1 *Cor.* 10: 16.

Both bread and wine are necessary to be received in. *Matt.* 26: 27. 1 *Cor.* 11: 26.

Self-examination commanded before partaking of. 1 *Cor.* 11: 28, 31.

Newness of heart and life necessary to the worthy partaking of. 1 *Cor.* 5: 7, 8.

Partakers of, should be wholly separate unto God. 1 *Cor.* 10: 21.

Was continually partaken of, by the Primitive Church. *Acts* 2: 42. *Acts* 20: 7.

Unworthy partakers of

Are guilty of the body and blood of Christ. 1 *Cor.* 11: 27.

Discern not the Lord's body. 1 *Cor.* 11: 29.

Are visited with judgments. 1 *Cor.* 11: 30.

COMPASSION AND SYMPATHY

Christ set an example of. *Luke* 19: 41, 42.

Exhortation to. *Rom.* 12: 15. 1 *Pet.* 3: 8.

Exercise towards

The afflicted. *Job* 6: 14. *Heb.* 13: 3.

The chastened. *Isa.* 22: 4. *Jer.* 9: 1.

Enemies. *Ps.* 35: 13.

The poor. *Prov.* 19: 17.

The weak. 2 *Cor.* 11: 29. *Gal.* 6: 2.

Saints. 1 *Cor.* 12: 25, 26.

Inseparable from love to God. 1 *John* 3: 17.

Motives to

The compassion of God. *Matt.* 18: 27, 33.

The sense of our infirmities. *Heb.* 5: 2.

The wicked made to feel, for saints. *Ps.* 106: 46.

Promise to those who shew. *Prov.* 19: 17.

Illustrated. *Luke* 10: 33. *Luke* 15: 20.

Exemplified. PHARAOH'S DAUGHTER, *Exod.* 2: 6. SHOBI, etc., 2 *Sam.* 17: 27–29. ELIJAH, 1 *Kings* 17: 18, 19. NEHEMIAH, *Neh.* 1: 4. JOB'S FRIENDS, *Job* 2: 11. JOB, *Job* 30: 25. DAVID, *Ps.* 35: 13, 14. JEWS, *John* 11: 19. PAUL, 1 *Cor.* 9: 22.

COMPASSION AND SYMPATHY OF CHRIST, THE

Necessary to his priestly office. *Heb.* 5: 2, with verse 7.

Manifested for the

Weary and heavy-laden. *Matt.* 11: 28–30.

Weak in faith. *Isa.* 40: 11. *Isa.* 42: 3, with *Matt.* 12: 20.

Tempted. *Heb.* 2: 18.

Afflicted. *Luke* 7: 13. *John* 11: 33, 35.

Diseased. *Matt.* 14: 14. *Mark* 1: 41.

Poor. *Mark* 8: 2.

Perishing sinners. *Matt.* 9: 36. *Luke* 19: 41.

An encouragement to prayer. *Heb.* 4: 15. Saints should imitate. 1 *Pet.* 3: 8.

CONDEMNATION

The sentence of God against sin. *Matt.* 25: 41.

Universal, caused by the offence of Adam. *Rom.* 5: 12, 16, 18.

Inseparable consequence of sin. *Prov.* 12: 2. *Rom.* 6: 23.

Increased by

Impenitence. *Matt.* 11: 20–24.

Unbelief. *John* 3: 18, 19.

Pride. 1 *Tim.* 3: 6.

Oppression. *Jas.* 5: 1–5.

Hypocrisy. *Matt.* 23: 14.
Conscience testifies to the justice of. *Job* 9: 20. *Rom.* 2: 1. *Titus* 3: 11.
The law testifies to the justice of. *Rom.* 3: 19.
According to men's deserts. *Matt.* 12: 37. 2 *Cor.* 11: 15.
Saints are delivered from, by Christ. *John* 3: 18. *John* 5: 24. *Rom.* 8: 1, 33, 34.
Of the wicked, an example. 2 *Pet.* 2: 6. *Jude* 7.
Chastisements are designed to rescue us from. 1 *Cor.* 11: 32.
Apostates ordained unto. *Jude* 4.
Unbelievers remain under. *John* 3: 18, 36.
The law is the ministration of. 2 *Cor.* 3: 9.

CONDUCT, CHRISTIAN

Believing God. *Mark* 11: 22. *John* 14: 1.
Fearing God. *Eccles.* 12: 13. 1 *Pet.* 2: 17.
Loving God. *Deut.* 6: 5. *Matt.* 22: 37.
Following God. *Eph.* 5: 1. 1 *Pet.* 1: 15, 16.
Obeying God. *Eccles.* 12: 13. *Luke* 1: 6.
Rejoicing in God. *Ps.* 33: 1. *Hab.* 3: 18.
Believing in Christ. *John* 6: 29. *Gal.* 2: 20.
Loving Christ. *John* 21: 15. *Eph.* 6: 24.
Following the example of Christ. *John* 13: 15. 1 *Pet.* 2: 21–24.
Obeying Christ. *John* 14: 21. *John* 15: 14.

Living

To Christ. *Rom.* 14: 8. 2 *Cor.* 5: 15.

Godly in Christ Jesus. 2 *Tim.* 3: 12.
Unto righteousness. *Rom.* 6: 18. 1 *Pet.* 2: 24.
Soberly, righteously, and godly. *Titus* 2: 12.

Walking

Worthy of God. 1 *Thess.* 2: 12.
Worthy of the Lord. *Col.* 1: 10.
In the Spirit. *Gal.* 5: 25.
After the Spirit. *Rom.* 8: 1.
In newness of life. *Rom.* 6: 4.
Worthy of our vocation. *Eph.* 4: 1.
As children of light. *Eph.* 5: 8.
Rejoicing in Christ. *Phil.* 3: 1. *Phil.* 4: 4.
Loving one another. *John* 15: 12. *Rom.* 12: 10. 1 *Cor.* 13: 3. *Eph.* 5: 2. *Heb.* 13: 1.
Striving for the faith. *Phil.* 1: 27. *Jude* 3.
Putting away all sin. 1 *Cor.* 5: 7. *Heb.* 12: 1.
Abstaining from all appearance of evil. 1 *Thess.* 5: 22.
Perfecting holiness. *Matt.* 5: 48. 2 *Cor.* 7: 1. 2 *Tim.* 3: 17.
Hating defilement. *Jude* 23.
Following after that which is good. *Phil.* 4: 8. 1 *Thess.* 5: 15. 1 *Tim.* 6: 11.
Overcoming the world. 1 *John* 5: 4, 5.
Adorning the gospel. *Phil.* 1: 27. *Titus* 2: 10.
Showing a good example. 1 *Tim.* 4: 12. 1 *Pet.* 2: 12.
Abounding in the work of the Lord. 1 *Cor.* 15: 58. 2 *Cor.* 8: 7. 1 *Thess.* 4: 1.
Shunning the wicked. *Ps.* 1: 1. 2 *Thess.* 3: 6.

Controlling the body. 1 *Cor.* 9: 27. *Col.* 3: 5.

Subduing the temper. *Eph.* 4: 26. *Jas.* 1: 19.

Submitting to injuries. *Matt.* 5: 39–41. 1 *Cor.* 6: 7.

Forgiving injuries. *Matt.* 6: 14. *Rom.* 12: 20.

Living peaceably with all. *Rom.* 12: 18. *Heb.* 12: 14.

Visiting the afflicted. *Matt.* 25: 36. *Jas.* 1: 27.

Doing as we would be done by. *Matt.* 7: 12. *Luke* 6: 31.

Sympathizing with others. *Rom.* 12: 15. 1 *Thess.* 5: 14.

Honouring others. *Ps.* 15: 4. *Rom.* 12: 10.

Fulfilling domestic duties. *Eph.* 6: 1–8. 1 *Pet.* 3: 1–7.

Submitting to Authorities. *Rom.* 13: 1–7.

Being liberal to others. *Acts* 20: 35. *Rom.* 12: 13.

Being contented. *Phil.* 4: 11. *Heb.* 13: 5.

Blessedness of maintaining. *Ps.* 1: 1–3. *Ps.* 19: 9–11. *Ps.* 50: 23. *Matt.* 5: 3–12. *John* 15: 10.

CONFESSING CHRIST

Influences of the Holy Spirit necessary to. 1 *Cor.* 12: 3. 1 *John* 4: 2.

A test of being saints. 1 *John* 2: 23. 1 *John* 4: 2, 3.

An evidence of union with God. 1 *John* 4: 15.

Necessary to salvation. *Rom.* 10: 9, 10.

Ensures his confessing us. *Matt.* 10: 32.

The fear of man prevents. *John* 7: 13. *John* 12: 42, 43.

Persecution should not prevent us from. *Mark* 8: 35. 2 *Tim.* 2: 12.

Must be connected with faith. *Rom.* 10: 9.

Consequences of not. *Matt.* 10: 33.

Exemplified. NATHANAEL, *John* 1: 49. PETER, *John* 6: 68, 69. *Acts* 2: 22–36. MAN BORN BLIND, *John* 9: 25, 33. MARTHA, *John* 11: 27. PETER AND JOHN, *Acts* 4: 7–12. APOSTLES, *Acts* 5: 29–32, 42. STEPHEN, *Acts* 7: 52, 59. PAUL, *Acts* 9: 29. TIMOTHY, 1 *Tim.* 6: 12. JOHN, *Rev.* 1: 9. CHURCH IN PERGAMOS, *Rev.* 2: 13. MARTYRS, *Rev.* 20: 4.

CONFESSION OF SIN

God requires. *Lev.* 5: 5. *Hos.* 5: 15.

God regards. *Job* 33: 27, 28. *Dan.* 9: 20, etc.

Exhortations to. *Joshua* 7: 19. *Jer.* 3: 13.

Promises to. *Lev.* 26: 40–42. *Prov.* 28: 13.

Should be accompanied with

Submission to punishment. *Lev.* 26: 41. *Neh.* 9: 33.

Prayer for forgiveness. 2 *Sam.* 24: 10. *Ps.* 25: 11. *Ps.* 51: 1. *Jer.* 14: 7–9, 21.

Self-abasement. *Isa.* 64: 5, 6. *Jer.* 3: 25.

Godly sorrow. *Ps.* 38: 18. *Lam.* 1: 20.

Forsaking sin. *Prov.* 28: 13.

Restitution. *Num.* 5: 6, 7.

Should be full and unreserved. *Ps.* 32: 5. *Ps.* 51: 3. *Ps.* 106: 6.

Followed by pardon. *Ps.* 32: 5. 1 *John* 1: 9.

Illustrated. *Luke* 15: 21. *Luke* 18: 13.

Exemplified. AARON, *Num.* 12: 11. ISRAELITES, *Num.* 21: 6, 7. 1 *Sam.* 7: 6. 1 *Sam.* 12: 19.

SAUL, 1 *Sam*. 15: 24. DAVID, 2 *Sam*. 24: 10. EZRA, *Ezra* 9: 6. NEHEMIAH, *Neh*. 1: 6, 7. LEVITES, *Neh*. 9: 4, 33, 34. JOB, *Job* 7: 20. DANIEL, *Dan*. 9: 4. PETER, *Luke* 5: 8. THIEF, *Luke* 23: 41.

CONSCIENCE

Witnesses in man. *Prov*. 20: 27. *Rom*. 2: 15.

Accuses of sin. *Gen*. 42: 21. 1 *Sam*. 24: 5. *Matt*. 27: 3. *Luke* 9: 7.

We should have the approval of. *Job* 27: 6. *Acts* 24: 16. *Rom*. 9: 1. *Rom*. 14: 22.

The blood of Christ alone can purify. *Heb*. 9: 14. *Heb*. 10: 2–10, 22.

Keep the faith in purity of. 1 *Tim*. 1: 19. 1 *Tim*. 3: 9.

Of saints, pure and good. *Heb*. 13: 18. 1 *Pet*. 3: 16, 21.

Submit to authority for. *Rom*. 13: 5.

Suffer patiently for. 1 *Pet*. 2: 19.

Testimony of, a source of joy. 2 *Cor*. 1: 12. 1 *John* 3: 21.

Of others, not to be offended. *Rom*. 14: 21. 1 *Cor*. 10: 28–32.

Ministers should commend themselves to that of their people. 2 *Cor*. 4: 2. 2 *Cor*. 5: 11.

Of the wicked, seared. 1 *Tim*. 4: 2.

Of the wicked, defiled. *Titus* 1: 15.

Without spiritual illumination, a false guide. *Acts* 23: 1, with *Acts* 26: 9.

CONTEMPT

Sin of. *Job* 31: 13, 14. *Prov*. 12: 21.

Folly of. *Prov*. 11: 12.

A characteristic of the wicked. *Prov*. 18: 3. 2 *Tim*. 3: 3.

Forbidden towards

Parents. *Prov*. 23: 22.

Christ's little ones. *Matt*. 18: 10.

Weak brethren. *Rom*. 14: 3.

Young ministers. 1 *Cor*. 16: 11.

Believing masters. 1 *Tim*. 6: 2.

The poor. *Jas*. 2: 1–3.

Self-righteousness prompts to. *Isa*. 65: 5. *Luke* 18: 9, 11.

Pride and prosperity prompt to. *Ps*. 123: 4.

Ministers should give no occasion for. 1 *Tim*. 4: 12.

Of ministers, is a despising of God. *Luke* 10: 16. 1 *Thess*. 4: 8.

Towards the church

Often turned into respect. *Isa*. 60: 14.

Often punished. *Ezek*. 28: 26.

To be met with patience. 1 *Sam*. 10: 27.

Causes saints to cry unto God. *Neh*. 4: 4. *Ps*. 123: 3.

The wicked exhibit, toward

Christ. *Ps*. 22: 6. *Isa*. 53: 3. *Matt*. 27: 29.

Saints. *Ps*. 119: 141. 1 *Cor*. 4: 10.

Authorities. 2 *Pet*. 2: 10. *Jude* 8.

Parents. *Prov*. 15: 3, 20.

The afflicted. *Job* 19: 18.

The poor. *Ps*. 14: 6. *Eccles*. 9: 16.

Saints sometimes guilty of. *Jas*. 2: 6.

Exemplified. HAGAR, *Gen*. 16: 4. CHILDREN OF BELIAL, 1 *Sam*. 10: 27. NABAL, 1 *Sam*. 25: 10,

11. MICHAL, 2 *Sam.* 6: 16. SAN-BALLAT, etc., *Neh.* 2: 19. *Neh.* 4: 2, 3. FALSE TEACHERS, 2 *Cor.* 10: 10.

CONTENTMENT

With godliness is great gain. *Ps.* 37: 16. 1 *Tim.* 6: 6.

Saints should exhibit

In their respective callings. 1 *Cor.* 7: 20.

With appointed wages. *Luke* 3: 14.

With what things they have. *Heb.* 13: 5.

With food and raiment. 1 *Tim.* 6: 8.

God's promises should lead to. *Heb.* 13: 5.

The wicked want. *Isa.* 5: 8.

Exemplified. BARZILLAI, 2 *Sam.* 19: 33–37. SHUNAMMITE, 2 *Kings* 4: 13. DAVID, *Ps.* 16: 6. AGUR, *Prov.* 30: 8, 9. PAUL, *Phil.* 4: 11, 12.

CONVERSION

By God. 1 *Kings* 18: 37. *John* 6: 44. *Acts* 21: 19.

By Christ. *Acts* 3: 26. *Rom.* 15: 18.

By the power of the Holy Ghost. *Prov.* 1: 23.

Is of grace. *Acts* 11: 21, with verse 23.

Follows repentance. *Acts* 3: 19. *Acts* 26: 20.

Is the result of faith. *Acts* 11: 21.

Through the instrumentality of

The scriptures. *Ps.* 19: 7. 2 *Tim.* 3: 15.

Ministers. *Acts* 26: 18. 1 *Thess.* 1: 9.

Self-examination. *Ps.* 119: 59. *Lam.* 3: 40.

Affliction. *Ps.* 78: 34.

Of sinners, a cause of joy

To God. *Ezek.* 18: 23. *Luke* 15: 32.

To saints. *Acts* 15: 3. *Gal.* 1: 23, 24.

Is necessary. *Matt.* 18: 3.

Commanded. *Job* 36: 10.

Exhortations to. *Prov.* 1: 23. *Isa.* 31: 6. *Isa.* 55: 7. *Jer.* 3:7. *Ezek.* 33: 11.

Promises connected with. *Neh.* 1: 9. *Isa.* 1: 27. *Jer.* 3: 14. *Ezek.* 18:27.

Pray for. *Ps.* 80: 7. *Ps.* 85: 4. *Jer.* 31: 18. *Lam.* 5: 21.

Is accompanied by confession of sin, and prayer. 1 *Kings* 8: 35.

Danger of neglecting. *Ps.* 7: 12. *Jer.* 44: 5, 11. *Ezek.* 3: 19.

Duty of leading sinners to. *Ps.* 51: 13.

Encouragement for leading sinners to. *Dan.* 12: 3. *Jas.* 5: 19, 20.

Of Gentiles, predicted. *Isa.* 2: 2. *Isa.* 11: 10. *Isa.* 60: 5. *Isa.* 66: 12.

Of Israel, predicted. *Ezek.* 36: 25–27. *Rom.* 11: 26.

COUNSELS AND PURPOSES OF GOD, THE

Are great. *Jer.* 32: 19.

Are wonderful. *Isa.* 28: 29.

Are immutable. *Ps.* 33: 11. *Prov.* 19: 21. *Jer.* 4: 28. *Rom.* 9: 11. *Heb.* 6: 17.

Are sovereign. *Isa.* 40: 13, 14. *Dan.* 4: 35.

Are eternal. *Eph.* 3: 11.

Are faithfulness and truth. *Isa.* 25: 1.

None can disannul. *Isa.* 14: 27.

Shall be performed. *Isa.* 14: 24. *Isa.* 46: 11.

The sufferings and death of Christ were according to. *Acts* 2: 23. *Acts* 4: 28.

Saints called, and saved according to. *Rom.* 8: 28. 2 *Tim.* 1: 9.

The union of all saints in Christ, is according to. *Eph.* 1: 9, 10.

The works of God according to. *Eph.* 1: 11.

Should be declared by ministers. *Acts* 20: 27.

Attend to. *Jer.* 49: 20. *Jer.* 50: 45.

Secret, not to be searched into. *Deut.* 29: 29. *Matt.* 24: 36. *Acts* 1: 7.

The wicked
Understand not. *Mic.* 4: 12.
Despise. *Isa.* 5: 19.
Reject. *Luke* 7: 30.

COURTS OF JUSTICE
Have authority from God. *Rom.* 13: 1–5.

Superior court
Held first by Moses alone in the wilderness. *Exod.* 18: 13–20.

Consisted subsequently of priests and Levites. *Deut.* 17: 9, with *Mal.* 2: 7.

Presided over by the governor or the high priest. *Deut.* 17: 12. *Judges* 4: 4, 5.

Held at the seat of government. *Deut.* 17: 8.

Decided on all appeals and difficult cases. *Exod.* 18:26. *Deut.* 1: 17. *Deut.* 17: 8, 9.

Decisions of, conclusive. *Deut.* 17: 10, 11.

Inferior
In all cities. *Deut.* 16: 18. 2 *Chron.* 19: 5–7.

Held at the gates. *Gen.* 34: 20. *Deut.* 16: 18. *Deut.* 21: 19. *Job* 5:4.

Judges of, appointed by the governor. *Exod.* 18: 21, 25. *Deut.* 1: 9–15. 2 *Sam.* 15: 3.

All minor cases decided by. *Exod.* 18: 26. 2 *Sam.* 15: 4.

All transfers of property made before. *Gen.* 23: 17–20. *Ruth* 4: 1, 2.

Re-established by Jehoshaphat. 2 *Chron.* 19: 5–10.

Re-established by Ezra. *Ezra* 7: 25.

Sanhedrin or court of the seventy
Probably derived from the seventy elders appointed by Moses. *Exod.* 24: 9. *Num.* 11: 16, 17, 24–30.

Mentioned in the latter part of sacred history. *Luke* 22: 66. *John* 11: 47. *Acts* 5: 27.

Consisted of chief priests, etc. *Matt.* 26: 57, 69.

Presided over by high priest. *Matt.* 26: 62–66.

Sat in high priest's palace. *Matt.* 26: 57, 58.

of the Romans in Judea
Presided over by the governor or deputy. *Matt.* 27: 2, 11. *Acts* 18: 12.

Place of, called the hall of judgment. *John* 18: 28, 33. *John* 19: 9.

Never interfered in any dispute about minor matters or about religion. *Acts* 18: 14, 15.

Could alone award death. *John* 18: 31.

Never examined their own citizens by torture. *Acts* 22: 25–29.

Appeals from, made to the emperor. *Acts* 25: 11. *Acts* 26: 32. *Acts* 28: 19.

Generally held in the morning. *Jer.* 21: 12. *Matt.* 27: 1. *Luke* 22: 66.

Sometimes held in synagogues. *Matt.* 10: 17. *Acts* 22: 19. *Acts* 26: 11. *Jas.* 2: 2. (Greek)

Provided with

Judges. *Deut.* 16: 18.

Officers. *Deut.* 16: 18. *Matt.* 5: 25.

Tormentors of executioners. *Matt.* 18: 34.

Judges of

Called elders. *Deut.* 25: 7. 1 *Sam.* 16: 4.

Called magistrates. *Luke* 12: 58.

Rode often on white asses. *Judges* 5: 10.

To judge righteously. *Lev.* 19: 15. *Deut.* 1: 16.

To judge without respect of persons. *Exod.* 23: 3, 6. *Lev.* 19: 15. *Deut.* 1: 17. *Prov.* 22: 22.

To investigate every case. *Deut.* 19: 18.

Not to take bribes. *Exod.* 23: 8. *Deut.* 16: 19.

To judge as for God. 2 *Chron.* 19: 6, 7, 9.

To decide according to law. *Ezek.* 44: 24.

To promote peace. *Zech.* 8: 16.

Sat on the judgment-seat while hearing causes. *Exod.* 18: 13. *Judges* 5: 10. *Isa.* 28: 6. *Matt.* 27: 19.

Examined the parties. *Acts* 24: 8.

Conferred together before giving judgment. *Acts* 5: 34–40. *Acts* 25: 12. *Acts* 26: 30, 31.

Pronounced the judgment of the court. *Matt.* 26: 65, 66. *Luke* 23: 24. *Acts* 5: 40.

Both the accusers and accused required to appear before. *Deut.* 25: 1. *Acts* 25: 16.

Cases in, were opened by

The complainant. 1 *Kings* 3: 17–21. *Acts* 16: 19–21.

An advocate. *Acts* 24: 1.

The accused

Stood before the judge. *Num.* 35: 12. *Matt.* 27: 11.

Permitted to plead their own cause. 1 *Kings* 3: 22. *Acts* 24: 10. *Acts* 26: 1.

Might have advocates. *Prov.* 31: 8, 9. *Isa.* 1: 17.

Exhorted to confess. *Joshua* 7: 19.

Examined on oath. *Lev.* 5: 1. *Matt.* 26: 63.

Sometimes examined by torture. *Acts* 22: 24, 29.

Sometimes treated with insult. *Matt.* 26: 67, *John* 18: 22, 23. *Acts* 23: 2, 3.

The evidence of two or more witnesses required in. *Deut.* 17: 6. *Deut.* 19: 15. *John* 8: 17. 2 *Cor.* 13: 1.

Witnesses sometimes laid their hands on the criminal's head before punishment. *Lev.* 24: 14.

False witnesses in to receive the punishment of the accused. *Deut.* 19: 19.

Corruption and bribery often

practised in. *Isa.* 10: 1.
Amos 5: 12. *Amos* 8: 6.

The judgment of

Not given till accused was
heard. *John* 7: 51.

Recorded in writing. *Isa.*
10: 1 (marg.).

Immediately executed.
Deut. 25: 2. *Joshua* 7: 25.
Mark 15: 15–20.

Witnesses first to execute.
Deut. 17: 7. *Acts* 7: 58.

Allusions to. *Job* 5: 4. *Ps.*
127: 5. *Matt.* 5: 22.

Illustrative of the last judgment. *Matt.* 19: 28. *Rom.*
14: 10. 1 *Cor.* 6: 12.

COVENANT, THE

Christ, the substance of. *Isa.*
42: 6. *Isa.* 49: 8.

Christ, the Mediator of. *Heb.*
8: 6. *Heb.* 9: 15. *Heb.* 12: 24.

Christ, the Messenger of. *Mal.*
3: 1.

Made with

Abraham. *Gen.* 15: 7–18.
Gen. 17: 2–14. *Luke* 1: 72–
75. *Acts* 3: 25. *Gal.* 3: 16.

Isaac. *Gen.* 17: 19, 21. *Gen.*
26: 3, 4.

Jacob. *Gen.* 28: 13, 14, with
1 *Chron.* 16: 16, 17.

Israel. *Exod.* 6: 4. *Acts*
3: 25.

David. 2 *Sam.* 23: 5. *Ps.*
89: 3, 4.

Renewed under the gospel *Jer.*
31: 31–33. *Rom.* 11: 27. *Heb.*
8: 8–10, 13.

Fulfilled in Christ. *Luke* 1:
68–79.

Confirmed in Christ. *Gal.* 3:
17.

Ratified by the blood of Christ.
Heb. 9: 11–14, 16–23.

Is a covenant of peace. *Isa.*
54: 9, 10. *Ezek.* 34: 25. *Ezek.*
37: 26.

Is unalterable. *Ps.* 89: 34. *Isa.*
54: 10. *Isa.* 59: 21. *Gal.* 3: 17.

Is everlasting. *Ps.* 111: 9. *Isa.*
55: 3. *Isa.* 61: 8. *Ezek.* 16: 60–
63. *Heb.* 13: 20.

All saints interested in. *Ps.*
25: 14. *Ps.* 89: 29–37. *Heb.* 8:
10.

The wicked have no interest in.
Eph. 2: 12.

Blessings connected with. *Isa.*
56: 4–7. *Heb.* 8: 10–12.

God is faithful to. *Deut.* 7: 9.
1 *Kings* 8: 23. *Neh.* 1: 5. *Dan.*
9: 4.

God is ever mindful of. *Ps.*
105: 8. *Ps.* 111: 5. *Luke* 1: 72.

Be mindful of. 1 *Chron.* 16:
15.

Caution against forgetting.
Deut. 4: 23.

Plead, in prayer. *Ps.* 74: 20.
Jer. 14: 21.

Punishment for despising.
Heb. 10: 29, 30.

COVETOUSNESS

Comes from the heart. *Mark*
7: 22, 23.

Engrosses the heart. *Ezek.*
33: 31. 2 *Pet.* 2: 14.

Is idolatry. *Eph.* 5: 5. *Col.* 3:
5.

Is the root of all evil. 1 *Tim.*
6: 10.

Is never satisfied. *Eccles.* 5:
10. *Hab.* 2: 5.

Is vanity. *Ps.* 39: 6. *Eccles.*
4: 8.

Is inconsistent

In saints. *Eph.* 5: 3. *Heb.*
13: 5.

Specially in ministers. 1
Tim. 3: 3.

Leads to

Injustice and oppression. *Prov.* 28: 20. *Mic.* 2: 2.

Foolish and hurtful lusts. 1 *Tim.* 6: 9.

Departure from the faith. 1 *Tim.* 6: 10.

Lying. 2 *Kings* 5: 22–25.

Murder. *Prov.* 1: 18, 19. *Ezek.* 22: 12.

Theft. *Joshua* 7: 21.

Poverty. *Prov.* 28: 22.

Misery. 1 *Tim.* 6: 10.

Domestic affliction. *Prov.* 15: 27.

Abhorred by God. *Ps.* 10: 3.

Forbidden. *Exod.* 20: 17.

A characteristic of the wicked. *Rom.* 1: 29.

A characteristic of the slothful. *Prov.* 21: 26.

Commended by the wicked alone. *Ps.* 10: 3.

Hated by saints. *Exod.* 18: 21. *Acts* 20: 33.

To be mortified by saints. *Col.* 3: 5.

Woe denounced against. *Isa.* 5: 8. *Hab.* 2: 9.

Punishment of. *Job* 20: 15. *Isa.* 57: 17. *Jer.* 22: 17–19. *Mic.* 2: 2, 3.

Excludes from heaven. 1 *Cor.* 6: 10. *Eph.* 5: 5.

Beware of. *Luke* 12: 15.

Avoid those guilty of. 1 *Cor.* 5: 11.

Pray against. *Ps.* 119: 36.

Reward of those who hate. *Prov.* 28: 16.

Shall abound in the last days. 2 *Tim.* 3: 2. 2 *Pet.* 2: 1–3.

Exemplified. LABAN, *Gen.* 31: 41. ACHAN, *Joshua* 7: 21. ELI'S SONS, 1 *Sam.* 2: 12–14. SAMUEL'S SONS, 1 *Sam.* 8: 3. SAUL, 1 *Sam.* 15: 9, 19. AHAB, 1 *Kings* 21: 2, etc. GEHAZI, 2 *Kings* 5: 20–24. NOBLES OF THE JEWS, *Neh.* 5: 7. *Isa.* 1: 23. JEWISH PRIESTS, *Isa.* 56: 11. *Jer.* 6: 13. BABYLON, *Jer.* 51: 13. YOUNG MAN, *Matt.* 19: 22. JUDAS, *Matt.* 26: 14, 15. *John* 12: 6. PHARISEES, *Luke* 16: 14. ANANIAS, etc., *Acts* 5: 1–10. DEMETRIUS, *Acts* 19: 27. FELIX, *Acts* 24: 26. BALAAM, *Num.* 22: 21. 2 *Pet.* 2: 15, with *Jude* 11.

DEATH, SPIRITUAL

Alienation from God is. *Eph.* 4: 18.

Carnal-mindedness is. *Rom.* 8: 6.

Walking in trespass and sins is. *Eph.* 2: 1. *Col.* 2: 13.

Spiritual ignorance is. *Isa.* 9: 2. *Matt.* 4: 16. *Luke* 1: 79. *Eph.* 4: 18.

Unbelief is. *John* 6: 53. 1 *John* 5: 12.

Living in pleasure is. 1 *Tim.* 5: 6.

Hypocrisy is. *Rev.* 3: 1, 2.

Is a consequence of the fall. *Rom.* 5: 15.

Is the state of all men by nature. *Matt.* 8: 22. *John* 5: 25. *Rom.* 6: 13.

The fruits of, are dead works. *Heb.* 6: 1. *Heb.* 9: 14.

A call to arise from. *Eph.* 5: 14.

Deliverance from, is through Christ. *John* 5: 24, 25. *Eph.* 2: 5. 1 *John* 5: 12.

Saints are raised from. *Rom.* 6: 13.

Love of the brethren, a proof of being raised from. 1 *John* 3: 14.

Illustrated. *Ezek.* 37: 2, 3. *Luke* 15: 24.

DEATH, NATURAL

By Adam. *Gen.* 3: 19. 1 *Cor.* 15: 21, 22.

Consequence of sin. *Gen.* 2: 17. *Rom.* 5: 12.

Lot of all. *Eccles.* 8: 8. *Heb.* 9: 27.

Ordered by God. *Deut.* 32: 39. *Job* 14: 5.

Puts an end to earthly projects. *Eccles.* 9: 10.

Strips of earthly possessions. *Job* 1: 21. 1 *Tim.* 6: 7.

Levels all ranks. *Job* 1: 21. *Job* 3: 17–19.

Conquered by Christ. *Rom.* 6: 9. *Rev.* 1: 18.

Abolished by Christ. 2 *Tim.* 1: 10.

Shall finally be destroyed by Christ. *Hos.* 13: 14. 1 *Cor.* 15: 26.

Christ delivers from the fear of. *Heb.* 2: 15.

Regard, as at hand. *Job* 14: 1, 2. *Ps.* 39: 4, 5. *Ps.* 90: 9. 1 *Pet.* 1: 24.

Prepare for. 2 *Kings* 20: 1.

Pray to be prepared for. *Ps.* 39: 4, 13. *Ps.* 90: 12.

Consideration of, a motive to diligence. *Eccles.* 9: 10. *John* 9: 4.

When averted for a season, is a motive to increased devotedness. *Ps.* 56: 12, 13. *Ps.* 116: 7–9. *Ps.* 118: 17. *Isa.* 38: 20.

Enoch and Elijah were exempted from. *Gen.* 5: 24, with *Heb.* 11: 5. 2 *Kings* 2: 11.

All shall be raised from. *Acts* 24: 15.

None subject to, in heaven. *Luke* 20: 36. *Rev.* 21: 4.

Illustrates the change produced in conversion. *Rom.* 6: 2. *Col.* 2: 20.

Is described as

A sleep. *Deut.* 31: 16. *John* 11: 11.

The earthly house of this tabernacle being dissolved. 2 *Cor.* 5: 1.

Putting off this tabernacle. 2 *Pet.* 1: 14.

God requiring the soul. *Luke* 12: 20.

Going the way whence there is no return. *Job* 16: 22.

Gathering to our people. *Gen.* 49: 33.

Going down into silence. *Ps.* 115: 17.

Yielding up the ghost. *Acts* 5: 10.

Returning to dust. *Gen.* 3: 19. *Ps.* 104: 29.

Being cut down. *Job* 14: 2.

Fleeing as a shadow. *Job* 14: 2.

Departing. *Phil.* 1: 23.

DEATH, ETERNAL

The necessary consequence of sin. *Rom.* 6: 16, 21. *Rom.* 8: 13. *Jas.* 1: 15.

The wages of sin. *Rom.* 6: 23.

The portion of the wicked. *Matt.* 25: 41, 46. *Rom.* 1: 32.

The way to, described. *Matt.* 7: 13.

Self-righteousness leads to. *Prov.* 14: 12.

God alone can inflict. *Matt.* 10: 28. *Jas.* 4: 12.

Is described as

Banishment from God. 2 *Thess.* 1: 9.

Society with the devil, etc. *Matt.* 25: 41.

A lake of fire. *Rev.* 19: 20. *Rev.* 21: 8.

The worm that dieth not. *Mark* 9: 44.

Outer darkness. *Matt.* 25:
30.

A mist of darkness for ever.
2 *Pet.* 2: 17.

Indignation, wrath, etc.
Rom. 2: 8, 9.

Is called

Destruction. *Rom.* 9: 22. 2
Thess. 1: 9.

Perishing. 2 *Pet.* 2: 12.

The wrath to come. 1 *Thess.*
1: 10.

The second death. *Rev.* 2:
11.

A resurrection to damnation.
John 5: 29.

A resurrection to shame, &c.
Dan. 12: 2.

Damnation of hell. *Matt.*
23: 33.

Everlasting punishment.
Matt. 25: 46.

Shall be inflicted by Christ.
Matt. 25: 33, 41. 2 *Thess.* 1: 7,
8.

Christ, the only way of escape
from. *John* 3: 16. *John* 8: 51.

Saints shall escape. *Rev.* 2: 11.
Rev. 21: 27.

Strive to preserve others from.
Jas. 5: 20.

Illustrated. *Luke* 16: 23–26.

DEATH OF CHRIST, THE

Foretold. *Isa.* 53: 8. *Dan.* 9:
26. *Zech.* 13: 7. *Ps.* 22.

Appointed by God. *Isa.* 53:
6, 10. *Acts* 2: 23.

Necessary for the redemption
of man. *Luke* 24: 46. *John*
12: 24. *Acts* 17: 3.

Acceptable, as a sacrifice to
God. *Matt.* 20: 28. *Eph.* 5:
2. 1 *Thess.* 5: 10.

Was voluntary. *Isa.* 53: 12.
Matt. 26: 53. *John* 10: 17, 18.

Was undeserved. *Isa.* 53: 9.

Mode of

Foretold by Christ. *Matt.*
20: 18, 19. *John* 12: 32, 33.

Prefigured. *Num.* 21: 8,
with *John* 3: 14.

Ignominious. *Heb.* 12: 2.

Accursed. *Deut.* 21: 23. *Gal.*
3: 13.

Exhibited his humility. *Phil.*
2: 8.

A stumbling-block to Jews.
1 *Cor.* 1: 23.

Foolishness to Gentiles. 1
Cor. 1: 18, 23.

Demanded by the Jews. *Matt.*
27: 22, 23.

Inflicted by the Gentiles. *Matt.*
27: 26–35.

In the company of malefactors.
Isa. 53: 12, with *Matt.* 27: 38.

Accompanied by preternatural
signs. *Matt.* 27: 45, 51–53.

Emblematical of the death unto
sin. *Rom.* 6: 3–8. *Gal.* 2: 20.

Commemorated in the sacra-
ment of the Lord's Supper.
Luke 22: 19, 20.

DEATH OF SAINTS, THE

A sleep in Christ. 1 *Cor.* 15:
18. 1 *Thess.* 4: 14.

Is blessed. *Rev.* 14: 13.

Is gain. *Phil.* 1: 21.

Is full of

Faith. *Heb.* 11: 13.

Peace. *Isa.* 57: 2.

Hope. *Prov.* 14: 32.

Sometimes desired. *Luke* 2:
29.

Waited for. *Job* 14: 14.

Met with resignation. *Gen.*
50: 24. *Joshua* 23: 14. 1 *Kings*
2: 2.

Met without fear. *Ps.* 23: 4.

Precious in God's sight. *Ps.*
116: 15.

God preserves them unto. *Ps.*
48: 14.

God is with them in. *Ps.* 23: 4.

Removes from coming evil 2 *Kings* 22: 20. *Isa.* 57: 1.

Leads to

Rest. *Job* 3: 17. *Rev.* 14: 13.

Comfort. *Luke* 16: 25.

Christ's presence. 2 *Cor.* 5: 8. *Phil.* 1: 23.

A crown of life. 2 *Tim.* 4: 8. *Rev.* 2: 10.

A joyful resurrection. *Isa.* 26: 19. *Dan.* 12: 2.

Disregarded by the wicked. *Isa.* 57: 1.

Survivors consoled for. 1 *Thess.* 4: 13.

The wicked wish theirs to resemble. *Num.* 23: 10.

Illustrated. *Luke* 16: 22.

Exemplified. ABRAHAM, *Gen.* 25: 8, ISAAC, *Gen.* 35: 29. JACOB, *Gen.* 49: 33. AARON, *Num.* 20: 28. MOSES, *Deut.* 34: 5. JOSHUA, *Joshua* 24: 29. ELISHA, 2 *Kings* 13: 14, 20. ONE THIEF, *Luke* 23: 43. DORCAS, *Acts* 9: 37.

DEATH OF THE WICKED, THE

Is in their sins. *Ezek.* 3: 19. *John* 8: 21.

Is without hope. *Prov.* 11: 7.

Sometimes without fear. *Jer.* 34: 5, with 2 *Chron.* 36: 11–13.

Frequently sudden and unexpected. *Job* 21: 13, 23. *Job* 27: 21. *Prov.* 29: 1.

Frequently marked by terror. *Job* 18: 11–15. *Job* 27: 19–21. *Ps.* 73: 19.

Punishment follows. *Isa.* 14: 9. *Acts* 1: 25.

The remembrance of them perishes in. *Job* 18: 17. *Ps.* 34: 16. *Prov.* 10: 7.

God has no pleasure in. *Ezek.* 18: 23, 32.

Like the death of beasts. *Ps.* 49: 14.

Illustrated. *Luke* 12: 20. *Luke* 16: 22, 23.

Exemplified. KORAH, etc., *Num.* 16: 32. ABSALOM, 2 *Sam.* 18: 9, 10. AHAB, 1 *Kings* 22: 34. JEZEBEL, 2 *Kings* 9: 33. ATHALIAH, 2 *Chron.* 23: 15. HAMAN, *Esther* 7: 10. BELSHAZZAR, *Dan.* 5: 30. JUDAS, *Matt.* 27: 5, with *Acts* 1: 18. ANANIAS, etc., *Acts* 5: 5, 9, 10, HEROD, *Acts* 12: 23.

DECEIT

Is falsehood. *Ps.* 119: 118.

The tongue, the instrument of. *Rom.* 3: 13.

Comes from the heart. *Mark* 7: 22.

Characteristic of the heart. *Jer.* 17: 9.

God abhors. *Ps.* 5: 6.

Forbidden. *Prov.* 24: 28. 1 *Pet.* 3: 10.

Christ was perfectly free from. *Isa.* 53: 9, with 1 *Pet.* 2: 22.

Saints

Free from. *Ps.* 24: 4. *Zeph.* 3: 13. *Rev.* 14: 5.

Purpose against. *Job* 27: 4.

Avoid. *Job* 31: 5.

Shun those addicted to. *Ps.* 101: 7.

Pray for deliverance from those who use. *Ps.* 43: 1. *Ps.* 120: 2.

Delivered from those who use. *Ps.* 72: 14.

Should beware of those who teach. *Eph.* 5: 6. *Col.* 2: 8.

Should lay aside, in seeking truth. 1 *Pet.* 2: 1.

Ministers should lay aside. 2 *Cor.* 4: 2. 1 *Thess.* 2: 3.

The wicked

Are full of. *Rom.* 1: 29.

Devise. *Ps.* 35: 20. *Ps.* 38: 12. *Prov.* 12: 5.

Utter. *Ps.* 10: 7. *Ps.* 36: 3.

Work. *Prov.* 11: 18.

Increase in. 2 *Tim.* 3: 13.

Use, to each other. *Jer.* 9: 5.

Use to themselves. *Jer.* 37: 9. *Obad.* 3: 7.

Delight in. *Prov.* 20: 17.

False teachers

Are workers of. 2 *Cor.* 11: 13.

Preach. *Jer.* 14: 14. *Jer.* 23: 26.

Impose on others by. *Rom.* 16: 18. *Eph.* 4: 14.

Sport themselves with. 2 *Pet.* 2: 13.

Hypocrites devise. *Job* 15: 35.

Hypocrites practise. *Hos.* 11: 12.

False witnesses use. *Prov.* 12: 17.

A characteristic of Antichrist. 2 *John* 7.

A characteristic of the Apostacy. 2 *Thess.* 2: 10.

Evil of

Keeps from knowledge of God. *Jer.* 9: 6.

Keeps from turning to God. *Jer.* 8: 5.

Leads to pride and oppression. *Jer.* 5: 27, 28.

Leads to lying. *Prov.* 11: 25.

Often accompanied by fraud and injustice. *Ps.* 10: 7. *Ps.* 43: 1.

Hatred often concealed by. *Prov.* 26: 24–26.

The folly of fools is. *Prov.* 14: 8.

The kisses of an enemy are. *Prov.* 27: 6.

Blessedness of being free from. *Ps.* 24: 4, 5. *Ps.* 32: 2.

Punishment of. *Ps.* 55: 23. *Jer.* 9: 7–9.

Exemplified. THE DEVIL, *Gen.* 3: 1, 4, 5. REBECCA AND JACOB, *Gen.* 27: 9, 19. LABAN, *Gen.* 31: 7. JOSEPH'S BRETHREN, *Gen.* 37: 31, 32. PHARAOH, *Exod.* 8: 29. DAVID, 1 *Sam.* 21: 13. JOB'S FRIENDS, *Job* 6: 15. DOEG, *Ps.* 52: 2, compared with the title. HEROD, *Matt.* 2: 8. PHARISEES, *Matt.* 22: 16. CHIEF PRIESTS, *Mark* 14: 1. LAWYER, *Luke,* 10: 25.

DECISION

Necessary to the service of God. *Luke* 9: 62.

Exhortations to. *Joshua* 24: 14, 15.

Exhibited in

Seeking God with the heart. 2 *Chron.* 15: 12.

Keeping the commandments of God. *Neh.* 10: 29.

Being on the Lord's side. *Exod.* 32: 26.

Following God fully. *Num.* 14: 24. *Num.* 32: 12.

Serving God. *Isa.* 56: 6.

Loving God perfectly. *Deut.* 6: 5.

Blessedness of. *Joshua* 1: 7.

Opposed to

A divided service. *Matt.* 6: 24.

Double-mindedness. *Jas.* 1: 8.

Halting between two opinions. 1 *Kings* 18: 21.

Turning to the right or left. *Deut.* 5: 32.

Not setting the heart aright. *Ps.* 78: 8, 37.

Exemplified. MOSES, *Exod.*
32: 26. CALEB, *Num.* 13: 30.
JOSHUA, *Joshua* 24: 15. RUTH,
Ruth 1: 16. ASA, 2 *Chron.* 15:
8. DAVID, *Ps.* 17: 3. PETER,
John 6: 68. PAUL, *Acts* 21: 13.
ABRAHAM, *Heb.* 11: 8.

DELIGHTING IN GOD

Commanded. *Ps.* 37: 4.
Reconciliation leads to. *Job*
22: 21, 26.
Observing the sabbath leads to.
Isa. 58: 13, 14.

Saints experience, in
Communion with God.
Song of Sol. 2: 3.
The law of God. *Ps.* 1: 2.
Ps. 119: 24, 35.
The goodness of God. *Neh.*
9: 25.
The comforts of God. *Ps.*
94: 19.

Hypocrites
Pretend to. *Isa.* 58: 2.
In heart despise. *Job* 27: 10.
Jer. 6: 10.
Promises to. *Ps.* 37: 4.
Blessedness of. *Ps.* 112: 1.

DENIAL OF CHRIST

In doctrine. *Mark* 8: 38. 2
Tim. 1: 8.
In practice. *Phil.* 3: 18, 19.
Titus 1: 16.
A characteristic of false teach-
ers. 2 *Pet.* 2: 1. *Jude* 4.
Is the spirit of Antichrist. 1
John 2: 22, 23. 1 *John* 4: 3.
Christ will deny those guilty of.
Matt. 10: 33. 2 *Tim.* 2: 12.
Leads to destruction. 2 *Pet.*
2: 1. *Jude* 4, 15.
Exemplified. PETER, *Matt.* 26:
69–75. THE JEWS, *John* 18: 40.
Acts 3: 13, 14.

DESPAIR

Produced in the wicked by
divine judgments. *Deut.* 28:
34, 67. *Rev.* 9: 6. *Rev.* 16:
10.

Leads to
Continuing in sin. *Jer.* 2:
25. *Jer.* 18: 12.
Blasphemy. *Isa.* 8: 21. *Rev.*
16: 10, 11.
Shall seize upon the wicked at
the appearing of Christ.
Rev. 6: 16.
Saints sometimes tempted to.
Job 7: 6. *Lam.* 3: 18.
Sainst enabled to overcome.
2 *Cor.* 4: 8, 9.
Trust in God, a preservative
against. *Ps.* 42: 5, 11.
Exemplified. CAIN, *Gen.* 4: 13,
14. AHITHOPHEL, 2 *Sam.* 17: 23.
JUDAS, *Matt.* 27: 5.

DEVIL, THE

Sinned against God. 2 *Pet.* 2:
4. 1 *John* 3: 8.
Cast out of heaven. *Luke*
10: 18.
Cast down to hell. 2 *Pet.* 2: 4.
Jude 6.
The author of the fall. *Gen.*
3: 1, 6, 14, 24.
Tempted Christ. *Matt.* 4: 3–10.
Perverts the scriptures. *Matt.*
4: 6, with *Ps.* 91: 11, 12.
Opposes God's work. *Zech.*
3: 1. 1 *Thess.* 2: 18.
Hinders the gospel. *Matt.* 13:
19. 2 *Cor.* 4: 4.
Works lying wonders. 2 *Thess.*
2: 9. *Rev.* 16: 14.
Assumes the form of an angel
of light. 2 *Cor.* 11: 14.

The wicked
Are the children of. *Matt.*
13: 38. *Acts* 13: 10. 1 *John*
3: 10.

Turn aside after. 1 *Tim.* 5: 15.

Do the lusts of. *John* 8: 44.

Possessed by. *Luke* 22: 3. *Acts* 5: 3. *Eph.* 2: 2.

Blinded by. 2 *Cor.* 4: 4.

Deceived by. 1 *Kings* 22: 21, 22. *Rev.* 20: 7, 8.

Ensnared by. 1 *Tim.* 3: 7. 2 *Tim.* 2: 26.

Troubled by. 1 *Sam.* 16: 14.

Punished, together with. *Matt.* 25: 41.

Saints

Afflicted by, only as God permits. *Job* 1: 12. *Job* 2: 4–7.

Tempted by. 1 *Chron.* 21: 1. 1 *Thess.* 3: 5.

Sifted by. *Luke* 22: 31.

Should resist. *Jas.* 4: 7. 1 *Pet.* 5: 9.

Should be armed against. *Eph.* 6: 11–16.

Should be watchful against. 2 *Cor.* 2: 11.

Overcome. 1 *John* 2: 13. *Rev.* 12: 11.

Shall finally triumph over. *Rom.* 16: 20.

Triumph over, by Christ

Predicted. *Gen.* 3: 15. *Ps.* 68: 18.

In resisting his temptations. *Matt.* 4: 11.

In casting out the spirits of. *Luke* 11: 20. *Luke* 13: 32.

In empowering his disciples to cast out. *Matt.* 10: 1. *Mark* 16: 17.

In destroying the works of. 1 *John* 3: 8.

Completed by his death. *Col.* 2: 15. *Heb.* 2: 14.

Illustrated. *Luke* 11: 21, 22.

Character of,

Presumptuous. *Job* 1: 6. *Matt.* 4: 5, 6.

Proud. 1 *Tim.* 3: 6.

Powerful. *Eph.* 2: 2. *Eph.* 6: 12.

Wicked. 1 *John* 2: 13.

Malignant. *Job* 1: 9. *Job* 2: 4.

Subtle. *Gen.* 3: 1, with 2 *Cor.* 11: 3.

Deceitful. 2 *Cor.* 11: 14. *Eph.* 6: 11.

Fierce and cruel. *Luke* 8: 29. *Luke* 9: 38, 42. 1 *Pet.* 5: 8.

Active in doing evil. *Job* 1: 7. *Job* 2: 2.

Cowardly. *Jas.* 4: 7.

The Apostacy is of. 2 *Thess.* 2: 9. 1 *Tim.* 4: 1.

Shall be condemned at the judgment. *Jude* 6. *Rev.* 20: 10.

Everlasting fire is prepared for. *Matt.* 25: 41.

Compared to, A FOWLER, *Ps.* 91: 3, FOWLS, *Matt.* 13: 4. A SOWER OF TARES. *Matt.* 13: 25, 28. A WOLF, *John* 10: 12. A ROARING LION, 1 *Pet.* 5: 8.

DEVOTEDNESS TO GOD

A characteristic of saints. *Ps.* 119: 38.

Christ, an example of. *John* 4: 34. *John* 17: 4.

Grounded upon

The mercies of God. *Rom.* 12: 1.

The goodness of God. 1 *Sam.* 12: 24.

The call of God. 1 *Thess.* 2: 12.

The death of Christ. 2 *Cor.* 5: 15.

Our creation. *Ps.* 86: 9.

Our preservation. *Isa.* 46: 4.

Our redemption. 1 *Cor.* 6: 19, 20.

Should be

With our spirit. 1 *Cor.* 6: 20. 1 *Pet.* 4: 6.

With our bodies. *Rom.* 12: 1. 1 *Cor.* 6: 20.

With our members. *Rom.* 6: 12, 13.

With our substance. *Exod.* 22: 29. *Prov.* 3: 9.

Unreserved. *Matt.* 6: 24. *Luke* 14: 33.

Abounding. 1 *Thess.* 4: 1.

Persevering. *Luke* 1: 74, 75. *Luke* 9: 62.

In life and death. *Rom.* 14: 8. *Phil.* 1: 20.

Should be exhibited in

Loving God. *Deut.* 6: 5. *Luke* 10: 27.

Serving God. 1 *Sam.* 12: 24. *Rom.* 12: 11.

Walking worthy of God. 1 *Thess.* 2: 12.

Doing all to God's glory. 1 *Cor.* 10: 31.

Bearing the cross. *Mark* 8: 34.

Self-denial. *Mark* 8: 34.

Living to Christ. 2 *Cor.* 5: 15.

Giving up all for Christ. *Matt.* 19: 21, 28, 29.

Want of, condemned. *Rev.* 3: 16.

Exemplified. JOSHUA, *Joshua* 24: 15. PETER, ANDREW, JAMES, JOHN. *Matt.* 4: 20—22. JOANNA, etc., *Luke* 8: 3. PAUL, *Phil.* 1: 21. TIMOTHY, *Phil.* 2: 19—22. EPAPHRODITUS, *Phil.* 2: 30.

DILIGENCE

Christ, an example. *Mark* 1: 35. *Luke* 2: 49.

Required by God in

Seeking him. 1 *Chron.* 22: 19. *Heb.* 11: 6.

Obeying him. *Deut.* 6: 17. *Deut.* 11: 13.

Hearkening to him. *Isa.* 55: 2.

Striving after perfection. *Phil.* 3: 13, 14.

Cultivating Christian graces. 2 *Pet.* 1: 5.

Keeping the soul. *Deut.* 4: 9.

Keeping the heart. *Prov.* 4: 23.

Labours of love. *Heb.* 6: 10—12.

Following every good work. 1 *Tim.* 5: 10.

Guarding against defilement. *Heb.* 12: 15.

Seeking to be found spotless. 2 *Pet.* 3: 14.

Making our calling, etc., sure. 2 *Pet.* 1: 10.

Self-examination. *Ps.* 77: 6.

Lawful business. *Prov.* 27: 22. *Eccles.* 9: 10.

Teaching religion. 2 *Tim.* 4: 2. *Jude* 3.

Instructing children. *Deut.* 6: 7. *Deut.* 11: 19.

Discharging official duties. *Deut.* 19: 18.

Saints should abound in. 2 *Cor.* 8: 7.

In the service of God

Should be persevered in. *Gal.* 6: 9.

Is not in vain. 1 *Cor.* 15: 58.

Preserves from evil. *Exod.* 15: 26.

Leads to assured hope. *Heb.* 6: 11.

God rewards. *Deut.* 11: 14. *Heb.* 11: 6.

In temporal matters, leads to

Favour. *Prov.* 11: 27.

Prosperity. *Prov.* 10: 4. *Prov.* 13: 4.

Honour. *Prov.* 12: 24. *Prov.* 22: 29.

Illustrated. *Prov.* 6: 6–8.

Exemplified. JACOB, *Gen.* 31: 40. RUTH *Ruth* 2: 17. HEZEKIAH, 2 *Chron.* 31: 21 NEHEMIAH, etc., *Neh.* 4: 6. PSALMIST, *Ps* 119: 60. APOSTLES, *Acts* 5: 42. APOLLOS *Acts* 18: 25. TITUS, 2 *Cor.* 8: 22. PAUL, *Thess.* 2: 9. ONESIPHORUS, 2 *Tim.* 1: 17

DISCIPLINE OF THE CHURCH

Ministers authorised to establish. *Matt.* 16: 19. *Matt.* 18: 18.

Consists in

Maintaining sound doctrine. 1 *Tim.* 1: 3. *Titus* 1: 13.

Ordering its affairs. 1 *Cor.* 11: 34. *Titus* 1: 5.

Rebuking offenders. 1 *Tim.* 5: 20. 2 *Tim.* 4: 2.

Removing obstinate offenders. 1 *Cor.* 5: 3–5, 13. 1 *Tim.* 1: 20.

Should be submitted to. *Heb.* 13: 17.

Is for edification. 2 *Cor.* 10: 8. 2 *Cor.* 13: 10.

Decency and order, the objects of. 1 *Cor.* 14: 40.

Exercise, in a spirit of charity. 2 *Cor.* 2: 6–8.

DISOBEDIENCE TO GOD

Provokes his anger. *Ps.* 78: 10, 40. *Isa.* 3: 8.

Forfeits his favour. 1 *Sam.* 13: 14.

Forfeits his promised blessings. *Joshua* 5: 6. 1 *Sam.* 2: 30. *Jer.* 18: 10.

Brings a curse. *Deut.* 11: 28. *Deut.* 28: 15, &c.

A characteristic of the wicked. *Eph.* 5: 6. *Titus* 1: 16. *Titus* 3: 3.

The wicked persevere in. *Jer.* 22: 21.

Heinousness of, illustrated. *Jer.* 35: 14, &c.

Men prone to excuse. *Gen.* 3: 12, 13.

Shall be punished. *Isa.* 42: 24, 25. *Heb.* 2: 2.

Acknowledge the punishment of, to be just. *Neh.* 9: 32, 33. *Dan.* 9: 10, 11, 14.

Warnings against. 1 *Sam.* 12: 15. *Jer.* 12: 17.

Bitter results of, illustrated. *Jer.* 9: 13, 15.

Exemplified. ADAM AND EVE, *Gen.* 3: 6, 11. PHARAOH, *Exod.* 5: 2. NADAB, etc., *Lev.* 10: 1. MOSES, etc., *Num.* 20: 8, 11, 24. SAUL, 1 *Sam.* 28: 18. THE PROPHET, 1 *Kings* 13: 20–23. ISRAEL, 2 *Kings* 18: 9–12. JONAH, *Jonah* 1: 2, 3.

DIVISIONS

Forbidden in the church. 1 *Cor.* 1: 10.

Condemned in the church. 1 *Cor.* 1: 11–13. 1 *Cor.* 11: 18.

Unbecoming in the church. 1 *Cor.* 11: 24, 25.

Are contrary to the

Unity of Christ. 1 *Cor.* 1: 13. 1 *Cor.* 12: 13.

Desire of Christ. *John* 17: 21–23.

Purpose of Christ. *John* 10: 16.

Spirit of the primitive church. 1 *Cor.* 11: 16.

Are a proof of a carnal spirit.
1 *Cor.* 3: 3.

Avoid those who cause. *Rom.*
16: 17.

Evil of, illustrated. *Matt.* 12:
25.

DIVORCE

Law of marriage against. *Gen.*
2: 24. *Matt.* 19: 6.

Permitted

By the Mosaic law. *Deut.*
24: 1.

On account of hardness of
heart. *Matt.* 19: 8.

Often sought by the Jews.
Mic. 2: 9. *Mal.* 2: 14.

Sought on slight grounds.
Matt. 5: 31. *Matt.* 19: 3.

Not allowed to those who
falsely accused their wives.
Deut. 22: 18, 19.

Women

Could obtain. *Prov.* 2: 17,
with *Mark* 10: 12.

Could marry after. *Deut.*
24: 2.

Responsible for vows after.
Num. 30: 9.

Married after, could not return to first husband. *Deut.*
24: 3, 4. *Jer.* 3: 1.

Afflicted by. *Isa.* 54: 4, 6.

Priests not to marry women
after. *Lev.* 21: 14.

Of servants, regulated by law.
Exod. 21: 7, 11.

Of captives, regulated by law.
Deut. 21: 13, 14.

Forced on those who had
idolatrous wives. *Ezra* 10:
2–17. *Neh.* 13: 23, 30.

Jews condemned for love of.
Mal. 2: 14–16.

Forbidden by Christ except
for adultery. *Matt.* 5: 32.
Matt. 19: 9.

Prohibition of, offended the
Jews. *Matt.* 19: 10.

Illustrative of God's casting
off the Jewish church. *Isa.*
50: 1. *Jer.* 3: 8.

DOCTRINES OF THE GOSPEL, THE

Are from God. *John* 7: 16.
Acts 13: 12.

Are taught by scripture. 2
Tim. 3: 16.

Are godly. 1 *Tim.* 6: 3. *Titus*
1: 1.

Immorality condemned by.
1 *Tim.* 1:9–11.

Lead to fellowship with the
Father and with the son. 1
John 1: 3. 2 *John* 9.

Lead to holiness. *Rom.* 6: 17–
22. *Titus* 2: 12.

Bring no reproach on. 1 *Tim.*
6: 1. *Titus* 2: 5.

Ministers should

Be nourished up in. 1 *Tim.*
4: 6.

Attend to. 1 *Tim.* 4: 13, 16.

Hold, in sincerity. 1 *Cor.*
2: 17. *Titus* 2: 7.

Hold, stedfastly. 2 *Tim.* 1:
13. *Titus* 1: 9.

Continue in. 1 *Tim.* 4: 16.

Speak things which become.
Titus 2: 1.

Saints obey, from the heart.
Rom. 6: 17.

Saints abide in. *Acts* 2: 42.
2 *John* 9.

A faithful walk adorns. *Titus*
2: 10.

The obedience of saints leads to
surer knowledge of. *John* 7:
17.

Those who oppose, are

Proud. 1 *Tim.* 6: 3, 4.

Ignorant. 1 *Tim.* 6: 4.

Doting about questions, &c. 1 *Tim.* 6: 4.

Not to be received. 2 *John* 10.

To be avoided. *Rom.* 16: 17.

Not endured by the wicked. 2 *Tim.* 4: 3.

DOCTRINES, FALSE

A hindrance to growth in grace. *Eph.* 4: 14.

Destructive to faith. 2 *Tim.* 2: 18.

Hateful to God. *Rev.* 2: 14, 15.

Unprofitable and vain. *Titus* 3: 9. *Heb.* 13: 9.

Should be avoided by

Ministers. 1 *Tim.* 1: 4. 1 *Tim.* 6: 20.

Saints. *Eph.* 4: 14. *Col.* 2: 8.

All men. *Jer.* 23: 16. *Jer.* 29: 8.

The wicked love. 2 *Tim.* 4: 3, 4.

The wicked given up to believe. 2 *Thess.* 2: 11.

Teachers of,

Not to be countenanced. 2 *John* 10.

Should be avoided. *Rom.* 16: 17, 18.

Bring reproach on religion. 2 *Pet.* 2: 2.

Speak perverse things. *Acts* 20: 30.

Attract many. *Acts* 20: 30. 2 *Pet.* 2: 2.

Deceive many. *Matt.* 24: 5.

Shall abound in the latter days. 1 *Tim.* 4: 1.

Pervert the gospel of Christ. *Gal.* 1: 6, 7.

Shall be exposed. 2 *Tim.* 3: 9.

Teachers of, are described as

Cruel. *Acts* 20: 29.

Deceitful. 2 *Cor.* 11: 13.

Covetous. *Titus* 1: 11. 2 *Pet.* 2: 3.

Ungodly. *Jude* 4, 8.

Proud and ignorant. 1 *Tim.* 6: 3, 4.

Corrupt and reprobate. 2 *Tim.* 3: 8.

Try, by scripture. *Isa.* 8: 20. 1 *John* 4: 1.

Curse on those who teach. *Gal.* 1: 8, 9.

Punishment of those who teach. *Mic.* 3: 6, 7. 2 *Pet.* 2: 1, 3.

DRUNKENNESS

Forbidden. *Eph.* 5: 18.

Caution against. *Luke* 21: 34.

Is a work of the flesh. *Gal.* 5: 21.

Is debasing. *Isa.* 28: 8.

Is inflaming. *Isa.* 5: 11.

Overcharges the heart. *Luke* 21: 34.

Takes away the heart. *Hos.* 4: 11.

Leads to

Poverty. *Prov.* 21: 17. *Prov.* 23: 21.

Strife. *Prov.* 23: 29, 30.

Woe and sorrow. *Prov.* 23: 29, 30.

Error. *Isa.* 28: 7.

Contempt of God's works. *Isa.* 5: 12.

Scorning. *Hos.* 7: 5.

Rioting and wantonness. *Rom.* 13: 13.

The wicked addicted to. *Dan.* 5: 1–4.

False teachers often addicted to. *Isa.* 56: 12.

Folly of yielding to. *Prov.* 20: 1.

Avoid those given to. *Prov.* 23: 20. 1 *Cor.* 5: 11.

Denunciations against

Those given to. *Isa.* 5: 11, 12. *Isa.* 28: 1–3.

Those who encourage. *Hab.* 2: 15.

Excludes from heaven. 1 *Cor.* 6: 10. *Gal.* 5: 21.

Punishment of. *Deut.* 21: 20, 21. *Joel* 1: 5, 6. *Amos* 6: 7. *Matt.* 24: 49–51.

Exemplified. NOAH, *Gen.* 9: 21. NABAL, 1 *Sam.* 25: 36. URIAH, 2 *Sam.* 11: 13. ELAH, 1 *Kings* 16: 9, 10. BENHADAD, 1 *Kings* 20: 16. BELSHAZZAR, *Dan.* 5: 4. CORINTHIANS, 1 *Cor.* 11: 21.

EARLY RISING

Christ set an example of. *Mark* 1: 35. *Luke* 21: 38. *John* 8: 2.

Requisite for

Redeeming time. *Eph.* 5: 16.

Devotion. *Ps.* 5: 3. *Ps.* 59: 16. *Ps.* 63: 1. *Ps.* 88: 13. *Isa.* 26: 9.

Communion with Christ. *Song of Sol.* 7: 12.

Executing God's commands. *Gen.* 22: 3.

Discharge of daily duties. *Prov.* 31: 15.

Neglect of, leads to poverty. *Prov.* 6: 9–11.

Practised by the wicked, for

Deceit. *Prov.* 27: 14.

Drunkenness. *Isa.* 5: 11.

Corrupting their doings. *Zeph.* 3: 7.

Executing plans of evil. *Mic.* 2: 1.

Illustrates spiritual diligence. *Rom.* 13: 11, 12.

Exemplified. ABRAHAM, *Gen.* 19: 27. ISAAC, etc., *Gen.* 26: 31. JACOB, *Gen.* 28: 18. JOSHUA, etc., *Joshua* 3: 1. GIDEON, *Judges* 6: 38. SAMUEL, 1 *Sam.* 15: 12. DAVID, 1 *Sam.* 17: 20. SERVANT OF ELISHA, 2 *Kings* 6: 15. MARY, etc., *Mark* 16: 2. APOSTLES, *Acts* 5: 21.

EDIFICATION

Described. *Eph.* 4: 12–16.

Is the object of

The ministerial office. *Eph.* 4: 11, 12.

Ministerial gifts. 1 *Cor.* 14: 3–5, 12.

Ministerial authority. 2 *Cor.* 10: 8. 2 *Cor.* 13: 10.

The Church's union in Christ. *Eph.* 4: 16.

The gospel, the instrument of. *Acts* 20: 32.

Love leads to. 1 *Cor.* 8: 1.

Exhortation to. *Jude* 20, 21.

Mutual, commanded. *Rom.* 14: 19. 1 *Thess.* 5: 11.

All to be done to. 2 *Cor.* 12: 19. *Eph.* 4: 29.

Use self-denial to promote, in others. 1 *Cor.* 10: 23, 33.

The peace of the Church favours. *Acts* 9: 31.

Foolish questions opposed to. 1 *Tim.* 1: 4.

ELECTION

Of Christ, as Messiah. *Isa.* 42: 1. 1 *Pet.* 2: 6.

Of good angels. 1 *Tim.* 5: 21.

Of Israel. *Deut.* 7: 6. *Isa.* 45: 4.

Of ministers. *Luke* 6: 13. *Acts* 9: 15.

Of churches. 1 *Pet.* 5: 13.

Of saints, is

Of God. 1 *Thess.* 1: 4. *Titus* 1: 1.

By Christ. *John* 13: 18. *John* 15: 16.

In Christ. *Eph.* 1: 4.

Personal. *Matt.* 20: 16, with *John* 6: 44. *Acts.* 22: 14. 2 *John* 13.

According to the purpose of God. *Rom.* 9: 11. *Eph.* 1: 11.

According to the foreknowledge of God. *Rom.* 8: 29. 1 *Pet.* 1: 2.

Eternal. *Eph.* 1: 4.

Sovereign. *Rom.* 9: 15, 16. 1 *Cor.* 1: 27. *Eph.* 1: 11.

Irrespective of merit. *Rom.* 9: 11.

Of grace. *Rom.* 11: 5.

Recorded in heaven. *Luke* 10: 20.

For the glory of God. *Eph.* 1: 6.

Through faith. 2 *Thess.* 2: 13.

Through sanctification of the Spirit. 1 *Pet.* 1: 2. 2 *Thess.* 2: 13.

To adoption. *Eph.* 1: 5.

To salvation. 2 *Thess.* 2: 13.

To conformity with Christ. *Rom.* 8: 29.

To good works. *Eph.* 2: 10.

To spiritual warfare. 2 *Tim.* 2: 4.

To eternal glory. *Rom.* 9: 23.

Ensures to saints

Effectual calling. *Rom.* 8: 30.

Divine teaching. *John* 17: 6.

Belief in Christ. *Acts* 13: 48.

Acceptance with God. *Rom.* 11: 7.

Protection. *Mark* 13: 20.

Vindication of their wrongs. *Luke* 18: 7.

Working of all things for good. *Rom.* 8: 28.

Blessedness. *Ps.* 33: 12. *Ps.* 65: 4.

The inheritance. *Isa.* 65: 9. 1 *Pet.* 1: 4, 5.

Should lead to cultivation of graces. *Col.* 3: 12.

Should be evidenced by diligence. 2 *Pet.* 1: 10.

Saints may have assurance of. 1 *Thess.* 1: 4.

Exemplified. ISAAC, *Gen.* 21: 12. ABRAM, *Neh.* 9: 7. ZERUBBABEL, *Hag.* 2: 23. APOSTLES, *John* 13: 18. *John* 15: 19. JACOB, *Rom.* 9: 12, 13. RUFUS, *Rom.* 16: 13. PAUL, *Gal.* 1: 15.

EMBLEMS OF THE HOLY SPIRIT, THE

Water. *John* 3: 5. *John* 7: 38, 39.

Cleansing. *Ezek.* 16: 9. *Ezek.* 36: 25. *Eph.* 5: 26. *Heb.* 10: 22.

Fertilizing. *Ps.* 1: 3. *Isa.* 27: 3, 6. *Isa.* 44: 3, 4. *Isa.* 58: 11.

Refreshing. *Ps.* 46: 4. *Isa.* 41: 17, 18.

Abundant. *John* 7: 37, 38.

Freely given. *Isa.* 55: 1. *John* 4: 14. *Rev.* 22: 17.

Fire. *Matt.* 3: 11.

Purifying. *Isa.* 4: 4. *Mal.* 3: 2, 3.

Illuminating. *Exod.* 13: 21. *Ps.* 78: 14.

Searching. *Zeph.* 1: 12, with 1 *Cor.* 2: 10.

Wind. *Song of Sol.* 4: 16.

Independent. *John* 3: 8. 1 *Cor.* 12: 11.

Powerful. 1 *Kings* 19: 11, with *Acts* 2: 2.

Sensible in its effects. *John* 3: 8.

Reviving. *Ezek.* 37: 9, 10, 14.

Oil. *Ps.* 45: 7.

  Healing. *Isa.* 1: 6. *Luke* 10: 34. *Rev.* 3: 18. ●

  Comforting. *Isa.* 61: 3. *Heb.* 1: 9.

  Illuminating. *Zech.* 4: 2, 3, 11–14. *Matt.* 25: 3, 4. 1 *John* 2: 20, 27.

  Consecrating. *Exod.* 29: 7. *Exod.* 30: 30. *Isa.* 61: 1.

Rain and dew. *Ps.* 72: 6.

  Fertilizing. *Ezek.* 34: 26, 27. *Hos.* 6: 3. *Hos.* 10: 12. *Hos.* 14: 5.

  Refreshing. *Ps.* 68: 9. *Isa.* 18: 4.

  Abundant. *Ps.* 133: 3.

  Imperceptible. 2 *Sam.* 17: 12, with *Mark* 4: 26–28.

A dove. *Matt.* 3: 16.

  Gentle. *Matt.* 10: 16, with *Gal.* 5: 22.

A voice. *Isa.* 6: 8.

  Speaking. *Matt.* 10: 20.

  Guiding. *Isa.* 30: 21, with *John* 16: 13.

  Warning. *Heb.* 3: 7–11.

A seal. *Rev.* 7: 2.

  Impressing. *Job* 38: 14, with 2 *Cor.* 3: 18.

  Securing. *Eph.* 1: 13, 14. *Eph.* 4: 30.

  Authenticating. *John* 6: 27. 2 *Cor.* 1: 22.

Cloven tongues. *Acts* 2: 3, 6: 11.

ENEMIES

Christ prayed for his. *Luke* 23: 34.

The lives of, to be spared. 1 *Sam.* 24: 10. 2 *Sam.* 16: 10, 11.

The goods of, to be taken care of. *Exod.* 23: 4, 5.

Should be

  Loved. *Matt.* 5: 44.

Prayed for. *Matt.* 5: 44. *Acts* 7: 60.

Assisted. *Prov.* 25: 21, with *Rom.* 12: 20.

Overcome by kindness. 1 *Sam.* 26: 21. *Prov.* 25: 22, with *Rom.* 12: 20.

Rejoice not at the misfortunes of. *Job* 31: 29.

Rejoice not at the fallings of. *Prov.* 24: 17.

Desire not the death of. 1 *Kings* 3: 11.

Curse them not. *Job* 31: 30.

Be affectionately concerned for. *Ps.* 35: 13.

The friendship of, deceitful. 2 *Sam.* 20: 9, 10. *Prov.* 26: 26. *Prov.* 27: 6. *Matt.* 26: 48, 49.

God defends against. *Ps.* 59: 9. *Ps.* 61: 3.

God delivers from. 1 *Sam.* 12: 11. *Ezra* 8: 31. *Ps.* 18: 48.

Made to be at peace with saints. *Prov.* 16: 7.

Pray for deliverance from. 1 *Sam.* 12: 10. *Ps.* 17: 9. *Ps.* 59: 1. *Ps.* 64: 1.

Of saints, God will destroy. *Ps.* 60: 12.

Praise God for deliverance from. *Ps.* 136: 24.

ENVY

Forbidden. *Prov.* 3: 31. *Rom.* 13: 13.

Produced by foolish disputations. 1 *Tim.* 6: 4.

Excited by good deeds of others. *Eccles.* 4: 4.

A work of the flesh. *Gal.* 5: 21. *Jas.* 4: 5.

Hurtful to the envious. *Job* 5: 2. *Prov.* 14: 30.

None can stand before. *Prov.* 27: 4.

A proof of carnal-mindedness. 1 *Cor.* 3: 1, 3.

Inconsistent with the gospel. *Jas.* 3: 14.

Hinders growth in grace. 1 *Pet.* 2: 1, 2.

The wicked

Are full of. *Rom.* 1: 29.

Live in. *Titus* 3: 3.

Leads to every evil work. *Jas.* 3: 16.

Prosperity of the wicked should not excite. *Ps.* 37: 1, 35. *Ps.* 73: 3, 17–20.

Punishment of. *Ps.* 106: 16, 17. *Isa.* 26: 11.

Exemplified. CAIN, *Gen.* 4: 5. PHILISTINES, *Gen.* 26: 14. LABAN'S SONS, *Gen.* 31: 1. JOSEPH'S BRETHREN, *Gen.* 37: 11. JOSHUA, *Num.* 11: 28, 29. AARON, etc., *Num.* 12: 2. KORAH, etc., *Num.* 16: 3, with *Ps.* 106: 16. SAUL, 1 *Sam.* 18: 8. SANBALLAT, etc., *Neh.* 2: 10. HAMAN, *Esther* 5: 13. EDOMITES, *Ezek.* 35: 11. PRINCES OF BABYLON, *Dan.* 6: 3, 4. CHIEF PRIESTS, *Mark* 15: 10. JEWS, *Acts* 13: 45. *Acts* 17: 5.

EXAMPLE OF CHRIST, THE

Is perfect. *Heb.* 7: 26.

Conformity to, required in

Holiness. 1 *Pet.* 1: 15, 16, with *Rom.* 1: 6.

Righteousness. 1 *John* 2: 6.

Purity. 1 *John* 3: 3.

Love. *John* 13: 34. *Eph.* 5: 2. 1 *John* 3: 16.

Humility. *Luke* 22: 27. *Phil.* 2: 5, 7.

Meekness. *Matt.* 11: 29.

Lowliness of heart. *Matt.* 11: 29.

Obedience. *John* 15: 10.

Self-denial. *Matt.* 16: 24. *Rom.* 15: 3.

Ministering to others. *Matt.* 20: 28. *John* 13: 14, 15.

Benevolence. *Acts* 20: 35. 2 *Cor.* 8: 7, 9.

Forgiving injuries. *Col.* 3: 13.

Overcoming sin. 1 *Pet.* 4: 1.

Overcoming the world. *John* 16: 33, with 1 *John* 5: 4.

Being not of the world. *John* 17: 16.

Being guileless. 1 *Pet.* 2: 21, 22.

Suffering wrongfully. 1 *Pet.* 2: 21–23.

Suffering for righteousness. *Heb.* 12: 3, 4.

Saints predestinated to follow. *Rom.* 8: 29.

Conformity to, progressive. 2 *Cor.* 3: 18.

EXCELLENCY AND GLORY OF CHRIST, THE

As God. *John* 1: 1–5. *Phil.* 2: 6, 9, 10.

As the Son of God. *Matt.* 3: 17. *Heb.* 1: 6, 8.

As One with the Father. *John* 10: 30, 38.

As the First-born. *Col.* 1: 15, 18.

As the First-begotten. *Heb.* 1: 6.

As Lord of lords, &c. *Rev.* 17: 14.

As the image of God. *Col.* 1: 15. *Heb.* 1: 3.

As Creator. *John* 1: 3. *Col.* 1: 16. *Heb.* 1: 2.

As the Blessed of God. *Ps.* 45: 2.

As Mediator. 1 *Tim.* 2: 5. *Heb.* 8: 6.

As Prophet. *Deut.* 18: 15, 16, with *Acts* 3: 22.

As Priest. *Ps.* 110: 4. *Heb.* 4: 15.

As King. *Isa.* 6: 1–5, with *John* 12: 41.

As Judge. *Matt.* 16: 27. *Matt.* 25: 31–33.

As Shepherd. *Isa.* 40: 10, 11. *John* 10: 11, 14.

As Head of the Church. *Eph.* 1: 22.

As the true Light. *Luke* 1: 78, 79. *John* 1: 4, 9.

As the foundation of the Church. *Isa.* 28: 16.

As the way. *John* 14: 6. *Heb.* 10: 19, 20.

As the truth. 1 *John* 5: 20. *Rev.* 3: 7.

As the life. *John* 11: 25. *Col.* 3: 4. 1 *John* 5: 11.

As incarnate. *John* 1: 14.

In his words. *Luke* 4: 22. *John* 7: 46.

In his works. *Matt.* 13: 54. *John* 2: 11.

In his sinless perfection. *Heb.* 7: 26–28.

In the fulness of his grace and truth. *Ps.* 45: 2, with *John* 1: 14.

In his transfiguration. *Matt.* 17: 2, with 2 *Pet.* 1: 16–18.

In his exaltation. *Acts* 7: 55, 56. *Eph.* 1: 21.

In the calling of the Gentiles. *Ps.* 72: 17. *John* 12: 21, 23.

In the restoration of the Jews. *Ps.* 102: 16.

In his triumph. *Isa.* 63: 1–3, with *Rev.* 19: 11, 16.

Followed his sufferings. 1 *Pet.* 1: 10, 11.

Followed his resurrection. 1 *Pet.* 1: 21.

Is unchangeable. *Heb.* 1: 10–12.

Is incomparable. *Song of Sol.* 5: 10. *Phil.* 2: 9.

Imparted to saints. *John* 17: 22. 2 *Cor.* 3: 18.

Celebrated by the redeemed. *Rev.* 5: 8–14. *Rev.* 7: 9–12.

Revealed in the gospel. *Isa.* 40: 5.

Saints shall rejoice at the revelation of. 1 *Pet.* 4: 13.

Saints shall behold, in heaven. *John* 17: 24.

EXCELLENCY AND GLORY OF THE CHURCH, THE

Derived from God. *Isa.* 28: 5.

Derived from Christ. *Isa.* 60: 1. *Luke* 2: 39.

Result from the favour of God. *Isa.* 43: 4.

God delights in. *Ps.* 45: 11. *Isa.* 62: 3–5.

Saints delight in. *Isa.* 66: 11.

Consist in its

Being the seat of God's worship. *Ps.* 96: 6.

Being the temple of God. 1 *Cor.* 3: 16, 17. *Eph.* 2: 21, 22.

Being the body of Christ. *Eph.* 1: 22, 23.

Being the bride of Christ. *Ps.* 45: 13, 14. *Rev.* 19: 7, 8. *Rev.* 21: 2.

Being established. *Ps.* 48: 8. *Isa.* 33: 20.

Eminent position. *Ps.* 48: 2. *Isa.* 2: 2.

Graces of character. *Song of Sol.* 2: 14.

Perfection of beauty. *Ps.* 50: 2.

Members being righteous. *Isa.* 60: 21. *Rev.* 19: 8.

Strength and defence. *Ps.* 48: 12, 13.

Sanctification. *Eph.* 5: 26, 27.

Augmented by increase of its members. *Isa.* 49: 18. *Isa.* 60: 4–14.

Are abundant. *Isa.* 66: 11.

Sin obscures. *Lam.* 2: 14, 15.

FAITH

Is the substance of things hoped for. *Heb.* 11: 1.

Is the evidence of things not seen. *Heb.* 11: 1.

Commanded. *Mark* 11: 22. 1 *John* 3: 23.

The objects of, are

God. *Mark* 11: 22. *John* 14: 1.

Christ. *John* 6: 29. *John* 14: 1. *Acts* 20: 21.

Writings of Moses. *John* 5: 46. *Acts* 24: 14.

Writings of the prophets. 2 *Chron.* 20: 20. *Acts* 26: 27.

The gospel. *Mark* 1: 15.

Promise of God. *Rom.* 4: 21. *Heb.* 11: 13.

In Christ, is

The gift of God. *Rom.* 12: 3. *Eph.* 2: 8. *Eph.* 6: 23. *Phil.* 1: 29.

The work of God. *Acts* 11: 21. 1 *Cor.* 2: 5.

Precious. 2 *Pet.* 1: 1.

Most holy. *Jude* 20.

Fruitful. 1 *Thess.* 1: 3.

Accompanied by repentance. *Mark* 1: 15. *Luke* 24: 47.

Followed by conversion. *Acts* 11: 21.

Christ is the Author and Finisher of. *Heb.* 12: 2.

Is a gift of the Holy Ghost. 1 *Cor.* 12: 9.

The scriptures designed to produce. *John* 20: 31. 2 *Tim.* 3: 15.

Preaching designed to produce.
John 17: 20. *Acts* 8: 12. *Rom.* 10: 14, 15, 17. 1 *Cor.* 3: 5.

Through it is

Remission of sins. *Acts* 10: 43. *Rom.* 3: 25.

Justification. *Acts* 13: 39. *Rom.* 3: 21, 22, 28, 30. *Rom.* 5: 1. *Gal.* 2: 16.

Salvation. *Mark* 16: 16. *Acts* 16: 31.

Sanctification. *Acts* 15: 9. *Acts* 26: 18.

Spiritual light. *John* 12: 36, 46.

Spiritual life. *John* 20: 31. *Gal.* 2: 20.

Eternal life. *John* 3: 15, 16. *John* 6: 40, 47.

Rest in heaven. *Heb.* 4: 3.

Edification. 1 *Tim.* 1: 4. *Jude* 20.

Preservation. 1 *Pet.* 1: 5.

Adoption. *John* 1: 12. *Gal.* 3: 26.

Access to God. *Rom.* 5: 2. *Eph.* 3: 12.

Inheritance of the promises. *Gal.* 3: 22. *Heb.* 6: 12.

The gift of the Holy Ghost. *Acts* 11: 15–17. *Gal.* 3: 14. *Eph.* 1: 13.

Impossible to please God without. *Heb.* 11: 6.

Justification is by, to be of grace. *Rom.* 4: 16.

Essential to the profitable reception of the gospel. *Heb.* 4: 2.

Necessary in the Christian warfare. 1 *Tim.* 1: 18, 19. 1 *Tim.* 6: 12.

The gospel effectual in those who have. 1 *Thess.* 2: 13.

Excludes self-justification. *Rom.* 10: 3, 4.

Excludes boasting. *Rom.* 3: 27.

Works by love. *Gal.* 5: 6. 1 *Tim.* 1: 5. *Philem.* 5.

Produces

Hope. *Rom.* 5: 2.

Joy. *Acts* 16: 34. 1 *Pet.* 1: 8.

Peace. *Rom.* 15: 13.

Confidence. *Isa.* 28: 16, with 1 *Pet.* 2: 6.

Boldness in preaching. *Ps.* 116: 10, with 2 *Cor.* 4: 13.

Christ is precious to those having. 1 *Pet.* 2: 7.

Christ dwells in the heart by. *Eph.* 3: 17.

Necessary in prayer. *Matt.* 21: 22. *Jas.* 1: 6.

Those who are not Christ's have not. *John* 10: 26, 27.

An evidence of the new birth. 1 *John* 5: 1.

By it saints

Live. *Gal.* 2: 20.

Stand. *Rom.* 11: 20. 2 *Cor.* 1: 24.

Walk. *Rom.* 4: 12. 2 *Cor.* 5: 7.

Obtain a good report. *Heb.* 11: 2.

Overcome the world. 1 *John* 5: 4, 5.

Resist the devil. 1 *Pet.* 5: 9.

Overcome the devil. *Eph.* 6: 16.

Are supported. *Ps.* 27: 13. 1 *Tim.* 4: 10.

Saints die in. *Heb.* 11: 13.

Saints should

Be full of. *Acts* 6: 5. *Acts* 11: 24.

Be sincere in. 1 *Tim.* 1: 5. 2 *Tim.* 1: 5.

Abound in. 2 *Cor.* 8: 7.

Continue in. *Acts* 14: 22. *Col.* 1: 23.

Be strong in. *Rom.* 4: 20.

Stand fast in. 1 *Cor.* 16: 13.

Be grounded and settled in. *Col.* 1: 23.

Hold, with a good conscience. 1 *Tim.* 1: 19.

Pray for the increase of. *Luke* 17: 5.

Have full assurance of. 2 *Tim.* 1: 12. *Heb.* 10: 22.

True, evidenced by its fruits. *Jas.* 2: 21–25.

Without fruits, is dead. *Jas.* 2: 17, 20, 26.

Examine whether you be in. 2 *Cor.* 13: 5.

All difficulties overcome by. *Matt.* 17: 20. *Matt.* 21: 21. *Mark* 9: 23.

All things should be done in. *Rom.* 14: 22.

Whatsoever is not of, is sin. *Rom.* 14: 23.

Often tried by affliction. 1 *Pet.* 1: 6, 7.

Trial of, works patience. *Jas.* 1: 3.

The wicked often profess. *Acts* 8: 13, 21.

The wicked destitute of. *John* 10: 25. *John* 12: 37. *Acts* 19: 9. 2 *Thess.* 3: 2.

Protection of, illustrated. A SHIELD, *Eph.* 6: 16. A BREASTPLATE, 1 *Thess.* 5: 8.

Exemplified. CALEB, *Num.* 13: 30. JOB, *Job* 19: 25. SHADRACH, etc., *Dan.* 3: 17. DANIEL, *Dan.* 6: 10, 23. PETER, *Matt.* 16: 16. WOMAN WHO WAS A SINNER, *Luke* 7: 50. NATHANAEL, *John* 1: 49. SAMARITANS, *John* 4: 39. MARTHA, *John* 11: 27. THE DISCIPLES, *John* 16: 30. THOMAS, *John* 20: 28. STEPHEN, *Acts* 6: 5. PRIESTS, *Acts* 6: 7. ETHIOPIAN. *Acts* 8: 37. BARNABAS, *Acts* 11: 4 SERGIUS PAULUS, *Acts* 13: 12. PHILIPPIAN JAILOR,

Acts 16: 31, 34. ROMANS, *Rom.* 1: 8. COLOSSIANS, *Col.* 1: 4. THESSALONIANS, 1 *Thess.* 1: 3. LOIS, 2 *Tim.* 1: 5. PAUL, 2 *Tim.* 4: 7. ABEL, *Heb.* 11: 4. ENOCH, *Heb.* 11: 5. NOAH, *Heb.* 11: 7. ABRAHAM, *Heb.* 11: 8, 17. ISAAC, *Heb.* 11: 20. JACOB, *Heb.* 11: 21. JOSEPH, *Heb.* 11: 22. MOSES, *Heb.* 11: 24, 27. RAHAB, *Heb.* 11: 31. GIDEON, etc., *Heb.* 11: 32, 33, 39.

FAITHFULNESS

A characteristic of saints. *Eph.* 1: 1. *Col. 1: 2. 1 Tim.* 6: 2. *Rev.* 17: 14.

Exhibited in
The service of God. *Matt.* 21: 45.

Declaring the word of God. *Jer.* 23: 28. 2 *Cor.* 2: 17. 2 *Cor.* 4: 2.

The care of dedicated things. 2 *Chron.* 31: 12.

Helping the brethren. 3 *John* 5.

Administering justice. *Deut.* 1: 16.

Bearing witness. *Prov.* 14: 5.

Reproving others. *Prov.* 27: 6. *Ps.* 141: 5.

Situations of trust. 2 *Kings* 12: 15. *Neh.* 13: 13. *Acts* 6: 1–3.

Doing work. 2 *Chron.* 34: 12.

Keeping secrets. *Prov.* 11: 13.

Conveying messages. *Prov.* 13: 17. *Prov.* 25: 13.

All things. 1 *Tim.* 3: 11.

The smallest matters. *Luke* 16: 10–12.

Should be unto death. *Rev.* 2: 10.

The mercy of God toward us,

designed to lead to. 1 *Cor.* 7: 25.

Especially required in
Ministers. 1 *Cor.* 4: 2. 2 *Tim.* 2: 2.

The wives of ministers. 1 *Tim.* 3: 11.

The children of ministers. *Titus* 1: 6.

Difficulty of finding. *Prov.* 20: 6.

The wicked devoid of. *Ps.* 5: 9.

Associate with those who exhibit. *Ps.* 101: 6.

Blessedness of. 1 *Sam.* 26: 23. *Prov.* 28: 20.

Blessedness of, illustrated. *Matt.* 24: 45, 46. *Matt.* 25: 21, 23.

Exemplified, JOSEPH, *Gen.* 39: 22, 23. MOSES, *Num.* 12: 7, with *Heb.* 3: 2, 5. DAVID, 1 *Sam.* 22: 14. HANANIAH, *Neh.* 7: 2. ABRAHAM, *Neh.* 9: 8. GAL. 3: 9. DANIEL, *Dan.* 6: 4. PAUL, *Acts* 20: 20, 27. TIMOTHY, 1 *Cor.* 4: 17. TYCHICUS, *Eph.* 6: 21. EPAPHRAS, *Col.* 1: 7. ONESIMUS. *Col.* 4: 9. SILVANUS, 1 *Pet.* 5: 12. ANTIPAS, *Rev.* 2: 13.

FAITHFULNESS OF GOD, THE

Is part of his character. *Isa.* 49: 7. 1 *Cor.* 1: 9. 1 *Thess.* 5: 24.

Declared to be
Great. *Lam.* 3: 23.

Established. *Ps.* 89: 2.

Incomparable. *Ps.* 89: 8.

Unfailing. *Ps.* 89: 33. 2 *Tim.* 2: 13.

Infinite. *Ps.* 36: 5.

Everlasting. *Ps.* 119: 90. *Ps.* 146: 6.

Should be pleaded in prayer. *Ps.* 143: 1.

Should be proclaimed. *Ps.* 40: 10. *Ps.* 89: 1.

Manifested

In his counsels. *Isa.* 25: 1.

In afflicting his saints. *Ps.* 119: 75.

In fulfilling his promises. 1 *Kings* 8: 20. *Ps.* 132: 11. *Mic.* 7: 20. *Heb.* 10: 23.

In keeping his covenant. *Deut.* 7: 9. *Ps.* 111: 5.

In his testimonies. *Ps.* 119: 138.

In executing his judgments. *Jer.* 23: 20. *Jer.* 51: 29.

In forgiving sins. 1 *John* 1: 9.

To his saints. *Ps.* 89: 24. 2 *Thess.* 3: 3.

Saints encouraged to depend on. 1 *Pet.* 4: 19.

Should be magnified. *Ps.* 89: 5. *Ps.* 92: 2.

FALL OF MAN, THE

By the disobedience of Adam. *Gen.* 3: 6, 11, 12, with *Rom.* 5: 12, 15, 19.

Through temptation of the devil. *Gen.* 3: 1–5. 2 *Cor.* 11: 3. 1 *Tim.* 2: 14.

Man in consequence of;

Made in the image of Adam. *Gen.* 5: 3, with 1 *Cor.* 15: 48, 49.

Born in sin. *Job.* 25: 4. *Ps.* 51: 5. *Isa.* 48: 8. *John* 3: 6.

A child of the devil. *Matt.* 13: 38. *John* 8: 44. 1 *John* 3: 8, 10.

A child of wrath. *Eph.* 2: 3.

Evil in heart. *Gen.* 6: 5. *Gen.* 8: 21. *Jer.* 16: 12. *Matt.* 15: 19.

Blinded in heart. *Eph.* 4: 18.

Corrupt and perverse in his ways. *Gen.* 6: 12. *Ps.* 10: 5. *Rom.* 3: 12–16.

Depraved in mind. *Rom.* 8. 5–7. *Eph.* 4: 17. *Col.* 1: 21. *Titus* 1: 15.

Without understanding. *Ps.* 14: 2, 3, with *Rom.* 3: 11. *Rom.* 1: 31.

Receives not the things of God. 1 *Cor.* 2: 14.

Comes short of God's glory. *Rom.* 3: 23.

Defiled in conscience. *Titus* 1: 15. *Heb.* 10: 22.

Intractable. *Job* 11: 12.

Estranged from God. *Gen.* 3: 8. *Ps.* 58: 3. *Eph.* 4: 18. *Col.* 1: 21.

In bondage to sin. *Rom.* 6: 19. *Rom.* 7: 5, 23. *Gal.* 5: 17. *Titus* 3: 3.

In bondage to the devil. 2 *Tim.* 2: 26. *Heb.* 2: 14, 15.

Constant in evil. *Ps.* 10: 5. 2 *Pet.* 2: 14.

Conscious of guilt. *Gen.* 3: 7, 8, 10.

Unrighteous. *Eccles.* 7: 20. *Rom.* 3: 10.

Abominable. *Job* 15: 16. *Ps.* 14: 3.

Turned to his own way. *Isa.* 53: 6.

Loves darkness. *John* 3: 19.

Corrupt, &c, in speech. *Rom.* 3: 13, 14.

Destructive. *Rom.* 3: 15, 16.

Devoid of the fear of God. *Rom.* 3: 18.

Totally depraved. *Gen.* 6: 5. *Rom.* 7: 18.

Dead in sin. *Eph.* 2: 1. *Col.* 2: 13.

All men partake of the effects of. 1 *Kings* 8: 46. *Gal.* 3: 22. 1 *John* 1: 8. 1 *John* 5: 19.

Punishment consequent upon

Banishment from paradise. *Gen.* 3: 24.

Condemnation to labour and sorrow. *Gen.* 3: 16, 19. *Job* 5: 6, 7.

Temporal death. *Gen.* 3: 19. *Rom.* 5: 12. 1 *Cor.* 15: 22.

Eternal death. *Job* 21: 30. *Rom.* 5: 18, 21. *Rom.* 6: 23.

Cannot be remedied by man. *Prov.* 20: 9. *Jer.* 2: 22. *Jer.* 13: 23.

Remedy for, provided by God. *Gen.* 3: 15.

FAMILIES

Of saints blessed. *Ps.* 128: 3, 6.

Should

Be taught the scriptures. *Deut.* 4: 9, 10.

Worship God together. 1 *Cor.* 16: 19.

Be duly regulated. *Prov.* 31: 27. 1 *Tim.* 3: 4, 5, 12.

Live in unity. *Gen.* 45: 24. *Ps.* 133: 1.

Live in mutual forbearance. *Gen.* 50: 17–21. *Matt.* 18: 21, 22.

Rejoice together before God. *Deut.* 14: 26.

Deceivers and liars should be removed from. *Ps.* 101: 7.

Warned against departing from God. *Deut.* 29: 18.

Punishment of irreligious. *Jer.* 10: 25.

Good—Exemplified, ABRAHAM, *Gen.* 18: 19. JACOB, *Gen.* 35: 2. JOSHUA, *Joshua* 24: 15. DAVID, 2 *Sam.* 6: 20. JOB, *Job* 1: 5. LAZARUS OF BETHANY, *John* 11: 1–5. CORNELIUS, *Acts* 10: 2, 33. LYDIA, *Acts* 16: 15. JAILOR OF PHILIPPI, *Acts* 16: 31–34.

CRISPUS, *Acts* 18: 8. LOIS, 2 *Tim.* 1: 5.

FASTING

Spirit of, explained. *Isa.* 58: 6, 7.

Not to be made a subject of display. *Matt.* 6: 16–18.

Should be unto God. *Zech.* 7: 5. *Matt.* 6: 18.

For the chastening of the soul. *Ps.* 69: 10.

For the humbling of the soul. *Ps.* 35: 13.

Observed on occasions of

Judgments of God. *Joel* 1: 14. *Joel* 2: 12.

Public calamities. 2 *Sam.* 1: 12.

Afflictions of the Church. *Luke* 5: 33–35.

Afflictions of others. *Ps.* 35: 13. *Dan.* 6: 18.

Private afflictions. 2 *Sam.* 12: 16.

Approaching danger. *Esther* 4: 16.

Ordination of ministers. *Acts* 13: 3. *Acts* 14: 23.

Accompanied by

Prayer. *Ezra* 8: 23. *Dan.* 9: 3.

Confession of sin. 1 *Sam.* 7: 6. *Neh.* 9: 1, 2.

Mourning. *Joel* 2: 12.

Humiliation. *Deut.* 9: 18. *Neh.* 9: 1.

Promises connected with. *Isa.* 58: 8–12. *Matt.* 6: 18.

Of hypocrites

Described. *Isa.* 58: 4, 5.

Ostentatious. *Matt.* 6: 16.

Boasted of, before God. *Luke* 18: 12.

Rejected. *Isa.* 58: 3. *Jer.* 14: 12.

Extraordinary—Exemplified,

OUR LORD, *Matt.* 4: 2. MOSES,
Exod. 34: 28. *Deut.* 9: 9, 18.
ELIJAH, 1 *Kings* 19: 8.

National—Exemplified, ISRAEL,
Judges 20: 26. *Ezra* 8: 21.
Esther 4: 3, 16. *Jer.* 36: 9.
MEN OF JABESH-GILEAD, 1 *Sam.*
31: 13. NINEVITES, *Jonah* 3: 5–
8.

Of Saints—Exemplified, DAVID,
2 *Sam.* 12: 16. *Ps.* 109: 24.
NEHEMIAH, *Neh.* 1: 4. ESTHER,
Esther 4: 16. DANIEL, *Dan.* 9:
3. DISCIPLES OF JOHN, *Matt.* 9:
14. ANNA, *Luke* 2: 37. CORNE-
LIUS, *Acts* 10: 30. PRIMITIVE
CHRISTIANS, *Acts* 13: 2. APOS-
TLES, 2 *Cor.* 6: 5. PAUL, 2 *Cor.*
11: 27. *Acts* 27: 21.

Of the Wicked—Exemplified,
ELDERS OF JEZREEL, 1 *Kings*
21: 12. AHAB, 1 *Kings* 21: 27.
PHARISEES, *Mark* 2: 18. *Luke*
18: 12.

FATHERLESS, THE

Find mercy in God. *Hos.*
14: 3.

God will

Be a father of. *Ps.* 68: 5.
Be a helper of. *Ps.* 10: 14.
Hear the cry of. *Exod.* 22:
23.
Execute the judgment of.
Deut. 10: 18. *Ps.* 10: 18.
Punish those who oppress.
Exod. 22: 24. *Isa.* 10: 1–3.
Mal. 3: 5.
Punish those who judge not.
Jer. 5: 28, 29.

Visit, in affliction. *Jas.* 1: 27.
Let them share in our blessings.
Deut. 14: 29.
Defend. *Ps.* 82: 3. *Isa.* 1: 17.
Wrong not, in judgment. *Deut.*
24: 17.
Defraud not. *Prov.* 23: 10.

Afflict not. *Exod.* 22: 22.
Oppress not. *Zech.* 7: 10.
Do no violence to. *Jer.* 22: 3.
Blessedness of taking care of.
Deut. 14: 29. *Job* 29: 12, 13.
Jer. 7: 6, 7.

The wicked

Rob. *Isa.* 10: 2.
Overwhelm. *Job* 6: 27.
Vex. *Ezra* 22: 7.
Oppress. *Job* 24: 3.
Murder. *Ps.* 94: 6.
Judge not for. *Isa.* 1: 23.
Jer. 5: 28.

A curse on those who oppress.
Deut. 27: 19.
Promises with respect to. *Jer.*
49: 11.
A type of Zion in affliction.
Lam. 5: 3.
Exemplified, LOT, *Gen.* 11: 27,
28. DAUGHTERS OF ZELOPHEHAD,
Num. 27: 1–5. JOTHAM, *Judges*
9: 16–21. MEPHIBOSHETH, 2
Sam. 9: 3. JOASH, 2 *Kings* 11:
1–12. ESTHER, *Esther* 2: 7.

FAVOUR OF GOD, THE

Christ the especial object of.
Luke 2: 52.

Is the source of

Mercy. *Isa.* 60: 10.
Spiritual life. *Ps.* 30: 5.
Spiritual wisdom leads to.
Prov. 8: 35.
Mercy and truth lead to. *Prov.*
3: 3, 4.

Saints

Obtain. *Prov.* 12: 2.
Encompassed by. *Ps.* 5: 12.
Strengthened by. *Ps.* 30: 7.
Victorious through. *Ps.* 44:
3.
Preserved through. *Job* 10:
12.
Exalted in. *Ps.* 89: 17.

Sometimes tempted to doubt. *Ps.* 77: 7.

Domestic blessings traced to. *Prov.* 18: 22.

Disappointment of enemies an assured evidence of. *Ps.* 41: 11.

Given in answer to prayer. *Job* 33: 26.

Pray for. *Ps.* 106: 4. *Ps.* 119: 58.

Plead, in prayer. *Exod.* 33: 13. *Num.* 11: 15.

To be acknowledged. *Ps.* 85: 1.

The wicked

Uninfluenced by. *Isa.* 26: 10.

Do not obtain. *Isa.* 27: 11. *Jer.* 16: 13.

Exemplified, NAPHTALI, *Deut.* 33: 23. SAMUEL, 1 *Sam.* 2: 26. JOB, *Job* 10: 12. THE VIRGIN MARY, *Luke* 1: 28, 30. DAVID, *Acts* 7: 46.

FEAR, GODLY

God is the object of. *Isa.* 8: 13.

God is the author of. *Jer.* 32: 39, 40.

Searching the scriptures gives the understanding of. *Prov.* 2: 3–5.

Described as

Hatred of evil. *Prov.* 8: 13.

Wisdom. *Job* 28: 28. *Ps.* 111: 10.

A treasure to saints. *Prov.* 15: 16. *Isa.* 33: 6.

A fountain of life. *Prov.* 14: 27.

Sanctifying. *Ps.* 19: 9.

Filial and reverential. *Heb.* 12: 9, 28.

Commanded. *Deut.* 13: 4. *Ps.* 22: 23. *Eccles.* 12: 13. 1 *Pet.* 2: 17.

Motives to,

The holiness of God. *Rev.* 15: 4.

The greatness of God. *Deut.* 10: 12, 17.

The goodness of God. 1 *Sam.* 12: 24.

The forgiveness of God. *Ps.* 130: 4.

Wondrous works of God. *Joshua* 4: 23, 24.

Judgments of God. *Rev.* 14: 7.

A characteristic of saints. *Mark* 3: 16.

Should accompany the joy of saints. *Ps.* 2: 11.

Necessary to

The worship of God. *Ps.* 5: 7. *Ps.* 89: 7.

The service of God. *Ps.* 2: 11. *Heb.* 12: 28.

Avoiding of sin. *Exod.* 20: 20.

Righteous government. 2 *Sam.* 23: 3.

Impartial administration of justice. 2 *Chron.* 19: 6–9.

Perfecting holiness. 2 *Cor.* 7: 1.

Those who have

Afford pleasure to God. *Ps.* 147: 11.

Are pitied by God. *Ps.* 103: 13.

Are accepted of God. *Acts* 10: 35.

Receive mercy from God. *Ps.* 103: 11, 17. *Luke* 1: 50.

Are blessed. *Ps.* 112: 1. *Ps.* 115: 13.

Confide in God. *Ps.* 115: 11. *Prov.* 14: 26.

Depart from evil. *Prov.* 16: 6.

Converse together of holy things. *Mal.* 3: 16.

Should not fear man. *Isa.* 8: 12, 13. *Matt.* 10: 28.

Desires of, fulfilled by God. *Ps.* 145: 19.

Days of, prolonged. *Prov.* 10: 27.

Should be

Prayed for. *Ps.* 86: 11.

Exhibited in our callings. *Col.* 3: 22.

Exhibited in giving a reason for our hope. 1 *Pet.* 3: 15.

Constantly maintained. *Deut.* 14: 23. *Joshua* 4: 24. *Prov.* 23: 17.

Taught to others. *Ps.* 34: 11.

Advantages of. *Prov.* 15: 16. *Prov.* 19: 23. *Eccles.* 8: 12, 13.

The wicked destitute of. *Ps.* 36: 1. *Prov.* 1: 29. *Jer.* 2: 19. *Rom.* 3: 18.

Exemplified, ABRAHAM, *Gen.* 22: 12. JOSEPH, *Gen.* 39: 9. *Gen.* 42: 18. OBADIAH 1 *Kings* 18: 12. NEHEMIAH, *Neh.* 5: 15. JOB, *Job* 1: 1, 8. PRIMITIVE CHRISTIANS, *Acts* 9: 31. CORNELIUS, *Acts* 10: 2. NOAH, *Heb.* 11: 7.

FEAR, UNHOLY

A characteristic of the wicked. *Rev.* 21: 8.

Is described as

A fear of idols. 2 *Kings* 17: 38.

A fear of man. 1 *Sam.* 15: 24. *John* 9: 22.

A fear of judgments. *Isa.* 2: 19. *Luke* 21: 26. *Rev.* 8: 16, 17.

A fear of future punishment. *Heb.* 10: 27.

Overwhelming. *Exod.* 15: 16. *Job* 15: 21, 24.

Consuming. *Ps.* 73: 19.

A guilty conscience leads to.

Gen. 3: 8, 10. *Ps.* 53: 5. *Prov.* 28: 1.

Seizes the wicked. *Job* 15: 24. *Job* 18: 11.

Surprises the hyprocrite. *Isa.* 33: 14, 18.

The wicked judicially filled with. *Lev.* 26: 16, 17. *Deut.* 28: 65–67. *Jer.* 49: 5.

Shall be realised. *Prov.* 1: 27. *Prov.* 10: 24.

God mocks. *Prov.* 1: 26.

Saints sometimes tempted to. *Ps.* 55: 5.

Saints delivered from. *Prov.* 1: 33. *Isa.* 14: 3.

Trust in God, a preservative from. *Ps.* 27: 1.

Exhortations against. *Isa.* 8: 12. *John* 14: 27.

Exemplified, ADAM, *Gen.* 3: 10. CAIN, *Gen.* 4: 14. MIDIANITES, *Judges* 7: 21, 22. PHILISTINES, 1 *Sam.* 14: 15. SAUL, 1 *Sam.* 28: 5, 20. ADONIJAH'S GUESTS, 1 *Kings* 1: 49. HAMAN, *Esther* 7: 6. AHAZ, *Isa.* 7: 2. BELSHAZZAR, *Dan.* 5: 6. PILATE. *John* 19: 8. FELIX, *Acts* 24: 25.

FLATTERY

Saints should not use. *Job* 32: 21, 22.

Ministers should not use. 1 *Thess.* 2: 5.

The wicked use, to

Others. *Ps.* 5: 9. *Ps.* 12: 2.

Themselves. *Ps.* 36: 2.

Hypocrites use, to

God. *Ps.* 78: 36.

Those in authority. *Dan.* 11: 34.

False prophets and teachers use. *Ezek.* 12: 24, with *Rom.* 16: 18.

Wisdom, a preservative against. *Prov.* 4: 5.

Worldly advantage obtained by. *Dan.* 11: 21, 32.

Seldom gains respect. *Prov.* 28: 23.

Avoid those given to. *Prov.* 20: 19.

Danger of. *Prov.* 7: 21–23. *Prov.* 29: 5.

Punishment of. *Job* 17: 5. *Ps.* 12: 3.

Exemplified. WOMEN OF TEKOAH, 2 *Sam.* 14: 17, 20. ABSALOM, 2 *Sam.* 15: 2–6. FALSE PROPHETS, 1 *Kings* 22: 13. DARIUS'S COURTIERS, *Dan.* 6: 7. PHARISEES, etc., *Mark* 12: 14. TYRIANS, etc., *Acts* 12: 22.

FOOLS

All men are, by nature. *Titus* 3: 3.

Deny God. *Ps.* 14: 1. *Ps.* 53: 1.

Blaspheme God. *Ps.* 74: 18. •

Reproach God. *Ps.* 74: 22.

Make a mock at sin. *Prov.* 14: 9.

Despise instruction. *Prov.* 1: 7. *Prov.* 15: 5.

Despise wisdom. *Prov.* 1: 7.

Hate knowledge. *Prov.* 1: 22.

Delight not in understanding. *Prov.* 18: 2.

Sport themselves in mischief. *Prov.* 10: 23.

Walk in darkness. *Eccles.* 2: 14.

Hate to depart from evil. *Prov.* 13: 19.

Worship of, hateful to God. *Eccles.* 5: 1.

Are

Corrupt and abominable. *Ps.* 14: 1.

Self-sufficient. *Prov.* 12: 15. *Rom.* 1: 22.

Self-confident. *Prov.* 14: 16.

Self-deceivers. *Prov.* 14: 8.

Mere professors of religion. *Matt.* 25: 2–12.

Full of words. *Eccles.* 10: 14.

Given to meddling. *Prov.* 20: 3.

Slanderers. *Prov.* 10: 18.

Liars. *Prov.* 10: 18.

Slothful. *Eccles.* 4: 5.

Angry. *Eccles.* 7: 9.

Contentious. *Prov.* 18: 6.

A grief to parents. *Prov.* 17: 25. *Prov.* 19: 13.

Come to shame. *Prov.* 3: 35.

Destroy themselves by their speech. *Prov.* 10: 8, 14. *Eccles.* 10: 12.

The company of, ruinous. *Prov.* 13: 20.

Lips of, a snare to the soul. *Prov.* 18: 7.

Cling to their folly. *Prov.* 26: 11. *Prov.* 27: 22.

Worship idols. *Jer.* 10: 8. *Rom.* 1: 22, 23.

Trust to their own hearts. *Prov.* 28: 26.

Depend upon their wealth. *Luke* 12: 20.

Hear the gospel and obey it not. *Matt.* 7: 26.

The mouth of, pours out folly. *Prov.* 15: 2.

Honour is unbecoming for. *Prov.* 26: 1, 8.

God has no pleasure in. *Eccles.* 5: 4.

Shall not stand in the presence of God. *Ps.* 5: 5.

Avoid them. *Prov.* 9: 6. *Prov.* 14: 7.

Exhorted to seek wisdom. *Prov.* 8: 5.

Punishment of. *Ps.* 107: 17. *Prov.* 19: 29. *Prov.* 26: 10.

Exemplified, REHOBOAM, 1 *Kings* 12: 8. ISRAEL, *Jer.* 4: 22. PHARISEES, *Matt.* 23: 17, 19.

FORGETTING GOD

A characteristic of the wicked. *Prov.* 2: 17. *Isa.* 65: 11.
Backsliders are guilty of. *Jer.* 3: 21, 22.

Is forgetting his

Covenant. *Deut.* 4: 23. 2 *Kings* 17: 38.
Works. *Ps.* 78: 7, 11. *Ps.* 106: 13.
Benefits. *Ps.* 103: 2. *Ps.* 106: 7.
Word. *Heb.* 12: 5. *Jas.* 1: 25.
Law. *Ps.* 119: 153, 176. *Hos.* 4: 6.
Church. *Ps.* 137: 5.
Past deliverances. *Judges* 8: 34. *Ps.* 78: 42.
Power to deliver. *Isa.* 51: 13–15.
Encouraged by false teachers. *Jer.* 23: 27.
Prosperity often leads to. *Deut.* 8: 12–14. *Hos.* 13: 6.
Trials should not lead to. *Ps.* 44: 17–20.
Resolve against. *Ps.* 119: 16, 93.
Cautions against. *Deut.* 6: 12. *Deut.* 8: 11.
Exhortation to those guilty of. *Ps.* 50: 22.
Punishment of. *Job* 8: 12, 13. *Ps.* 9: 17. *Isa.* 17: 10, 11. *Ezek.* 23: 35. *Hos.* 8: 14.

FORGIVENESS OF INJURIES

Christ set an example of. *Luke* 23: 34.
Commanded. *Mark* 11: 25. *Rom.* 12: 19.
To be unlimited. *Matt.* 18: 22. *Luke* 17: 4.
A characteristic of saints. *Ps.* 7: 4.

Motives to,

The mercy of God. *Luke* 6: 36.
Our need of forgiveness. *Mark* 11: 25.
God's forgiveness of us. *Eph.* 4: 32.
Christ's forgiveness of us. *Col.* 3: 13.
A glory to saints. *Prov.* 19: 11.

Should be accompanied by

Forbearance. *Col.* 3: 13.
Kindness. *Gen.* 45: 5–11. *Rom.* 12: 20.
Blessing and prayer. *Matt.* 5: 44.
Promises to. *Matt.* 6: 14. *Luke* 6: 37.
No forgiveness without. *Matt.* 6: 15. *Jas.* 2: 13.
Illustrated. *Matt.* 18: 23–35.
Exemplified, JOSEPH, *Gen.* 50: 20, 21. DAVID, 1 *Sam.* 24: 7. 2 *Sam.* 18: 5. 2 *Sam.* 19: 23. SOLOMON, 1 *Kings* 1: 53. STEPHEN, *Acts* 7: 60. PAUL, 2 *Tim.* 4: 16.

FORSAKING GOD

Idolaters guilty of. 1 *Sam.* 8: 8. 1 *Kings* 11: 33.
The wicked guilty of. *Deut.* 28: 20.
Backsliders guilty of. *Jer.* 15: 6.

Is forsaking

His house. 2 *Chron.* 29: 6.
His covenant. *Deut.* 29: 25. 1 *Kings* 19: 10. *Jer.* 22: 9. *Dan.* 11: 30.
His commandments. *Ezra* 9: 10.
The right way. 2 *Pet.* 2: 15.
Trusting in man is. *Jer.* 17: 5.
Leads men to follow their own devices. *Jer.* 2: 13.

Prosperity tempts to. *Deut.* 31: 20. *Deut.* 32: 15.

Wickedness of. *Jer.* 2: 13. *Jer.* 5: 7.

Unreasonableness and ingratitude of. *Jer.* 2: 5, 6.

Brings confusion. *Jer.* 17: 13.

Followed by remorse. *Ezek.* 6: 9.

Brings down his wrath. *Ezra* 8: 22.

Provokes God to forsake men. *Judges* 10: 13. 2 *Chron.* 15: 2. 2 *Chron.* 24: 20, 24.

Resolve against. *Joshua* 24: 16. *Neh.* 10: 29–39.

Curse pronounced upon. *Jer.* 17: 5.

Sin of, to be confessed. *Ezra* 9: 10.

Warnings against. *Joshua* 24: 20. 1 *Chron.* 28: 9.

Punishment of. *Deut.* 28: 20. 2 *Kings* 22: 16, 17. *Isa.* 1: 28. *Jer.* 1: 16. *Jer.* 5: 19.

Exemplified, CHILDREN OF ISRAEL, 1 *Sam.* 12: 10. SAUL, 1 *Sam.* 15: 11. AHAB, 1 *Kings* 18: 18. AMON, 2 *Kings* 21: 22. KINGDOM OF JUDAH, 2 *Chron.* 12: 1, 5. 2 *Chron.* 21: 10. *Isa.* 1: 4. *Jer.* 15: 6. KINGDOM OF ISRAEL, 2 *Chron.* 13: 11, with 2 *Kings* 17: 7–18. MANY DISCIPLES, *John* 6: 66. PHYGELLUS, etc., 2 *Tim.* 1: 15. BALAAM, 2 *Pet.* 2: 15.

GIFTS OF GOD, THE

All blessings are. *Jas.* 1: 17. 2 *Pet.* 1: 3.

Are dispensed according to his will. *Eccles.* 2: 26. *Dan.* 2: 21. *Rom.* 12: 6. 1 *Cor.* 7: 7.

Are free and abundant. *Num.* 14: 8. *Rom.* 8: 32.

Spiritual,
  Christ the chief of. *Isa.* 42:
  6. *Isa.* 55: 4. *John* 3: 16. *John* 4: 10. *John* 6: 32, 33.

  Are through Christ. *Ps.* 68: 18, with *Eph.* 4: 7, 8. *John* 6: 27.

  The Holy Ghost. *Luke* 11: 13. *Acts* 8: 20.

  Grace. *Ps.* 84: 11. *Jas.* 4: 6.

  Wisdom. *Prov.* 2: 6. *Jas.* 1: 5.

  Repentance. *Acts* 11: 18.

  Faith. *Eph.* 2: 8. *Phil.* 1: 29.

  Righteousness. *Rom.* 5: 16, 17.

  Strength and power. *Ps.* 68: 35.

  A new heart. *Ezek.* 11: 19.

  Peace. *Ps.* 29: 11.

  Rest. *Matt.* 11: 28. 2 *Thess.* 1: 7.

  Glory. *Ps.* 84: 11. *John* 17: 22.

  Eternal life. *Rom.* 6: 23.

  Not repented of by him. *Rom.* 11: 29.

  To be used for mutual profit. 1 *Pet.* 4: 10.

  Pray for. *Matt.* 7: 7, 11. *John* 16: 23, 24.

  Acknowledge. *Ps.* 4: 7. *Ps.* 21: 2.

Temporal,
  Life. *Isa.* 42: 5.

  Food and raiment. *Matt.* 6: 25–33.

  Rain and fruitful seasons. *Gen.* 27: 28. *Lev.* 26: 4, 5. *Isa.* 30: 23.

  Wisdom, 2 *Chron.* 1: 12.

  Peace. *Lev.* 26: 6. 1 *Chron.* 22: 9.

  All good things. *Ps.* 34: 10. 1 *Tim.* 6: 17.

  To be used and enjoyed. *Eccles.* 3: 13. *Eccles.* 5: 19, 20. 1 *Tim.* 4: 4, 5.

Should cause us to remember God. *Deut.* 8: 18.

All creatures partake of. *Ps.* 136: 25. *Ps.* 145: 15, 16.

Pray for. *Zech.* 10: 1. *Matt.* 6: 11.

Illustrated. *Matt.* 25: 15–30.

GIFT OF THE HOLY SPIRIT, THE

By the Father. *Neh.* 9: 20. *Luke* 11: 13.

By the Son. *John* 20: 22.

To Christ without measure. *John* 3: 34.

Given

According to promise. *Acts* 2: 38, 39.

Upon the exaltation of Christ. *Ps.* 68: 18. *John* 7: 39.

Through the intercession of Christ. *John* 14: 16.

In answer to prayer. *Luke* 11: 13. *Eph.* 1: 16, 17.

For instruction. *Neh.* 9: 20.

For comfort of saints. *John* 14: 16.

To those who repent and believe. *Acts* 2: 38.

To those who obey God. *Acts* 5: 32.

To the Gentiles. *Acts* 10: 44, 45. *Acts* 11: 17. *Acts* 15: 8.

Is abundant. *Ps.* 68: 9. *John* 7: 38, 39.

Is permanent. *Is.* 59: 21. *Hag.* 2: 5. 1 *Pet.* 4: 14.

Is fructifying. *Isa.* 32: 15.

Received through faith. *Gal.* 3: 14.

An evidence of union with Christ. 1 *John* 3: 24. 1 *John* 4: 13.

An earnest of the inheritance of the saints. 2 *Cor.* 1: 22. 2 *Cor.* 5: 5. *Eph.* 1: 14.

A pledge of the continued favour of God. *Ezek.* 39: 29.

GLORIFYING GOD

Commanded. 1 *Chron.* 16: 28. *Ps.* 22: 23. *Isa.* 42: 12.

Due to him. 1 *Chron.* 16: 29.

For his

Holiness. *Ps.* 99: 9. *Rev.* 15: 4.

Mercy and truth. *Ps.* 115: 1. *Rom.* 15: 9.

Faithfulness and truth. *Isa.* 25: 1.

Wondrous works. *Matt.* 15: 31. *Acts* 4: 21.

Judgments. *Isa.* 25: 3. *Ezek.* 28: 22. *Rev.* 14: 7.

Deliverances. *Ps.* 50: 15.

Grace to others. *Acts* 11: 18. 2 *Cor.* 9: 13. *Gal.* 1: 24.

Obligation of saints to. 1 *Cor.* 6: 20.

Is acceptable through Christ. *Phil.* 1: 11. 1 *Pet.* 4: 11.

Christ, an example of. *John* 17: 4.

Accomplished by

Relying on his promises. *Rom.* 4: 20.

Praising him. *Ps.* 50: 23.

Doing all to him. 1 *Cor.* 10: 31.

Dying for him. *John* 21: 19.

Confessing Christ. *Phil.* 3: 11.

Suffering for Christ. 1 *Pet.* 4: 14, 16.

Glorifying Christ. *Acts* 19: 17. 2 *Thess.* 1: 12.

Bringing forth fruits of righteousness. *John* 15: 8. *Phil.* 1: 11.

Patience in affliction. *Isa.* 24: 15.

Faithfulness. 1 *Pet.* 4: 11.

Required in body and spirit. 1 *Cor.* 6: 20.

Shall be universal. *Ps.* 86: 9. *Rev.* 5: 13.

Saints should

Resolve on. *Ps.* 69: 30. *Ps.* 118: 28.

Unite in. *Ps.* 34: 3. *Rom.* 15: 6.

Persevere in. *Ps.* 86: 12.

All the blessings of God are designed to lead to. *Isa.* 60: 21. *Isa.* 61: 3.

The holy example of saints may lead others to. *Matt.* 5: 16. 1 *Pet.* 2: 12.

All, by nature, fail in. *Rom.* 3: 23.

The wicked averse to. *Dan.* 5: 23. *Rom.* 1: 21.

Punishment for not. *Dan.* 5: 23, 30. *Mal.* 2: 2. *Acts* 12: 23. *Rom.* 1: 21.

Heavenly hosts engaged in. *Rev.* 4: 11.

Exemplified, DAVID, *Ps.* 57: 5. THE MULTITUDE, *Matt.* 9: 8. *Matt.* 15: 31. THE VIRGIN MARY, *Luke* 1: 46. ANGELS, *Luke* 2: 14. SHEPHERDS, *Luke* 2: 20. MAN SICK OF THE PALSY, *Luke* 5: 25. WOMAN WITH INFIRMITY, *Luke* 13: 13. LEPER, *Luke* 17: 15. BLIND MAN, *Luke* 18: 43. CENTURION, *Luke* 23: 47. THE CHURCH AT JERUSALEM, *Acts* 11: 18. GENTILES AT ANTIOCH, *Acts* 13: 48. ABRAHAM, *Rom.* 4: 20. PAUL, *Rom.* 11: 36.

GLORY

God is, to his people. *Ps.* 3: 3. *Zech.* 2: 5.

Christ is, to his people. *Isa.* 60: 1. *Luke* 2: 32.

The gospel ordained to be, to saints. 1 *Cor.* 2: 7.

Of the gospel, exceeds that of the law. 2 *Cor.* 3: 9, 10.

The joy of saints is full of. 1 *Pet.* 1: 8.

Spiritual,

Is given by God. *Ps.* 84: 11.

Is given by Christ. *John* 17: 22.

Is the work of the Holy Ghost. 2 *Cor.* 3: 18.

Eternal

Procured by the death of Christ. *Heb.* 2: 10.

Accompanies salvation by Christ. 2 *Tim.* 2: 10.

Inherited by saints. 1 *Sam.* 2: 8. *Ps.* 73: 24. *Prov.* 3: 35. *Col.* 3: 4. 1 *Pet.* 5: 10.

Saints called to. 2 *Thess.* 2: 14. 1 *Pet.* 5: 10.

Saints afore prepared unto. *Rom.* 9: 23.

Enhanced by present afflictions. 2 *Cor.* 4: 17.

Present afflictions not worthy to be compared with. *Rom.* 8: 18.

Of the Church, shall be rich and abundant. *Isa.* 60: 11–13.

The bodies of saints shall be raised in. 1 *Cor.* 15: 43. *Phil.* 3: 21.

Saints shall be, of their ministers. 1 *Thess.* 2: 19, 20

Afflictions of ministers are, to saints. *Eph.* 3: 13.

Temporal,

Is given by God. *Dan.* 2: 37.

Passeth away. 1 *Pet.* 1: 24.

The devil tries to seduce by. *Matt.* 4: 8.

Of hypocrites turned to shame. *Hos.* 4: 7.

Seek not, from man. *Matt.* 6: 2. 1 *Thess.* 2: 6.

Of the wicked

Is in their shame. *Phil. 3:* 19.

Ends in destruction. *Isa. 5:* 14.

GLORY OF GOD, THE

Exhibited in Christ. *John 1:* 14. 2 *Cor.* 4: 6. *Heb.* 1: 3.

Exhibited in

His name. *Deut.* 28: 58. *Neh.* 9: 5.

His majesty. *Job 37:* 22. *Ps.* 93: 1. *Ps.* 104: 1. *Ps.* 145: 5, 12. *Isa.* 2: 10.

His power. *Exod.* 15: 1, 6. *Rom.* 6: 4.

His works. *Ps.* 19: 1. *Ps.* 111: 3.

His holiness. *Exod.* 15: 11.

Described as

Great. *Ps.* 138: 5.

Eternal. *Ps.* 104: 31.

Rich. *Eph.* 3: 16.

Highly exalted. *Ps.* 8: 1. *Ps.* 113: 4.

Exhibited to

Moses. *Exod.* 34: 5–7, with *Exod.* 33, 18–23.

Stephen. *Acts* 7: 55.

His Church. *Deut.* 5: 24. *Ps.* 102: 16.

Enlightens the Church. *Isa.* 60: 1, 2. *Rev.* 21: 11, 23.

Saints desire to behold. *Ps.* 63: 2. *Ps.* 90: 16.

God is jealous of. *Isa.* 42: 8.

Reverence. *Isa.* 59: 19.

Plead in prayer. *Ps.* 79: 9.

Declare. 1 *Chron.* 16: 24. *Ps.* 145: 5, 11.

Magnify. *Ps.* 57: 5.

The earth is full of. *Isa.* 6: 3.

The knowledge of, shall fill the earth. *Hab.* 2: 14.

GLUTTONY

Christ was falsely accused of. *Matt.* 11: 19.

The wicked addicted to. *Phil.* 3: 19. *Jude* 12.

Leads to

Carnal security. *Isa.* 22: 13, with 1 *Cor.* 15: 32. *Luke* 12: 19.

Poverty. *Prov.* 23: 21.

Of princes, ruinous to their people. *Eccles.* 10: 16, 17.

Is inconsistent in saints. 1 *Pet.* 4: 3.

Caution against. *Prov.* 23: 2, 3. *Luke* 21: 34. *Rom.* 13: 13, 14.

Pray against temptations to. *Ps.* 141: 4.

Punishment of. *Num.* 11: 33, 34, with *Ps.* 78: 31. *Deut.* 21: 21. *Amos* 6: 4, 7.

Danger of, illustrated. *Luke* 12: 45, 46.

Exemplified. ESAU, *Gen.* 25: 30–34, with *Heb.* 12: 16, 17. ISRAEL, *Num.* 11: 4, with *Ps.* 78: 18. SONS OF ELI, 1 *Sam.* 2: 12–17. BELSHAZZAR, *Dan.* 5: 1.

GOD

Is a spirit. *John* 4: 24. 2 *Cor.* 3: 17.

Is declared to be

Light. *Isa.* 60: 19. *Jas.* 1: 17. 1 *John* 1: 5.

Love. 1 *John* 4: 8, 16.

Invisible. *Job* 23: 8, 9. *John* 1: 18. *John* 5: 37. *Col.* 1: 15. 1 *Tim.* 1: 17.

Unsearchable. *Job* 11: 7. *Job* 37: 23. *Ps.* 145: 3. *Isa.* 40: 28. *Rom.* 11: 33.

Incorruptible. *Rom.* 1: 23.

Eternal. *Deut.* 33: 27. *Ps.* 90: 2. *Rev.* 4: 8–10.

Immortal. 1 *Tim.* 1: 17. 1 *Tim.* 6: 16.

Omnipotent. *Gen.* 17: 1. *Exod.* 6: 3

Omniscient. *Ps.* 139: 1–6. *Prov.* 5: 21.

Omnipresent. *Ps.* 139: 7. *Jer.* 23: 23.

Immutable. *Ps.* 102: 26, 27. *Jas.* 1: 17.

Only wise. *Rom.* 16: 27. 1 *Tim.* 1: 17.

Glorious. *Exod.* 15: 11. *Ps.* 145: 5.

Most High. *Ps.* 83: 18. *Acts* 7: 48.

Perfect. *Matt.* 5: 48.

Holy. *Ps.* 99: 9. *Isa.* 5: 16.

Just. *Deut.* 32: 4. *Isa.* 45: 21.

True. *Jer.* 10: 10. *John* 17: 3.

Upright. *Ps.* 25: 8. *Ps.* 92: 15.

Righteous. *Ezra* 9: 15. *Ps.* 145: 17.

Good. *Ps.* 25: 8. *Ps.* 119: 68.

Great. 2 *Chron.* 2: 5. *Ps.* 86: 10.

Gracious. *Exod.* 34: 6. *Ps.* 116: 5.

Faithful. 1 *Cor.* 10: 13. 1 *Pet.* 4: 19.

Merciful *Exod.* 34: 6, 7. *Ps.* 86: 5.

Long-suffering. *Num.* 14: 18. *Mic.* 7: 18.

Jealous. *Joshua* 24: 19. *Nahum* 1: 2.

Compassionate. 2 *Kings* 13: 23.

A consuming fire. *Heb.* 12: 29.

None beside him. *Deut.* 4: 35. *Isa.* 44: 6.

None before him. *Isa.* 43: 10.

None like to him. *Exod.* 9: 14.

Deut. 33: 26. 2 *Sam.* 7: 22. *Isa.* 46: 5, 9. *Jer.* 10: 6.

None good but he. *Matt.* 19: 17.

Fills heaven and earth. 1 *Kings* 8: 27. *Jer.* 23: 24.

Should be worshipped in spirit and in truth. *John* 4: 24.

GOODNESS OF GOD, THE

Is part of his character. *Ps.* 25: 8. *Nahum* 1: 7. *Matt.* 19: 17.

Declared to be

Great. *Neh.* 9: 35. *Zech.* 9: 17.

Rich. *Ps.* 104: 24. *Rom.* 2: 4.

Abundant. *Exod.* 34: 6. *Ps.* 33: 5.

Satisfying. *Ps.* 65: 4. *Jer.* 31: 12, 14.

Enduring. *Ps.* 23: 6. *Ps.* 52: 1.

Universal. *Ps.* 145: 9. *Matt.* 5: 45.

Manifested

To his Church. *Ps.* 31: 19. *Lam.* 3: 25.

In doing good. *Ps.* 119: 68. *Ps.* 145: 9.

In supplying temporal wants. *Acts* 14: 17.

In providing for the poor. *Ps.* 68: 10.

In forgiving sins. 2 *Chron.* 30: 18. *Ps.* 86: 5.

Leads to repentance. *Rom.* 2: 4.

Recognise, in his dealings. *Ezra* 8: 18. *Neh.* 2: 18.

Pray for the manifestation of. 2 *Thess.* 1: 11.

Despise not. *Rom.* 2: 4.

Reverence. *Jer.* 33: 9. *Hos.* 3: 5.

Magnify. *Ps.* 107: 8. *Jer.* 33: 11.

Urge others to confide in. *Ps.* 34: 8.

The wicked disregard. *Neh.* 9: 35.

GOSPEL, THE

Described. *Luke* 2: 10, 11.

Foretold. *Isa.* 41: 27. *Isa.* 52: 7, with *Rom.* 10: 15. *Isa.* 61: 1–3.

Preached under the Old Testament. *Heb.* 4: 2.

Exhibits the grace of God. *Acts* 11: 3. *Acts* 20: 32.

The knowledge of the glory of God is by. 2 *Cor.* 4: 4, 6.

Life and immortality are brought to light by. 2 *Tim.* 1: 10.

Is the power of God unto salvation. *Rom.* 1: 16. 1 *Cor.* 1: 18. 1 *Thess.* 1: 5.

Is truth. *Col.* 1: 5.

Is glorious. 2 *Cor.* 4: 4.

Is everlasting. 1 *Pet.* 1: 25. *Rev.* 14: 6.

Preached by Christ. *Matt.* 4: 23. *Mark* 1: 14.

Ministers have dispensation to preach. 1 *Cor.* 9: 17.

Preached beforehand to Abraham. *Gen.* 22: 18, with *Gal.* 3: 8.

Preached to

The Jews first. *Luke* 24: 47. *Acts* 13: 46. *Acts* 14: 1. *Acts* 16: 3. *Acts* 17: 1, and 2. *Acts* 18: 4. *Acts* 19: 8. *Acts* 28: 17.

The Gentiles. *Mark* 13: 10. *Gal.* 2: 2.

The poor. *Matt.* 11: 5. *Luke* 4: 18.

Every creature. *Mark* 16: 15. *Col.* 1: 23.

Must be believed. *Mark* 1: 15. *Heb.* 4: 2.

Brings peace. *Luke* 2: 10, 14. *Eph.* 6: 15.

Produces hope. *Col.* 1: 23.

Saints have fellowship in. *Phil.* 1: 5.

There is fulness of blessing in. *Rom.* 15: 29.

Those who receive, should

Adhere to the truth of. *Gal.* 1: 6, 7. *Gal.* 2: 14.

Not be ashamed of. *Rom.* 1: 16.

Live in subjection to. 2 *Cor.* 9: 13.

Have their conversation becoming. *Phil.* 1: 27.

Earnestly contend for the faith of. *Phil.* 1: 17, 27. *Jude* 3.

Sacrifice friends and property for. *Mark* 10: 29.

Sacrifice life itself for. *Mark* 8: 35.

Profession of, attended by afflictions. 2 *Tim.* 1: 8.

Promises to sufferers for. *Mark* 8: 35. *Mark* 10: 30.

Be careful not to hinder. 1 *Cor.* 9: 12.

Is hid to them that are lost. 2 *Cor.* 4: 3.

Testifies to the final judgment. *Rom.* 2: 16.

Let him who preaches another, be accursed. *Gal.* 1: 8.

Awful consequences of not obeying. 2 *Thess.* 1: 8, 9.

Is called, the

Dispensation of the grace of God. *Eph.* 3: 2.

Gospel of peace. *Eph.* 6: 15.

Gospel of God. *Rom.* 1: 1. 1 *Thess.* 2: 8. 1 *Pet.* 4: 17.

Gospel of Jesus Christ.

Rom. 1: 9, 16. 2 *Cor.* 2: 12.
1 *Thess.* 3: 2.

Gospel of the grace of God. *Acts* 20: 24.

Gospel of the kingdom. *Matt.* 24: 14.

Gospel of salvation. *Eph.* 1: 13.

Glorious gospel of Christ. 2 *Cor.* 4: 4.

Preaching of Jesus Christ. *Rom.* 16: 25.

Mystery of Christ. *Eph.* 3: 4.

Mystery of the gospel. *Eph.* 6: 19.

Word of God. 1 *Thess.* 2: 13.

Word of Christ. *Col.* 3: 16.

Word of grace. *Acts* 14: 3. *Acts* 20: 32.

Word of salvation. *Acts* 13: 26.

Word of reconciliation. 2 *Cor.* 5: 19.

Word of truth. *Eph.* 1: 13. 2 *Cor.* 6: 7.

Word of faith. *Rom.* 10: 8.

Word of life. *Phil.* 2: 16.

Ministration of the Spirit. 2 *Cor.* 3: 8.

Doctrine according to godliness. 1 *Tim.* 6: 3.

Form of sound words. 2 *Tim.* 1: 13.

Rejection of, by many, foretold. *Isa.* 53: 1, with *Rom.* 10: 15, 16.

Rejection of, by the Jews, a means of blessing to the Gentiles. *Rom.* 11: 28.

GRACE

God is the God of all. 1 *Pet.* 5: 10.

God is the Giver of. *Ps.* 84: 11.

God's throne, the throne of. *Heb.* 4: 16.

The Holy Ghost is the Spirit of. *Zech.* 12: 10. *Heb.* 10: 29.

Was upon Christ. *Luke* 2: 40.

Christ spake with. *Ps.* 45: 2, with *Luke* 4: 22.

Christ was full of. *John* 1: 14.

Came by Christ. *John* 1: 17. *Rom.* 5: 15.

Given by Christ. 1 *Cor.* 1: 4.

Riches of, exhibited in God's kindness through Christ. *Eph.* 2: 7.

Glory of, exhibited in our acceptance in Christ. *Eph.* 1: 6.

Is described as

Great. *Acts* 4: 33.

Sovereign. *Rom.* 5: 21.

Rich. *Eph.* 1: 7. *Eph.* 2: 7.

Exceeding. 2 *Cor.* 9: 14.

Manifold. 1 *Pet.* 4: 10.

All-sufficient. 2 *Cor.* 12: 9.

All-abundant. *Rom.* 5: 15, 17, 20.

True. 1 *Pet.* 5: 12.

Glorious. *Eph.* 1: 6.

Not in vain. 1 *Cor.* 15: 10.

The gospel, a declaration of. *Acts* 20: 24, 32.

Is the source of

Election. *Rom.* 11: 5.

The call of God. *Gal.* 1: 15.

Justification. *Rom.* 3: 24. *Titus* 3: 7.

Faith. *Acts* 18: 27.

Forgiveness of sins. *Eph.* 1: 7.

Salvation. *Acts* 15: 11. *Eph.* 2: 5, 8.

Consolation. 2 *Thess.* 2: 16.

Hope. 2 *Thess.* 2: 16.

Necessary to the service of God. *Heb.* 12: 28.

God's work completed in saints by. 2 *Thess.* 1: 11, 12.

The success and completion of the work of God to be attributed to. *Zech.* 4: 7.

Inheritance of the promises by. *Rom.* 4: 16.

Justification by, opposed to that by works. *Rom.* 4: 4, 5. *Rom.* 11: 6. *Gal.* 5: 4.

Saints

Are heirs of. 1 *Pet.* 3: 7.

Are under. *Rom.* 6: 14.

Receive, from Christ. *John* 1: 16.

Are what they are by. 1 *Cor.* 15: 10. 2 *Cor.* 1: 12.

Abound in gifts of. *Acts* 4: 33. 2 *Cor.* 8: 1. 2 *Cor.* 9: 8, 14.

Should be established in. *Heb.* 13: 9.

Should be strong in. 2 *Tim.* 2: 1.

Should grow in. 2 *Pet.* 3: 18.

Should speak with. *Eph.* 4: 29. *Col.* 4: 6.

Specially given

To ministers. *Rom.* 12: 3, 6. *Rom.* 15: 15. 1 *Cor.* 3: 10. *Gal.* 2: 9. *Eph.* 3: 7.

To the humble. *Prov.* 3: 34, with *Jas.* 4: 6.

To those who walk uprightly. *Ps.* 84: 11.

Gospel of, not to be received in vain. 2 *Cor.* 6: 1.

Pray for,

For yourselves. *Heb.* 4: 16.

For others. 2 *Cor.* 13: 14. *Eph.* 6: 24.

Beware lest you fail of. *Heb.* 12: 15.

Manifestation of, in others, a cause of gladness. *Acts* 11: 23.

Special manifestation of, at the second coming of Christ. 1 *Pet.* 1: 13.

Not to be abused. *Rom.* 6: 1, 15.

Antinomians abuse. *Jude* 4.

HAPPINESS OF SAINTS IN THIS LIFE

Is in God. *Ps.* 73: 25.

Only found in the ways of wisdom. *Prov.* 3: 17, 18.

Is derived from

Fear of God. *Ps.* 128: 1, 2. *Prov.* 28: 14.

Trust in God. *Prov.* 16: 20. *Phil.* 4: 6, 7.

Obedience to God. *Ps.* 40: 8. *John* 13: 17.

Salvation. *Deut.* 33: 29. *Isa.* 12: 2, 3.

Hope in the Lord. *Ps.* 146: 5.

Hope of glory. *Rom.* 5: 2.

God being their Lord. *Ps.* 144: 15.

God being their help. *Ps.* 146: 5.

Praising God. *Ps.* 135: 3.

Their mutual love. *Ps.* 133: 1.

Divine chastening. *Job* 5: 17. *Jas.* 5: 11.

Suffering for Christ. 2 *Cor.* 12: 10. 1 *Pet.* 3: 14. 1 *Pet.* 4: 13, 14.

Having mercy on the poor. *Prov.* 14: 21.

Finding wisdom. *Prov.* 3: 13.

Retaining wisdom. *Prov.* 3: 18.

Is abundant and satisfying. *Ps.* 36: 8. *Ps.* 63: 5.

HAPPINESS OF THE WICKED, THE

Is limited to this life. *Ps.* 17: 14. *Luke* 16: 25.

Is short. *Job* 20: 5.

Is uncertain. *Luke* 12: 20.

Is vain. *Eccles.* 2: 1. *Eccles.* 7: 6.

Is derived from

Their wealth. *Job* 21: 13. *Ps.* 52: 7.

Their power. *Job* 21: 7. *Ps.* 37: 35.

Their worldly prosperity. *Ps.* 17: 14. *Ps.* 73: 3, 4. 7.

Gluttony. *Isa.* 22: 13. *Hab.* 1: 16.

Drunkenness. *Isa.* 5: 11. *Isa.* 56: 12.

Vain pleasure. *Job* 21: 12. *Isa.* 5: 12.

Successful oppression. *Hab.* 1: 15.

Marred by jealousy. *Esther* 5: 13.

Often interrupted by judgments. *Num.* 11: 33. *Job* 15: 21. *Ps.* 73: 18–20. *Jer.* 25: 10, 11.

Leads to sorrow. *Prov.* 14: 13.

Leads to recklessness. *Isa.* 22: 13.

Sometimes a stumbling-block to saints. *Ps.* 73: 3, 16. *Jer.* 12: 1. *Hab.* 1: 13.

Saints often permitted to see the end of. *Ps.* 73: 17–20.

Envy not. *Ps.* 37: 1.

Woe against. *Amos* 6: 1. *Luke* 6: 25.

Illustrated. *Ps.* 37: 35, 36. *Luke* 12: 16– 20. *Luke* 16: 19, 25.

Exemplified, ISRAEL, *Num.* 11: 33. HAMAN, *Esther* 5: 9–11. BELSHAZZAR, *Dan.* 5: 1. HEROD, *Acts* 12: 21–23.

HATRED

Forbidden. *Lev.* 19: 17. *Col.* 3: 8.

Is murder. 1 *John* 3: 15.

A work of the flesh. *Gal.* 5: 20.

Often cloaked by deceit. *Prov.* 10: 18. *Prov.* 26: 26.

Leads to deceit. *Prov.* 26: 24, 25.

Stirs up strife. *Prov.* 10: 12.

Embitters life. *Prov.* 15: 17.

Inconsistent with

The knowledge of God. 1 *John* 2: 9, 11.

The love of God. 1 *John* 4: 20.

Liars prone to. *Prov.* 26: 28.

The wicked exhibit,

Towards God. *Rom.* 1: 30.

Towards saints. *Ps.* 25: 19. *Prov.* 29: 10.

Towards each other. *Titus* 3: 3.

Christ experienced. *Ps.* 35: 19, with *John* 15: 25.

Saints should

Expect. *Matt.* 10: 22.

Not marvel at. 1 *John* 3: 13.

Return good for. *Exod.* 23: 5. *Matt.* 5: 44.

Not rejoice in the calamities of those who exhibit. *Job* 31: 29, 30. *Ps.* 35: 13, 14.

Give no cause for. *Prov.* 25: 17.

Punishment of. *Ps.* 34: 21. *Ps.* 44: 7. *Ps.* 89: 23. *Amos* 1: 11.

We should exhibit, against

False ways. *Ps.* 119: 104, 128.

Lying. *Ps.* 119: 163.

Evil. *Ps.* 97: 10. *Prov.* 8: 13.

Backsliding. *Ps.* 101: 3.

Hatred and opposition to God. *Ps.* 139: 21, 22.

Exemplified, CAIN, *Gen.* 4: 5, 8. ESAU, *Gen.* 27: 41. JOSEPH'S BRETHREN, *Gen.* 37: 4. MEN OF GILEAD, *Judges* 11: 7. SAUL, 1 *Sam.* 18: 8, 9. AHAB, 1 *Kings* 22: 8. HAMAN, *Esther* 3: 5, 6. ENEMIES OF THE JEWS, *Esther* 9: 1, 5. *Ezek.* 35: 5, 6. CHALDEANS, *Dan.* 3: 12. ENEMIES OF DANIEL, *Dan.* 6: 4–15. HERODIAS,

Matt. 14: 3, 8. THE JEWS, *Acts* 23: 12, 14.

HATRED TO CHRIST

Is without cause. *Ps.* 69: 4, with *John* 15: 25.

Is on account of his testimony against the world. *John* 7: 7.

Involves

Hatred to his Father. *John* 15: 23, 24.

Hatred to his people. *John* 15: 18.

Punishment of. *Ps.* 2: 2, 9. *Ps.* 21: 8.

No escape for those who persevere in. 1 *Cor.* 15: 25. *Heb.* 10: 29–31.

Illustrated. *Luke* 19: 12–14, 17.

Exemplified, CHIEF PRIESTS, etc., *Matt.* 27: 1, 2. *Luke* 22: 5. JEWS, *Matt.* 27: 22, 23. SCRIBES, etc., *Mark* 11: 18. *Luke* 11: 53, 54.

HEART, THE

Issues of life are out of. *Prov.* 4: 23.

God

Tries. 1 *Chron.* 29: 17. *Jer.* 12: 3.

Knows. *Ps.* 44: 21. *Jer.* 20: 12.

Searches. 1 *Chron.* 28: 9. *Jer.* 17: 10.

Understands the thoughts of. 1 *Chron.* 28: 9. *Ps.* 139: 2.

Ponders. *Prov.* 21: 2. *Prov.* 24: 12.

Influences. 1 *Sam.* 10: 26. *Ezra* 6: 22. *Ezra* 7: 27. *Prov.* 21: 1. *Jer.* 20: 9.

Creates a new. *Ezra* 36: 26.

Prepares. 1 *Chron.* 29: 18. *Prov.* 16: 1.

Opens. *Acts* 16: 14.

Enlightens. 2 *Cor.* 4: 6.

Strengthens. *Ps.* 27: 14.

Establishes. *Ps.* 112: 8. 1 *Thess.* 3: 13

Should be

Prepared unto God. 1 *Sam.* 7: 3.

Given to God. *Prov.* 23: 26.

Perfect with God. 1 *Kings* 8: 61.

Applied unto wisdom. *Ps.* 90: 12. *Prov.* 2: 2.

Guided in the right way. *Prov.* 23: 19.

Purified. *Jas.* 4: 8.

Single. *Eph.* 6: 5. *Col.* 3: 22.

Tender. *Eph.* 4: 32.

Kept with diligence. *Prov.* 4: 23.

We should

Believe with. *Acts* 8: 37. *Rom.* 10: 10.

Serve God with all. *Deut.* 11: 13.

Keep God's statutes with all. *Deut.* 26: 16.

Walk before God with all. 1 *Kings* 2: 4.

Trust in God with all. *Prov.* 3: 5.

Love God with all. *Matt.* 22: 37.

Return to God with all. *Deut.* 30: 2.

Do the will of God from. *Eph.* 6: 6.

Sanctify God in. 1 *Pet.* 3: 15.

No man can cleanse. *Prov.* 20: 9.

Faith, the means of purifying. *Acts* 15: 9.

Renewal of, promised under the gospel. *Ezek.* 11: 19. *Ezek.* 36: 26. *Heb.* 3: 10.

When broken and contrite, not despised by God. *Ps.* 51: 17.

Pray that it may be

Cleansed. *Ps.* 51: 10.

Inclined to God's testimonies. *Ps.* 119: 36.

Sound in God's statutes. *Ps.* 119: 80.

United to fear God. *Ps.* 86: 11.

Directed into the love of God. 2 *Thess.* 3: 5.

Harden not, against God. *Ps.* 95: 8, with *Heb.* 4: 7.

Harden not, against the poor. *Deut.* 15: 7.

Regard not iniquity in. *Ps.* 66: 18.

Take heed lest it be deceived. *Deut.* 11: 16.

Know the plague of. 1 *Kings* 8: 38.

He that trusteth in, is a fool *Prov.* 28: 26.

HEART, CHARACTER OF THE RENEWED

Inclined to seek God. 2 *Chron.* 11: 16.

Prepared to seek God. 2 *Chron.* 19: 3. *Ezra* 7: 10. *Ps.* 10: 17.

Fixed on God. *Ps.* 57: 7. *Ps.* 112: 7.

Joyful in God. 1 *Sam.* 2: 1. *Zech.* 10: 7.

Perfect with God. 1 *Kings* 8: 61. *Ps.* 102: 2.

Upright. *Ps.* 97: 11. *Ps.* 125: 4.

Clean. *Ps.* 73: 1.

Pure. *Ps.* 24: 4. *Matt.* 5: 8.

Tender. 1 *Sam.* 24: 5. 2 *Kings* 22: 19.

Single and sincere. *Acts* 2: 46. *Heb.* 10: 22.

Honest and good. *Luke* 8: 15.

Broken, contrite. *Ps.* 34: 18. *Ps.* 51: 17.

Obedient. *Ps.* 119: 112. *Rom.* 6: 17.

Filled with the law of God. *Ps.* 40: 8. *Ps.* 119: 11.

Awed by the word of God. *Ps.* 119: 161.

Filled with the fear of God. *Jer.* 32: 40.

Meditative. *Ps.* 4: 4. *Ps.* 77: 6.

Circumcised. *Deut.* 30: 6. *Rom.* 2: 29.

Void of fear. *Ps.* 27: 3.

Desirous of God. *Ps.* 84: 2.

Enlarged. *Ps.* 119: 32. 2 *Cor.* 6: 11.

Faithful to God. *Neh.* 9: 8.

Confident in God. *Ps.* 112: 7.

Sympathizing. *Jer.* 4: 19. *Lam.* 3: 51.

Prayerful. 1 *Sam.* 1: 13. *Ps.* 27: 8.

Inclined to obedience. *Ps.* 119: 112.

Wholly devoted to God *Ps.* 9: 1. *Ps.* 119: 10, 69, 145.

Zealous. 2 *Chron.* 17: 6. *Jer.* 20: 9.

Wise. *Prov.* 10: 8. *Prov.* 14: 33. *Prov.* 23: 15.

A treasury of good. *Matt.* 12: 35.

HEART, CHARACTER OF THE UNRENEWED

Hateful to God. *Prov.* 6: 16, 18. *Prov.* 11: 20.

Full of evil. *Eccles.* 9: 3.

Full of evil imaginations. *Gen.* 6: 5. *Gen.* 8: 21. *Prov.* 6: 18.

Full of vain thoughts. *Jer.* 4: 14.

Fully set to do evil. *Eccles.* 8: 11.

Desperately wicked. *Jer.* 17: 9.

Far from God. *Isa.* 29: 13, with *Matt.* 15: 8.

Not perfect with God. 1 *Kings* 15: 3. *Acts* 8: 21. *Prov.* 6: 18.

Not prepared to seek God. 2 *Chron.* 12: 14.

A treasury of evil. *Matt.* 12: 35. *Mark* 7: 21.

Darkened. *Rom.* 1: 21.

Prone to error. *Ps.* 95: 10.

Prone to depart from God. *Deut.* 29: 18. *Jer.* 17: 5.

Impenitent. *Rom.* 2: 5.

Unbelieving. *Heb.* 3: 12.

Blind. *Eph.* 4: 18.

Uncircumcised. *Lev.* 26: 41. *Acts* 7: 51.

Of little worth. *Prov.* 10: 20.

Deceitful. *Jer.* 17: 9.

Deceived. *Isa.* 44: 20. *Jas.* 1: 26.

Divided. *Hos.* 10: 2.

Double. 1 *Chron.* 12: 33. *Ps.* 12: 2.

Hard. *Ezek.* 3: 7. *Mark* 10: 5. *Rom.* 2: 5.

Haughty. *Prov.* 18: 12. *Jer.* 48: 29.

Influenced by the devil. *John* 13: 2.

Carnal. *Rom.* 8: 7.

Covetous. *Jer.* 22: 17. 2 *Pet.* 2: 14.

Despiteful. *Ezek.* 25: 15.

Ensnaring. *Eccles.* 7: 26.

Foolish. *Prov.* 12: 23. *Prov.* 22: 15.

Froward. *Ps.* 101: 4. *Prov.* 6: 14. *Prov.* 17: 20.

Fretful against the Lord. *Prov.* 19: 3.

Idolatrous. *Ezra* 14: 3, 4.

Mad. *Eccles.* 9: 3.

Mischievous. *Ps.* 28: 3. *Ps.* 140: 2.

Proud. *Ps.* 101: 5. *Jer.* 49: 16.

Rebellious. *Jer.* 5: 23.

Perverse. *Prov.* 12: 8.

Stiff. *Ezek.* 2: 4.

Stony. *Ezek.* 11: 19. *Ezek.* 36: 26.

Stout. *Isa.* 10: 12. *Isa.* 46: 12.

Elated by sensual indulgence. *Hos.* 13: 6.

Elated by prosperity. 2 *Chron.* 26: 16. *Dan.* 5: 20.

Studieth destruction. *Prov.* 24: 2.

Often judicially stupefied. *Isa.* 6: 10. *Acts* 28: 26, 27.

Often judicially hardened. *Exod.* 4: 21. *Joshua* 11: 20.

HEATHEN, THE

Are without God and Christ. *Eph.* 2: 12.

Described as

Ignorant. 1 *Cor.* 1: 21. *Eph.* 4: 18.

Idolatrous. *Ps.* 135: 15. *Rom.* 1: 23, 25.

Worshippers of the devil. 1 *Cor.* 10: 20.

Curel. *Ps.* 74: 20. *Rom.* 1: 31.

Filthy. *Ezra* 6: 21. *Eph.* 4: 19. *Eph.* 5: 12.

Persecuting. *Ps.* 2: 1, 2. 2 *Cor.* 11: 26.

Scoffing at saints. *Ps.* 79: 10.

Degradation of. *Lev.* 25: 44.

Have

Evidence of the power of God. *Rom.* 1: 19, 20.

Evidence of the goodness of God. *Acts* 14: 17.

The testimony of conscience. *Rom.* 2: 14, 15.

Evil of imitating. 2 *Kings* 16: 3. *Ezek.* 11: 12.

Cautions against imitating. *Jer.* 10: 2. *Matt.* 6: 7.

Danger of intercourse with. *Ps.* 106: 35.

Employed to chastise the Church. *Lev.* 26: 33. *Jer.* 49: 14. *Lam.* 1: 3. *Ezek.* 7: 24. *Ezek.* 25: 7. *Dan.* 4: 27. *Hab.* 1: 5–9.

The Church shall be avenged of.

Ps. 149: 7. *Jer.* 10: 25. *Obad.* 15.

God

Rules over. 2 *Chron.* 20: 6. *Ps.* 47: 8.

Brings to nought the counsels of. *Ps.* 33: 10.

Will be exalted among. *Ps.* 46: 10. *Ps.* 102: 15.

Punishes. *Ps.* 44: 2. *Joel* 3: 11–13. *Mic.* 5: 15. *Hab.* 3: 12. *Zech.* 14: 18.

Will finally judge. *Rom.* 2: 12–16.

Given to Christ. *Ps.* 2: 8. *Dan.* 7: 14.

Salvation of, foretold. *Gen.* 12: 3, with *Gal.* 3: 8. *Isa.* 2: 2–4. *Isa.* 52: 10. *Isa.* 60: 1–8.

Salvation provided for. *Acts* 28: 28. *Rom.* 15: 9–12.

The glory of God to be declared amongst. 1 *Chron.* 16: 24. *Ps.* 96: 3.

The gospel to be preached to. *Matt.* 24: 14. *Matt.* 28: 19. *Rom.* 16: 26. *Gal.* 1: 16.

Necessity for preaching to. *Rom.* 10: 14.

The gospel received by. *Acts* 11: 1. *Acts* 13: 48. *Acts* 15: 3, 23.

Baptism to be administered to. *Matt.* 28: 19.

The Holy Ghost poured out upon. *Acts* 10: 44, 45. *Acts* 15: 8.

Praise God for success of the gospel amongst. *Ps.* 98: 1–3. *Acts* 11: 18.

Pray for. *Ps.* 67: 2–5.

Aid missions to. 2 *Cor.* 11: 9. 3 *John* 6, 7.

Conversion of, acceptable to God. *Acts* 10: 35. *Rom.* 15: 16.

HEAVEN

Created by God. *Gen.* 1: 1. *Rev.* 10: 6.

Everlasting. *Ps.* 89: 29. 2 *Cor.* 5: 1.

Immeasurable. *Jer.* 31: 37.

High. *Ps.* 103: 11. *Isa.* 57: 15.

Holy. *Deut.* 26: 15. *Ps.* 20: 6. *Isa.* 57: 15.

God's dwelling-place. 1 *Kings* 8: 30. *Matt.* 6: 9.

God's throne. *Isa.* 66: 1, with *Acts* 7: 49.

God

Is the Lord of. *Dan.* 5: 23. *Matt.* 11: 25.

Reigns in. *Ps.* 11: 4. *Ps.* 135: 6. *Dan.* 4: 35.

Fills. 1 *Kings* 8: 27. *Jer.* 23: 24.

Answers his people from. 1 *Chron.* 21: 26. 2 *Chron.* 7: 14. *Neh.* 9: 27. *Ps.* 20: 6.

Sends his judgments from. *Gen.* 19: 24. 1 *Sam.* 2: 10. *Dan.* 4: 13, 14. *Rom.* 1: 18.

Christ

As Mediator, entered into. *Acts* 3: 21. *Heb.* 6: 20. *Heb.* 9: 12, 24.

Is all-powerful in. *Matt.* 28: 18. 1 *Pet.* 3: 22.

Angels are in. *Matt.* 18: 10. *Mark* 24: 36.

Names of saints are written in. *Luke* 10: 20. *Heb.* 12: 23.

Saints rewarded in. *Matt.* 5: 12. 1 *Pet.* 1: 4.

Repentance occasions joy in. *Luke* 15: 7.

Lay up treasure in. *Matt.* 6: 20. *Luke* 12: 33.

Flesh and blood cannot inherit. 1 *Cor.* 15: 50.

Happiness of, described. *Rev.* 7: 16, 17.

Is called

A garner. *Matt.* 3: 12.

The kingdom of Christ and of God. *Eph.* 5: 5.

The Father's house. *John* 14: 2.

A heavenly country. *Heb.* 11: 16.

A rest. *Heb.* 4: 9.

Paradise. *2 Cor.* 12: 2, 4.

The wicked excluded from. *Gal.* 5: 21. *Eph.* 5: 5. *Rev.* 22: 15.

Enoch and Elijah were translated into. *Gen.* 5: 24, with *Heb.* 11: 5. 2 *Kings* 2: 11.

HEEDFULNESS

Commanded. *Exod.* 23: 13. *Prov.* 4: 25—27.

Necessary

In the care of the soul. *Deut.* 4: 9.

In the house and worship of God. *Eccles.* 5: 1.

In what we hear. *Mark* 4: 24.

In how we hear. *Luke* 8: 18.

In keeping God's commandments. *Joshua* 22: 5.

In conduct. *Eph.* 5: 15.

In speech. *Prov.* 13: 3. *Jas.* 1: 19.

In worldly company. *Ps.* 39: 1. *Col.* 4: 5.

In giving judgment. 1 *Chron.* 19: 6, 7.

Against sin. *Heb.* 12: 15, 16.

Against unbelief. *Heb.* 3: 12.

Against idolatry. *Deut.* 4: 15, 16.

Against false christs, and false prophets. *Matt.* 24: 4, 5, 23, 24.

Against false teachers. *Phil.* 3: 2. *Col* 2: 8. 2 *Pet.* 3: 16, 17.

Against presumption. 1 *Cor.* 10: 12.

Promises to. 1 *Kings* 2: 4. 1 *Chron.* 22: 13.

A place of torment. *Luke* 16: 23. *Rev.* 14: 10, 11.

Described as

Everlasting punishment. *Matt.* 25: 46.

Everlasting fire. *Matt.* 25: 41.

Everlasting burnings. *Isa.* 33: 14.

A furnace of fire. *Matt.* 13: 42, 50.

A lake of fire. *Rev.* 20: 15.

Fire and brimstone. *Rev.* 14: 10.

Unquenchable fire. *Matt.* 3: 12.

Devouring fire. *Isa.* 33: 14.

Prepared for the devil, etc. *Matt.* 25: 41.

Devils are confined in, until the judgment-day. 2 *Pet.* 2: 4. *Jude* 6.

Punishment of, is eternal. *Isa.* 33: 14. *Rev.* 20: 10.

The wicked shall be turned into. *Ps.* 9: 17.

Human power cannot preserve from. *Ezek.* 32: 27.

The body suffers in. *Matt.* 5: 29. *Matt.* 10: 28.

The soul suffers in. *Matt.* 10: 28.

The wise avoid. *Prov.* 15: 24.

Endeavour to keep others from. *Prov.* 23: 14. *Jude* 23.

The society of the wicked leads to. *Prov.* 5: 5. *Prov.* 9: 18.

The beast, false prophets, and the devil shall be cast into. *Rev.* 19: 20. *Rev.* 20: 10.

The powers of, cannot prevail against the Church. *Matt.* 16: 18.

Illustrated. *Isa.* 30: 33.

HOLINESS

Commanded. *Lev.* 11: 45. *Lev.* 20: 7.

Christ

Desires, for his people. *John* 17: 17.

Effects, in his people. *Eph.* 5: 25–27.

An example of. *Heb.* 7: 26. 1 *Pet.* 2: 21, 22.

The character of God, the standard of. *Lev.* 19: 2, with 1 *Pet.* 1: 15, 16.

The character of Christ, the standard of. *Rom.* 8: 29. 1 *John* 2: 6.

The gospel the way of. *Isa.* 35: 8.

Necessary to God's worship. *Ps.* 24: 3, 4.

None shall see God without. *Heb.* 12: 14.

Saints

Elected to. *Rom.* 8: 29. *Eph.* 1: 4.

Called to. 1 *Thess.* 4: 7. 2 *Tim.* 1: 9.

New, created in. *Eph.* 4: 24.

Possess. 1 *Cor.* 3: 17. *Heb.* 3: 1.

Have their fruit unto. *Rom.* 6: 22.

Should follow after. *Heb.* 12: 14.

Should serve God in. *Luke* 1: 74, 75.

Should yield their members as instruments of. *Rom.* 6: 13, 19.

Should present their bodies to God in. *Rom.* 12: 1.

Should have their conversation in. 1 *Pet.* 1: 15. 2 *Pet.* 3: 11.

Should continue in. *Luke* 1: 75.

Should seek perfection in. 2 *Cor.* 7: 1.

Shall be presented to God in. *Col.* 1: 22. 1 *Thess.* 3: 13.

Shall continue in, for ever. *Rev.* 22: 11.

Behaviour of aged women should be as becomes. *Titus* 2: 3.

Promise to women who continue in. 1 *Tim.* 2: 15.

Promised to the Church. *Isa.* 35: 8. *Obad.* 17. *Zech.* 14: 20, 21.

Becoming in the Church. *Ps.* 93: 5.

The Church is the beauty of. 1 *Chron.* 16: 29. *Ps.* 29: 2.

The word of God the means of producing. *John* 17: 17. 2 *Tim.* 3: 16, 17.

Is the result of

The manifestation of God's grace. *Titus* 2: 3, 11, 12.

Subjection to God. *Rom.* 6: 22.

Union with Christ. *John* 15: 4, 5.

Required in prayer. 1 *Tim.* 2: 8.

Ministers should

Possess. *Titus* 1: 8.

Avoid everything inconsistent with. *Lev.* 21: 6. *Isa.* 52: 11.

Be examples of. 1 *Tim.* 4: 12.

Exhort to. *Heb.* 12: 14. 1 *Pet.* 1: 14–16.

Motives to;

The glory of God. *John* 15: 8. *Phil.* 1: 11.

The mercies of God. *Rom.* 12: 1, 2.

The dissolution of all things. *2 Pet.* 3: 11.

Chastisements are intended to produce, in saints. *Heb.* 12: 10.

Should lead to separation from the wicked. *Num.* 16: 21, 26. *2 Cor.* 6: 17, 18.

Hypocrites pretend to. *Isa.* 65: 5.

The wicked are without. 1 *Tim.* 1: 9. *2 Tim.* 3: 2.

Exemplified. DAVID, *Ps.* 86: 2. ISRAEL, *Jer.* 2: 3. JOHN THE BAPTIST, *Mark* 6: 20. PROPHETS, *Luke* 1: 70. PAUL, 1 *Thess.* 2: 10. WIVES OF PATRIARCHS, 1 *Pet.* 3: 5.

HOLINESS OF GOD, THE

Is incomparable. *Exod.* 15: 11. 1 *Sam.* 2: 3.

Exhibited in his

Character. *Ps.* 22: 3. *John* 17: 11.

Name. *Isa.* 57: 15. *Luke* 1: 49.

Words. *Ps.* 60: 6. *Jer.* 23: 9.

Works. *Ps.* 145: 17.

Kingdom. *Ps.* 47: 8.

Is pledged for the fulfilment of

His promises. *Ps.* 89: 35.

His judgments. *Amos* 4: 2.

Saints are commanded to imitate. *Lev.* 11: 44, with 1 *Pet.* 1: 15, 16.

Saints should praise. *Ps.* 30: 4.

Should produce reverential fear. *Rev.* 15: 4.

Requires holy service. *Joshua* 24: 19. *Ps.* 93: 5.

Heavenly hosts adore. *Isa.* 6: 3. *Rev.* 4: 8.

Should be magnified. 1 *Chron.* 16: 10. *Ps.* 48: 1. *Ps.* 99: 3, 5. *Rev.* 15: 4.

HOLY SPIRIT, THE, IS GOD

As Jehovah. *Exod.* 17: 7, with *Heb.* 3: 7–9. *Num.* 12: 6, with 2 *Pet.* 1: 21.

As Jehovah of hosts. *Isa.* 6: 3, 8–10, with *Acts* 28: 25.

As Jehovah, Most High. *Ps.* 78: 17, 21, with *Acts* 7: 51.

Being invoked as Jehovah. *Luke* 2: 26–29. *Acts* 4: 23–25, with *Acts* 1: 16, 20. 2 *Thess.* 3: 5.

As called God. *Acts* 5: 3, 4.

As eternal. *Heb.* 9: 14.

As omnipresent. *Ps.* 139: 7–13.

As omniscient. 1 *Cor.* 2: 10.

As omnipotent. *Luke* 1: 35. *Rom.* 15: 19.

As the Spirit of glory and of God. 1 *Pet.* 4: 14.

As Creator. *Gen.* 1: 26, 27, with *Job* 33: 4.

As equal to, and one with the Father. *Matt.* 28: 19. 2 *Cor.* 13: 14.

As Sovereign Disposer of all things. *Dan.* 4: 35, with 1 *Cor.* 12: 6, 11.

As Author of the new birth. *John* 3: 5, 6, with 1 *John* 5: 4.

As raising Christ from the dead. *Acts* 2: 24, with 1 *Pet.* 3: 18. *Heb.* 13: 20, with *Rom.* 1: 4.

As inspiring scripture. 2 *Tim.* 3: 16, with 2 *Pet.* 1: 21.

As the source of wisdom. 1 *Cor.* 12: 8.

As the source of miraculous power. *Matt.* 12: 28, with *Luke* 11: 20. *Acts* 19: 11, with *Rom.* 15: 19.

As appointing and sending ministers. *Acts* 13: 2, 4, with *Matt.* 9: 38. *Acts* 20: 28.

As directing where the gospel

should be preached. *Acts* 16: 6, 7, 10.

As dwelling in saints. *John* 14: 17, with 1 *Cor*. 14: 25. 1 *Cor*. 3: 16, with 1 *Cor*. 6: 19.

As Comforter of the Church. *Acts* 9: 31, with 2 *Cor*. 1: 3.

As sanctifying the Church. *Ezek*. 37: 28, with *Rom*. 15: 16.

As the Witness. *Heb*. 10: 15, with 1 *John* 5: 9.

HOLY SPIRIT, THE COMFORTER, THE

Proceeds from the Father. *John* 15: 26.

Given
By the Father. *John* 14: 16.
By Christ. *Isa*. 61: 3.
Through Christ's intercession. *John* 14: 16.
Sent in the name of Christ. *John* 14: 26.
Sent by Christ from the Father. *John* 15: 26. *John* 16: 7.

As such he
Communicates joy to saints. *Rom*. 14: 17. *Gal*. 5: 22. 1 *Thess*. 1: 6.
Edifies the Church. *Acts* 9: 31.
Testifies of Christ. *John* 15: 26.
Imparts the love of God. *Rom*. 5: 3–5.
Imparts hope. *Rom*. 15: 13. *Gal*. 5: 5.
Teaches saints. *John* 14: 26.
Dwells with, and in saints. *John* 14: 17.
Abides for ever with saints. *John* 14: 16.
Is known by saints. *John* 14: 17.
The world cannot receive. *John* 14: 17.

HOLY SPIRIT, THE TEACHER, THE

Promised. *Prov*. 1: 23.
As the Spirit of wisdom. *Isa*. 11: 2. *Isa*. 40: 13, 14.

Given
In answer to prayer. *Eph*. 1: 16, 17.
To saints. *Neh*. 9: 20. 1 *Cor*. 2: 12, 13.
Necessity for. 1 *Cor*. 2: 9, 10.

As such he
Reveals the things of God. 1 *Cor*. 10: 13.
Reveals the things of Christ. *John* 16: 14.
Brings the words of Christ to remembrance. *John* 14: 26.
Directs in the way of godliness. *Isa*. 30: 21. *Ezek*. 36: 27.
Teaches saints to answer persecutors. *Mark* 13: 11. *Luke* 12: 12.
Enables ministers to teach. 1 *Cor*. 12: 8.
Guides into all truth. *John* 14: 26. *John* 16: 13.
Attend to the instruction of. *Rev*. 2: 7, 11, 29.
The natural man will not receive the things of. 1 *Cor*. 2: 14.

HOPE

In God. *Ps*. 39: 7. 1 *Pet*. 1: 21.
In Christ. 1 *Cor*. 15: 19. 1 *Tim*. 1: 1.
In God's promises. *Acts* 26: 6, 7. *Titus* 1: 2.
In the mercy of God. *Ps*. 33: 18.
Is the work of the Holy Ghost. *Rom*. 15: 13. *Gal*. 5: 5.

Obtained through

Grace. *2 Thess.* 2: 16.

The word. *Ps.* 119: 81.

Patience and comfort of the scripture. *Rom.* 15: 4.

The gospel. *Col.* 1: 5, 23.

Faith. *Rom.* 5: 1, 2. *Gal.* 5: 5.

The result of experience. *Rom.* 5: 4.

Described as

Good. *2 Thess.* 2: 16.

Lively. *1 Pet.* 1: 3.

Sure and stedfast. *Heb.* 6: 19.

Gladdening. *Prov.* 10: 28.

Blessed. *Titus* 2: 13.

Makes not ashamed. *Rom.* 5: 5.

Triumphs over difficulties. *Rom.* 4: 18.

Is an encouragement to boldness in preaching. *2 Cor.* 3: 12.

Saints

Are called to. *Eph.* 4: 4.

Rejoice in. *Rom.* 5: 2. *Rom.* 12: 12.

Have all, the same. *Eph.* 4: 4.

Have, in death. *Prov.* 14: 32.

Should abound in. *Rom.* 15: 13.

Should look for the object of. *Titus* 2: 13.

Should not be ashamed of. *Ps.* 119: 116.

Should hold fast. *Heb.* 3: 6.

Should not be moved from. *Col.* 1: 23.

Should continue in. *Ps.* 71: 14. *1 Pet.* 1: 13.

Connected with faith and love. *1 Cor.* 13: 13.

Objects of;

Salvation. *1 Thess.* 5: 8.

Righteousness. *Gal.* 5: 5.

Christ's glorious appearing. *Titus* 2: 13.

A resurrection. *Acts* 23: 6. *Acts* 24: 15.

Eternal life. *Titus* 1: 2. *Titus* 3: 7.

Glory. *Rom.* 5: 2. *Col.* 1: 27.

Leads to purity. *1 John* 3: 3.

Leads to patience. *Rom.* 8: 25. *1 Thess.* 1: 3.

Seek for full assurance of. *Heb.* 6: 11.

Be ready to give an answer concerning. *1 Pet.* 3: 15.

Encouragement to. *Hos.* 2: 15. *Zech.* 9: 12.

Encourage others to. *Ps.* 130: 7.

Happiness of. *Ps.* 146: 5.

Life is the season of. *Eccles.* 9: 4. *Isa.* 38: 18.

The wicked have no ground for. *Eph.* 2: 12.

Of the wicked

Is in their worldly possessions. *Job* 31: 24.

Shall make them ashamed. *Isa.* 20: 5, 6. *Zech.* 9: 5.

Shall perish. *Job* 8: 13. *Job* 11: 20. *Prov.* 10: 28.

Shall be extinguished in death. *Job* 27: 8.

Illustrated by, AN ANCHOR, *Heb.* 6: 19. A HELMET, *1 Thess.* 5: 8.

Exemplified. DAVID, *Ps.* 39: 7. PAUL, *Acts* 24: 15. ABRAHAM, *Rom.* 4: 18. THESSALONIANS, *1 Thess.* 1: 3.

HOSPITALITY

Commanded. *Rom.* 12: 13. *1 Pet.* 4: 9.

Required in ministers. *1 Tim.* 3: 2. *Titus* 1: 8.

A test of Christian character. *1 Tim.* 5: 10.

Specially to be shown to

Strangers. *Heb.* 13: 2.

The poor. *Isa.* 58: 7. *Luke* 14: 13.

Enemies. 2 *Kings* 6: 22, 23. *Rom.* 12: 20.

Encouragement to. *Luke* 14: 14. *Heb.* 13: 2.

Exemplified. MELCHIZEDEK *Gen.* 14: 18. ABRAHAM, *Gen.* 18: 3–8. LOT, *Gen.* 19: 2, 3. LABAN, *Gen.* 24: 31. JETHRO, *Exod.* 2: 20. MANOAH, *Judges* 13: 15. SAMUEL, 1 *Sam.* 9: 22. DAVID, 2 *Sam.* 6: 19. BARZILLAI, 2 *Sam.* 19: 32. SHUNAMMITE, 2 *Kings* 4: 8. NEHEMIAH, *Neh.* 5: 17. JOB, *Job* 31: 17, 32. ZACCHEUS, *Luke* 19: 6. SAMARITANS, *John* 4: 40. LYDIA, *Acts* 16: 15. JASON, *Acts* 17: 7. MNASON, *Acts* 21: 16. PEOPLE OF MELITA, *Acts* 28: 2. PUBLIUS, *Acts* 28: 7. GAIUS, 3 *John* 5, 6.

HUMAN NATURE OF CHRIST, THE

Was necessary to his mediatorial office. 1 *Tim.* 2: 5. *Heb.* 2: 17.

Is proved by his

Conception in the Virgin's womb. *Matt.* 1: 18. *Luke* 1: 31.

Birth. *Matt.* 1: 16, 25. *Matt.* 2: 2. *Luke* 2: 7, 11.

Partaking of flesh and blood. *John* 1: 14. *Heb.* 2: 14.

Having a human soul. *Matt.* 26: 38. *Luke* 23: 46. *Acts* 2: 31.

Circumcision. *Luke* 2: 21.

Increase in wisdom and stature. *Luke* 2: 52.

Weeping. *Luke* 19: 41. *John* 11: 35.

Hungering. *Matt.* 4: 2. *Matt.* 21: 18.

Thirsting. *John* 4: 7. *John* 19: 28.

Sleeping. *Matt.* 8: 24. *Mark* 4: 38.

Being subject to weariness. *John* 4: 6.

Being a man of sorrows. *Isa.* 53: 3, 4. *Luke* 22: 44. *John* 11: 33. *John* 12: 27.

Being buffeted. *Matt.* 26: 67. *Luke* 22: 64.

Enduring indignities. *Luke* 23: 11.

Being scourged. *Matt.* 27: 26. *John* 19: 1.

Being nailed to the cross. *Ps.* 22: 16, with *Luke* 23: 33.

Death. *John* 19: 30.

Side being pierced. *John* 19: 34.

Burial. *Matt.* 27: 59, 60. *Matt.* 15: 46.

Resurrection. *Acts* 3: 15. 2 *Tim.* 2: 8.

Was like our own in all things except sin. *Acts* 3: 22. *Phil.* 2: 7, 8. *Heb.* 2: 17.

Was without sin. *Heb.* 7: 26, 28. 1 *John* 3: 5.

Was submitted to the evidence of the senses. *Luke* 24: 39. *John* 20: 27. 1 *John* 1: 1, 2.

Was of the seed of

The woman. *Gen.* 3: 15. *Isa.* 7: 14. *Jer.* 31: 22. *Luke* 1: 31. *Gal.* 4: 4.

Abraham. *Gen.* 22: 18, with *Gal.* 3: 16. *Heb.* 2: 16.

David. 2 *Sam.* 7: 12, 16. *Ps.* 89: 35, 36. *Jer.* 23: 5. *Matt.* 22: 42. *Mark* 10: 47. *Acts* 2: 30. *Acts* 13: 23. *Rom.* 1: 3.

Genealogy of. *Matt.* 1: 1, etc.
Luke 3: 23, etc.

Attested by himself. *Matt.* 8:
20. *Matt.* 16: 13.

Confession of, a test of belonging to God. *John* 4: 2.

Acknowledged by men. *Mark*
6: 3. *John* 7: 27. *John* 19: 5.
Acts 2: 22.

Denied by Antichrist. 1 *John*
4: 3. 2 *John* 7.

HUMILITY

Necessary to the service of God.
Mic. 6: 8.

Christ an example of. *Matt.*
11: 29. *John* 13: 14, 15. *Phil.*
2: 5–8.

A characteristic of saints. *Ps.*
34: 2.

They who have

Regarded by God. *Ps.* 138:
6. *Isa.* 66: 2.

Heard by God. *Ps.* 9: 12.
Ps. 10: 17.

Enjoy the presence of God.
Isa. 57: 15.

Delivered by God. *Job* 22:
29.

Lifted up by God. *Jas.* 4:
10.

Exalted by God. *Luke* 14:
11, *Luke* 18: 14.

Are greatest in Christ's kingdom. *Matt.* 18: 4.

Receive more grace. *Prov.*
3: 34. *Jas.* 4: 6.

Upheld by honour. *Prov.*
18: 12. *Prov.* 29: 23.

Is before honour. *Prov.* 15:
33.

Leads to riches, honour, and
life. *Prov.* 22: 4.

Saints should

Put on. *Col.* 3: 12.

Be clothed with. 1 *Pet.* 5: 5.

Walk with. *Eph.* 4: 1, 2.

Beware of false. *Col.* 2: 18,
23.

Afflictions intended to produce.
Lev. 26: 41. *Deut.* 8: 3. *Lam.*
3: 20.

Want of, condemned. 2 *Chron.*
33: 23. 2 *Chron.* 36: 12. *Jer.*
44: 10. *Dan.* 5: 22.

Temporal judgments averted by.
2 *Chron.* 7: 14. 2 *Chron.* 12:
6, 7.

Excellency of. *Prov.* 16: 19.

Blessedness of. *Matt.* 5: 3.

Exemplified. ABRAHAM, *Gen.*
18: 27. JACOB, *Gen.* 32: 10.
MOSES, *Exod.* 3: 11. *Exod.* 4:
10. JOSHUA, *Joshua* 7: 6. GIDEON, *Judges* 6: 15. DAVID, 1
Chron. 29: 14. HEZEKIAH, 2
Chron. 32: 26. MANASSEH, 2
Chron. 33: 12. JOSIAH, 2 *Chron.*
34: 27. JOB, *Job* 40: 4. *Job* 42:
6. ISAIAH, *Isa.* 6: 5. JEREMIAH,
Jer. 1: 6. JOHN THE BAPTIST,
Matt. 3: 14. CENTURION, *Matt.*
8: 8. WOMAN OF CANAAN, *Matt.*
15: 27. ELIZABETH, *Luke* 1: 43.
PETER, *Luke* 5: 8. PAUL, *Acts*
20: 19.

HUMILITY OF CHRIST, THE

Declared by himself. *Matt.*
11: 29.

Exhibited in his

Taking our nature. *Phil.* 2:
7. *Heb.* 2: 16.

Birth. *Luke* 2: 4–7.

Subjection to his parents.
Luke 2: 51.

Station in life. *Matt.* 13:
55. *John* 9: 29.

Poverty. *Luke* 9: 58. 2 *Cor.*
8: 9.

Partaking of our infirmities.
Heb. 4: 15. *Heb.* 5: 7.

Submitting to ordinances. *Matt.* 3: 13–15.

Becoming a servant. *Matt.* 20: 28. *Luke* 22: 27. *Phil.* 2: 7.

Associating with the despised. *Matt.* 9: 10, 11. *Luke* 15: 1, 2.

Refusing honours. *John* 5: 41. *John* 6: 15.

Entry into Jerusalem. *Zech.* 9: 9, with *Matt.* 21: 5, 7.

Washing his disciples' feet. *John* 13: 5.

Obedience. *John* 6: 38. *Heb.* 10: 9.

Submitting to sufferings. *Isa.* 50: 6. *Isa.* 53: 7, with *Acts* 8: 32. *Matt.* 26: 37–39.

Exposing himself to reproach and contempt. *Ps.* 22: 6. *Ps.* 69: 9, with *Rom.* 15: 3. *Isa.* 53: 3.

Death. *John* 10: 15, 17, 18. *Phil.* 2: 8. *Heb.* 12: 2.

Saints should imitate. *Phil.* 2: 5–8.

On account of, He was despised. *Mark* 6: 3. *John* 9: 29.

His exaltation, the result of. *Phil.* 2: 9.

HUSBANDS

Should have but one wife. *Gen.* 2: 24. 1 *Tim.* 3: 2, 12.

Have authority over their wives. *Gen.* 3: 16. 1 *Cor.* 11: 3. *Eph.* 5: 23.

Duty of, to wives;

To respect them. 1 *Pet.* 3: 7.

To love them. *Eph.* 5: 25, etc. *Col.* 3: 19.

To regard them as themselves. *Gen.* 2: 23, with *Matt.* 19: 5.

To be faithful to them. *Prov.* 5: 19. *Mal.* 2: 14, 15.

To dwell with them for life. *Gen.* 2: 24. *Matt.* 19: 3–9.

To comfort them. 1 *Sam.* 1: 8.

To consult with them. *Gen.* 31: 4–7.

Not to leave them, though unbelieving. 1 *Cor.* 7: 11, 12, 14, 16.

Duties of, not to interfere with their duties to Christ. *Luke* 14: 26, with *Matt.* 19: 29.

Good—Exemplified. ISAAC, *Gen.* 24: 67. ELKANAH, 1 *Sam.* 1: 4, 5.

Bad—Exemplified. SOLOMON, 1 *Kings* 11: 1. AHASUERUS, *Esther* 1: 10, 11.

HYPOCRITES

God knows and detects. *Isa.* 29: 15, 16.

Christ knew and detected. *Matt.* 22: 18.

God has no pleasure in. *Isa.* 9: 17.

Shall not come before God. *Job* 13: 16.

Described as

Wilfully blind. *Matt.* 23: 17, 19, 26.

Vile. *Isa.* 32: 6.

Self-righteousness. *Isa.* 65: 5. *Luke* 18: 11.

Covetous. *Ezek.* 33: 31. 2 *Pet.* 2: 3.

Ostentatious. *Matt.* 6: 2, 5, 16. *Matt.* 23: 5.

Censorious. *Matt.* 7: 3–5. *Luke* 13: 14, 15.

Regarding tradition more than the word of God. *Matt.* 15: 1–3.

Exact in minor, but neglecting important duties. *Matt.* 23: 23, 24.

Having but a form of godliness. 2 *Tim.* 3: 5.

Seeking only outward purity. *Luke* 11: 39.

Professing but not practising. *Ezek.* 33: 31, 32. *Matt.* 23: 3. *Rom.* 2: 17–23.

Using but lip-worship. *Isa.* 29: 13, with *Matt.* 15: 8.

Glorying in appearance only. 2 *Cor.* 5: 12.

Trusting in privileges. *Jer.* 7: 4. *Matt.* 3: 9.

Apparently zealous in the things of God. *Isa.* 58: 2.

Zealous in making proselytes. *Matt.* 23: 15.

Devouring widows' houses. *Matt.* 23: 14.

Loving pre-eminence. *Matt.* 23: 6, 7.

Worship of, not acceptable to God. *Isa.* 1: 11–15. *Isa.* 58: 3–5. *Matt.* 15: 9.

Joy of, but for a moment. *Job* 20: 5.

Hope of, perishes. *Job* 8: 13. *Job* 27: 8, 9.

Heap up wrath. *Job* 36: 13.

Fearfulness shall surprise. *Isa.* 33: 14.

Destroy others by slander. *Prov.* 11: 9.

In power, are a snare. *Job* 34: 30.

The Apostacy to abound with. 1 *Tim.* 4: 2.

Beware of the principles of. *Luke* 12: 1.

Spirit of, hinders growth in grace. 1 *Pet.* 2: 1.

Woe to. *Isa.* 20: 15. *Matt.* 23: 13.

Punishment of. *Job* 15: 34. *Isa.* 10: 6. *Jer.* 42: 20, 22. *Matt.* 24: 51.

Illustrated. *Matt.* 23: 27, 28. *Luke* 11: 44.

Exemplified. CAIN, *Gen.* 4: 3. ABSALOM, 2 *Sam.* 15: 7, 8. THE JEWS, *Jer.* 3: 10. PHARISEES, etc. *Matt.* 16: 3. JUDAS, *Matt.* 26: 49. HERODIANS, *Mark* 12: 13, 15. ANANIAS, *Acts* 5: 1–8. SIMON, *Acts* 8: 13–23.

IDLENESS AND SLOTH

Forbidden. *Rom.* 12: 11. *Heb.* 6: 12.

Produce apathy. *Prov.* 12: 27. *Prov.* 26: 15.

Akin to extravagance. *Prov.* 18: 9.

Accompanied by conceit. *Prov.* 26: 16.

Lead to

Poverty. *Prov.* 10: 4. *Prov.* 20: 13.

Want. *Prov.* 20: 4. *Prov.* 24: 34.

Hunger. *Prov.* 19: 15. *Prov.* 24: 34.

Bondage. *Prov.* 12: 24.

Disappointment. *Prov.* 13: 4. *Prov.* 21: 25.

Ruin. *Prov.* 24: 30, 31. *Eccles.* 10: 18.

Tattling and meddling. 1 *Tim.* 5: 13.

Effects of, afford instruction to others. *Prov.* 24: 30–32.

Remonstrance against. *Prov.* 6: 6, 9.

False excuses for. *Prov.* 20: 4. *Prov.* 22: 13.

Illustrated. *Prov.* 26: 14. *Matt.* 25: 18, 26.

Exemplified. WATCHMEN, *Isa.* 56: 10. ATHENIANS, *Acts* 17: 21. THESSALONIANS, 2 *Thess.* 3: 11.

IDOLATRY

Forbidden. *Exod.* 20: 2, 3. *Deut.* 5: 7.

Consists in

Making images. *Exod.* 20: 4. *Deut.* 5: 8.

Bowing down to images. *Exod.* 20: 5. *Deut.* 5: 9.

Worshipping images. *Isa.* 44: 17. *Dan.* 3: 5, 10, 15.

Sacrificing to images. *Ps.* 106: 38. *Acts* 7: 41.

Worshipping other gods. *Deut.* 30: 17. *Ps.* 81: 9.

Mentioning other gods. *Exod.* 23: 13.

Walking after other gods. *Deut.* 8: 19.

Speaking in the name of other gods. *Deut.* 18: 20.

Looking to other gods. *Hos.* 3: 1.

Serving other gods. *Deut.* 7: 4. *Jer.* 5: 19.

Fearing other gods. 2 *Kings* 17: 35.

Sacrificing to other gods. *Exod.* 22: 20.

Worshipping the true God by an image, etc. *Exod.* 32: 4–6, with *Ps.* 106: 19, 20.

Worshipping angels. *Col.* 2: 18.

Worshipping the host of heaven. *Deut.* 4: 19. *Deut.* 17: 3.

Worshipping devils. *Matt.* 4: 9, 10. *Rev.* 9: 20.

Worshipping dead men. *Ps.* 106: 28.

Setting up idols in the heart. *Ezek.* 14: 3, 4.

Covetousness. *Eph.* 5: 5. *Col.* 3: 5.

Sensuality. *Phil.* 3: 19.

Is changing the glory of God into an image. *Rom.* 1: 23, with *Acts* 17: 29.

Is changing the truth of God into a lie. *Rom.* 1: 25, with *Isa.* 41: 20.

Is a work of the flesh. *Gal.* 5: 19, 20.

Incompatible with the service of God. *Gen.* 35: 2, 3. *Joshua* 24: 23. 1 *Sam.* 7: 3. 1 *Kings* 18: 21. 2 *Cor.* 6: 15, 16.

Described as

An abomination to God. *Deut.* 7: 25.

Hateful to God. *Deut.* 16: 22. *Jer.* 44: 4.

Vain and foolish. *Ps.* 115: 4–8. *Isa.* 44: 19. *Jer.* 10: 3.

Bloody. *Ezek.* 23: 39.

Abominable. 1 *Pet.* 4: 3.

Unprofitable. *Judges* 10: 14. *Isa.* 46: 7.

Defiling. *Ezek.* 20: 7. *Ezek.* 36: 18.

They who practise,

Forget God. *Deut.* 8: 19. *Jer.* 18: 15.

Go astray from God. *Ezek.* 44: 10.

Pollute the name of God. *Ezek.* 20: 39.

Defile the sanctuary of God. *Ezek.* 5: 11.

Are estranged from God. *Ezek.* 14: 5.

Forsake God. 2 *Kings* 22: 17. *Jer.* 16: 11.

Hate God. 2 *Chron.* 19: 2, 3.

Provoke God. *Deut.* 31: 30. *Isa.* 65: 3. *Jer.* 25: 6.

Are vain in their imaginations. *Rom.* 1: 21.

Are ignorant and foolish. *Rom.* 1: 21, 22.

Inflame themselves. *Isa.* 57: 5.

Hold fast their deceit. *Jer.* 8: 5.

Carried away by it. 1 *Cor.* 12: 2.

Go after it in heart. *Ezek.* 20: 16.

Are mad upon it. *Jer.* 50: 38.

Boast of it. *Ps.* 97: 7.

Have fellowship with devils. 1 *Cor.* 10: 20.

Ask counsel of their idols. *Hos.* 4: 12.

Look to idols for deliverance. *Isa.* 44: 17. *Isa.* 45: 20.

Swear by their idols. *Amos* 8: 14.

Objects of, numerous. 1 *Cor.* 8: 5.

Objects of, described as

Strange gods. *Gen.* 35: 2, 4. *Joshua* 24: 20.

Other gods. *Judges* 2: 12, 17. 1 *Kings* 14: 9.

New gods. *Deut.* 32: 17. *Judges* 5: 8.

Gods that cannot save. *Isa.* 45: 20.

Gods that have not made the heavens. *Jer.* 10: 11.

No gods. *Jer.* 5: 7. *Gal.* 4: 8.

Molten gods. *Exod.* 34: 17. *Lev.* 19: 4.

Molten images. *Deut.* 27: 15. *Hab.* 2: 18.

Graven images. *Isa.* 45: 20. *Hos.* 11: 2.

Senseless idols. *Deut.* 4: 28. *Ps.* 115: 5, 7.

Dumb idols. *Hab.* 2: 18. 1 *Cor.* 12: 2.

Dumb stones. *Hab.* 2: 19.

Stocks. *Jer.* 3: 9. *Hos.* 4: 12.

Abominations. *Isa.* 44: 19. *Jer.* 32: 34.

Images of abomination. *Ezek.* 7: 20.

Idols of abomination. *Ezek.* 16: 36.

Stumbling-blocks. *Ezek.* 14: 3.

Teachers of lies. *Hab.* 2: 18.

Wind and confusion. *Isa.* 41: 29.

Nothing. *Isa.* 41: 24. 1 *Cor.* 8: 4.

Helpless. *Jer.* 10: 5.

Vanity. *Jer.* 18: 15.

Vanities of the Gentiles. *Jer.* 14: 22.

Making idols for the purpose of, described and ridiculed. *Isa.* 44: 10–20.

Obstinate sinners judicially given up to. *Deut.* 4: 28. *Deut.* 28: 64. *Hos.* 4: 17.

Warnings against. *Deut.* 4: 15–19.

Exhortations to turn from. *Ezek.* 14: 6. *Ezek.* 20: 7. *Acts* 14: 15.

Renounced on conversion. 1 *Thess.* 1: 9.

Saints should

Keep from. *Joshua* 23: 7. 1 *John* 5: 21.

Flee from. 1 *Cor.* 10: 14.

Not have anything connected with, in their houses. *Deut.* 7: 26.

Not partake of anything connected with. 1 *Cor.* 10: 19, 20.

Not have religious intercourse with those who practise. *Joshua* 23: 7. 1 *Cor.* 5: 11.

Not covenant with those who practise. *Exod.* 34: 12, 15. *Deut.* 7: 2.

Not intermarry with those who practise. *Exod.* 34: 16. *Deut.* 7: 3.

Testify against. *Acts* 14: 15. *Acts* 19: 26.

Refuse to engage in, though

threatened with death. *Dan.* 3: 18.

Saints preserved by God from. 1 *Kings* 19: 18, with *Rom.* 11: 4.

Saints refuse to receive the worship of. *Acts* 10: 25, 26. *Acts* 14: 11–15.

Angels refuse to receive the worship of. *Rev.* 22: 8, 9.

Destruction of promised. *Ezek.* 36: 25. *Zech.* 13: 2.

Everything connected with, should be destroyed. *Exod.* 34: 13. *Deut.* 7: 5. 2 *Sam.* 5: 21. 2 *Kings* 23: 14.

Woe denounced against. *Hab.* 2: 19.

Curse denounced against. *Deut.* 27: 15.

Punishment of;

Judicial death. *Deut.* 17: 2–5.

Dreadful judgments which end in death. *Jer.* 8: 2. *Jer.* 16: 1–11.

Banishment. *Jer.* 8: 3. *Hos.* 8: 5–8. *Amos* 5: 26, 27.

Exclusion from heaven. 1 *Cor.* 6: 9, 10. *Eph.* 5: 5. *Rev.* 22: 15.

Eternal torments. *Rev.* 14: 9–11. *Rev.* 21: 8.

Exemplified. ISRAEL, *Exod.* 32: 1. 2 *Kings* 17: 12. PHILISTINES, *Judges* 16: 23. MICAH, *Judges* 17: 4, 5. JEROBOAM, 1 *Kings* 12: 28. MAACHAH, 1 *Kings* 15: 13. AHAB, 1 *Kings* 16: 31. JEZE-EBEL, 1 *Kings* 18: 19. SEN-NACHERIB, 2 *Kings* 19: 37. MANASSEH, 2 *Kings* 21: 4–7. AMON, 2 *Kings* 21: 21. AHAZ, 2 *Chron.* 28: 3. JUDAH, *Jer.* 11: 13. NEBUCHADNEZZAR, *Dan.* 3: 1. BELSHAZZAR, *Dan.* 5: 23. PEOPLE OF LYSTRA, *Acts* 14: 11,

12. ATHENIANS, *Acts* 17: 16. EPHESIANS, *Acts* 19: 28.

Zeal against—Exemplified. ASA, 1 *Kings* 15: 12. JOSIAH, 2 *Kings* 23: 5. JEHOSHAPHAT, 2 *Chron.* 17: 6. ISRAEL, 2 *Chron.* 31: 1. MANASSEH, 2 *Chron.* 33: 15.

IGNORANCE OF GOD

Ignorance of Christ is. *John* 8: 19.

Evidenced by

Want of love. 1 *John* 4: 8.

Not keeping his commands. 1 *John* 2: 4.

Living in sin. *Titus* 1: 16. 1 *John* 3: 6.

Leads to

Error. *Matt.* 22: 29.

Idolatry. *Isa.* 44: 19. *Acts* 17: 29, 30.

Alienation from God. *Eph.* 4: 18.

Sinful lusts. 1 *Thess.* 4: 5. 1 *Pet.* 1: 14.

Persecuting saints. *John* 15: 21. *John* 16: 3.

Is no excuse for sin. *Lev.* 4: 2. *Luke* 12: 48.

The wicked, in a state of. *Jer.* 9: 3. *John* 15: 21. *John* 17: 25. *Acts* 17: 30.

The wicked choose. *Job* 21: 14. *Rom.* 1: 28.

Punishment of. *Ps.* 79: 6. 2 *Thess.* 1: 8.

Ministers should

Compassionate those in. *Heb.* 5: 2.

Labour to remove. *Acts* 17: 23.

Exemplified. PHARAOH, *Exod.* 5: 2. ISRAELITES. *Ps.* 95: 10. *Isa.* 1: 3. FALSE PROPHETS, *Isa.* 56: 10, 11. JEWS, *Luke* 23: 34.

NICODEMUS, *John* 3: 10. GEN-
TILES, *Gal.* 4: 8. PAUL, 1 *Tim.*
1: 13.

INDUSTRY

Commanded. *Eph.* 4: 28. 1
Thess. 4: 11.
Required of man in a state of
innocence. *Gen.* 2: 15.
Required of man after the fall.
Gen. 3: 23.
To be suspended on the sabbath.
Exod. 20: 10.
Characteristic of godly women.
Prov. 31: 13, etc.
Early rising necessary to.
Prov. 31: 15.

▌Requisite to supply

Our own wants. *Acts* 20: 34.
1 *Thess.* 2: 9.
Wants of others. *Acts* 20:
35. *Eph.* 4: 28.
The slothful devoid of. *Prov.*
24: 30, 31.

Leads to

Increase of substance. *Prov.*
13: 11.
Affection of relatives. *Prov.*
31: 28.
General commendation.
Prov. 31: 31.
Illustrated. *Prov.* 6: 6–8.
Exemplified. RACHEL, *Gen.* 29:
9. JACOB, *Gen.* 31: 6. JETHRO'S
DAUGHTERS, *Exod.* 2: 16. RUTH,
Ruth 2: 2, 3. JEROBOAM, 1
Kings 11: 28. DAVID, 1 *Sam.*
16: 11. JEWISH ELDERS, *Ezra* 6:
14, 15. DORCAS, *Acts* 9: 39.
PAUL, *Acts* 18: 3. 1 *Cor.* 4: 12.

INDWELLING OF THE HOLY SPIRIT, THE

In his Church, as his temple.
1 *Cor.* 3: 16.
In the body of saints, as his temple. 1 *Cor.* 6: 19. 2 *Cor.* 6:
16.
Promised to saints. *Ezek.* 36:
27.
Saints enjoy. *Isa.* 63: 11. 2
Tim. 1: 14.
Saints full of. *Acts* 6: 5. *Eph.*
5: 18.

Is the means of

Quickening. *Rom.* 8: 11.
Guiding. *John* 16: 13. *Gal.*
5: 18.
Fructifying. *Gal.* 5: 22.
A proof of being Christ's.
Rom. 8: 9.
A proof of adoption. *Rom.* 8:
15. *Gal.* 4: 6.
Is abiding. 1 *John* 2: 27.

Those who have not,

Are sensual. *Jude* 19.
Are without Christ. *Rom.*
8: 9.
Opposed by the carnal nature.
Gal. 5: 17.

INGRATITUDE TO GOD

A characteristic of the wicked.
Rom. 1: 21.
Inexcusable. *Isa.* 1: 2, 3. *Rom.*
1: 21.
Unreasonable. *Jer.* 2: 5, 6, 31.
Mic. 6: 2, 3.
Exceeding folly of. *Deut.* 32:
6.
Guilt of. *Ps.* 106: 7, 21. *Jer.*
2: 11–13.
Prosperity likely to produce.
Deut. 31: 20. *Deut.* 32: 15. *Jer.*
5: 7–11.
Warnings against. *Deut.* 8:
11–14. 1 *Sam.* 12: 24, 25.
Punishment of. *Neh.* 9: 20–27.
Hos. 2: 8, 9.
Illustrated. *Isa.* 5: 1–7. *Ezra*
16: 1–15.
Exemplified. ISRAEL, *Deut.* 32:
18. SAUL, 1 *Sam.* 15: 17–19.

DAVID, 2 *Sam.* 12: 7–9. NEBU-CHADNEZZAR, *Dan.* 5: 18–21. LEPERS, *Luke* 17: 17, 18.

INGRATITUDE

A characteristic of the wicked. *Ps.* 38: 20. 2 *Tim.* 3: 2.

Often exhibited

By relations. *Job* 19: 14.
By servants. *Job* 19: 15, 16.
To benefactors. *Ps.* 109: 5. *Eccles.* 9: 15.
To friends in distress. *Ps.* 38: 11.

Saints avoid the guilt of. *Ps.* 7: 4, 5.

Should be met with

Prayer. *Ps.* 35: 12, 13. *Ps.* 109: 4.
Faithfulness. *Gen.* 31: 38–42.
Persevering love. 2 *Cor.* 12: 15.

Punishment of. *Prov.* 17: 13. *Jer.* 18: 20, 21.
Exemplified. LABAN, *Gen.* 31: 6, 7. CHIEF BUTLER, *Gen.* 40:23. ISRAEL, *Exod.* 17: 4. MEN OF KEILAH, 1 *Sam.* 23: 5, 12. SAUL, 1 *Sam.* 24: 17. NABAL, 1 *Sam.* 25: 5–11, 21. ABSALOM, 2 *Sam.* 15: 6. JOASH, 2 *Chron.* 24: 22.

INJUSTICE

Forbidden. *Lev.* 19: 15, 35. *Deut.* 16: 19.

Specially to be avoided towards

The poor. *Exod.* 23: 6. *Prov.* 22: 16.
The stranger and fatherless. *Exod.* 22: 21, 22. *Deut.* 24: 17. *Jer.* 22: 3.
Servants. *Job* 31: 13, 14.

Of the least kind, condemned. *Luke* 16: 10.

God

Regards. *Eccles.* 5: 8.
Approves not of. *Lam.* 3: 35, 36.
Abominates. *Prov.* 17: 15. *Prov.* 20: 10.
Hears the cry of those who suffer. *Jas.* 5: 4.
Provoked to avenge. *Ps.* 12: 5.

Brings a curse. *Deut.* 27: 17, 19.
A bad example leads to. *Exod.* 23: 2.
Intemperance leads to. *Prov.* 31: 5.
Covetousness leads to. *Jer.* 6: 13.

Saints should

Hate. *Prov.* 29: 27.
Testify against. *Ps.* 58: 1, 2. *Mic.* 3: 8, 9.
Bear, patiently. 1 *Cor.* 6: 7.
Take no vengeance for. *Matt.* 5: 39.

The wicked

Deal with. *Isa.* 26: 10.
Judge with. *Ps.* 82: 2. *Eccles.* 3: 16. *Hab.* 1: 4.
Practise, without shame. *Jer.* 6: 13, 15. *Zeph.* 3: 5.

Punishment of. *Prov.* 11: 7. *Prov.* 28: 8. *Amos* 5: 11, 12. *Amos* 8: 5, 8. 1 *Thess.* 4: 6.
Exemplified. POTIPHAR, *Gen.* 39: 20. SONS OF SAMUEL, 1 *Sam.* 8: 3. AHAB, 1 *Kings* 21: 10, 15, 16. JEWS, *Isa.* 59: 14. PRINCES, etc. *Dan.* 6: 4. JUDAS, *Matt.* 27: 4. PILATE, *Matt.* 27: 24–26. PRIESTS, etc. *Acts* 4: 3. FESTUS, *Acts* 24: 27.

INSPIRATION OF THE HOLY SPIRIT, THE

Foretold. *Joel* 2: 28, with *Acts* 2: 16–18.

All scripture given by. *2 Tim.*
3: 16. *2 Pet.* 1: 21.

Design of;

To reveal future events. *Acts*
1: 16. *Acts* 28: 25.

To reveal the mysteries of
God. *Amos* 3: 7. *1 Cor.* 2:
10.

To give power to ministers.
Mic. 3: 8. *Acts* 1: 8.

To direct ministers. *Ezek.*
3: 24–27. *Acts* 11: 12. *Acts*
13: 2.

To control ministers. *Acts*
16: 6.

To testify against sin. *2
Kings* 17: 13. *Neh.* 9: 30.
Mic. 3: 8. *John* 16: 8, 9.

Modes of;

Various. *Heb.* 1: 1.

By secret impulse. *Judges*
13: 25. *2 Pet.* 1: 21.

By a voice. *Isa.* 6: 8. *Acts*
8: 29. *Rev.* 1: 10.

By visions. *Num.* 12: 6.
Ezek. 11: 24.

By dreams. *Num.* 12: 6.
Dan. 7: 1.

Necessary to prophesying.
Num. 11: 25–27. *2 Chron.* 20:
14–17.

Is irresistible. *Amos* 3: 8.

Despisers of, punished. *2
Chron.* 36: 15, 16. *Zech.* 7: 12.

JEWS, THE

Descendants of Abraham. *Ps.*
105: 6. *John* 8: 33. *Rom.* 9: 7.

The people of God. *Deut.* 32:
9. *2 Sam.* 7: 24. *Isa.* 51: 16.

Separated to God. *Exod.* 33:
16. *Num.* 23: 9. *Deut.* 4: 34.

Beloved for their fathers' sake.
Deut. 4: 37. *Deut.* 10: 15, with
Rom. 11: 28.

Christ descended from. *John*
4: 22. *Rom.* 9: 5.

The Objects of

God's love. *Deut.* 7: 8.
Deut. 23: 5. *Jer.* 31: 3.

God's choice. *Deut.* 7: 6.

God's protection. *Ps.* 105:
15. *Zech.* 2: 8.

The covenant established with.
Exod. 6: 4. *Exod.* 24: 6–8.
Exod. 34: 27.

Promises respecting, made to

Abraham. *Gen.* 12: 1–3.
Gen. 13: 14–17. *Gen.* 15: 18.
Gen. 17: 7, 8.

Isaac. *Gen.* 26: 2–5, 24.

Jacob. *Gen.* 18: 12–15. *Gen.*
35: 9–12.

Themselves. *Exod.* 6: 7, 8.
Exod. 19: 5, 6. *Deut.* 26: 18,
19.

Privileges of. *Ps.* 76: 1, 2.
Rom. 3: 1; 2. *Rom.* 9: 4, 5.

Punished for

Idolatry. *Isa.* 65: 3–7.

Unbelief. *Rom.* 11: 20.

Breaking covenant. *Isa.* 24:
5. *Jer.* 11: 10.

Transgressing the law. *Isa.*
1: 4, 7. *Isa.* 24: 5, 6.

Changing the ordinances.
Isa. 24: 5.

Killing the prophets. *Matt.*
23: 37, 38.

Imprecating upon themselves
the blood of Christ. *Matt.*
27: 25.

Scattered among the nations.
Deut. 28: 64. *Ezek.* 6: 8. *Ezek.*
36: 19.

Despised by the nations. *Ezek.*
36: 3.

Their country trodden under
foot by the Gentiles. *Deut.*
28: 49–52. *Luke* 21: 24.

Their house left desolate. *Matt.*
24: 38.

Deprived of civil and religious privileges. *Hos.* 3: 4.

Denunciations against those who

Cursed. *Gen.* 27: 29. *Num.* 24: 9.

Contended with. *Isa.* 41: 11. *Isa.* 49: 25.

Oppressed. *Isa.* 49: 26. *Isa.* 51: 21–23.

Hated. *Ps.* 129: 5. *Ezek.* 35: 5, 6.

Aggravated the afflictions of. *Zech.* 1: 14, 15.

Slaughtered. *Ps.* 79: 1–7. *Ezek.* 35: 5, 6.

God, mindful of. *Ps.* 98: 3. *Isa.* 49: 15, 16.

Christ was sent to. *Matt.* 15: 24. *Matt.* 21: 37. *Acts* 3: 20, 22, 26.

Compassion of Christ for. *Matt.* 23: 37. *Luke* 19: 41.

The gospel preached to, first. *Matt.* 10: 6. *Luke* 24: 47. *Acts* 1: 8.

Blessedness of blessing. *Gen.* 27: 29.

Blessedness of favouring. *Gen.* 12: 3. *Ps.* 122: 6.

Pray importunately for. *Ps.* 122: 6. *Isa.* 62: 1, 6, 7. *Jer.* 31: 7. *Rom.* 10: 1.

Saints remember. *Ps.* 102: 14. *Ps.* 137: 5. *Jer.* 51: 50.

Promises respecting,

The pouring out of the Spirit upon them. *Ezek.* 39: 29. *Zech.* 12: 10.

The removal of their blindness. *Rom.* 11: 25. 2 *Cor.* 3: 14–16.

Their return and seeking to God. *Hos.* 3: 5.

Their humiliation for the rejection of Christ. *Zech.* 12: 10.

Pardon of sin. *Isa.* 44: 22. *Rom.* 11: 27.

Salvation. *Isa.* 59: 20, with *Rom.* 11: 26.

Sanctification. *Jer.* 33: 8. *Ezek.* 36: 25. *Zech.* 12: 1, 9.

Joy occasioned by conversion of. *Isa.* 44: 23. *Isa.* 49: 13. *Isa.* 52: 8, 9. *Isa.* 66: 10.

Blessing to the Gentiles by conversion of. *Isa.* 2: 1–5. *Isa.* 60: 5. *Isa.* 66: 19. *Rom.* 11: 12, 15.

Re-union of. *Jer.* 3: 18. *Ezek.* 37: 16, 17, 20–22. *Hos.* 1: 11. *Mic.* 2: 12. *Isa.* 11: 11–12.

Restoration to their own land. *Isa.* 11: 15, 16. *Isa.* 14: 1–3. *Isa.* 27: 12, 13. *Jer.* 16: 14, 15. *Ezek.* 36: 24. *Ezek.* 37: 21, 25. *Ezek.* 39: 25, 28. *Luke* 21: 24.

Gentiles assisting in their restoration. *Isa.* 49: 22, 23. *Isa.* 60: 10, 14. *Isa.* 61: 4–6.

Subjection of Gentiles to. *Isa.* 60: 11, 12, 14.

Future glory of. *Isa.* 60: 19. *Isa.* 62: 3, 4. *Zeph.* 3: 19, 20. *Zech.* 2: 5.

Future prosperity of. *Isa.* 60: 6, 7, 9, 17. *Isa.* 61: 4–6. *Hos.* 14: 5, 6.

That Christ shall appear amongst. *Isa.* 59: 20. *Zech.* 14: 4.

That Christ shall dwell amongst. *Ezek.* 43: 7, 9. *Zech.* 2: 11.

That Christ shall reign over. *Ezek.* 34: 23. *Ezek.* 37: 24, 25. *Isa.* 9: 7.

Conversion of, illustrated. *Ezek.* 37: 1–14. *Rom.* 11: 24.

JOY OF GOD OVER HIS PEOPLE, THE

Greatness of, described. *Zeph.* 3: 17.

On account of their

Repentance. *Luke* 15: 7, 10.
Faith. *Heb.* 11: 5, 6.
Fear of him. *Ps.* 147: 11.
Praying to him. *Prov.* 15: 8.
Hope in his mercy. *Ps.* 147: 11.
Meekness. *Ps.* 149: 4.
Uprightness. 1 *Chron.* 29: 17. *Prov.* 11: 20.

Leads him to

Prosper them. *Deut.* 30: 9.
Do them good. *Deut.* 28: 63. *Jer.* 32: 41.
Deliver them. 2 *Sam.* 22: 20.
Comfort them. *Isa.* 65: 19.
Give them the inheritance. *Num.* 14: 8.
Illustrated. *Isa.* 62: 5. *Luke* 15: 23, 24.
Exemplified. SOLOMON, 1 *Kings* 10: 9.

JOY

God gives. *Eccles.* 2: 26. *Ps.* 4: 7.
Christ appointed to give. *Isa.* 61: 3.
Is a fruit of the Spirit. *Gal.* 5: 22.
The gospel, good tidings of. *Luke* 2: 10, 11.
God's word affords. *Neh.* 8: 12. *Jer.* 15: 16.
The gospel, to be received with. 1 *Thess.* 1: 6.
Promised to saints. *Ps.* 132: 16. *Isa.* 35: 10. *Isa.* 55: 12. *Isa.* 56: 7.
Prepared for saints. *Ps.* 97: 11.
Enjoined to saints. *Ps.* 32: 11. *Phil.* 3: 1.

Fulness of, in God's presence. *Ps.* 16: 11.
Vanity of seeking, from earthly things. *Eccles.* 2: 10, 11. *Eccles.* 11: 8.

Experienced by

Believers. *Luke* 24: 52. *Acts* 16: 34.
Peace-makers. *Prov.* 12: 20.
The just. *Prov.* 21: 15.
The wise, and discreet. *Prov.* 15: 23.
Parents of good children. *Prov.* 23: 24.
Increased to the meek. *Isa.* 29: 19.

Of saints is

In God. *Ps.* 89: 16. *Ps.* 149: 2. *Hab.* 3: 18. *Rom.* 5: 11.
In Christ. *Luke* 1: 47. *Phil.* 3: 3.
In the Holy Ghost. *Rom.* 14: 17.
For election. *Luke* 10: 20.
For salvation. *Ps.* 21: 1. *Isa.* 61: 10.
For deliverance from bondage. *Ps.* 105: 43. *Jer.* 31: 10–13.
For manifestation of goodness. 2 *Chron.* 7: 10.
For temporal blessings. *Joel* 2: 23, 24.
For supplies of grace. *Isa.* 12: 3.
For divine protection. *Ps.* 5: 11. *Ps.* 16: 8, 9.
For divine support. *Ps.* 28: 7. *Ps.* 63: 7.
For the victory of Christ. *John* 16: 33.
For the hope of glory. *Rom.* 5: 2.
For the success of the gospel. *Acts* 15: 3.

Of saints, should be

Great. *Zech.* 9: 9. *Acts* 8: 8.

Abundant. 2 *Cor.* 8: 2.

Exceeding. *Ps.* 21: 6. *Ps.* 68: 3.

Animated. *Ps.* 32: 11. *Luke* 6: 23.

Unspeakable. 1 *Pet.* 1: 8.

Full of glory. 1 *Pet.* 1: 8.

Constant. 2 *Cor.* 6: 10. *Phil.* 4: 4.

For evermore. 1 *Thess.* 5: 16.

With awe. *Ps.* 2: 11.

In hope. *Rom.* 12: 12.

In sorrow. 2 *Cor.* 6: 10.

Under trials. *Jas.* 1: 2. 1 *Pet.* 1: 6.

Under persecutions. *Matt.* 5: 11, 12. *Luke* 6: 22, 23. *Heb.* 10: 34.

Under calamities. *Hab.* 3: 17, 18.

Expressed in hymns. *Eph.* 5: 19. *Jas.* 5: 13.

Afflictions of saints succeeded by. *Ps.* 30: 5. *Ps.* 126: 5. *Isa.* 35: 10. *John* 16: 20.

Pray for restoration of. *Ps.* 51: 8, 12. *Ps.* 85: 6.

Promote, in the afflicted. *Job* 29: 13.

Of saints, made full by

The favour of God. *Acts* 2: 28.

Faith in Christ. *Rom.* 15: 13.

Abiding in Christ. *John* 15: 10, 11.

The word of Christ. *John* 17: 13.

Answers to prayer. *John* 16: 24.

Communion of saints. 2 *Tim.* 1: 4. 1 *John* 1: 3, 4. 2 *John* 12.

Saints should afford, to their ministers. *Phil.* 2: 2. *Philem.* 20.

Ministers should

Esteem their people as their. *Phil.* 4: 1. 1 *Thess.* 2: 20.

Promote, in their people. 2 *Cor.* 1: 24. *Phil.* 1: 25.

Pray for, for their people. *Rom.* 15: 13.

Have, in the faith and holiness of their people. 2 *Cor.* 7: 4. 1 *Thess.* 3: 9. 3 *John* 4.

Come to their people with. *Rom.* 15: 32.

Finish their course with. *Acts* 20: 24.

Desire to render an account with. *Phil.* 2: 16. *Heb.* 13: 17.

Serve God with. *Ps.* 100: 2.

Liberality in God's service should cause. 1 *Chron.* 29: 9, 17.

Is strengthening to saints. *Neh.* 8: 10.

Saints should engage in all religious services with. *Ezra* 6: 6: 22. *Ps.* 42: 4.

Saints should have, in all their undertakings. *Deut.* 12: 18.

Saints shall be presented to God with exceeding. 1 *Pet.* 4: 13, with *Jude* 24.

The coming of Christ will afford to saints exceeding. 1 *Pet.* 4: 13.

Shall be the final reward of saints at the judgment-day. *Matt.* 25: 21.

Of the wicked

Is derived from earthly pleasures. *Eccles.* 2: 10. *Eccles.* 11: 9.

Is derived from folly. *Prov.* 15: 21.

Is delusive. *Prov.* 14: 13.

Is short-lived. *Job* 20: 5. *Eccles.* 7: 6.

Should be turned into mourning. *Jas.* 4: 9.

Shall be taken away. *Isa.* 16: 10.

Holy—Illustrated. *Isa.* 9: 3. *Matt.* 13: 44.

Holy—Exemplified. HANNAH, 1 *Sam.* 2: 1. DAVID, 1 *Chron.* 29: 9. WISE MEN, *Matt.* 2: 10. THE VIRGIN MARY, *Luke* 1: 47. ZACCHEUS, *Luke* 19: 6. CONVERTS, *Acts* 2: 46. *Acts* 13: 52. PETER, etc. *Acts* 5: 41. SAMARITANS, *Acts* 8: 8. JAILOR, *Acts* 16: 34.

JUDGMENT, THE

Predicted in the Old Testament. 1 *Chron.* 16: 33. *Ps.* 9: 7. *Ps.* 96: 13. *Eccles.* 3: 17.

A first principle of the gospel. *Heb.* 6: 2.

A day appointed for. *Acts* 17: 31. *Rom.* 2: 16.

Time of, unknown to us. *Mark* 13: 32.

Called, the

Day of wrath. *Rom.* 2: 5. *Rev.* 6: 17.

Revelation of the righteous judgment of God. *Rom.* 2: 5.

Day of judgment and perdition of ungodly men. 2 *Pet.* 3: 7.

Day of destruction. *Job* 21: 30.

Judgment of the great day. *Jude* 6.

Shall be administered by Christ. *John* 5: 22, 27. *Acts* 10: 42. *Rom.* 14: 10. 2 *Cor.* 5: 10.

Saints shall sit with Christ in. 1 *Cor.* 6: 2. *Rev.* 20: 4.

Shall take place at the coming of Christ. *Matt.* 25: 31. 2 *Tim.* 4: 1.

Of Heathens, by the law of conscience. *Rom.* 2: 12, 14, 15.

Of Jews, by the law of Moses. *Rom.* 2: 12.

Of Christians, by the gospel. *Jas.* 2: 12.

Shall be held upon

All nations. *Matt.* 25: 32.

All men. *Heb.* 9: 27. *Heb.* 12: 23.

Small and great. *Rev.* 20: 12.

The righteous and wicked. *Eccles.* 3: 17.

Quick and dead. 2 *Tim.* 4: 1. 1 *Pet.* 4: 5.

Shall be in righteousness. *Ps.* 98: 9. *Acts* 17: 31.

The books shall be opened at. *Dan.* 7: 10.

Shall be of all

Actions. *Eccles.* 11: 9. *Eccles.* 12: 14. *Rev.* 20: 13.

Words. *Matt.* 12: 36, 37. *Jude* 15.

Thoughts. *Eccles.* 12: 14. 1 *Cor.* 4: 5.

None, by nature, can stand in. *Ps.* 130: 3. *Ps.* 143: 2. *Rom.* 3: 19.

Saints shall, through Christ, be enabled to stand in. *Rom.* 8: 33, 34.

Christ will acknowledge saints at. *Matt.* 25: 34—40. *Rev.* 3: 5.

Perfect love will give boldness in. 1 *John* 4: 17.

Saints shall be rewarded at. 2 *Tim.* 4: 8. *Rev.* 11: 18.

The wicked shall be condemned in. *Matt.* 7: 22, 23. *Matt.* 25: 41.

Final punishment of the wicked will succeed. *Matt.* 13: 40—42. *Matt.* 25: 46.

The word of Christ shall be a

witness against the wicked in. *John* 12: 48.

The certainty of, a motive to

Repentance. *Acts* 17: 30, 31.

Faith. *Isa.* 28: 16, 17.

Holiness. 2 *Cor.* 5: 9, 10. 2 *Pet.* 3: 11, 14.

Prayer and watchfulness. *Mark* 13: 33.

Warn the wicked of. *Acts* 24: 25. 2 *Cor.* 5: 11.

The wicked dread. *Acts* 24: 25. *Heb.* 10: 27.

Neglected advantages increase condemnation at. *Matt.* 11: 20–24. *Luke* 11: 31, 32.

Devils shall be condemned at. 2 *Pet.* 2: 4. *Jude* 6.

JUDGMENTS

Are from God. *Deut.* 32: 39. *Job* 12: 23. *Amos* 3: 6. *Mic.* 6: 9.

Different kinds of;

Blotting out the name. *Deut.* 29: 20.

Abandonment by God. *Hos.* 4: 17.

Cursing men's blessings. *Mal.* 2: 2.

Pestilence. *Deut.* 28: 21, 22. *Amos* 4: 10.

Enemies. 2 *Sam.* 24: 13.

Famine. *Deut.* 28: 38–40. *Amos* 4: 7–9.

Famine of hearing the word. *Amos* 8: 11.

The sword. *Exod.* 22: 24. *Jer.* 19: 7.

Captivity. *Deut.* 28: 41. *Ezek.* 39: 23.

Continued sorrows. *Ps.* 32: 10. *Ps.* 78: 32, 33. *Ezek.* 24: 23.

Desolation. *Ezek.* 33: 29. *Joel* 3: 19.

Destruction. *Job* 31: 3. *Ps.*

34: 16. *Prov.* 2: 22. *Isa.* 11: 4.

Inflicted upon

Nations. *Gen.* 15: 14. *Jer.* 51: 20, 21.

Individuals. *Deut.* 29: 20. *Jer.* 23: 34.

False gods. *Exod.* 12: 12. *Num.* 33: 4.

Posterity of sinners. *Exod.* 20: 5. *Ps.* 37: 28. *Lam.* 5: 7.

All enemies of saints. *Jer.* 30: 16.

Sent for correction. *Job* 37: 13. *Jer.* 30: 11.

Sent for the deliverance of saints. *Exod.* 6: 6.

Are sent, as punishment for

Disobedience to God. *Lev.* 26: 14–16. 2 *Chron.* 7: 19, 20.

Despising the warnings of God. 2 *Chron.* 36: 16. *Prov.* 1: 24–31. *Jer.* 44: 4–6.

Murmuring against God. *Num.* 14: 29.

Idolatry. 2 *Kings* 22: 17. *Jer.* 16: 18.

Iniquity. *Isa.* 26: 21. *Ezek.* 24: 13, 14.

Persecuting saints. *Deut.* 32: 43.

Sins of rulers. 1 *Chron.* 21: 2, 12.

Manifest the righteous character of God. *Exod.* 9: 14–16. *Ezek.* 39: 21. *Dan.* 9: 14.

Are in all the earth. 1 *Chron.* 16: 14.

Are frequently tempered with mercy. *Jer.* 4: 27. *Jer.* 5: 10, 15–18. *Amos* 9: 8.

Should lead to

Humiliation. *Joshua* 7: 6. 2 *Chron.* 12: 6. *Lam.* 3: 1–20. *Joel* 1: 13. *Jonah* 3: 5, 6.

Prayer. 2 *Chron.* 20: 9.

Contrition. *Neh.* 1: 4. *Esther* 4: 3. *Isa.* 22: 12.

Learning righteousness. *Isa.* 26: 9.

Should be a warning to others. *Luke* 13: 35.

May be averted by

Humiliation. *Exod.* 33: 3, 4, 14. 2 *Chron.* 7: 14.

Prayer. *Judges* 3: 9–11. 2 *Chron.* 7: 13, 14.

Forsaking iniquity. *Jer.* 18: 7, 8.

Turning to God. *Deut.* 30: 1–3.

Saints

Preserved during. *Job* 5: 19, 20. *Ps.* 91: 7. *Isa.* 26: 20. *Ezek.* 9: 6. *Rev.* 7: 3.

Provided for, during. *Gen.* 47: 12. *Ps.* 33: 19. *Ps.* 37: 19.

Pray for those under. *Exod.* 32: 11–13. *Num.* 11: 2. *Dan.* 9: 3.

Sympathise with those under. *Jer.* 9: 1. *Jer.* 13: 17. *Lam.* 3: 48.

Acknowledge the justice of. 2 *Sam.* 24: 17. *Ezra* 9: 13. *Neh.* 9: 33. *Jer.* 14: 7.

Upon nations—Exemplified. THE OLD WORLD, *Gen.* 6: 7, 17. SODOM, etc. *Gen.* 19: 24. EGYPT, *Exod.* 9: 14. ISRAEL, *Num.* 14: 29, 35. *Num.* 21: 6. PEOPLE OF ASHDOD, 1 *Sam.* 5: 6. PEOPLE OF BETHSHEMESH, 1 *Sam.* 6: 19. AMALEKITES, 1 *Sam.* 15: 3.

Upon individuals—Exemplified. CAIN, *Gen.* 4: 11, 12. CANAAN, *Gen.* 9: 25. KORAH, etc. *Num.* 16: 33–35. ACHAN, *Joshua* 7: 25. HOPHNI, etc. 1 *Sam.* 2: 34. SAUL, 1 *Sam.* 15: 23. UZZAH, 2 *Sam.* 6: 7. JEROBOAM, 1 *Kings* 13: 4. AHAB, 1 *Kings* 22: 38. GEHAZI, 2 *Kings* 5: 27. JEZEBEL, 2 *Kings* 9: 35. NEBUCHADNEZZAR, *Dan.* 4: 31. BELSHAZZAR, *Dan.* 5: 30. ZACHARIAS, *Luke* 1: 20. ANANIAS, etc., *Acts* 5: 1–10. HEROD, *Acts* 12: 23. ELYMAS, *Acts* 13 11.

Preservation during—Exemplified, NOAH, *Gen.* 7: 1, 16. LOT, *Gen.* 19: 15–17. JOSEPH, etc. *Gen.* 45: 7. ELIJAH, 1 *Kings* 17: 9. ELISHA, etc. 2 *Kings* 4: 38–41. SHUNAMMITE, 2 *Kings* 8: 1, 2.

JUSTICE

Commanded. *Deut.* 16: 20. *Isa.* 56: 1.

Christ, an example of. *Ps.* 98: 9. *Isa.* 11: 4. *Jer.* 23: 5.

Specially required in rulers. 2 *Sam.* 23: 3. *Ezek.* 45: 9.

To be done

In executing judgment. *Deut.* 16: 18. *Jer.* 21: 12.

In buying and selling. *Lev.* 19: 36. *Deut.* 25: 15.

To the poor. *Prov.* 29: 14. *Prov.* 31: 9.

To the fatherless and widows. *Isa.* 1: 17.

To servants. *Col.* 4: 1.

Gifts impede. *Exod.* 23: 8.

God

Requires. *Mic.* 6: 8.

Sets the highest value on. *Prov.* 21: 3.

Delights in. *Prov.* 11: 1.

Gives wisdom to execute. 1 *Kings* 3: 11, 12. *Prov.* 2: 6, 9.

Displeased with the want of. *Eccles.* 5: 8.

Brings its own reward. *Jer.* 22: 15.

Saints should

Study the principles of. *Phil.* 4: 8.

Receive instruction in. *Prov.* 1: 3.

Pray for wisdom to execute. 1 *Kings* 3: 9.

Always do. *Ps.* 119: 121. *Ezek.* 18: 8, 9.

Take pleasure in doing. *Prov.* 21: 15.

Teach others to do. *Gen.* 18: 19.

Promises to. *Isa.* 33: 15, 16. *Jer.* 7: 5, 7.

The wicked

Scorn. *Prov.* 19: 28.

Abhor. *Mic.* 3: 9.

Call not for. *Isa.* 59: 4.

Banish. *Isa.* 59: 14.

Pass over. *Luke* 11: 42.

Afflict those who act with. *Job* 12: 4. *Amos* 5: 12.

Exemplified. MOSES, *Num.* 16: 15. SAMUEL, 1 *Sam.* 12: 4. DAVID, 2 *Sam.* 8: 15. SOLOMON, 1 *Kings* 3: 16–27. JOSIAH, *Jer.* 22: 15. JOSEPH, *Luke* 23: 50, 51. APOSTLES, 1 *Thess.* 2: 10.

JUSTICE OF GOD, THE

Is a part of his character. *Deut.* 32: 4. *Isa.* 45: 21.

Declared to be

Plenteous. *Job* 37: 23.

Incomparable. *Job* 4: 17.

Incorruptible. *Deut.* 10: 17. 2 *Chron.* 19: 7.

Impartial. 2 *Chron.* 19: 7. *Jer.* 32: 19.

Unfailing. *Zeph.* 3: 5.

Undeviating. *Job* 8: 3. *Job* 34: 12.

Without respect of persons. *Rom.* 2: 11. *Col.* 3: 25. 1 *Pet.* 1: 17.

The habitation of his throne.
Ps. 89: 14.

Not to be sinned against. *Jer.* 50: 7.

Denied by the ungodly. *Ezek.* 33: 17, 20.

Exhibited in

Forgiving sins. 1 *John* 1: 9.

Redemption. *Rom.* 3: 26.

His government. *Ps.* 9: 4. *Jer.* 9: 24.

His judgments. *Gen.* 18: 25. *Rev.* 19: 2.

All his ways. *Ezek.* 18: 25, 29.

The final judgment. *Acts* 17: 31.

Acknowledge. *Ps.* 51: 4, with *Rom.* 3: 4.

Magnify. *Ps.* 98: 9. *Ps.* 99: 3, 4.

JUSTIFICATION BEFORE GOD

Promised in Christ. *Isa.* 45: 25. *Isa.* 53: 11.

Is the act of God. *Isa.* 50: 8. *Rom.* 8: 33.

Under the law

Requires perfect obedience. *Lev.* 18: 5, with *Rom.* 10: 5. *Rom.* 2: 13, *Jas.* 2: 10.

Man cannot attain to. *Job* 9: 2, 3, 20. *Job* 25: 4. *Ps.* 130: 3. *Ps.* 143: 2, with *Rom.* 3: 20. *Rom.* 9: 31, 32.

Under the Gospel,

Is not of works. *Acts* 13: 39. *Rom.* 8: 3. *Gal.* 2: 6. *Gal.* 3: 11.

Is not of faith and works united. *Acts* 15, 1–29. *Rom.* 3: 28. *Rom.* 11: 6. *Gal.* 2: 14–21. *Gal.* 5: 4.

Is by faith alone. *John* 5: 24. *Acts* 13: 39. *Rom.* 3: 30. *Rom.* 5: 1. *Gal.* 2: 16.

Is of grace. *Rom.* 3: 24.

Rom. 4: 16. *Rom.* 5: 17–21.

In the name of Christ. 1 *Cor.* 6: 11.

By imputation of Christ's righteousness. *Isa.* 61: 10. *Jer.* 23: 6. *Rom.* 3: 22. *Rom.* 5: 18. 1 *Cor.* 1: 30. 2 *Cor.* 5: 21.

By the blood of Christ. *Rom.* 5: 9.

By the resurrection of Christ. *Rom.* 4: 25. 1 *Cor.* 15: 17.

Blessedness of. *Ps.* 32: 1, 2, with *Rom.* 4: 6–8.

Frees from condemnation. *Isa.* 50: 8, 9. *Isa.* 54: 17, with *Rom.* 8: 33, 34.

Entitles to an inheritance. *Titus* 3: 7.

Ensures glorification. *Rom.* 8: 30.

The wicked shall not attain to. *Exod.* 23: 7.

By faith,

Revealed under the old dispensation. *Hab.* 2: 4, with *Rom.* 1: 17.

Excludes boasting. *Rom.* 3: 27. *Rom.* 4: 2. 1 *Cor.* 1: 29, 31.

Does not make void the law. *Rom.* 3: 30, 31. 1 *Cor.* 9: 21.

Typified. *Zech.* 3: 4, 5.

Illustrated. *Luke* 18: 14.

Exemplified. ABRAHAM, *Gen.* 15: 6. PAUL, *Phil.* 3: 8, 9.

KINGS

God chooses. *Deut.* 17: 15. 1 *Chron.* 28: 4–6.

God ordains. *Rom.* 13: 1.

God anoints. 1 *Sam.* 16: 12. 2 *Sam.* 12: 7.

Set up by God. 1 *Sam.* 12: 13. *Dan.* 2: 21.

Removed by God. 1 *Kings* 11: 11. *Dan.* 2: 21.

Christ is the Prince of. *Rev.* 1: 5.

Christ is the King of. *Rev.* 17: 14.

Reign by direction of Christ. *Prov.* 8: 15.

Supreme judges of nations. 1 *Sam.* 8: 5.

Resistance to, is resistance to the ordinance of God. *Rom.* 13: 2.

Able to enforce their commands. *Eccles.* 8: 4.

Numerous subjects, the honour of. *Prov.* 14: 28.

Not saved by their armies. *Ps.* 33: 16.

Dependent on the earth. *Eccles.* 5: 9.

Should

Fear God. *Deut.* 17: 19.

Serve Christ. *Ps.* 2: 10–12.

Keep the law of God. 1 *Kings* 2: 3.

Study the scriptures. *Deut.* 17: 19.

Promote the interests of the Church. *Ezra* 1: 2–4. *Ezra* 6: 1–12.

Nourish the Church. *Isa.* 49: 23.

Rule in the fear of God. 2 *Sam.* 23: 3.

Maintain the cause of the poor and oppressed. *Prov.* 31: 8, 9.

Investigate all matters. *Prov.* 25: 2.

Not pervert judgment. *Prov.* 31: 5.

Prolong their reign by hating covetousness. *Prov.* 28: 16.

Throne of, established by righteousness and justice. *Prov.* 16: 12. *Prov.* 29: 14.

Specially warned against

Impurity. *Prov.* 31: 3.

Lying. *Prov.* 17: 7.

Heakening to lies. *Prov.* 29: 12.

Intemperance. *Prov.* 31: 4, 5.

The gospel to be preached to. *Acts* 9: 15. *Acts* 26: 27, 28.

Without understanding, are oppressors. *Prov.* 28: 16.

Often reproved by God. 1 *Chron.* 16: 21.

Judgments upon, when opposed to Christ. *Ps.* 2: 2, 5, 9.

When good,

Regard God as their strength. *Ps.* 99: 4.

Speak righteously. *Prov.* 16: 10.

Love righteous lips. *Prov.* 16: 13.

Abhor wickedness. *Prov.* 16: 12.

Discountenance evil. *Prov.* 20: 8.

Punish the wicked. *Prov.* 20: 26.

Favour the wise. *Prov.* 14: 35.

Honour the diligent. *Prov.* 22: 29.

Befriend the good. *Prov.* 22: 11.

Are pacified by submission. *Prov.* 16: 14. *Prov.* 25: 15.

Evil counsellors should be removed from. 2 *Chron.* 22: 3, 4, with *Prov.* 25: 5.

Curse not, even in thought. *Exod.* 22: 28. *Eccles.* 10: 20.

Speak no evil of. *Job* 34: 18. 2 *Pet.* 2: 10.

Pay tribute to. *Matt.* 22: 21. *Rom.* 13: 6, 7.

Be not presumptuous before. *Prov.* 25: 6.

Should be

Honoured. *Rom.* 13: 7. 1 *Pet.* 2: 17.

Feared. *Prov.* 24: 21.

Reverenced. 1 *Sam.* 24: 8. 1 *Kings* 1: 23, 31.

Obeyed. *Rom.* 13: 1, 5. 1 *Pet.* 2: 13.

Prayed for. 1 *Tim.* 2: 1, 2.

Folly of resisting. *Prov.* 19: 12. *Prov.* 20: 2.

Punishment for resisting the lawful authority of. *Rom.* 13: 2.

Guilt and danger of stretching out the hand against. 1 *Sam.* 26: 9. 2 *Sam.* 1: 14.

They that walk after the flesh despise. 2 *Pet.* 2: 10. *Jude* 8.

GOOD—Exemplified. DAVID, 2 *Sam.* 8: 15. ASA, 1 *Kings* 15: 11. JEHOSHAPHAT, 1 *Kings* 22: 43. AMAZIAH, etc. 2 *Kings* 15: 3. UZZIAH, etc. 2 *Kings* 15: 34. HEZEKIAH, 2 *Kings* 18: 3. JOSIAH, 2 *Kings* 22: 2. MANASSEH, 2 *Chron.* 33: 12–16.

LANGUAGE

Of all mankind one at first. *Gen.* 11: 1, 6.

Called

Speech. *Mark* 14: 70. *Acts* 14: 11.

Tongue. *Acts* 1: 19. *Rev.* 5: 9.

Confusion of,

A punishment for presumption, etc. *Gen.* 11: 2–6.

Originated the varieties in. *Gen.* 11: 7.

Scattered men over the earth. *Gen.* 11: 8, 9.

Divided men into separate nations. *Gen.* 10: 5, 20, 31.

Great variety of, spoken by men. 1 *Cor.* 14: 10.

Ancient kingdoms often comprehended nations of different. *Esther* 1: 22. *Dan.* 3: 4. *Dan.* 6: 25.

Kinds of, mentioned;

Hebrew. 2 *Kings* 18: 28. *Acts* 26: 14.

Chaldee. *Dan.* 1: 4.

Syriac. 2 *Kings* 18: 26. *Ezra* 4: 7.

Greek. *Acts* 21: 37.

Latin. *Luke* 23: 38.

Lycaonian. *Acts* 14: 11.

Arabic, etc. *Acts* 2: 11.

Egyptian. *Ps.* 81: 5. *Ps.* 114: 1. *Acts* 2: 10.

Of some nations difficult. *Ezra* 3: 5, 6.

The term barbarian applied to those who spoke a strange. 1 *Cor.* 14: 11.

Power of speaking different,

A gift of the Holy Ghost. 1 *Cor.* 12: 10.

Promised. *Mark* 16: 17.

Given on the day of Pentecost. *Acts* 2: 3, 4.

Followed receiving the gospel. *Acts* 10: 44–46.

Conferred by laying on of the apostles' hands. *Acts* 8: 17, 18. *Acts* 19: 6.

Necessary to spread of the gospel. *Acts* 2: 7–11.

A sign to unbelievers. 1 *Cor.* 14: 22.

Sometimes abused. 1 *Cor.* 14: 2–12, 23.

Interpretation of,

Antiquity of engaging persons for. *Gen.* 42: 23.

A gift of the Holy Ghost. 1 *Cor.* 12: 10.

Most important in the early church. 1 *Cor.* 14: 5, 13, 27, 28.

The Jews punished by being given up to people of a strange. *Deut.* 28: 49. *Isa.* 28: 11. *Jer.* 5: 15.

LAW OF GOD, THE

Is absolute and perpetual. *Matt.* 5: 18.

Given

To Adam. *Gen.* 2: 16, 17, with *Rom.* 5: 12–14.

To Noah. *Gen.* 9: 6.

To the Israelites. *Exod.* 20: 2, etc. *Ps.* 75: 5.

Through Moses. *Exod.* 31: 18. *John* 7: 19.

Through the ministration of angels. *Acts* 7: 53. *Gal.* 3: 19. *Heb.* 2: 2.

Described as

Pure. *Ps.* 19: 8.

Spiritual. *Rom.* 7: 14.

Holy, just, and good. *Rom.* 7: 12.

Exceeding broad. *Ps.* 119: 96.

Perfect. *Ps.* 19: 7. *Rom.* 12: 2.

Truth. *Ps.* 119: 142.

Not grievous. 1 *John* 5: 3.

Requires obedience of the heart. *Ps.* 51: 6. *Matt.* 5: 28. *Matt.* 22: 37.

Requires perfect obedience. *Deut.* 27: 26. *Gal.* 3: 10. *Jas.* 2: 10.

Love is the fulfilling of. *Rom.* 13: 8, 10. *Gal.* 5: 14. *Jas.* 2: 8.

It is man's duty to keep. *Eccles.* 12: 13.

Man, by nature, not in subjection to. *Rom.* 7: 5. *Rom.* 8: 7.

Man cannot render perfect obedience to. 1 *Kings* 8: 46. *Eccles.* 7: 20. *Rom.* 3: 10.

Sin is a transgression of. 1 *John* 3: 4.

All men have transgressed. *Rom.* 3: 9, 19.

Man cannot be justified by. *Acts* 13: 39. *Rom.* 3: 20, 28. *Gal.* 2: 16. *Gal.* 3: 11.

Gives the knowledge of sin. *Rom.* 3: 20. *Rom.* 7: 7.

Worketh wrath. *Rom.* 4: 15.

Conscience testifies to. *Rom.* 2: 15.

Designed to lead to Christ. *Gal.* 3: 24.

Obedience to

A characteristic of saints. *Rev.* 12: 17.

A test of love. 1 *John* 5: 3.

Of prime importance. 1 *Cor.* 7: 19.

Blessedness of keeping. *Ps.* 119: 1. *Matt.* 5: 19. 1 *John* 3: 22, 24. *Rev.* 22: 14.

Christ

Came to fulfill. *Matt.* 5: 17.

Magnified. *Isa.* 42: 21.

Explained. *Matt.* 7: 12. *Matt.* 22: 37–40.

The love of, produces peace. *Ps.* 119: 165.

Saints

Freed from the bondage of. *Rom.* 6: 14. *Rom.* 7: 4, 6. *Gal.* 3: 13.

Freed from the curse of. *Gal.* 3: 13.

Have, written on their hearts. *Jer.* 31: 33, with *Heb.* 8: 10.

Love. *Ps.* 119: 97, 113.

Delight in. *Ps.* 119: 77. *Rom.* 7: 22.

Prepare their hearts to seek. *Ezra* 7: 10.

Pledge themselves to walk in. *Neh.* 10: 29.

Keep. *Ps.* 119: 55.

Pray to understand. *Ps.* 119: 18.

Pray for power to keep. *Ps.* 119: 34.

Should remember. *Mal.* 4: 4.

Should make, the subject of their conversation. *Exod.* 13: 9.

Lament over the violation of, by others. *Ps.* 119: 136.

The wicked

Despise. *Amos* 2: 4.

Forget. *Hos.* 4: 6.

Forsake. 2 *Chron.* 12: 1. *Jer.* 9: 13.

Refuse to hear. *Isa.* 30: 9. *Jer.* 6: 19.

Refuse to walk in. *Ps.* 78: 10.

Cast away. *Isa.* 5: 24.

Is the rule of life to saints. 1 *Cor.* 9: 21. *Gal.* 5: 13, 14.

Is the rule of the judgment. *Rom.* 2: 12.

To be used lawfully. 1 *Tim.* 1: 8.

Established by faith. *Rom.* 3: 31.

Punishment for disobeying. *Neh.* 9: 26, 27. *Isa.* 65: 11–13. *Jer.* 9: 13–16.

LIBERALITY

Pleasing to God. 2 *Cor.* 9: 7. *Heb.* 13: 16.

God never forgets. *Heb.* 6: 10.

Christ set an example of. 2 *Cor.* 8: 9.

Characteristic of saints. *Ps.* 112: 9. *Isa.* 32: 8.

Unprofitable, without love. 1 *Cor.* 13: 3.

Should be exercised

In the service of God. *Exod.* 35: 21–29.

Toward saints. *Rom.* 12: 13. *Gal.* 6: 10.

Toward servants. *Deut.* 15: 12–14.

Toward the poor. *Deut.* 15: 11. *Isa.* 58: 7.

Toward strangers. *Lev.* 25: 35.

Toward enemies. *Prov.* 25: 21.

Toward all men. *Gal.* 6: 10.

In lending to those in want. *Matt.* 5: 42.

In giving alms. *Luke* 12: 33.

In relieving the destitute. *Isa.* 58: 7.

In forwarding missions. *Phil.* 4: 14–16.

In rendering personal services. *Phil.* 2: 30.

Without ostentation. *Matt.* 6: 1–3.

With simplicity. *Rom.* 12: 8.

According to ability. *Deut.* 16: 10, 17. 1 *Cor.* 16: 2.

Willingly. *Exod.* 25: 2. 2 *Cor.* 8: 12.

Abundantly. 2 *Cor.* 8: 7. 2 *Cor.* 9: 11–13.

Exercise of, provokes others to. 2 *Cor.* 9: 2.

Labour to be enabled to exercise. *Acts* 20: 35. *Eph.* 4: 28.

Want of,

Brings many a curse. *Prov.* 28: 27.

A proof of not loving God. 1 *John* 3: 17.

A proof of not having faith. *Jas.* 2: 14–16.

Blessings connected with. *Ps.* 41: 1. *Prov.* 22: 9. *Acts* 20: 35.

Promises to. *Ps.* 112: 9. *Prov.* 11: 25. *Prov.* 28: 27. *Eccles.* 11: 1, 2. *Isa.* 58: 10.

Exhortations to. *Luke* 3: 11. *Luke* 11: 41. *Acts* 20: 35. 1 *Cor.* 16: 1. 1 *Tim.* 6: 17, 18.

Exemplified. PRINCES OF IS-RAEL, *Num.* 7: 2. BOAZ, *Ruth* 2: 16. DAVID, 2 *Sam.* 9: 7, 10. BARZILLAI, etc. 2 *Sam.* 17: 28. ARAUNAH, 2 *Sam.* 24: 22. SHUNAMMITE, 2 *Kings* 4: 8, 10. JUDAH, 2 *Chron.* 24: 10, 11. NEHEMIAH, *Neh.* 7: 70. JEWS, *Neh.* 7: 71, 72. JOB, *Job* 29: 15, 16. NEBUZAR-ADAN, *Jer.* 40: 4, 5. JOANNA, etc., *Luke* 8: 3. ZACCHEUS, *Luke* 19: 8. PRIMITIVE CHRISTIANS, *Acts* 2: 45. BARNABAS, *Acts* 4: 36, 37. DORCAS, *Acts* 9: 36. CORNELIUS, *Acts* 10: 2. CHURCH OF ANTIOCH, *Acts* 11: 29, 30. LYDIA, *Acts* 16: 15. PAUL, *Acts* 20: 34. PEOPLE OF MALTA, *Acts* 28: 2. STEPHANAS, etc., 1 *Cor.* 16: 17.

Extraordinary—Exemplified. ISRAELITES, *Exod.* 36: 5. POOR WIDOW, *Mark* 12: 42–44. CHURCHES OF MACEDONIA, 2 *Cor.* 8: 1–5.

LIBERTY, CHRISTIAN

Foretold. *Isa.* 42: 7. *Isa.* 61: 1.

Conferred

By God. *Col.* 1: 13.

By Christ. *Gal.* 4: 3–5. *Gal.* 5:1.

By the Holy Ghost. *Rom.* 8: 15. 2 *Cor.* 3: 17.

Through the gospel. *John* 8: 32.

Confirmed by Christ. *John* 8: 36.

Proclaimed by Christ. *Isa.* 61: 1. *Luke* 4: 18.

The service of Chirst is. 1 *Cor.* 7: 22.

Is freedom from

The law. *Rom.* 7: 6. *Rom.* 8: 2.

The curse of the law. *Gal.* 3: 13.

The fear of death. *Heb.* 2: 15.

Sin. *Rom.* 6: 7, 18.

Corruption. *Rom.* 8: 21.

Bondage of man. 1 *Cor.* 9: 19.

Jewish ordinances. *Gal.* 4: 3. *Col.* 2: 20.

Called the glorious liberty of the children of God. *Rom.* 8: 21.

Saints are called to. *Gal.* 5: 13.

Saints should

Praise God for. *Ps.* 116: 16, 17.

Assert. 1 *Cor.* 10: 29.

Walk in. *Ps.* 119: 45.

Stand fast in. *Gal.* 2: 5. *Gal.* 5: 1.

Not abuse. *Gal.* 5: 13. 1 *Pet.* 2: 16.

Not offend others by. 1 *Cor.* 8: 9. 1 *Cor.* 10: 29, 32.

The gospel is the law of. *John* 1: 25. *Jas.* 2: 12.

False teachers

Promise, to others. 2 *Pet.* 2: 19.

Abuse. *Jude* 4.

Try to destroy. *Gal.* 2: 4.

The wicked, devoid of. *John* 8: 34, with *Rom.* 6: 20.

Typified. *Lev.* 25: 10–17. *Gal.* 4: 22–26, 31.

LIFE, NATURAL

God is the Author of. *Gen.* 2: 7. *Acts* 17: 28.

God preserves. *Ps.* 36: 6. *Ps.* 66: 9.

Is in the hand of God. *Job* 12: 10. *Dan.* 5: 23.

Forfeited by sin. *Gen.* 2: 17. *Gen.* 3: 17–19.

Of others, not to be taken away. *Exod.* 20: 13.

Described as

Vain. *Eccles.* 6: 12.

Limited. *Job* 7: 1. *Job* 14: 5.

Short. *Job* 14: 1. *Ps.* 89: 47.

Uncertain. *Jas.* 4: 13–15.

Full of trouble. *Job* 14: 1.

God's loving-kindness better than. *Ps.* 63: 3.

The value of. *Job* 2: 4. *Matt.* 6: 25.

Preserved by discretion. *Prov.* 13: 3.

Sometimes prolonged, in answer to prayer. *Isa.* 38: 2–5. *Jas.* 5: 15.

Obedience to God, tends to prolong. *Deut.* 30: 20.

Obedience to parents, tends to prolong. *Exod.* 20: 12. *Prov.* 4: 10.

Cares and pleasure of, dangerous. *Luke* 8: 14. *Luke* 21: 34. 2 *Tim.* 2: 4.

Saints have true enjoyment of. *Ps.* 128: 2. 1 *Tim.* 4: 8.

Of saints, specially protected by God. *Job* 2: 6. *Acts* 18: 10. 1 *Pet.* 3: 13.

Of the wicked, not especially protected by God. *Job* 36: 6. *Ps.* 78: 50.

The wicked have their portion of good, during. *Ps.* 17: 14. *Luke* 6: 24. *Luke* 16: 25.

Should be spent in

The fear of God. 1 *Pet.* 1: 17.

The service of God. *Luke* 1: 75.

Living unto God. *Rom.* 14: 8. *Phil.* 1: 21.

Peace. *Rom.* 12: 18. 1 *Tim.* 2: 2.

Doing good. *Eccles.* 3: 12.

Should be taken all due care of. *Matt.* 10: 23. *Acts* 27: 34.

Should be laid down, if necessary, for Christ. *Matt.* 10: 39. *Luke* 14: 26. *Acts* 20: 24.

Should be laid down, if necessary, for the brethren. *Rom.* 16: 4. 1 *John* 3: 16.

Be thankful for

The preservation of. *Ps.* 103: 4. *John* 2: 6.

The supply of its wants. *Gen.* 48: 15.

The dissatisfied despise. *Eccles.* 2: 17.

We know not what is good for us in. *Eccles.* 6: 12.

Be not over-anxious to provide for its wants. *Matt.* 6: 25.

The enjoyment of, consists not in abundance of possessions. *Luke* 12: 15.

Is compared to

An eagle hasting to the prey. *Job* 9: 26.

A pilgrimage. *Gen.* 47: 9.

A tale told. *Ps.* 90: 9.

A swift post. *Job* 9: 25.

A swift ship. *Job* 9: 26.

A hand-breadth. *Ps.* 39: 5.

A shepherd's tent removed. *Isa.* 38: 12.

A dream. *Ps.* 73: 20.

A sleep. *Ps.* 90: 5.

A vapour. *Jas.* 4: 14.

A shadow. *Eccles.* 6: 12.

A thread cut by the weaver. *Isa.* 38: 12.

A weaver's shuttle. *Job* 7: 6.

A flower. *Job* 14: 2.

Grass. 1 *Pet.* 1: 24.

Water spilt on the ground. 2 *Sam.* 14: 14.

Wind. *Job* 7: 7.

Shortness of, should lead to spiritual improvement. *Deut.* 32: 29. *Ps.* 90: 12.

Sometimes judicially shortened. 1 *Sam.* 2: 32, 33. *Job* 36: 16.

Miraculously restored by Christ. *Matt.* 9: 18, 25. *Luke* 7: 15, 22. *John* 11: 43.

LIFE, SPIRITUAL

God is the Author of. *Ps.* 36: 9. *Col.* 2: 13.

Christ is the Author of. *John* 5: 21, 25. *John* 6: 33, 51–53. *John* 14: 6. 1 *John* 4: 9.

The Holy Ghost is the Author of. *Ezek.* 37: 14, with *Rom.* 8: 9–13.

The word of God is the instrument of. *Isa.* 55: 3. 2 *Cor.* 3: 6. 1 *Pet.* 4: 6.

Is hidden with Christ. *Col.* 3: 3.

The fear of God is. *Prov.* 14: 27. *Prov.* 19: 23.

Spiritual-mindedness is. *Rom.* 8: 6.

Is maintained by

Christ. *John* 6: 57. 1 *Cor.* 10: 3, 4.

Faith. *Gal.* 2: 20.

The word of God. *Deut.* 8: 3, with *Matt.* 4: 4.

Prayer. *Ps.* 69: 32.

Has its origin in the new-birth. *John* 3: 3–8.

Has its infancy. *Luke* 10: 21. 1 *Cor.* 3: 1, 2. 1 *John* 2: 12.

Has its youth. 1 *John* 2: 13, 14.

Has its maturity. *Eph.* 4: 13. 1 *John* 2: 13, 14.

Is described as

A life unto God. *Rom.* 6: 11. *Gal.* 2: 19.

A life according to God. 1 *Pet.* 4: 6.

Newness of life. *Rom.* 6: 4.

Living in the Spirit. *Gal.* 5: 25.

Revived by God. *Ps.* 85: 6. *Hos.* 6: 2.

Evidenced by love to the brethren. 1 *John* 3: 14.

All saints have. *Eph.* 2: 1, 5. *Col.* 2: 13.

Should animate the services of saints. *Rom.* 12: 1. 1 *Cor.* 14: 15.

Saints praise God for. *Ps.* 119: 175.

Seek to grow in. *Eph.* 4: 15. 1 *Pet.* 2: 2.

Pray for the increase of. *Ps.* 119: 25. *Ps.* 143: 11.

The wicked alienated from. *Eph.* 4: 18.

Lovers of pleasure destitute of. 1 *Tim.* 5: 6.

Hypocrites destitute of. *Jude* 12. *Rev.* 3: 1.

Illustrated. *Ezek.* 37: 9, 10. *Luke* 15: 24.

LIFE, ETERNAL

Christ is. 1 *John* 1: 2. 1 *John* 5: 20.

Revealed by Christ. *John* 6: 68. 2 *Tim.* 1: 10.

To know God and Christ is. *John* 17: 3.

Given

By God. *Ps.* 133: 3. *Rom.* 6: 23.

By Christ. *John* 6: 27. *John* 10: 28.

In Christ. 1 *John* 5: 11.

Through Christ. *Rom.* 5: 21. *Rom.* 6: 23.

To all given to Christ. *John* 17: 2.

To those who believe in God. *John* 5: 24.

To those who believe in Christ. *John* 3: 15, 16. *John* 6: 40, 47.

To those who hate life for Christ. *John* 12: 25.

In answer to prayer. *Ps.* 21: 4.

Revealed in the scriptures. *John* 5: 39.

Results from

Drinking the water of life. *John* 4: 14.

Eating the bread of life. *John* 6: 50–58.

Eating of the tree of life. *Rev.* 2: 7.

They who are ordained to, believe the gospel. *Acts* 13: 48.

Saints

Have promises of. 1 *Tim.* 4: 8. 2 *Tim.* 1: 1. *Titus* 1: 2. 1 *John* 2: 25.

Have hope of. *Titus* 1: 2. *Titus* 3: 7.

May have assurance of. 2 *Cor.* 5: 1. 1 *John* 5: 13.

Shall reap, through the Spirit. *Gal.* 6: 8.

Shall inherit. *Matt.* 19: 29.

Look for the mercy of God unto. *Jude* 21.

Should lay hold of. 1 *Tim.* 6: 12, 19.

Are preserved unto. *John* 10: 28, 29.

Shall rise unto. *Dan.* 12: 2. *John* 5: 29.

Shall go into. *Matt.* 25: 46.

Shall reign in. *Dan.* 7: 18. *Rom.* 5: 17.

The self-righteous think to inherit, by works. *Mark* 10: 17.

Cannot be inherited by works. *Rom.* 2: 7, with *Rom.* 3: 10–19.

The wicked

Have not. 1 *John* 3: 15.

Judge themselves unworthy of. *Acts* 13: 46.

Exhortation to seek. *John* 6: 27.

LONG-SUFFERING OF GOD, THE

Is part of his character. *Exod.* 34: 6. *Num.* 14: 18. *Ps.* 86: 15.

Salvation, the object of. *2 Pet.* 3: 15.

Through Christ's intercession. *Luke* 13: 8.

Should lead to repentance. *Rom.* 2: 4. *2 Pet.* 3: 9.

An encouragement to repent. *Joel* 2: 13.

Exhibited in forgiving sins. *Rom.* 3: 25.

Exercised toward

His people. *Isa.* 30: 18. *Ezek.* 20: 17.

The wicked. *Rom.* 9: 22. 1 *Pet.* 3: 20.

Plead in prayer. *Jer.* 15: 15.

Limits set to. *Gen.* 6: 3. *Jer.* 44: 22.

The wicked

Abuse. *Eccles.* 8: 11. *Matt.* 24: 48, 49.

Despise. *Rom.* 2: 4.

Punished for despising. *Neh.* 9: 30. *Matt.* 24: 48–51. *Rom.* 2: 5.

Illustrated. *Luke* 13: 6–9.

Exemplified. MANASSEH, 2 *Chron.* 33: 10–13. ISRAEL, *Ps.* 78: 38. *Isa.* 48: 9. JERUSALEM, *Matt.* 23: 37. PAUL, 1 *Tim.* 1: 16.

LOVE OF GOD, THE

Is a part of his character. 2 *Cor.* 13: 11. 1 *John* 4: 8.

Christ, the especial object of. *John* 15: 9. *John* 17: 26.

Christ abides in. *John* 15: 10.

Described as

Sovereign. *Deut.* 7: 8. *Deut.* 10: 15.

Great. *Eph.* 2: 4.

Abiding. *Zeph.* 3: 17.

Unfailing. *Isa.* 49: 15, 16.

Unalienable. *Rom.* 8: 39.

Constraining. *Hos.* 11: 4.

Everlasting. *Jer.* 31: 3.

Irrespective of merit. *Deut.* 7: 7. *Job* 7: 17.

Manifested towards

Perishing sinners. *John* 3: 16. *Titus* 3: 4.

His saints. *John* 16: 27. *John* 17: 23. 2 *Thess.* 2: 16. 1 *John* 4: 16.

The destitute. *Deut.* 10: 18.

The cheerful giver. 2 *Cor.* 9: 7.

Exhibited in

The giving of Christ. *John* 3: 16.

The sending of Christ. 1 *John* 4: 9.

Christ's dying for us while sinners. *Rom.* 5: 8. 1 *John* 4: 10.

Election. *Mal.* 1: 2, 3. *Rom.* 9: 11–13.

Adoption. 1 *John* 3: 1.

Redemption. *Isa.* 43: 3, 4. *Isa.* 63: 9.

Freeness of salvation. *Titus* 3: 4–7.

Forgiving sin. *Isa.* 38: 17.

Quickening souls. *Eph.* 2: 4, 5.

Drawing us to himself. *Hos.* 11: 4.

Temporal blessings. *Deut.* 7: 13.

Chastisements. *Heb.* 12: 6.

Defeating evil counsels. *Deut.* 23: 5.

Shed abroad in the heart by the Holy Ghost. *Rom.* 5: 5.

Saints know and believe. 1 *John* 4: 16.

Saints should abide in. *Jude* 21.

Perfected in saints

By obedience. 1 *John* 2: 5.

By brotherly love. 1 *John* 4: 12.

The source of our love to him. 1 *John* 4: 19.

To be sought in prayer. 2 *Cor.* 13: 14.

LOVE OF CHRIST, THE

To the Father. *Ps.* 91: 14. *John* 14: 31.

To his Church. *Song of Sol.* 4: 8, 9. *Song of Sol.* 5: 1. *John* 15: 9. *Eph.* 5: 25.

To those who love him. *Prov.* 8: 17. *John* 14: 21.

Manifested in his

Coming to seek the lost. *Luke* 19: 10.

Praying for his enemies. *Luke* 23: 34.

Giving himself for us. *Gal.* 2: 20.

Dying for us. *John* 15: 13. 1 *John* 3: 16.

Washing away our sins. *Rev.* 1: 5.

Interceding for us. *Heb.* 7: 25. *Heb.* 9: 24.

Sending the Spirit. *Ps.* 68: 18. *John* 16: 7.

Rebukes and chastisements. *Rev.* 3: 19.

Passeth knowledge. *Eph.* 3: 19.

To be imitated. *John* 13: 34. *John* 15: 12. *Eph.* 5: 2. 1 *John* 3: 16.

To saints, is

Unquenchable. *Song of Sol.* 8: 7.

Constraining. 2 *Cor.* 5: 14.

Unchangeable. *John* 13: 1.

Indissoluble. *Rom.* 8: 35.

Obedient saints abide in. *John* 15: 10.

Saints obtain victory through. *Rom.* 8: 37.

Is the banner over his saints. *Song of Sol.* 2: 4.

Is the ground of his saints' love to him. *Luke* 7: 47.

To saints, shall be acknowledged even by enemies. *Rev.* 3: 9.

Illustrated. *Matt.* 18: 11–13.

Exemplified towards. PETER, *Luke* 22: 32, 61. LAZARUS, etc. *John* 11: 5, 36. HIS APOSTLES, *John* 13: 1, 34. JOHN, *John* 13: 23.

LOVE TO GOD

Commanded. *Deut.* 11: 1. *Joshua* 22: 5.

The first great commandment. *Matt.* 22: 38.

With all the heart. *Deut.* 6: 5, with *Matt.* 22: 37.

Better than all sacrifices. *Mark* 12: 33.

Produced by

The Holy Ghost. *Gal.* 5: 22. 2 *Thess.* 3: 5.

The love of God to us. 1 *John* 4: 19.

Answers to prayer. *Ps.* 116: 1.

Exhibited by Christ. *John* 14: 31.

A characteristic of saints. *Ps.* 5: 11.

Should produce

Joy. *Ps.* 5: 11.

Love to saints. 1 *John* 5: 1.

Hatred of sin. *Ps.* 97: 10.

Obedience to God. *Deut.* 30: 20. 1 *John* 5: 3.

Perfected in obedience. 1 *John* 2: 5.

Perfected, gives boldness. 1 *John* 4: 17, 18.

God, faithful to those who have. *Deut.* 7: 9.

They who have

Are known of him. 1 *Cor.* 8: 3.

Are preserved by him. *Ps.* 145: 20.

Are delivered by him. *Ps.* 91: 14.

Partake of his mercy. *Exod.* 20: 6. *Deut.* 7: 9.

Have all things working for their good. *Rom.* 8: 28.

Persevere in. *Jude* 21.

Exhort one another to. *Ps.* 31: 23.

Pray for. 2 *Thess.* 3: 5.

The love of the world is a proof of not having. 1 *John* 2: 15.

They who love not others, are without. 1 *John* 4: 20.

Hypocrites, without. *Luke* 11: 42. *John* 5: 42.

The uncharitable, without. 1 *John* 3: 17.

God tries the sincerity of. *Deut.* 13: 3.

Promises connected with. *Deut.* 11: 13–15. *Ps.* 69: 36. *Isa.* 56: 6, 7. *Jas.* 1: 12.

LOVE TO CHRIST

Exhibited by God. *Matt.* 17: 5. *John* 5: 20.

Exhibited by saints. 1 *Pet.* 1: 8.

His personal excellence is deserving of. *Song of Sol.* 5: 9–16.

His love to us a motive to. 2 *Cor.* 5: 14.

Manifested in

Seeking him. *Song of Sol.* 3: 2.

Obeying him. *John* 14: 15, 21, 23.

Ministering to him. *Matt.* 27: 55, with *Matt.* 25: 40.

Preferring him to all others. *Matt.* 10: 37.

Taking up the cross for him. *Matt.* 10: 38.

A characteristic of saints. *Song of Sol.* 1: 4.

An evidence of adoption. *John* 8: 42.

Should be

Sincere. *Eph.* 6: 24.

With the soul. *Song of Sol.* 1: 7.

In proportion to our mercies. *Luke* 7: 47.

Supreme. *Matt.* 10: 37.

Ardent. *Song of Sol.* 2: 5. *Song of Sol.* 8: 6.

Unquenchable. *Song of Sol.* 8: 7.

Even unto death. *Acts* 21: 13. *Rev.* 12: 11.

Promises to. 2 *Tim.* 4: 8. *Jas.* 1: 12.

Increase of, to be prayed for. *Phil.* 1: 9.

Pray for grace to those who have. *Eph.* 6: 24.

They who have

Are loved by the Father. *John* 14: 21, 23. *John* 16: 27.

Are loved by Christ. *Prov.* 8: 17. *John* 14: 21.

Enjoy communion with God and Christ. *John* 14: 23.

Decrease of, rebuked. *Rev.* 2: 4.

Want of, denounced. 1 *Cor.* 16: 22.

The wicked, destitute of. *Ps.* 35: 19, with *John* 15: 18, 25.

Exemplified. JOSEPH OF ARIMATHAEA, *Matt.* 27: 57–60. PENITENT WOMAN, *Luke* 7: 47. CERTAIN WOMEN, *Luke* 23: 28.

THOMAS, *John* 11: 16. MARY
MAGDALENE, *John* 20: 11.
PETER, *John* 21: 15—17. PAUL,
Acts 21: 13.

LOVE TO MAN

Is of God. 1 *John* 4: 7.
Commanded by God. 1 *John*
4: 21.
Commanded by Christ. *John*
13: 34. *John* 15: 12. 1 *John* 3:
23.
After the example of Christ.
John 13: 34. *John* 15: 12. *Eph.*
5: 2.
Taught by God. 1 *Thess.* 4: 9.
Faith worketh by. *Gal.* 5: 6.
A fruit of the Spirit. *Gal.* 5:
22. *Col.* 1: 8.
Purity of heart leads to. 1 *Pet.*
1: 22.
Explained. 1 *Cor.* 13: 4—7.
Is an active principle. 1 *Thess.*
1: 3. *Heb.* 6: 10.
Is an abiding principle. 1 *Cor.*
13: 8, 13.
Is the second great command-
ment. *Matt.* 22: 37—39.
Is the end of the commandment.
1 *Tim.* 1: 5.
Supernatural gifts are nothing
without. 1 *Cor.* 13: 1, 2.
The greatest sacrifices are noth-
ing without. 1 *Cor.* 13: 3.
Especially enjoined upon ministers. 1 *Tim.* 4: 12. 2 *Tim.*
2: 22.

Saints should

Put on. *Col.* 3: 14.
Follow after. 1 *Cor.* 14: 1.
Abound in. *Phil.* 1: 9. 1
Thess. 3: 12.
Continue in. 1 *Tim.* 2: 15.
Heb. 13: 1.
Provoke each other to. 2
Cor. 8: 7. 2 *Cor.* 9: 2. *Heb.*
10: 24.

Be sincere in. *Rom.* 12: 9.
2 *Cor.* 6: 6. 2 *Cor.* 8: 8. 1
John 3: 18.
Be disinterested in. 1 *Cor.*
10: 24. 1 *Cor.* 13: 5. *Phil.* 2:
4.
Be fervent in. 1 *Pet.* 1: 22.
1 *Pet.* 4: 8.
Should be connected with
brotherly-kindness. *Rom.* 12:
10. 1 *Pet.* 1: 7.
Should be with a pure heart.
1 *Pet.* 1: 22.
All things should be done with.
1 *Cor.* 16: 14.

Should be exhibited, toward

Saints. 1 *Pet.* 2: 17. 1 *John*
5: 1.
Ministers. 1 *Thess.* 5: 13.
Our families. *Eph.* 5: 25.
Titus 2: 4.
Fellow-countrymen. *Exod.*
32: 32. *Rom.* 9: 2, 3. *Rom.*
10: 1.
Strangers. *Lev.* 19: 34. *Deut.*
10: 19.
Enemies. *Exod.* 23: 4, 5.
2 *Kings* 6: 22. *Matt.* 5: 44.
Rom. 12: 14, 20. 1 *Pet.* 3: 9.
All men. *Gal.* 6: 10.

Should be exhibited, in

Ministering to the wants of
others. *Matt.* 25: 35. *Heb.*
6: 10.
Loving each other. *Gal.* 5:
13.
Relieving strangers. *Lev.*
25: 35. *Matt.* 25: 35.
Clothing the naked. *Isa.* 58:
7. *Matt.* 25: 36.
Visiting the sick, etc. *Job*
31: 16—22. *Jas.* 1: 27.
Sympathising. *Rom.* 12: 15,
1 *Cor.* 12: 26.
Supporting the weak. *Gal.*
6: 2. 1 *Thess.* 5: 14.
Covering the faults of others.

Prov. 10: 12, with 1 *Pet.* 4: 8.

Forgiving injuries. *Eph.* 4: 32. *Col.* 3: 13.

Forbearing. *Eph.* 4: 2.

Rebuking. *Lev.* 19: 17. *Matt.* 18: 15.

Necessary to true happiness. *Prov.* 15: 17.

The love of God is a motive to. *John* 13: 34. 1 *John* 4: 11.

An evidence of

Being in the light. 1 *John* 2: 10.

Discipleship with Christ. *John* 13: 35.

Spiritual life. 1 *John* 3: 14.

Is the fulfilling of the law. *Rom.* 13: 8–10. *Gal.* 5: 14. *Jas.* 2: 8.

Love to self is the measure of. *Mark* 12: 33.

Is good and pleasant. *Ps.* 133: 1, 2.

Is a bond of union. *Col.* 2: 2.

Is the bond of perfectness. *Col.* 3: 14.

Hypocrites, devoid of. 1 *John* 2: 9, 11. 1 *John* 4: 20.

The wicked, devoid of. 1 *John* 3: 10.

Exemplified. JOSEPH, *Gen.* 45: 15. RUTH, *Ruth* 1: 16, 17. JONATHAN, etc. 1 *Sam.* 20: 17, 41, 42. OBADIAH, 1 *Kings* 18: 4. CENTURION, *Luke* 7: 5. PRIMITIVE CHURCH, *Acts* 2: 46. *Heb.* 10: 33, 34. LYDIA, *Acts* 16: 15. AQUILA, etc. *Rom.* 16: 3, 4. PAUL, 2 *Cor.* 6: 11, 12. EPAPHRODITUS, *Phil.* 2: 25, 26, 30. PHILIPPIANS, *Phil.* 4: 15–19. COLOSSIANS, *Col.* 1: 4. THESSALONIANS, 1 *Thess.* 3: 6. ONESIPHORUS, 2 *Tim.* 1: 16–18. PHILEMON, *Philem.* 7–9. MOSES, *Heb.* 11: 25.

LOVING-KINDNESS OF GOD, THE

Is through Christ. *Eph.* 2: 7. *Titus* 3: 4–6.

Described as

Great. *Neh.* 9: 17.

Excellent. *Ps.* 36: 7.

Good. *Ps.* 69: 16.

Marvellous. *Ps.* 17: 7. *Ps.* 31: 21.

Multitudinous. *Isa.* 63: 7.

Everlasting. *Isa.* 54: 8.

Merciful. *Ps.* 117: 2.

Better than life. *Ps.* 63: 3.

Consideration of the dealings of God gives a knowledge of. *Ps.* 107: 43.

Saints

Betrothed in. *Hos.* 2: 19.

Drawn by. *Jer.* 31: 3.

Preserved by. *Ps.* 40: 11.

Quickened after. *Ps.* 119: 88.

Comforted by. *Ps.* 119: 76.

Look for mercy through. *Ps.* 51: 1.

Receive mercy through. *Isa.* 54: 8.

Are heard according to. *Ps.* 119: 149.

Are ever mindful of. *Ps.* 26: 3. *Ps.* 49: 9.

Should expect, in affliction. *Ps.* 42: 7, 8.

Crowned with. *Ps.* 103: 4.

Never utterly taken from saints. *Ps.* 89: 33. *Isa.* 54: 10.

Former manifestations of, to be pleaded in prayer. *Ps.* 25: 6. *Ps.* 89: 49.

Pray for the

Exhibition of. *Ps.* 17: 7. *Ps.* 143: 8.

Continuance of. *Ps.* 36: 10.

Extension of. *Gen.* 24: 12 2 *Sam.* 2: 6.

Praise God for. *Ps.* 92: 2. *Ps.* 138: 2.

Proclaim, to others. *Ps.* 40: 10.

LYING

Forbidden. *Lev.* 19: 11. *Col.* 3: 9.

Hateful to God. *Prov.* 6: 16–19.

An abomination to God. *Prov.* 12: 22.

A hindrance to prayer. *Isa.* 59: 2, 3.

The devil, the father of. *John* 8: 44.

The devil excites men to. 1 *Kings* 22: 22. *Acts* 5: 3.

Saints

Hate. *Ps.* 119: 163. *Prov.* 13: 5.

Avoid. *Isa.* 63: 8. *Zeph.* 3: 13.

Respect not those who practise. *Ps.* 40: 4.

Reject those who practise. *Ps.* 101: 7.

Pray to be preserved from. *Ps.* 119: 29. *Prov.* 30: 8.

Unbecoming in rulers. *Prov.* 17: 7.

The evil of rulers hearkening to. *Prov.* 29: 12.

False prophets addicted to. *Jer.* 23: 14. *Ezek.* 22: 28.

False witnesses addicted to. *Prov.* 14: 5, 25.

Antinomians guilty of. 1 *John* 1: 6. 1 *John* 2: 4.

Hypocrites addicted to. *Hos.* 11: 12.

Hypocrites, a seed of. *Isa.* 57: 4.

The wicked

Addicted to, from their infancy. *Ps.* 58: 3.

Love. *Ps.* 52: 3.

Delight in. *Ps.* 62: 4.

Seek after. *Ps.* 4: 2.

Prepare their tongues for. *Jer.* 9: 3, 5.

Bring forth. *Ps.* 7: 14.

Give heed to. *Prov.* 17: 4.

A characteristic of the Apostacy. 2 *Thess.* 2: 9. 1 *Tim.* 4: 2.

Leads to

Hatred. *Prov.* 26: 28.

Love of impure conversation. *Prov.* 17: 4.

Often accompanied by gross crimes. *Hos.* 4: 1, 2.

Folly of concealing hatred by. *Prov.* 10: 18.

Vanity of getting riches by. *Prov.* 21: 6.

Shall be detected. *Prov.* 12: 19.

Poverty preferable to. *Prov.* 19: 22.

Excludes from heaven. *Rev.* 21: 27. *Rev.* 22: 15.

They who are guilty of, shall be cast into hell. *Rev.* 21: 8.

Punishment for. *Ps.* 5: 6. *Ps.* 120: 3, 4. *Prov.* 19: 5. *Jer.* 50: 36.

Exemplified. THE DEVIL, *Gen.* 3: 4. CAIN, *Gen.* 4: 9. SARAH, *Gen.* 18: 15. JACOB, *Gen.* 27: 19. JOSEPH'S BRETHREN, *Gen.* 37: 31, 32. GIBEONITES, *Joshua* 9: 9–13. SAMSON, *Judges* 16: 10. SAUL, 1 *Sam.* 15: 13. MICHAL, 1 *Sam.* 19: 14. DAVID, 1 *Sam.* 21: 2. PROPHET OF BETHEL, 1 *Kings* 13: 18. GEHAZI, 2 *Kings* 5: 22. JOB'S FRIENDS, *Job* 13: 4. NINEVITES, *Nahum* 3: 1. PETER, *Matt.* 26: 72. ANANIAS, etc., *Acts* 5: 5. CRETANS, *Titus* 1: 12.

MAGISTRATES

Are appointed by God. *Rom.* 13: 1.

Are ministers of God. *Rom.* 13: 4, 6.

Purpose of their appointment. *Rom.* 13: 4. 1 *Pet.* 2: 14.

Are not a terror to the good, but to the evil. *Rom.* 13: 3.

To be wisely selected and appointed. *Exod.* 18: 21. *Ezra* 7: 25.

To be prayed for. 1 *Tim.* 2: 1, 2.

Should

Rule in the fear of God. 2 *Sam.* 23: 3. 2 *Chron.* 19: 7.

Know the law of God. *Ezra* 7: 25.

Be faithful to the Sovereign. *Dan.* 6: 4.

Enforce the laws. *Ezra* 7: 26.

Hate covetousness. *Exod.* 18: 21.

Not take bribes. *Exod.* 23: 8. *Deut.* 16: 19.

Defend the poor, etc. *Job* 29: 12, 16.

Judge for God, not for man. 2 *Chron.* 19: 6.

Judge righteously. *Deut.* 1: 16. *Deut.* 16: 18. *Deut.* 25: 1.

Be impartial. *Exod.* 23: 6. *Deut.* 1: 17.

Be diligent in ruling. *Rom.* 12: 8.

Subjection to the authority enjoined. *Rom.* 13: 1. 1 *Pet.* 2: 13, 14.

Wicked—Illustrated. *Prov.* 28: 15.

Good—Exemplified. JOSEPH, *Gen.* 41: 46. GIDEON, *Judges* 8: 35. SAMUEL, 1 *Sam.* 12: 3, 4. *Ezra* 10: 1–9. NEHEMIAH, *Neh.* 3: 15. JOB, *Job* 29: 16. DANIEL, *Dan.* 6: 3.

Wicked—Exemplified. SONS OF SAMUEL, 1 *Sam.* 8: 3. PILATE,

Matt. 27: 24, 26. MAGISTRATES IN PHILIPPI, *Acts* 16: 22, 23. GALLIO, *Acts* 18: 16, 17. FELIX, *Acts* 24: 26.

MALICE

Forbidden. 1 *Cor.* 14: 20. *Col.* 3: 8.

A hindrance to growth in grace. 1 *Pet.* 2: 1, 2.

Incompatible with the worship of God. 1 *Cor.* 5: 7, 8.

Christian liberty not to be made a cloak for. 1 *Pet.* 2: 16.

Saints avoid. *Job* 31: 29, 30. *Ps.* 35: 12–14.

The wicked

Speak with. 3 *John* 10.

Live in. *Titus* 3: 3.

Conceive. *Ps.* 7: 14.

Filled with. *Rom.* 1: 29.

Visit saints with. *Ps.* 83: 3. *Matt.* 22: 6.

Pray for those who injure you through. *Matt.* 5: 44.

Brings its own punishment. *Ps.* 7: 15, 16.

God requites. *Ps.* 10: 14. *Ezek.* 36: 5.

Punishment of. *Amos* 1: 11, 12. *Obad.* 10–15.

Exemplified. CAIN, *Gen.* 4: 5. ESAU, *Gen.* 27: 41. JOSEPH'S BRETHREN, *Gen.* 37: 19, 20. SAUL, 1 *Sam.* 18: 9–11. SANBALLAT, etc., *Neh.* 2: 10. HAMAN, *Esther* 3: 5, 6. EDOMITES, *Ezek.* 35: 5. PRESIDENTS, etc., *Dan.* 6: 4–9. HERODIAS, *Mark* 6: 19. SCRIBES, etc., *Mark* 11: 18. *Luke* 11: 54. DIOTREPHES, 3 *John* 10.

MARRIAGE

Divinely instituted. *Gen.* 2: 24.

A covenant relationship. *Mal.* 2: 4.

Designed for

The happiness of man. *Gen. 2: 18.*

Increasing the species. *Gen. 1: 28. Gen. 9: 1.*

Raising up a godly seed. *Mal. 2: 15.*

Preventing fornication. 1 *Cor. 7: 2.*

The expectation of the promised seed of the woman an incentive to, in the early age. *Gen. 3: 15,* with *Gen. 4: 1* (marg.).

Lawful in all. 1 *Cor. 7: 2, 28.* 1 *Tim. 5: 14.*

Honourable for all. *Heb. 13: 4.*

Should be only in the Lord. 1 *Cor. 7: 39.*

Expressed by

Joining together. *Matt. 19: 6.*

Making affinity. 1 *Kings 3: 1.*

Taking to wife. *Exod. 2: 1.*

Giving daughters to sons, and sons to daughters. *Deut. 7: 3. Ezra 9: 12.*

Indissoluble during the joint lives of the parties. *Matt. 19: 6. Rom. 7: 2, 3.* 1 *Cor. 7: 39.*

Early introduction of polygamy. *Gen. 4: 19.*

Contracted in patriarchal age with near relations. *Gen. 20: 12. Gen. 24: 24. Gen. 28: 2.*

Often contracted by parents for children. *Gen. 24: 49–51. Gen. 34: 6, 8.*

Should be with consent of parents. *Gen. 28: 8. Judges 14: 2, 3.*

Consent of the parties necessary to. *Gen. 24: 57, 58.* 1 *Sam. 18: 20.* 1 *Sam. 25: 41.*

Parents might refuse to give their children in. *Exod. 22: 17. Deut. 7: 3.*

The Jews

Forbidden to contract with their near relations. *Lev. 18: 6.*

Forbidden to contract with idolaters. *Deut. 7: 3, 4. Joshua 23: 12. Ezra 9: 11, 12.*

Often contracted with foreigners. 1 *Kings 11: 1. Neh. 13: 23.*

Sometimes guilty of polygamy. 1 *Kings 11: 1, 3.*

Careful in contracting for their children. *Gen. 24: 2, 3. Gen. 28: 1, 2.*

Betrothed themselves some time before. *Deut. 20: 7. Judges 14: 5, 7,* with 8 v. *Matt. 1: 18.*

Contracted when young. *Prov. 2: 17. Joel 1: 8.*

Often contracted in their own tribe. *Exod. 2: 1. Num. 36: 6–13. Luke 1: 5, 27.*

Obliged to contract with wife of brother who died without seed. *Deut. 25: 5. Matt. 22: 24.*

Considered being debarred from, a reproach. *Isa. 4: 1.*

Considered being debarred from, a cause of grief. *Judges 11: 38.*

Often punished by being debarred from. *Jer. 7: 34. Jer. 16: 9. Jer. 25: 10.*

Were allowed divorce from, because of hardness of their hearts. *Deut. 24: 1,* with *Matt. 19: 7, 8.*

Exempted from going to war immediately after. *Deut.* 20: 7.

Priest not to contract, with divorced or improper persons. *Lev.* 21: 7.

The high priest not to contract, with a widow or a divorced or profane person. *Lev.* 21: 14.

Contracted at the gate and before witnesses. *Ruth* 4: 1, 10, 11.

Modes of demanding women in. *Gen.* 24: 3, 4. *Gen.* 34: 6, 8. 1 *Sam.* 25: 39, 40.

Elder daughters usually given in, before the younger. *Gen.* 29: 26.

A dowry given to the woman's parents before. *Gen.* 29: 18. *Gen.* 34: 12. 1 *Sam.* 18: 27, 28. *Hos.* 3: 2.

Celebrated

With great rejoicing. *Jer.* 33: 11. *John* 3: 29.

With feasting. *Gen.* 29: 22. *Judges* 14: 10. *Matt.* 22: 2, 3. *John* 2: 1–10.

For seven days. *Judges* 14: 12.

A benediction pronounced after. *Gen.* 24: 60. *Ruth* 4: 11, 12.

The bride

Received presents before. *Gen.* 24: 53.

Given a handmaid at. *Gen.* 24: 59. *Gen.* 29: 24, 29.

Adorned with jewels for. *Isa.* 49: 18. *Isa.* 61: 10.

Gorgeously apparelled. *Ps.* 45: 13, 14.

Attended by bridesmaids. *Ps.* 45: 9.

Stood on the right of bridegroom. *Ps.* 45: 9.

Called to forget her father's house. *Ps.* 45: 10.

The bridegroom

Adorned with ornaments. *Isa.* 61: 10.

Attended by many friends. *Judges* 14: 11. *John* 3: 29.

Presented with gifts. *Ps.* 45: 12.

Crowned with garlands. *Song of Sol.* 3: 11.

Rejoiced over the bride. *Isa.* 62: 5.

Returned with the bride to his house at night. *Matt.* 25: 1–6.

Garments provided for guests at. *Matt.* 22: 12.

Infidelity of those contracted in, punished as if married. *Deut.* 22: 23, 24. *Matt.* 1: 19.

Illustrative of

God's union with the Jewish nation. *Isa.* 54: 5. *Jer.* 3: 14. *Hos.* 2: 19, 20.

Christ's union with his Church. *Eph.* 5: 23, 24, 32.

MARTYRDOM

Is death endured for the word of God, and testimony of Christ. *Rev.* 6: 9. *Rev.* 20: 4.

Saints

Forewarned of. *Matt.* 10: 21. *Matt.* 24: 9. *John* 16: 2.

Should not fear. *Matt.* 10: 28. *Rev.* 2: 10.

Should be prepared for. *Matt.* 16: 24, 25. *Acts* 21: 13.

Should resist sin unto. *Heb.* 12: 4.

Reward of. *Rev.* 2: 10. *Rev.* 6: 11.

Inflicted at the instigation of the devil. *Rev.* 2: 10, 13.

The Apostacy guilty of inflicting. *Rev.* 17: 6. *Rev.* 18: 24.

Of saints, shall be avenged. *Luke* 11: 50, 51. *Rev.* 18: 20–24.

Exemplified. ABEL, *Gen.* 4: 8, with 1 *John* 3: 12. PROPHETS AND SAINTS OF OLD, 1 *Kings* 18: 4. 1 *Kings* 19: 10. *Luke* 11: 50, 51. *Heb.* 11: 37. URIJAH, *Jer.* 26: 23. JOHN THE BAPTIST, *Mark* 6: 27. PETER, *John* 21: 18, 19. STEPHEN, *Acts* 7: 58. PRIMITIVE CHRISTIANS, *Acts* 9: 1, with *Acts* 22: 4. *Acts* 26: 10. JAMES, *Acts* 12: 2. ANTIPAS, *Rev.* 2: 13.

MASTERS

Authority of, established. *Col.* 3: 22. 1 *Pet.* 2: 18.

Christ set an example to. *John* 13: 14.

Should with their households,

Worship God. *Gen.* 35: 3.

Fear God. *Acts* 10: 2.

Serve God. *Joshua* 24: 15.

Observe the Sabbath. *Exod.* 20: 10. *Deut.* 5: 12–14.

Put away idols. *Gen.* 35: 2.

Should select faithful servants. *Gen.* 24: 2. *Ps.* 101: 6, 7.

Should receive faithful advice from servants. 2 *Kings* 5: 13, 14.

Duty of, towards servants;

To act justly. *Job* 31: 13, 15. *Col.* 4: 1.

To deal with them in the fear of God. *Eph.* 6: 9. *Col.* 4: 1.

To esteem them highly, if saints. *Philem.* 16.

To take care of them in sickness. *Luke* 7: 3.

To forbear threatening them. *Eph.* 6: 9.

Not to defraud them. *Gen.* 31: 7.

Not to keep back their wages. *Lev.* 19: 13. *Deut.* 24: 15.

Not to rule over them with rigour. *Lev.* 25: 43. *Deut.* 24: 14.

Benevolent, blessed. *Deut.* 15: 18.

Unjust, denounced. *Jer.* 22: 13. *Jas.* 5: 4:

Good—Exemplified. ABRAHAM, *Gen.* 18-: 19. JACOB, *Gen.* 35: 2. JOSHUA, *Joshua* 24, 15. DAVID, 2 *Sam.* 6: 20. CENTURION. *Luke* 7: 2, 3. CORNELIUS, *Acts* 10: 2.

Bad—Exemplified. EGYPTIANS, *Exod.* 1: 13, 14. NABAL, 1 *Sam.* 25: 17. AMALEKITE, 1 *Sam.* 30: 13.

MEEKNESS

Christ set an example of. *Ps.* 45: 4. *Matt.* 11: 29. *Matt.* 21: 5. 2 *Cor.* 10: 1.

A fruit of the Spirit. *Gal.* 5: 22, 23.

Saints should

Seek. *Zeph.* 2: 3.

Put on. *Col.* 3: 12, 13.

Receive the word of God with. *Jas.* 1: 21.

Exhibit, in conduct, etc. *Jas.* 3: 13.

Answer for their hope with. 1 *Pet.* 3: 15.

Shew, to all men. *Titus* 3: 2.

Restore the erring with. *Gal.* 6: 1.

Precious in the sight of God. 1 *Pet.* 3: 4.

Ministers should

Follow after. 1 *Tim.* 6: 11.

Instruct opposers with. *2 Tim.* 2: 24, 25.

Urge, on their people. *Titus* 3: 1, 2.

A characteristic of wisdom. *Jas.* 3: 17.

Necessary to a Christian walk. *Eph.* 4: 1, 2.

They who are gifted with,

Are preserved. *Ps.* 76: 9.

Are exalted. *Ps.* 147: 6.

Are guided and taught. *Ps.* 25: 9.

Are richly provided for. *Ps.* 22: 26.

Are beautified with salvation. *Ps.* 149: 4.

Increase their joy. *Isa.* 29: 19.

Shall inherit the earth. *Ps.* 37: 11.

The gospel to be preached to those who possess. *Isa.* 61: 1.

Blessedness of. *Matt.* 5: 5.

Exemplified. MOSES, *Num.* 12: 3. DAVID, 2 *Sam.* 16: 9–12. PAUL, 1 *Thess.* 2: 7.

MERCY

After the example of God. *Luke* 6: 36.

Enjoined. *Hos.* 12: 6. *Col.* 3: 12.

To be engraved on the heart. *Prov.* 3: 3.

Characteristic of saints. *Ps.* 37: 26. *Isa.* 57: 1.

Should be shewn

With cheerfulness. *Rom.* 12: 8.

To our brethren. *Zech.* 7: 9.

To the poor. *Prov.* 14: 31. *Dan.* 4: 27.

To animals. *Prov.* 12: 10.

Upholds the throne of kings. *Prov.* 20: 28.

Beneficial to those who exercise. *Prov.* 11: 17.

Blessedness of shewing. *Prov.* 14: 21. *Matt.* 5: 7.

Hypocrites devoid of. *Matt.* 23: 23.

Denunciations against those devoid of. *Hos.* 4: 1, 3. *Jas.* 2: 13.

MERCY OF GOD, THE

Is part of his character. *Exod.* 34: 6, 7. *Ps.* 62: 12. *Jonah* 4: 2. 2 *Cor.* 1: 3.

Described as

Great. *Num.* 14: 18. *Isa.* 54: 7.

Rich. *Eph.* 2: 4.

Manifold. *Neh.* 9: 27. *Lam.* 3: 32.

Plenteous. *Ps.* 86: 5, 15. *Ps.* 103: 8.

Abundant. 1 *Pet.* 1: 3.

Sure. *Isa.* 53: 3. *Mic.* 7: 20.

Everlasting. 1 *Chron.* 16: 34. *Ps.* 89: 28.

Tender. *Ps.* 25: 6. *Luke* 1: 78.

New every morning. *Lam.* 3: 23.

High as heaven. *Ps.* 36: 5. *Ps.* 103: 11.

Filling the earth. *Ps.* 119: 64.

Over all his works. *Ps.* 145: 9.

Is his delight. *Mic.* 7: 18.

Manifested

In the sending of Christ. *Luke* 1: 78.

In salvation. *Titus* 3: 5.

In long-suffering. *Lam.* 3: 22. *Dan.* 9: 9.

To his people. *Deut.* 32: 43. 1 *Kings* 8: 23.

To them that fear him. *Ps.* 103: 17. *Luke* 1: 50.

To returning backsliders. *Jer.* 3: 12. *Joel* 2: 13.

To repentant sinners. *Prov.* 28: 13. *Isa.* 55: 7.

To the afflicted. *Isa.* 49: 13. *Isa.* 54: 7.

To the fatherless. *Hos.* 14: 3.

To whom he will. *Hos.* 2: 23, with *Rom.* 9: 15, 18.

With everlasting kindness. *Isa.* 54: 8.

A ground of hope. *Ps.* 130: 7. *Ps.* 147: 11.

A ground of trust. *Ps.* 52: 8.

Should be

Sought for ourselves. *Ps.* 6: 2.

Sought for others. *Gal.* 6: 16. 1 *Tim.* 1: 2. 2 *Tim.* 1: 18.

Pleaded in prayer. *Ps.* 6: 4. *Ps.* 25: 6. *Ps.* 51: 1.

Rejoiced in. *Ps.* 31: 7.

Magnified. 1 *Chron.* 16: 34. *Ps.* 115: 1. *Ps.* 118: 1–4, 29. *Jer.* 33: 11.

Typified. MERCY-SEAT, *Exod.* 25: 17.

Exemplified. LOT, *Gen.* 19: 16, 19. EPAPHRODITUS, *Phil.* 2: 27. PAUL, 1 *Tim.* 1: 13.

MINISTERS

Called by God. *Exod.* 28: 1, with *Heb.* 5: 4.

Qualified by God. 2 *Cor.* 3: 5, 6.

Commissioned by Christ. *Matt.* 28: 19.

Sent by the Holy Ghost. *Acts* 13: 2, 4.

Have authority from God. 2 *Cor.* 10: 8. 2 *Cor.* 13: 10.

Authority of, is for edification. 2 *Cor.* 10: 8. 2 *Cor.* 13: 10.

Separated unto the gospel. *Rom.* 1: 1.

Entrusted with the gospel. 1 *Thess.* 2: 4.

Described as

Ambassadors for Christ. 2 *Cor.* 5: 20.

Ministers of Christ. 1 *Cor.* 4: 1.

Stewards of the mysteries of God. 1 *Cor.* 4: 1.

Defenders of the faith. *Phil.* 1: 7.

Specially protected by God. 2 *Cor.* 1: 10.

Necessity for. *Rom.* 10: 14.

Excellency of. *Rom.* 10: 15.

Labours of, vain, without God's blessing. 1 *Cor.* 3: 7. 1 *Cor.* 15: 10.

Compared to earthen vessels. 2 *Cor.* 4: 7.

Should be

Pure. *Isa.* 52: 11. 1 *Tim.* 3: 9.

Holy. *Lev.* 21: 6. *Titus* 1: 8.

Humble. *Acts* 20: 19.

Patient. 2 *Cor.* 6: 4. 2 *Tim.* 2: 24.

Blameless. 1 *Tim.* 3: 2. *Titus* 1: 7.

Willing. *Isa.* 6: 8. 1 *Pet.* 5: 2.

Disinterested. 2 *Cor.* 12: 14. 1 *Thess.* 2: 6.

Impartial. 1 *Tim.* 5: 21.

Gentle. 1 *Thess.* 2: 7. 2 *Tim.* 2: 24.

Devoted. *Acts* 20: 24. *Phil.* 1: 20, 21.

Strong in grace. 2 *Tim.* 2: 1.

Self-denying. 1 *Cor.* 9: 27.

Sober, just, and temperate. *Titus* 1: 8.

Hospitable. 1 *Tim.* 3: 2. *Titus* 1: 8.

Apt to teach. 1 *Tim.* 3: 2. 2 *Tim.* 2: 24.

Studious and meditative. 1 *Tim.* 4: 13, 15.

Watchful. 2 *Tim.* 4: 5.

Prayerful. *Eph.* 3: 14. *Phil.* 1: 4.

Strict in ruling their own families. 1 *Tim.* 3: 4, 12.

Affectionate to their people. *Phil.* 1: 7. 1 *Thess.* 2: 8, 11.

Ensamples to the flock. *Phil.* 3: 17. 2 *Thess.* 3: 9. 1 *Tim.* 4: 12. 1 *Pet.* 5: 3.

Should not be

Lords over God's heritage. 1 *Pet.* 5: 3.

Greedy of filthy lucre. *Acts* 20: 23. 1 *Tim.* 3: 3, 8. 1 *Pet.* 5: 2.

Contentious. 1 *Tim.* 3: 3. *Titus* 1: 7.

Crafty. 2 *Cor.* 4: 2.

Men-pleasers. *Gal.* 1: 10. 1 *Thess.* 2: 4.

Easily dispirited. 2 *Cor.* 4: 8, 9. 2 *Cor.* 6: 10.

Entangled by cares. *Luke* 9: 60. 2 *Tim.* 2: 4.

Given to wine. 1 *Tim.* 3: 3. *Titus* 1: 7.

Should seek the salvation of their flock. 1 *Cor.* 10: 33.

Should avoid giving unnecessary offence. 1 *Cor.* 10: 32, 33. 2 *Cor.* 6: 3.

Should make full proof of their ministry. 2 *Tim.* 4: 5.

Are bound, to

Preach the gospel to all. *Mark* 16: 15. 1 *Cor.* 1: 17.

Feed the Church. *Jer.* 3: 15. *John* 21: 15–17. *Acts* 20: 28. 1 *Pet.* 5: 2.

Build up the Church. 2 *Cor.* 12: 19. *Eph.* 4: 12.

Watch for souls. *Heb.* 13: 17.

Pray for their people. *Joel* 2: 17. *Col.* 1: 9.

Strengthen the faith of their people. *Luke* 22: 32. *Acts* 14: 22.

Teach. 2 *Tim.* 2: 2.

Exhort. *Titus* 1: 9. *Titus* 2: 15.

Warn affectionately. *Acts* 20: 31.

Rebuke. *Titus* 1: 13. *Titus* 2: 15.

Comfort. 2 *Cor.* 1: 4–6.

Convince gainsayers. *Titus* 1: 9.

War a good warfare. 1 *Tim.* 1: 18. 2 *Tim.* 4: 7.

Endure hardness. 2 *Tim.* 2: 3.

Should preach

Christ crucified. *Acts* 8: 5, 35. 1 *Cor.* 2: 2.

Repentance and faith. *Acts* 20: 21.

According to the oracles of God. 1 *Pet.* 4: 11.

Everywhere. *Mark* 16: 20. *Acts* 8: 4.

Not with enticing words of man's wisdom.. 1 *Cor.* 1: 17. 1 *Cor.* 2: 1, 4.

Not setting forth themselves. 2 *Cor.* 4: 5.

Without deceitfulness. 2 *Cor.* 2: 17. 2 *Cor.* 4: 2. 1 *Thess.* 2: 3, 5.

Fully, and without reserve. *Acts* 5: 20. *Acts* 20: 20, 27. *Rom.* 15: 19.

With boldness. *Isa.* 58: 1. *Ezek.* 2: 6. *Matt.* 10: 27, 28.

With plainness of speech. 2 *Cor.* 3: 12.

With zeal. 1 *Thess.* 2: 8.

With constancy. *Acts* 6: 4. 2 *Tim.* 4: 2.

With consistency. 2 *Cor.* 1: 18, 19.

With heedfulness. 1 *Tim.* 4: 16.

With good will and love. *Phil.* 1: 15–17.

Without charge, if possible. 1 *Cor.* 9: 18. 1 *Thess.* 2: 9.

Woe to those, who do not preach the gospel. 1 *Cor.* 9: 16.

When faithful,

Approve themselves as the ministers of God. 2 *Cor.* 6: 4.

Thank God for his gifts to their people. 1 *Cor.* 1: 4. *Phil.* 1: 3. 1 *Thess.* 3: 9.

Glory in their people. 2 *Cor.* 7: 4.

Rejoice in the faith and holiness of their people. 1 *Thess.* 2: 19, 20. 1 *Thess.* 3: 6–9.

Commend themselves to the consciences of men. 2 *Cor.* 4: 2.

Are rewarded. *Matt.* 24: 47. 1 *Pet.* 5: 4.

When unfaithful,

Described. *Isa.* 56: 10–12. *Titus* 1: 10, 11.

Deal treacherously with their people. *John* 10: 12.

Delude men. *Jer.* 6: 14.

Seek gain. *Mic.* 3: 11. 2 *Pet.* 2: 3.

Shall be punished. *Ezek.* 33: 6–8. *Matt.* 24: 48–51.

Their people are bound, to

Regard them as God's messengers. 1 *Cor.* 4: 1. *Gal.* 4: 14.

Attend to their instructions. *Mal.* 2: 7. *Matt.* 23: 3.

Follow their holy example. 1 *Cor.* 11: 1. *Phil.* 3: 17.

Imitate their faith. *Heb.* 13: 18.

Hold them in reputation. *Phil.* 2: 29. 1 *Thess.* 5: 13. 1 *Tim.* 5: 17.

Love them. 2 *Cor.* 8: 7. 1 *Thess.* 3: 6.

Pray for them. *Rom.* 15: 30. 2 *Cor.* 1: 11. *Eph.* 6: 19. *Heb.* 13: 18.

Obey them. 1 *Cor.* 16: 16. *Heb.* 13: 17.

Give them joy. 2 *Cor.* 1: 14. 2 *Cor.* 2: 3.

Help them. *Rom.* 16: 9. *Phil.* 4: 3.

Support them. 2 *Chron.* 31: 4. 1 *Cor.* 9: 7–11. *Gal.* 6: 6.

Pray for the increase of. *Matt.* 9: 38.

Faithful—Exemplified. THE ELEVEN APOSTLES, *Matt.* 28: 16–19. THE SEVENTY, *Luke* 10: 1, 17. MATTHIAS, *Acts* 1: 26. PHILIP, *Acts* 8: 5. BARNABAS, *Acts* 11: 23. SIMEON, etc., *Acts* 13: 1. PAUL, *Acts* 28: 31. TYCHICUS, *Eph.* 6: 21. TIMOTHY, *Phil.* 2: 22. EPAPHRODITUS, *Phil.* 2: 25. ARCHIPPUS, *Col.* 4: 17. TITUS, *Titus* 1: 5.

MIRACLES

Power of God necessary to. *John* 3: 2.

Described as

Marvellous things. *Ps.* 78: 12.

Marvellous works. *Isa.* 29: 14. *Ps.* 105: 5.

Signs and wonders. *Jer.* 32: 21. *John* 4: 48. 2 *Cor.* 12: 12.

Manifest

The glory of God. *John* 11: 4.

The glory of Christ. *John* 2: 11. *John* 11: 4.

The works of God. *John* 9: 3.

Were evidences of a divine commission. *Exod.* 4: 1–5. *Mark* 16: 20.

The Messiah was expected to perform. *Matt.* 11: 2, 3. *John* 7: 31.

Jesus was proved to be the Messiah by. *Matt.* 11: 4–6. *John* 5: 36. *Acts* 2: 22.

Jesus was followed on account of. *Matt.* 4: 23–25. *John* 6: 2, 26.

A gift of the Holy Ghost. 1 *Cor.* 12: 10.

Were performed

By the power of God. *Acts* 14: 3. *Acts* 15: 12. *Acts* 19: 11.

By the power of Christ. *Matt.* 10: 1.

By the power of the Holy Ghost. *Matt.* 12: 28. *Rom.* 15: 19.

In the name of Christ. *Mark* 16: 17. *Acts* 3: 16. *Acts* 4: 30.

First preaching of the gospel confirmed by. *Mark* 16: 20. *Heb.* 2: 4.

They who wrought, disclaimed all power of their own. *Acts* 3: 12.

Should produce faith. *John* 2: 23. *John* 20: 30, 31.

Should produce obedience. *Deut.* 11: 1–3. *Deut.* 29: 2, 3, 9.

Instrumental to the early propagation of the gospel. *Acts* 8: 6. *Rom.* 15: 18, 19.

Faith required in

Those who performed. *Matt.* 17: 20. *Matt.* 21: 21. *John* 14: 12. *Acts* 3: 16. *Acts* 6: 8.

Those for whom they were performed. *Matt.* 9: 28. *Mark* 9: 22–24. *Acts* 14: 9.

Should be remembered. 1 *Chron.* 16: 12. *Ps.* 105: 5.

Should be told to future generations. *Exod.* 10: 2. *Judges* 6: 13.

Insufficient, of themselves, to produce conversion. *Luke* 16: 31.

The wicked

Desire to see. *Luke* 11: 29. *Luke* 23: 8.

Often acknowledge. *John* 11: 47. *Acts* 4: 16.

Do not understand. *Ps.* 106: 7.

Do not consider. *Mark* 6: 52.

Forget. *Neh.* 9: 17. *Ps.* 78: 11.

Proof against. *Num.* 14: 22. *John* 12: 37.

Guilt of rejecting the evidence afforded by. *Matt.* 11: 20–24. *John* 15: 24.

MIRACLES OF CHRIST, THE

Water turned into wine. *John* 2: 6–10.

Nobleman's son healed. *John* 4: 46–53.

Centurion's servant healed. *Matt.* 8: 5–13.

Draughts of fishes. *Luke* 5: 4–6. *John* 21: 6.

Devils cast out. *Matt.* 8: 28–32. *Matt.* 9: 32, 33. *Matt.* 15: 22–28. *Matt.* 17: 14–18.

Peter's wife's mother healed. *Matt.* 8: 14, 15.

Lepers cleansed. *Matt.* 8: 3. *Luke* 17: 14.

Paralytic healed. *Mark* 2: 3–12.

Withered hand restored. *Matt.* 12: 10–13.

Impotent man healed. *John* 5: 5–9.

The dead raised to life. *Matt.* 9: 18, 19, 23–25. *Luke* 7: 12–15. *John* 11: 11–44.

Issue of blood stopped. *Matt.* 9: 20–22.

The blind restored to sight. *Matt.* 9: 27–30. *Mark* 8: 22–25. *John* 9: 1–7.

The deaf and dumb cured. *Mark* 7: 32–35.

The multitude fed. *Matt.* 14: 15–21. *Matt.* 15: 32–38.

His walking on the sea. *Matt.* 14: 25–27.

Peter walking on the sea. *Matt.* 14: 29.

Tempest stilled. *Matt.* 23: 26. *Matt.* 14: 32.

Sudden arrival of the ship. *John* 6: 21.

Tribute-money. *Matt.* 17: 27.

Woman healed of infirmity. *Luke* 13: 11–13.

Dropsy cured. *Luke* 14: 2–4.

Fig-tree blighted. *Matt.* 21: 19.

Malchus healed. *Luke* 22: 50, 51.

Performed before the messengers of John. *Luke* 7: 21, 22.

Many and divers diseases healed. *Matt.* 4: 23, 24. *Matt.* 14: 14. *Matt.* 15: 30. *Mark* 1: 34. *Luke* 6: 17–19.

His resurrection. *Luke* 24: 6, with *John* 10: 18.

His appearance to his disciples, the doors being shut. *John* 20: 19.

MIRACLES WROUGHT THROUGH SERVANTS OF GOD

Moses and Aaron:
    Rod turned into a serpent. *Exod.* 4: 3. *Exod.* 7: 10.

Rod restored. *Exod.* 4: 4.

Hand made leprous. *Exod.* 4: 6.

Hand healed. *Exod.* 4: 7.

Water turned into blood. *Exod.* 4: 9, 30.

River turned into blood. *Exod.* 7: 20.

Frogs brought. *Exod.* 8: 6.

Frogs removed. *Exod.* 8: 13.

Lice brought. *Exod.* 8: 17.

Flies brought. *Exod.* 8: 21–24.

Flies removed. *Exod.* 8: 31.

Murrain of beasts. *Exod.* 9: 3–6.

Boils and blains brought. *Exod.* 9: 10, 11.

Hail brought. *Exod.* 9: 23.

Hail removed. *Exod.* 9: 33.

Locusts brought. *Exod.* 10: 13.

Locusts removed. *Exod.* 10: 19.

Darkness brought. *Exod.* 10: 22.

The first-born destroyed. *Exod.* 12: 29.

The Red Sea divided. *Exod.* 14: 21, 22.

Egyptians overwhelmed. *Exod.* 14: 26–28.

Water sweetened. *Exod.* 15: 25.

Water from rock in Horeb. *Exod.* 17: 6.

Amalek vanquished. *Exod.* 17: 11–13.

Destruction of Korah. *Num.* 16: 28–32.

Water from rock in Kadesh. *Num.* 20: 11.

Healing by brazen serpent. *Num.* 21: 8, 9.

Joshua:
    Waters of Jordan divided. *Joshua* 3: 10–17.

Jordan restored to its course. *Joshua* 4: 18.

Jericho taken. *Joshua* 6: 6–20.

The sun and moon stayed. *Joshua* 10: 12–14.

Midianites destroyed. *Judges* 7: 16–22.

Samson:

A lion killed. *Judges* 14: 6.

Philistines killed. *Judges* 14: 19. *Judges* 15: 15.

The gates of Gaza carried away. *Judges* 16: 3.

Dagon's house pulled down. *Judges* 16: 30.

Samuel:

Thunder and rain in harvest. 1 *Sam.* 12: 18.

The prophet of Judah:

Jeroboam's hand withered. 1 *Kings* 13: 4.

The altar rent. 1 *Kings* 13: 5.

The withered hand restored. 1 *Kings* 13: 6.

Elijah:

Drought caused. 1 *Kings* 17: 1. *Jas.* 5: 17.

Meal and oil multiplied. 1 *Kings* 17: 14–16.

A child restored to life. 1 *Kings* 17: 22, 23.

Sacrifice consumed by fire. 1 *Kings* 18: 36, 38.

Men destroyed by fire. 2 *Kings* 1: 10–12.

Rain brought. 1 *Kings* 18: 41–45. *Jas.* 5: 18.

Waters of Jordan divided. 2 *Kings* 2: 8.

Elisha:

Waters of Jordan divided. 2 *Kings* 2: 14.

Waters healed. 2 *Kings* 2: 21, 22.

Children torn by bears. 2 *Kings* 2: 24.

Oil multiplied. 2 *Kings* 4: 1–7.

Child restored to life. 2 *Kings* 4: 32–35.

Naaman healed. 2 *Kings* 5: 10, 14.

Gehazi struck with leprosy. 2 *Kings* 5: 27.

Iron caused to swim. 2 *Kings* 6: 6.

Syrians smitten with blindness. 2 *Kings* 6: 18.

Syrians restored to sight. 2 *Kings* 6: 20.

A man restored to life. 2 *Kings* 13: 21.

Isaiah:

Hezekiah healed. 2 *Kings* 20: 7.

Shadow put back on the dial. 2 *Kings* 20: 11.

The seventy disciples:

Various miracles. *Luke* 10: 9, 17.

The apostles, etc.

Many miracles. *Acts* 2: 43. *Acts* 5: 12.

Peter:

Lame man cured. *Acts* 3: 7.

Death of Ananias. *Acts* 5: 5.

Death of Sapphira. *Acts* 5: 10.

The sick healed. *Acts* 5: 15, 16.

Eneas made whole. *Acts* 9: 34.

Dorcas restored to life. *Acts* 9: 40.

Stephen:

Great miracles. *Acts* 6: 8.

Philip:

Various miracles. *Acts* 8: 6, 7, 13.

Paul:

Elymas smitten with blindness. *Acts* 13: 11.

Lame man cured. *Acts* 14: 10.

An unclean spirit cast out. *Acts* 16: 18.

Special miracles. *Acts* 19: 11, 12.

Eutychus restored to life. *Acts* 20: 10–12.

Viper's bite made harmless. *Acts* 28: 5.

Father of Publius healed. *Acts* 28: 8.

Paul and Barnabas:

Various miracles. *Acts* 14: 3.

MIRACLES THROUGH EVIL AGENTS

Performed through the power of the devil. 2 *Thess.* 2: 9. *Rev.* 16: 14.

Wrought

In support of false religions. *Deut.* 13: 1, 2.

By false christs. *Matt.* 24: 24.

By false prophets. *Matt.* 24: 24. *Rev.* 19: 20.

A mark of the Apostacy. 2 *Thess.* 2: 3, 9. *Rev.* 13: 13.

Not to be regarded. *Deut.* 13: 3.

Deceive the ungodly. 2 *Thess.* 2: 10–12. *Rev.* 13: 14. *Rev.* 19: 20.

Exemplified. MAGICIANS OF EGYPT, *Exod.* 7: 11, 22. *Exod.* 8: 7. WITCH OF ENDOR, 1 *Sam.* 28: 7–14. SIMON MAGUS, *Acts* 8: 9–11.

MIRACULOUS GIFTS OF THE HOLY SPIRIT

Foretold. *Isa.* 35: 4–6. *Joel* 2: 28, 29.

Of different kinds. 1 *Cor.* 12: 4–6.

Enumerated. 1 *Cor.* 12: 8–10, 28.

Christ was endued with. *Matt.* 12: 28.

Poured out on the day of Pentecost. *Acts* 2: 1–4.

Communicated

Upon the preaching of the gospel. *Acts* 10: 44–46.

By the laying on of the Apostles' hands. *Acts* 8: 17, 18. *Acts* 19: 6.

For the confirmation of the gospel. *Mark* 16: 20. *Acts* 14: 3. *Rom.* 15: 19. *Heb.* 2: 4.

For the edification of the Church. 1 *Cor.* 12: 7. 1 *Cor.* 14: 12, 13.

Dispensed, according to his sovereign will. 1 *Cor.* 12: 11.

Were to be sought after. 1 *Cor.* 12: 31. 1 *Cor.* 14: 1.

Temporary nature of. 1 *Cor.* 13: 8.

Were not to be

Neglected. 1 *Tim.* 4: 14. 2 *Tim.* 1: 6.

Despised. 1 *Thess.* 5: 20.

Purchased. *Acts* 8: 20.

Might be possessed without saving grace. *Matt.* 7: 22, 23. 1 *Cor.* 13: 1, 2. *Heb.* 6: 5–6.

Counterfeited by Antichrist. *Matt.* 24: 24. 2 *Thess.* 2: 9. *Rev.* 13: 13, 14.

MISSIONARY-WORK BY MINISTERS

Commanded. *Matt.* 28: 19. *Mark* 16: 15.

Warranted by predictions concerning the Heathen, etc. *Isa.* 42: 10–12. *Isa.* 66: 19.

Is according to the purpose of God. *Luke* 24: 46, 47. *Gal.* 1: 15, 16. *Col.* 1: 25–27.

Directed by the Holy Ghost. *Acts* 13: 2.

Required. *Luke* 10: 2. *Rom.* 10: 14, 15.

The Holy Ghost calls to. *Acts* 13: 2.

Christ engaged in. *Matt.* 4: 17, 23. *Matt.* 11: 1. *Mark* 1: 38, 39. *Luke* 8: 1.

Christ sent his disciples to labour in. *Mark* 3: 14. *Mark* 6: 7.

Obligations to engage in. *Acts* 4: 19, 20. *Rom.* 1: 13–15. 1 *Cor.* 9: 16.

Excellency of. *Isa.* 52: 7, with *Rom.* 10: 15.

Worldly concerns should not delay. *Luke* 9: 59–62.

God qualifies for. *Exod.* 3: 11, 18. *Exod.* 4: 11, 12, 15.

God strengthens for. *Jer.* 1: 7–9.

Guilt and danger of shrinking from. *Jonah* 1: 3, 4.

Requires wisdom and meekness. *Matt.* 10: 16.

Be ready to engage in. *Isa.* 6: 8.

Aid those engaged in. 2 *Cor.* 11: 9. 3 *John* 5–8.

Harmony should subsist amongst those engaged in. *Gal.* 2: 9. 1 *Cor.* 15: 11.

Success of,

To be prayed for. *Eph.* 6: 18, 19. *Col.* 4: 3.

A cause of joy. *Acts* 15: 3.

A cause of praise. *Acts* 11: 18. *Acts* 21: 19, 20.

No limits to the sphere of. *Mark* 16: 15. *Rev.* 14: 6.

Opportunities for, not to be neglected. 1 *Cor.* 16: 9.

Exemplified. LEVITES, 2 *Chron.* 17: 8, 9. JONAH, *Jonah* 3: 2. THE SEVENTY, *Luke* 10: 1, 17. APOSTLES, *Mark* 6: 12. *Acts* 13: 2–5. PHILIP, *Acts* 8: 5. PAUL, etc., *Acts* 13: 2–4. SILAS, *Acts* 15: 40, 41. TIMOTHEUS, *Acts* 16: 3. NOAH, 2 *Pet.* 2: 5.

MISSIONARIES, ALL CHRISTIANS SHOULD BE AS

After the example of Christ. *Acts* 10: 38.

Women and children, as well as men. *Ps.* 8: 2. *Prov.* 31: 26. *Matt.* 21: 15, 16. *Phil.* 4: 3. 1 *Tim.* 5: 10. *Titus* 2: 3–5. 1 *Pet.* 3: 1.

The zeal of idolaters should provoke to. *Jer.* 7: 18.

The zeal of hypocrites should provoke to. *Matt.* 23: 15.

An imperative duty. *Judges* 5: 23. *Luke* 19: 40.

The principle on which. 2 *Cor.* 5: 14, 15.

However weak they may be. 1 *Cor.* 1: 27.

From their calling as saints. *Exod.* 19: 6. 1 *Pet.* 2: 9.

As faithful stewards. 1 *Pet.* 4: 10, 11.

In youth. *Ps.* 71: 17. *Ps.* 148: 12, 13.

In old age. *Deut.* 32: 7. *Ps.* 71: 18.

In the family. *Deut.* 6: 7. *Ps.* 78: 5–8. *Isa.* 38: 19. 1 *Cor.* 7: 16.

In their intercourse with the world. *Matt.* 5: 16. *Phil.* 2: 15, 16. 1 *Pet.* 2: 12.

In first giving their own selves to the Lord. 2 Cor. 8: 5.

In declaring what God has done for them. Ps. 66: 16. Ps. 116: 16–19.

In hating life for Christ. `Luke 14: 26.

In openly confessing Christ. Matt. 10: 32.

In following Christ. Luke 14: 27. Luke 18: 22.

In preferring Christ above all relations. Luke 14: 26.

In joyfully suffering for Christ. Heb. 10: 34.

In forsaking all for Christ. Luke 5: 11.

In a holy example. Matt. 5: 16. Phil. 2: 15. 1 Thess. 1: 7.

In holy conduct. 1 Pet. 2: 12.

In holy boldness. Ps. 119: 46.

In dedicating themselves to the service of God. Joshua 24: 15. Ps. 27: 4.

In devoting all property to God. 1 Chron. 29: 2, 3, 14, 16. Eccles. 11: 1. Matt. 6: 19, 20. Mark 12: 44. Luke 12: 33. Luke 18: 22, 28. Acts 2: 45. Acts 4: 32–34.

In holy conversation. Ps. 37: 30, with Prov. 10: 31. Prov. 15: 7. Eph. 4: 29. Col. 4: 6.

In talking of God and his works. Ps. 71: 24. Ps. 77: 12. Ps. 119: 27. Ps. 145: 11, 12.

In showing forth God's praises. Isa. 43: 21.

In inviting others to embrace the gospel. Ps. 34: 8. Isa. 2: 3. John 1: 46. John 4: 29.

In seeking the edification of others. Rom. 14: 19. Rom. 15: 2. 1 Thess. 5: 11.

In admonishing others. 1 Thess. 5: 14. 2 Thess. 3: 15.

In reproving others. Lev. 19: 17. Eph. 5: 11.

In teaching and exhorting. Ps. 34: 11. Ps. 51: 13. Col. 3: 16. Heb. 3: 13. Heb. 10: 25.

In interceding for others. Col. 4: 3. Heb. 13: 18. Jas. 5: 16.

In aiding ministers in their labours. Rom. 16: 3, 9. 2 Cor. 11: 9. Phil. 4: 14–16. 3 John 6.

In giving a reason for their faith. Exod. 12: 26, 27. Deut. 6: 20, 21. 1 Pet. 3: 15.

In encouraging the weak. Isa. 35: 3, 4. Rom. 14: 1. Rom. 15: 1. 1 Thess. 5: 14.

In visiting and relieving the poor, the sick, etc. Lev. 25: 35. Ps. 112: 9, with 2 Cor. 9: 9. Matt. 25: 36. Acts 20: 35. Jas. 1: 27.

With a willing heart. Exod. 35: 29. 1 Chron. 29: 9, 14.

With a superabundant liberality. Exod. 36: 5–7. 2 Cor. 8: 3.

Encouragement to. Prov. 11: 25, 30. 1 Cor. 1: 27. Jas. 5: 19, 20.

Blessedness of. Dan. 12: 3.

Illustrated. Matt. 25: 14. Luke 19: 13, etc., etc.

Exemplified. HANNAH, 1 Sam. 2: 1–10. CAPTIVE MAID, 2 Kings 5: 3. CHIEF OF THE FATHERS, etc., Ezra 1: 5. SHADRACH, etc., Dan. 3: 16–18. RESTORED DEMONIAC, Mark 5: 20. SHEPHERDS, Luke 2: 17. ANNA, Luke 2: 38. JOANNA, etc., Luke 8: 3. LEPER, Luke 17: 15. DISCIPLES, Luke 19: 37, 38. CENTURION, Luke 23: 47. ANDREW, John 1: 41, 42. PHILIP, John 1: 46. WOMAN OF SAMARIA, John 4: 29. BARNABAS, Acts 4: 36, 37. PERSECUTED SAINTS, Acts 8: 4. Acts 11: 19, 20. APOLLOS, Acts 18: 25. AQUILA, etc., Acts 18: 26. VARIOUS INDIVIDUALS, Rom. Chap. 16th. ONESIPHORUS, 2

Tim. 1: 16. PHILEMON, *Philem.* 1–6.

MURDER

Forbidden. *Exod.* 20: 13, with *Rom.* 13: 9.

Explained by Christ. *Matt.* 5: 21, 22.

Hatred is. 1 *John* 3: 15.

Is a work of the flesh. *Gal.* 5: 21.

Comes from the heart. *Matt.* 15: 19.

Defiles the

Hands. *Isa.* 59: 3.

Person and garments. *Lam.* 4: 13, 14.

Land. *Num.* 35: 33. *Ps.* 106: 38.

Not concealed from God. *Isa.* 26: 21. *Jer.* 2: 34.

Cries for vengeance. *Gen.* 4: 10.

God

Abominates. *Prov.* 6: 16, 17.

Makes inquisition for. *Ps.* 9: 12.

Will avenge. *Deut.* 32: 43. *Hos.* 1: 4.

Requires blood for. *Gen.* 9: 5. *Num.* 35: 33. 1 *Kings* 2: 32.

Rejects the prayers of those guilty of. *Isa.* 1: 15. *Isa.* 59: 2, 3.

Curses those guilty of. *Gen.* 4: 11.

The law made to restrain. 1 *Tim.* 1: 9.

Saints

Specially warned against. 1 *Pet.* 4: 15.

Deprecate the guilt of. *Ps.* 51: 14.

Should warn others against. *Gen.* 37: 22. *Jer.* 26: 15.

Connected with idolatry. *Ezek.* 22: 3, 4.

The wicked

Filled with. *Rom.* 1: 29.

Devise. *Gen.* 27: 41. *Gen.* 37: 18.

Intent on. *Jer.* 22: 17.

Lie in wait to commit. *Ps.* 10: 8–10.

Swift to commit. *Prov.* 1: 16. *Rom.* 3: 15.

Perpetrate. *Job* 24: 14. *Ezek.* 22: 3.

Have hands full of. *Isa.* 1: 15.

Encourage others to commit. *Prov.* 1: 11.

Characteristic of the devil. *John* 8: 44.

Punishment of. *Gen.* 4: 12–15. *Gen.* 9: 6. *Num.* 35: 30. *Jer.* 19: 4–9.

Punishment of, not commuted under the Law. *Num.* 35: 31.

Of saints, specially avenged. *Deut.* 32: 43. *Matt.* 23: 35. *Rev.* 18: 20, 24.

Excludes from heaven. *Gal.* 5: 21. *Rev.* 22: 15.

Exemplified. CAIN, *Gen.* 4: 8. ESAU, *Gen.* 27: 41. JOSEPH'S BRETHREN, *Gen.* 37: 20. PHARAOH, *Exod.* 1: 22. ABIMELECH, *Judges* 9: 5. MEN OF SHECHEM, *Judges* 9: 24. AMALEKITE, 2 *Sam.* 1: 16. RECHAB, etc., 2 *Sam.* 4: 5–7. DAVID, 2 *Sam.* 12: 9. ABSALOM, 2 *Sam.* 13: 29. JOAB, 1 *Kings* 2: 31, 32. BAASHA, 1 *Kings* 15: 27. ZIMRI, 1 *Kings* 16: 10. JEZEBEL, 1 *Kings* 21: 10. ELDERS OF JEZREEL, 1 *Kings* 21: 13. AHAB, 1 *Kings* 21: 19. HAZAEL, 2 *Kings* 8: 12, 15. ADRAMMELECH, etc., 2 *Kings* 19: 37. MANASSEH, 2 *Kings* 21: 16. ISHMAEL, *Jer.* 41: 7. PRINCES

OF ISRAEL, *Ezek.* 11: 6. PEOPLE OF GILEAD, *Hos.* 6: 8. THE HERODS, *Matt.* 2: 16. *Matt.* 14: 10. *Acts* 12: 2. HERODIAS AND HER DAUGHTER, *Matt.* 14: 8—11. CHIEF PRIESTS, *Matt.* 27: 1. JUDAS, *Matt.* 27: 4. BARABBAS, *Mark* 15: 7. JEWS, *Acts* 7: 52. 1 *Thess.* 2: 15.

MURMURING

Forbidden. 1 *Cor.* 10: 10. *Phil.* 2: 14.

Against

God. *Prov.* 19: 3.

The sovereignty of God. *Rom.* 9: 19, 20.

The service of God. *Mal.* 3: 14.

Christ. *John* 6: 41—43, 52.

Ministers of God. *Exod.* 17: 3. *Num.* 16: 41.

Disciples of Christ. *Mark* 7: 2. *Luke* 5: 30.

Unreasonableness of. *Lam.* 3: 39.

Tempts God. *Exod.* 17: 2.

Provokes God. *Num.* 14: 2, 11. *Deut.* 9: 8, 22.

Saints cease from. *Isa.* 29: 23, 24.

Characteristic of the wicked. *Jude* 16.

Guilt of encouraging others in. *Num.* 13: 31–33, with *Num.* 14: 36, 37.

Punishment of. *Num.* 11: 1. *Num.* 14: 27–29. *Num.* 16: 45, 46. *Ps.* 106: 25, 26.

Illustrated. *Matt.* 20: 11. *Luke* 15: 29, 30.

Exemplified. CAIN, *Gen.* 4: 13, 14. MOSES, *Exod.* 5: 22, 23. ISRAELITES, *Exod.* 14: 11. *Num.* 21: 5. AARON, etc., *Num.* 12: 1, 2, 8. KORAH, etc., *Num.* 16: 3. ELIJAH, 1 *Kings* 19: 4. JOB, *Job* 3: 1, etc. JEREMIAH, *Jer.* 20: 14—18. JONAH, *Jonah* 4: 8, 9. DISCIPLES, *Mark* 14: 4, 5. *John* 6: 61. PHARISEES, *Luke* 15: 2. *Luke* 19: 7. JEWS, *John* 6: 41—43. GRECIANS, *Acts* 6: 1.

MUSIC

Early invention of. *Gen.* 4: 21.

Divided into

Vocal. 2 *Sam.* 19: 35. *Acts* 16: 25.

Instrumental. *Dan.* 6: 18.

Designed to promote joy. *Eccles.* 2: 8, 10.

Vanity to all unsanctified. *Eccles.* 2: 8, 11.

Considered efficacious in mental disorders. 1 *Sam.* 16: 14–17, 23.

Effects produced on the prophets of old by. 1 *Sam.* 10: 5, 6. 2 *Kings* 3: 15.

Instruments of,

Cymbals. 1 *Chron.* 16: 5. *Ps.* 150: 5.

Cornet. *Ps.* 98: 6. *Hos.* 5: 8.

Dulcimer. *Dan.* 3: 5.

Flute. *Dan.* 3: 5.

Harp. *Ps.* 137: 2. *Ezek.* 26: 13.

Organ. *Gen.* 4: 21. *Job* 21: 12. *Ps.* 150: 4.

Pipe. 1 *Kings* 1: 40. *Isa.* 5: 12. *Jer.* 48: 36.

Psaltery. *Ps.* 33: 2. *Ps.* 71: 22.

Sackbut. *Dan.* 3: 5.

Tabret. 1 *Sam.* 10: 5. *Isa.* 24: 8.

Timbrel. *Exod.* 15: 20. *Ps.* 68: 25.

Trumpet. 2 *Kings* 11: 14. 2 *Chron.* 29: 27.

Viol. *Isa.* 14: 11. *Amos* 5: 23.

Made of fir wood. 2 *Sam.* 6: 5.

Made of almug wood. 1 *Kings* 10: 12.

Made of brass. 1 *Cor.* 13: 1.

Made of silver. *Num.* 10: 2.

Made of horns of animals. *Joshua* 6: 8.

Many, with strings. *Ps.* 33: 2. *Ps.* 150: 4.

Early invention of. *Gen.* 4: 21.

Invented by David. 1 *Chron.* 23: 5. 2 *Chron.* 7: 6.

The Jews celebrated for inventing. *Amos* 6: 5.

Often expensively ornamented. *Ezek.* 28: 13.

Great diversity of. *Eccles.* 2: 8.

Appointed to be used in the temple. 1 *Chron.* 16: 4–6. 1 *Chron.* 23: 5, 6. 1 *Chron.* 25: 1. 2 *Chron.* 29: 25.

Custom of sending away friends with. *Gen.* 31: 27.

The Jews used,

In sacred processions. 2 *Sam.* 6: 4, 5, 15. 1 *Chron.* 13: 6–8. 1 *Chron.* 15: 27, 28.

At laying foundation of temple. *Ezra* 3: 9, 10.

At consecration of temple. 2 *Chron.* 5: 11–13.

At coronation of kings. 2 *Chron.* 23: 11, 13.

At dedication of city walls. *Neh.* 12: 27, 28.

To celebrate victories. *Exod.* 15: 20. 1 *Sam.* 18: 6, 7.

In religious feasts. 2 *Chron.* 30: 21.

In private entertainments. *Isa.* 5: 12. *Amos* 6: 5.

In dances. *Matt.* 11: 17. *Luke* 15: 25.

In funeral ceremonies. *Matt.* 9: 23.

In commemorating great men. 2 *Chron.* 35: 25.

Used in idol worship. *Dan.* 3: 5.

The movements of armies regulated by. *Joshua* 6: 8. 1 *Cor.* 14: 8.

Generally put aside in times of affliction. *Ps.* 137: 2–4. *Dan.* 6: 18.

Illustrative

Of joy and gladness. *Zeph.* 3: 17. *Eph.* 5: 19.

Of heavenly felicity. *Rev.* 5: 8, 9.

Ceasing of calamities. *Isa.* 24: 8, 9. *Rev.* 18: 22.

NEW BIRTH, THE

The corruption of human nature requires. *John* 3: 6. *Rom.* 8: 7, 8.

None can enter heaven without. *John* 3: 3.

Effected by

God. *John* 1: 13. 1 *Pet.* 1: 3.

Christ. 1 *John* 2: 29.

The Holy Ghost. *John* 3: 6. *Titus* 3: 5.

Through the instrumentality of

The word of God. *Jas.* 1: 18. 1 *Pet.* 1: 23.

The resurrection of Christ. 1 *Pet.* 1: 3.

The ministry of the gospel. 1 *Cor.* 4: 15.

Is of the will of God. *Jas.* 1: 18.

Is of the mercy of God. *Titus* 3: 5.

Is for the glory of God. *Isa.* 43: 7.

Described as

A new creation. 2 *Cor.* 5:
17. *Gal.* 6: 15. *Eph.* 2: 10.

Newness of life. *Rom.* 6: 4.

A spiritual resurrection.
Rom. 6: 4–6. *Eph.* 2: 1, 5.
Col. 2: 12. *Col.* 3: 1.

A new heart. *Ezek.* 36: 26.

A new spirit. *Ezek.* 11: 19.
Rom. 7: 6.

Putting on the new man.
Eph. 4: 24.

The inward man. *Rom.* 7:
22. 2 *Cor.* 4: 16.

Circumcision of the heart.
Deut. 30: 6, with *Rom.* 2:
29. *Col.* 2: 11.

Partaking of the divine nature. 2 *Pet.* 1: 4.

The washing of regeneration.
Titus 3: 5.

All saints partake of. 1 *Pet.* 2:
2. 1 *John* 5: 1.

Produces

Likeness to God. *Eph.* 4:
24. *Col.* 3: 10.

Likeness to Christ. *Rom.* 8:
29.

Knowledge of God. *Jer.* 24:
7. *Col.* 3: 10.

Hatred of sin. 1 *John* 3: 9.
1 *John* 5: 18.

Victory over the world. 1
John 5: 4.

Delight in God's law. *Rom.*
7: 22.

Evidenced by

Faith in Christ. 1 *John* 5: 1.

Righteousness. 1 *John* 2:
29.

Brotherly love. 1 *John* 4: 7.

Connected with adoption. *Isa.*
43: 6, 7. *John* 1: 12, 13.

The ignorant cavil at. *John* 3:
4.

Manner of effecting—Illustrated. *John* 3: 8.

Preserves from satan's devices.
1 *John* 5: 18.

OBEDIENCE TO GOD

Commanded. *Deut.* 13: 4.

Without faith, is impossible.
Heb. 11: 6.

Includes

Obeying his voice. *Exod.*
19: 5. *Jer.* 7: 23.

Obeying his law. *Deut.* 11:
27. *Isa.* 42: 24.

Obeying Christ. *Exod.* 23:
21. 2 *Cor.* 10: 5.

Obeying the gospel. *Rom.*
1: 5. *Rom.* 6: 17. *Rom.* 10:
16, 17.

Keeping his commandments.
Eccles. 12: 13.

Submission to higher powers.
Rom. 13: 1.

Better than sacrifice. 1 *Sam.*
15: 22.

Justification obtained by that of
Christ. *Rom.* 5: 19.

Christ, an example of. *John*
15: 10. *Phil.* 2: 5–8. *Heb.* 5: 8.

Angels engaged in. *Ps.* 103: 20.

A characteristic of saints. 1
Pet. 1: 14.

Saints elected to. 1 *Pet.* 1: 2.

Obligations to. *Acts* 4: 19, 20.
Acts 5: 29.

Exhortations to. *Jer.* 26: 13.
Jer. 38: 20.

Should be

From the heart. *Deut.* 11:
13. *Rom.* 6: 17.

With willingness. *Ps.* 18: 44.
Isa. 1: 19.

Unreserved. *Joshua* 22: 2, 3.

Undeviating. *Deut.* 28: 14.

Constant. *Phil.* 2: 12.

Resolve upon. *Exod.* 24: 7.
Joshua 24: 24.

Confess your failure in. *Dan.*
9: 10.

Prepare the heart for. 1 *Sam.* 7: 3. *Ezra* 7: 10.

Pray to be taught. *Ps.* 119: 35. *Ps.* 143: 10.

Promises to. *Exod.* 23: 22. 1 *Sam.* 12: 14. *Isa.* 1: 19. *Jer.* 7: 23.

To be universal in the latter days. *Dan.* 7: 27.

Blessedness of. *Deut.* 11: 27. *Deut.* 28: 1–13. *Luke* 11: 28. *Jas.* 1: 25.

The wicked refuse. *Exod.* 5: 2. *Neh.* 9: 17.

Punishment of refusing. *Deut.* 11: 28. *Deut.* 28: 15–68. *Joshua* 5: 6. *Isa.* 1: 20.

Exemplified. NOAH, *Gen.* 6: 22. ABRAM, *Gen.* 12: 1–4, with *Heb.* 11: 8. *Gen.* 22: 3, 12. ISRAELITES, *Exod.* 12: 28. *Exod.* 24: 7. MOSES, *Exod.* 34: 4. CALEB, etc., *Num.* 32: 12. ASA, 1 *Kings* 15: 11. ELIJAH, 1 *Kings* 17: 5. HEZEKIAH, 2 *Kings* 18: 6. JOSIAH, 2 *Chron.* 35: 26. DAVID, *Ps.* 119: 166. ZERUBBABEL, etc., *Hag.* 1: 12. JOSEPH, *Matt.* 1: 24. WISE MEN, *Matt.* 2: 12. ZACHARIAS, etc., *Luke* 1: 6. PAUL, *Acts* 26: 19. SAINTS OF ROME, *Rom.* 16: 19.

OFFENCE

Occasions of, must arise. *Matt.* 18: 7.

Occasioning of, forbidden. 1 *Cor.* 10: 32.

Persecution, a cause of, to mere professors. *Matt.* 13: 21. *Matt.* 24: 10.

The wicked take, at

The low station of Christ. *Matt.* 13: 54–57.

Christ, as the corner-stone. *Isa.* 8: 14, with 1 *Pet.* 2: 8.

Christ, as the bread of life. *John* 6: 58–61.

Christ crucified. 1 *Cor.* 1: 23. *Gal.* 5: 11.

The righteousness of faith. *Rom.* 9: 32.

The necessity of inward purity. *Matt.* 15: 11, 12.

Blessedness of not taking, at Christ. *Matt.* 11: 6.

Saints warned against taking. *John* 16: 1.

Saints should

Be without. *Phil.* 1: 10.

Be cautious of giving. *Ps.* 73: 15. *Rom.* 14: 13. 1 *Cor.* 8: 9.

Have a conscience void of. *Acts* 24: 16.

Cut off what causes, to themselves. *Matt.* 5: 29, 30. *Mark* 9: 43–47.

Not let their liberty occasion, to others. 1 *Cor.* 8: 9.

Use self-denial rather than occasion. *Rom.* 14: 21. 1 *Cor.* 8: 13.

Avoid those who cause. *Rom.* 16: 17.

Reprove those who cause. *Exod.* 32: 21. 1 *Sam.* 2: 24.

Ministers should

Be cautious of giving. 2 *Cor.* 6: 3.

Remove that which causes. *Isa.* 57: 14.

All things that cause, shall be gathered out of Christ's kingdom. *Matt.* 13: 41.

Denunciation against those who cause. *Matt.* 18: 7. *Mark* 9: 42.

Punishment for occasioning. *Ezek.* 44: 12. *Mal.* 2: 8, 9. *Matt.* 18: 6.

Exemplified. AARON, *Exod.* 32: 2–6. BALAAM, etc., *Num.* 31:

16, with *Rev.* 2: 14. GIDEON, *Judges* 8: 27. SONS OF ELI, 1 *Sam.* 2: 12–17. JEROBOAM, 1 *Kings* 12: 26–30. OLD PROPHET, 1 *Kings* 13: 18–26. PRIESTS, *Mal.* 2: 8. PETER, *Matt.* 16: 23.

OFFENCES AGAINST THE HOLY SPIRIT

Exhortations against. *Eph.* 4: 30. 1 *Thess.* 5: 19.

Exhibited in

Tempting him. *Acts* 5: 9.

Vexing him. *Isa.* 63: 10.

Grieving him. *Eph.* 4: 30.

Quenching him. 1 *Thess.* 5: 19.

Lying to him. *Acts* 5: 3, 4.

Resisting him. *Acts* 7: 51.

Undervaluing his gifts. *Acts* 8: 19, 20.

Doing despite unto him. *Heb.* 10: 29.

Disregarding his testimony. *Neh.* 9: 30.

Blasphemy against him, unpardonable. *Matt.* 12: 31, 32. 1 *John* 5: 16.

OFFERINGS

To be made to God alone. *Exod.* 22: 20: *Judges* 13: 16.

Antiquity of. *Gen.* 4: 3, 4.

Different kinds of;

Burnt. *Lev.* 1: 3–17. *Ps.* 66: 15.

Sin. *Lev.* 4: 3–35. *Lev.* 6: 25. *Lev.* 10: 17.

Trespass. *Lev.* 5: 6–19. *Lev.* 6: 6. *Lev.* 7: 1.

Peace. *Lev.* 3: 1–17. *Lev.* 7: 11.

Heave. *Exod.* 29: 27, 28. *Lev.* 7: 14. *Num.* 15: 19.

Wave. *Exod.* 29: 26. *Lev.* 7: 30.

Meat. *Lev.* 2 ch. *Num.* 15: 4.

Drink. *Gen.* 35: 14. *Exod.* 29: 40. *Num.* 15: 5.

Thank. *Lev.* 7: 12. *Lev.* 22: 29. *Ps.* 50: 14.

Free-will. *Lev.* 23: 28. *Deut.* 16: 10. *Deut.* 23: 23.

Incense. *Exod.* 30: 8. *Mal.* 1: 11. *Luke* 1: 9.

First-fruits. *Exod.* 22: 29. *Deut.* 18: 4.

Tithe. *Lev.* 27: 30. *Num.* 18: 21. *Deut.* 14: 22.

Gifts. *Exod.* 35: 22. *Num.* 7: 2–88.

Jealousy. *Num.* 5: 15.

Personal, for redemption. *Exod.* 30: 13, 15.

Declared to be most holy. *Num.* 18: 9.

Required to be

Perfect. *Lev.* 22: 21.

The best of their kind. *Mal.* 1: 14.

Offered willingly. *Lev.* 22: 19.

Offered in righteousness. *Mal.* 3: 3.

Offered in love and charity. *Matt.* 5: 23, 24.

Brought in a clean vessel. *Isa.* 66: 20.

Brought to the place appointed by God. *Deut.* 12: 6. *Ps.* 27: 6. *Heb.* 9: 9.

Laid before the altar. *Matt.* 5: 23, 24.

Presented by the priest. *Heb.* 5: 1.

Brought without delay. *Exod.* 22: 29, 30.

Unacceptable without gratitude. *Ps.* 50: 8, 14.

Could not make the offerer perfect. *Heb.* 9: 9.

Things forbidden as;

The price of fornication. *Deut.* 23: 18.

The price of a dog. *Deut.* 23: 18.

Whatever was blemished. *Lev.* 22: 20.

Whatever was imperfect. *Lev.* 22: 24.

Whatever was unclean. *Lev.* 27: 11, 27.

Laid up in the temple. 2 *Chron.* 31: 12. *Neh.* 10: 37.

Hezekiah prepared chambers for. 2 *Chron.* 31: 11.

The Jews often

Slow in presenting. *Neh.* 13: 10–12.

Defrauded God of. *Mal.* 3: 8.

Gave the worst they had as. *Mal.* 1: 8, 13.

Rejected in, because of sin. *Isa.* 1: 13. *Mal.* 1: 10.

Abhorred, on account of the sins of the priests. 1 *Sam.* 2: 17.

Presented to idols. *Ezek.* 20: 28.

Made by strangers, to be the same as by the Jews. *Num.* 15: 14–16.

Many offences under the law, beyond the efficacy of. 1 *Sam.* 3: 14. *Ps.* 51: 16.

Illustrative of

Christ's offering of Himself. *Eph.* 5: 2.

The conversion of the Gentiles. *Rom.* 15: 16.

The conversion of the Jews. *Isa.* 66: 20.

PARABLES OF CHRIST, THE

Wise and foolish builders. *Matt.* 7: 24–27.

Children of the bride-chamber. *Matt.* 9: 15.

New cloth and old garment. *Matt.* 9: 16.

New wine and old bottles. *Matt.* 9: 17.

Unclean spirit. *Matt.* 12: 43.

Sower. *Matt.* 13: 3, 18. *Luke* 8: 5, 11.

Tares. *Matt.* 13: 24–30, 36–43.

Mustard-seed. *Matt.* 13: 31, 32. *Luke* 13: 19.

Leaven. *Matt.* 13: 33.

Treasure hid in a field. *Matt.* 13: 44.

Pearl of great price. *Matt.* 13: 45, 46.

Net cast into the sea. *Matt.* 13: 47–50.

Food defileth not. *Matt.* 15: 10–15.

Unmerciful servant. *Matt.* 18: 23–35.

Labourers hired. *Matt.* 20: 1–16.

Two sons. *Matt.* 21: 28–32.

Wicked husbandmen. *Matt.* 21: 33–45.

Marriage-feast. *Matt.* 22: 2–14.

Fig-tree leafing. *Matt.* 24: 32–34.

Man of the house watching. *Matt.* 24: 43.

Faithful, and evil servants. *Matt.* 24: 45–51.

Ten virgins. *Matt.* 25: 1–13.

Talents. *Matt.* 25: 14–30.

Kingdom, divided against itself. *Mark* 3: 24.

House, divided against itself. *Mark* 3: 25.

Strong man armed. *Mark* 3: 27. *Luke* 11: 21.

Seed growing secretly. *Mark* 4: 26–29.

Lighted candle. *Mark* 4: 21. *Luke* 11: 33–36.

Man taking a far journey. *Mark* 13: 34–37.

Blind leading the blind. *Luke* 6: 39.

Beam and mote. *Luke* 6: 41, 42.

Tree and its fruit. *Luke* 43–45.

Creditor and debtors. *Luke* 7: 41–47.

Good Samaritan. *Luke* 10: 30–37.

Importunate friend. *Luke* 11: 5–9.

Rich fool. *Luke* 12: 16–21.

Cloud and wind. *Luke* 12: 54–57.

Barren fig-tree. *Luke* 13: 6–9.

Men bidden to a feast. *Luke* 14: 7–11.

Builder of a tower. *Luke* 14: 28–30, 33.

King going to war. *Luke* 14: 31–33.

Savour of salt. *Luke* 14: 34, 35.

Lost sheep. *Luke* 15: 3–7.

Lost piece of silver. *Luke* 15: 8–10.

Prodigal son. *Luke* 15: 11–32.

Unjust steward. *Luke* 16: 1–8.

Rich man and Lazarus. *Luke* 16: 19–31.

Importunate widow. *Luke* 18: 1–8.

Pharisee and Publican. *Luke* 18: 9–14.

Pounds. *Luke* 19: 12–27.

Good Shepherd. *John* 10: 1–6.

Vine and branches. *John* 15: 1–5.

PARDON

Promised. *Isa.* 1: 18. *Jer.* 31: 34, with *Heb.* 8: 12. *Jer.* 50: 20.

None, without shedding of blood. *Lev.* 17: 11, with *Heb.* 9: 22.

Legal sacrifices, ineffectual for. *Heb.* 10: 4.

Outward purifications, ineffectual for. *Job* 9: 30, 31. *Jer.* 2: 22.

The blood of Christ, alone, is efficacious for. *Zech.* 13: 1, with 1 *John* 1: 7.

Is granted

By God alone. *Dan.* 9: 9. *Mark* 2: 7.

By Christ. *Mark* 2: 5. *Luke* 7: 48.

Through Christ. *Luke* 1: 69, 77. *Acts* 5: 31. *Acts* 13: 38.

Through the blood of Christ. *Matt.* 26: 28. *Rom.* 3: 25. *Col.* 1: 14.

For the name's sake of Christ. 1 *John* 2: 12.

According to the riches of grace. *Eph.* 1: 7.

On the exaltation of Christ. *Acts* 5: 31.

Freely. *Isa.* 43: 25.

Readily. *Neh.* 9: 17. *Ps.* 86: 5.

Abundantly. *Isa.* 55: 7. *Rom.* 5: 20.

To those who confess their sins. 2 *Sam.* 12: 13. *Ps.* 32: 5. 1 *John* 1: 9.

To those who repent. *Acts* 2: 38.

To those who believe. *Acts* 10: 43.

Should be preached in the name of Christ. *Luke* 24: 47.

Exhibits the

Compassion of God. *Mic.* 7: 18, 19.

Grace of God. *Rom.* 5: 15, 16.

Mercy of God. *Exod.* 34: 7. *Ps.* 51: 1.

Goodness of God. 2 *Chron.* 30: 18. *Ps.* 86: 5.

Forbearance of God. *Rom.* 3: 25.

Loving-kindness of God. *Ps.* 51: 1.

Justice of God. *1 John* 1: 9.

Faithfulness of God. *1 John* 1: 9.

Expressed by

Forgiving transgression. *Ps.* 32: 1.

Removing transgression. *Ps.* 103: 12.

Blotting out transgression. *Isa.* 44: 22.

Covering sin. *Ps.* 32: 1.

Blotting out sin. *Acts* 3: 19.

Casting sins into the sea. *Mic.* 7: 19.

Not imputing sin. *Rom.* 4: 8.

Not mentioning transgression. *Ezek.* 18: 22.

Remembering sins no more. *Heb.* 10: 17.

All saints enjoy. *Col.* 2: 13. 1 *John* 2: 12.

Blessedness of. *Ps.* 32: 1 with *Rom.* 4: 7.

Should lead to

Returning to God. *Isa.* 44: 22.

Loving God. *Luke* 7: 47.

Fearing God. *Ps.* 130: 4.

Praising God. *Ps.* 103: 2, 3.

Ministers are appointed to proclaim. *Isa.* 40: 1, 2. 2 *Cor.* 5: 19.

Pray for,

For yourselves. *Ps.* 25: 11, 18. *Ps.* 51: 1. *Matt.* 6: 12. *Luke* 11: 4.

For others. *Jas.* 5: 15. 1 *John* 5: 16.

Encouragement to pray for. 2 *Chron.* 7: 14.

Withheld from

The unforgiving. *Mark* 11: 26. *Luke* 6: 37.

The unbelieving. *John* 8: 21, 24.

The impenitent. *Luke* 13: 2–5.

Blasphemers against the Holy Ghost. *Matt.* 12: 32. *Mark* 3: 28, 29.

Apostates. *Heb.* 10: 26, 27. 1 *John* 5: 16.

Illustrated. *Luke* 7: 42. *Luke* 15: 20–24.

Exemplified. ISRAELITES, *Num.* 14: 20. DAVID, 2 *Sam.* 12: 13. MANASSEH, 2 *Chron.* 33: 13. HEZEKIAH, *Isa.* 38: 17. THE PARALYTIC, *Matt.* 9: 2. THE PENITENT *Luke* 7: 47.

PARENTS

Receive their children from God. *Gen.* 33: 5. 1 *Sam.* 1: 27. *Ps.* 127: 3.

Their duty to their children is

To love them. *Titus* 2: 4.

To bring them to Christ. *Matt.* 19: 13, 14.

To train them up for God. *Prov.* 22: 6. *Eph.* 6: 4.

To instruct them in God's word. *Deut.* 4: 9. *Deut.* 11: 19. *Isa.* 38: 19.

To tell them of God's judgments. *Joel* 1: 3.

To tell them of the miraculous works of God. *Exod.* 10: 2. *Ps.* 78: 4.

To command them to obey God. *Deut.* 32: 46. 1 *Chron.* 28: 9.

To bless them. *Gen.* 48: 15. *Heb.* 11: 20.

To pity them. *Ps.* 103: 13.

To provide for them. *Job*

42: 15. 2 *Cor.* 12: 14. 1 *Tim.* 5: 8.

To rule them. 1 *Tim.* 3: 4, 12.

To correct them. *Prov.* 13: 24. *Prov.* 19: 18. *Prov.* 23: 13. *Prov.* 29: 17. *Heb.* 12: 7.

Not to provoke them. *Eph.* 6: 4. *Col.* 3: 21.

Not to make unholy connexions for them. *Gen.* 24: 1–4. *Gen.* 28: 1, 2.

Wicked children, a cause of grief to. *Prov.* 10: 1. *Prov* 17: 25.

Should pray for their children

For their spiritual welfare. *Gen.* 17: 18. 1 *Chron.* 29: 19.

When in temptation. *Job* 1: 5.

When in sickness. 2 *Sam.* 12: 16. *Mark* 5: 23. *John* 4: 46, 49.

When faithful,

Are blessed by their children. *Prov.* 31: 28.

Leave a blessing to their children. *Ps.* 112: 2. *Prov.* 11: 21. *Isa.* 65: 23.

Sins of, visited on their children. *Exod.* 20: 5. *Isa.* 14: 20. *Lam.* 5: 7.

Negligence of, sorely punished. 1 *Sam.* 3: 13.

When wicked,

Instruct their children in evil. *Jer.* 9: 14. 1 *Pet.* 1: 18.

Set a bad example to their children. *Ezek.* 20: 18. *Amos* 2: 4.

Good—Exemplified. ABRAHAM, *Gen.* 18: 19. JACOB, *Gen.* 44: 20, 30. JOSEPH, *Gen.* 48, 13–20. MOTHER OF MOSES, *Exod.* 2: 2,

3. MANOAH, *Judges* 13: 8. HANNAH, 1 *Sam.* 1: 28. DAVID, 2 *Sam.* 18: 5, 33. SHUNAMMITE, 2 *Kings* 4: 19, 20. JOB, *Job* 1: 5. MOTHER OF LEMUEL, *Prov.* 31: 1. NOBLEMAN, *John* 4: 49. LOIS AND EUNICE, 2 *Tim.* 1: 5.

Bad—Exemplified. MOTHER OF MICAH, *Judges* 17: 3. ELI, 1 *Sam.* 3: 13. SAUL, 1 *Sam.* 20: 33. ATHALIAH, 2 *Chron.* 22: 3, MANASSEH, 2 *Chron.* 33: 6. HERODIAS. *Mark* 6: 24.

PATIENCE

God, is the God of. *Rom.* 15: 5.

Christ, an example of. *Isa.* 53: 7, with *Acts* 8: 32. *Matt.* 27: 14.

Enjoined. *Titus* 2: 2. 2 *Pet.* 1: 6.

Should have its perfect work. *Jas.* 1: 4.

Trials of saints lead to. *Rom.* 5: 3. *Jas.* 1: 3.

Produces

Experience. *Rom.* 5: 4.

Hope. *Rom.* 15: 4.

Suffering with, for well-doing, is acceptable with God. 1 *Pet.* 2: 20.

To be exercised in

Running the race set before us. *Heb.* 12: 1.

Bringing forth fruits. *Luke* 8: 15.

Well-doing. *Rom.* 2: 7. *Gal.* 6: 9.

Waiting for God. *Ps.* 37: 7. *Ps.* 40: 1.

Waiting for Christ. 1 *Cor.* 1: 7. 2 *Thess.* 3: 5.

Waiting for the hope of the gospel. *Rom.* 8: 25. *Gal.* 5: 5.

Waiting for God's salvation. *Lam.* 3: 26.

Bearing the yoke. *Lam.* 3: 27.

Tribulation. *Luke* 21: 19. *Rom.* 12: 12.

Necessary to the inheritance of the promises. *Heb.* 6: 12. *Heb.* 10: 36.

Exercise, towards all. 1 *Thess.* 5: 14.

They who are in authority, should exercise. *Matt.* 18: 26. *Acts* 26: 3.

Ministers should follow after. 1 *Tim.* 6: 11.

Ministers approved by. 2 *Cor.* 6: 4.

Should be accompanied by

Godliness. 2 *Pet.* 1: 6.

Faith. 2 *Thess.* 1: 4. *Heb.* 6: 12. *Rev.* 13: 10.

Temperance. 2 *Pet.* 1: 6.

Long-suffering. *Col.* 1: 11.

Joyfulness. *Col.* 1: 11.

Saints strengthened unto all. *Col.* 1: 11.

Commended. *Eccles.* 7: 8. *Rev.* 2: 2, 3.

Illustrated. *Jas.* 5: 7.

Exemplified. JOB, *Job* 1: 21. *Jas.* 5: 11. SIMEON, *Luke* 2: 25. PAUL, 2 *Tim.* 3: 10. ABRAHAM, *Heb.* 6: 15. PROPHETS, *Jas.* 5: 10. JOHN, *Rev.* 1: 9.

PEACE

God is the Author of. *Ps.* 147: 14. *Isa.* 45: 7. 1 *Cor.* 14: 33.

Results from

Heavenly wisdom. *Jas.* 3: 17.

The government of Christ. *Isa.* 2: 4.

Praying for rulers. 1 *Tim.* 2: 2.

Seeking the peace of those with whom we dwell. *Jer.* 29: 7.

Necessary to the enjoyment of life. *Ps.* 34: 12, 14, with 1 *Pet.* 3: 10, 11.

God bestows upon those who

Obey him. *Lev.* 26: 6.

Please him. *Prov.* 16: 7.

Endure his chastisements. *Job* 5: 17, 23, 24.

Is a bond of union. *Eph.* 4: 3.

The fruit of righteousness should be sown in. *Jas.* 3: 18.

The Church shall enjoy. *Ps.* 125: 5. *Ps.* 128: 6. *Isa.* 2: 4. *Hos.* 2: 18.

Stains should

Love. *Zech.* 8: 19.

Seek. *Ps.* 34: 14, with 1 *Pet.* 3: 11.

Follow. 2 *Tim.* 2: 22.

Follow the things which make for. *Rom.* 14: 19.

Cultivate. *Ps.* 120: 7.

Speak. *Esther* 10: 3.

Live in. 2 *Cor.* 13: 11.

Have, with each other. *Mark* 9: 50. 1 *Thess.* 5: 13.

Endeavour to have, with all men. *Rom.* 12: 18. *Heb.* 12: 14.

Pray for that of the Church. *Ps.* 122: 6–8.

Exhort others to. *Gen.* 45: 24.

Ministers should exhort to. 2 *Thess.* 3: 12.

Advantages of. *Prov.* 17: 1. *Eccles.* 4: 6.

Blessedness of. *Ps.* 133: 1.

Blessedness of promoting. *Matt.* 5: 9.

The wicked

Hypocritically speak. *Ps.* 28: 3.

Speak not. *Ps.* 35: 20.

Enjoy not. *Isa.* 48: 22. *Ezek.* 7: 25.

Opposed to. *Ps.* 120: 7.

Hate. *Ps.* 120: 6.

Shall abound in the latter days. *Isa.* 2: 4. *Isa.* 11: 13. *Isa.* 32: 18.

Exemplified. ABRAHAM, *Gen.* 13: 8, 9. ABIMELECH, *Gen.* 26: 29. MORDECAI, *Esther* 10: 3. DAVID, *Ps.* 120: 7.

PEACE, SPIRITUAL

God is the God of. *Rom.* 15: 33. 2 *Cor.* 13: 11. 1 *Thess.* 5: 23. *Heb.* 13: 20.

God ordains. *Isa.* 26: 12.

God speaks, to his saints. *Ps.* 85: 8.

Christ is the Lord of. 2 *Thess.* 3: 16.

Christ is the Prince of. *Isa.* 9: 6.

Christ gives. 2 *Thess.* 3: 16.

Christ guides into the way of. *Luke* 1: 79.

Christ is our. *Eph.* 2: 14.

Is through the atonement of Christ. *Isa.* 53: 5. *Eph.* 2: 14, 15. *Col.* 1: 20.

Bequeathed by Christ. *John* 14: 27.

Preached

By Christ. *Eph.* 2: 17.

Through Christ. *Acts* 10: 36.

By ministers. *Isa.* 52: 7, with *Rom.* 10: 15.

Announced by angels. *Luke* 2: 14.

Follows upon justification. *Rom.* 5: 1.

A fruit of the Spirit. *Rom.* 14: 17. *Gal.* 5: 22.

Divine wisdom is the way of. *Prov.* 3: 17.

Accompanies

Faith. *Rom.* 15: 13.

Righteousness. *Isa.* 32: 17.

Acquaintance with God. *Job* 22: 21.

The love of God's law. *Ps.* 119: 165.

Spiritual-mindedness. *Rom.* 8: 6.

Established by covenant. *Isa.* 54: 10. *Ezek.* 34: 25. *Mal.* 2: 5.

Promised to

The Church. *Isa.* 66: 12.

The Gentiles. *Zech.* 9: 10.

Saints. *Ps.* 72: 3, 7. *Isa.* 55: 12.

The meek. *Ps.* 37: 11.

Those who confide in God. *Isa.* 26: 3.

Returning backsliders. *Isa.* 57: 18, 19.

We should love. *Zech.* 8: 19.

The benediction of ministers should be. *Num.* 6: 26. *Luke* 10: 5.

Saints

Have, in Christ. *John* 16: 33.

Have, with God. *Isa.* 27: 5. *Rom.* 5: 1.

Enjoy. *Ps.* 119: 165.

Repose in. *Ps.* 4: 8.

Blessed with. *Ps.* 29: 11.

Kept in perfect. *Isa.* 26: 3.

Ruled by. *Col.* 3: 15.

Kept by. *Phil.* 4: 7.

Die in. *Ps.* 37: 37. *Luke* 2: 29.

Wish, to each other. *Gal.* 6: 16. *Phil.* 1: 2. *Col.* 1: 2. 1 *Thess.* 1: 1.

Of saints,

Great. *Ps.* 119: 165. *Isa.* 54: 13.

Abundant. *Ps.* 72: 7. *Jer.* 33: 6.

Secure. *Job* 34: 29.

Passeth all understanding. *Phil.* 4: 7.

Consummated after death. *Isa.* 57: 2.

The gospel is good tidings of. *Rom.* 10: 15.

The wicked

Know not the way of. *Isa.* 59: 8. *Rom.* 3: 17.

Know not the things of. *Luke* 19: 42.

Promise, to themselves. *Deut.* 29: 19.

Are promised, by false teachers. *Jer.* 6: 14.

There is none for. *Isa.* 48: 22. *Isa.* 57: 21.

Supports under trials. *John* 14: 27. *John* 16: 33.

PERFECTION

Is of God. *Ps.* 18: 32. *Ps.* 138: 8.

All saints have, in Christ. 1 *Cor.* 2: 6. *Phil.* 3: 15. *Col.* 2: 10.

God's perfection the standard of. *Matt.* 5: 48.

Implies,

Entire devotedness. *Matt.* 19: 21.

Purity and holiness in speech. *Jas.* 3: 2.

Saints commanded to aim at. *Gen.* 17: 1. *Deut.* 18: 13.

Saints claim not. *Job* 9: 20. *Phil.* 3: 12.

Saints follow after. *Prov.* 4: 18. *Phil.* 3: 12.

Ministers appointed to lead saints to. *Eph.* 4: 12. *Col.* 1: 28.

Exhortation to. 2 *Cor.* 7: 1. 2 *Cor.* 13: 11.

Impossibility of attaining to. 2 *Chron.* 6: 36. *Ps.* 119: 96.

The word of God is

The rule of. *Jas.* 1: 25.

Designed to lead us to. 2 *Tim.* 3: 16, 17.

Charity is the bond of. *Col.* 3: 14.

Patience leads to. *Jas.* 1: 4.

Pray for. *Heb.* 13: 20, 21. 1 *Pet.* 5: 10.

The Church shall attain to. *John* 17: 23. *Eph.* 4: 13.

Blessedness of. *Ps.* 37: 37. *Prov.* 2: 21.

PERSECUTION

Christ suffered. *Ps.* 69: 26. *John* 5: 16.

Christ voluntarily submitted to. *Isa.* 50: 6.

Christ was patient under. *Isa.* 53: 7.

Saints may expect. *Mark* 10: 30. *Luke* 21: 12. *John* 15: 20.

Saints suffer, for the sake of God. *Jer.* 15: 15.

Of saints, is a persecution of Christ. *Zech.* 2: 8, with *Acts* 9: 4, 5.

All that live godly in Christ, shall suffer. 2 *Tim.* 3: 12.

Originates in

Ignorance of God and Christ. *John* 16: 3.

Hatred to God and Christ. *John* 15: 20, 24.

Hatred to the gospel. *Matt.* 13: 21.

Pride. *Ps.* 10: 2.

Mistaken zeal. *Acts* 13: 50. *Acts* 26: 9–11.

Is inconsistent with the spirit of the gospel. *Matt.* 26: 52.

Men by nature addicted to. *Gal.* 4: 29.

Preachers of the gospel subject to. *Gal.* 5: 11.

Is sometimes unto death. *Acts* 22: 4.

God forsakes not his saints under. 2 *Cor.* 4: 9.

God delivers out of. *Dan.* 3: 25, 28. 2 *Cor.* 1: 10. 2 *Tim.* 3: 11.

Cannot separate from Christ. *Rom.* 8: 35.

Lawful means may be used to escape. *Matt.* 2: 13. *Matt.* 10: 23. *Matt.* 12: 14, 15.

Saints suffering, should

Commit themselves to God. 1 *Pet.* 4: 19.

Exhibit patience. 1 *Cor.* 4: 12.

Rejoice. *Matt.* 5: 12. 1 *Pet.* 4: 13.

Glorify God. 1 *Pet.* 4: 16.

Pray for deliverance. *Ps.* 7: 1. *Ps.* 119: 86.

Pray for those who inflict. *Matt.* 5: 44.

Return blessing for. *Rom.* 12: 14.

The hope of future blessedness supports under. 1 *Cor.* 15: 19, 32. *Heb.* 10: 34, 35.

Blessedness of enduring, for Christ's sake. *Matt.* 5: 10. *Luke* 6: 22.

Pray for those suffering. 2 *Thess.* 3: 2.

Hypocrites cannot endure. *Mark* 4: 17.

False teachers shrink from. *Gal.* 6: 12.

The wicked

Addicted to. *Ps.* 10: 2. *Ps.* 69: 26.

Active in. *Ps.* 143: 3. *Lam.* 4: 19.

Encourage each other in. *Ps.* 71: 11.

Rejoice in its success. *Ps.* 13: 4. *Rev.* 11: 10.

Punishment for. *Ps.* 7: 13. 2 *Thess.* 1: 6.

Illustrated. *Matt.* 21: 33–39.

Spirit of—Exemplified. PHARAOH, etc., *Exod.* 1: 8–14. SAUL, 1 *Sam.* 26: 18. JEZEBEL, 1 *Kings* 19: 2. ZEDEKIAH, etc., *Jer.* 38: 4–6. CHALDEANS, *Dan.* 3: 8, etc. PHARISEES, *Matt.* 12: 14. JEWS, *John* 5: 16. 1 *Thess.* 2: 15. HEROD, *Acts* 12: 1. GENTILES, *Acts* 14: 5. PAUL, *Phil.* 3: 6. 1 *Tim.* 1: 13.

Suffering of—Exemplified. MICAIAH, 1 *Kings* 22: 27. DAVID, *Ps.* 119: 161. JEREMIAH, *Jer.* 32: 2. DANIEL, *Dan.* 6: 5–17. PETER, etc., *Acts* 4: 3. APOSTLES, *Acts* 5: 18. THE PROPHETS, *Acts* 7: 52. PRIMITIVE CHURCH, *Acts* 13: 50. PAUL AND SILAS, *Acts* 16: 23. HEBREWS, *Heb.* 10: 33. SAINTS OF OLD, *Heb.* 11: 36.

PERSEVERANCE

An evidence of reconciliation with God. *Col.* 1: 21–23.

An evidence of belonging to Christ. *John* 8: 31. *Heb.* 3: 6, 14.

A characteristic of saints. *Prov.* 4: 18.

To be manifested in

Seeking God. 1 *Chron.* 16: 11.

Waiting upon God. *Hos.* 12: 6.

Prayer. *Rom.* 12: 12. *Eph.* 6: 18.

Well-doing. *Rom.* 2: 7. 2 *Thess.* 3: 13.

Continuing in the faith. *Acts* 14: 22. *Col.* 1: 23. 2 *Tim.* 4: 7.

Holding fast hope. *Heb.* 3: 6.

Maintained through

The power of God. *Ps.* 37:
24. *Phil.* 1: 6.

The power of Christ. *John*
10: 28.

The intercession of Christ.
Luke 22: 31, 32. *John* 17: 11.

The fear of God. *Jer.* 32: 40.

Faith. 1 *Pet.* 1: 5.

Promised to saints. *Job* 17: 9.

Leads to increase of knowledge.
John 8: 31, 32.

In well-doing

Leads to assurance of hope.
Heb. 6: 10, 11.

Is not in vain. 1 *Cor.* 15: 58.
Gal. 6: 9.

Ministers should exhort to.
Acts 13: 43. *Acts* 14: 22.

Encouragement to. *Heb.* 12:
2, 3.

Promises to. *Matt.* 10: 22.
Matt. 24: 13. *Rev.* 2: 26–28.

Blessedness of. *Jas.* 1: 25.

Want of,

Excludes from the benefits of
the gospel. *Heb.* 6: 4–6.

Punished. *John* 15: 6. *Rom.*
11: 22.

Illustrated. *Mark* 4: 5, 17.

PERSONALITY OF THE HOLY SPIRIT, THE

He creates and gives life. *Job*
33: 4.

He appoints and commissions
ministers. *Isa.* 48: 16. *Acts*
13: 2. *Acts* 20: 28.

He directs ministers where to
preach. *Acts* 8: 29. *Acts* 10:
19, 20.

He directs ministers where not
to preach. *Acts* 16: 6, 7.

He instructs ministers what to
preach. 1 *Cor.* 2: 13.

He spoke in, and by, the
Prophets. *Acts* 1: 16. 1 *Pet.* 1:
11, 12. 2 *Pet.* 1: 21.

He strives with sinners. *Gen.*
6: 3.

He reproves. *John* 16: 8.

He comforts. *Acts* 9: 31.

He helps our infirmities. *Rom.*
8: 26.

He teaches. *John* 14: 26. 1
Cor. 12: 3.

He guides. *John* 16: 13.

He sanctifies. *Rom.* 15: 16. 1
Cor. 6: 11.

He testifies of Christ. *John* 15:
26.

He glorifies Christ. *John* 16:
14.

He has a power of his own.
Rom. 15: 13.

He searches all things. *Rom.*
11: 33, 34, with 1 *Cor.* 2: 10,
11.

He works according to his own
will. 1 *Cor.* 12: 11.

He dwells with saints. *John* 14:
17.

He can be grieved. *Eph.* 4: 30.

He can be vexed. *Isa.* 63: 10.

He can be resisted. *Acts* 7: 51.

He can be tempted. *Acts* 5: 9.

PILGRIMS AND STRANGERS

Described. *John* 17: 16.

Saints are called to be. *Gen.*
12: 1, with *Acts* 7: 3. *Luke* 14:
26, 27, 33.

All saints are. *Ps.* 39: 12. 1
Pet. 1: 1.

Saints confess themselves. 1
Chron. 29: 15. *Ps.* 39: 12. *Ps.*
119: 19. *Heb.* 11: 13.

Saints as,

Have the example of Christ.
Luke 9: 58.

Are strengthened by God.
Deut. 33: 25. *Ps.* 84: 6, 7.

Are actuated by faith. *Heb.* 11: 9.

Have their faces towards Zion. *Jer.* 50: 5.

Keep the promises in view. *Heb.* 11: 13.

Forsake all for Christ. *Matt.* 19: 27.

Look for a heavenly country. *Heb.* 11: 16.

Look for a heavenly city. *Heb.* 11: 10.

Pass their sojourning in fear. 1 *Pet.* 1: 17.

Rejoice in the statutes of God. *Ps.* 119: 54.

Pray for direction. *Ps.* 43: 3. *Jer.* 50: 5.

Have a heavenly conversation. *Phil.* 3: 20.

Hate worldly fellowship. *Ps.* 120: 5, 6.

Are not mindful of this world. *Heb.* 11: 15.

Are not at home in this world. *Heb.* 11: 9.

Shine as lights in the world. *Phil.* 2: 15.

Invite others to go with them. *Num.* 10: 29.

Are exposed to persecution. *Ps.* 120: 5–7. *John* 17: 14.

Should abstain from fleshly lusts. 1 *Pet.* 2: 11.

Should have their treasure in heaven. *Matt.* 6: 19. *Luke* 12: 33. *Col.* 3: 1, 2.

Should not be over anxious about worldly things. *Matt.* 6: 25.

Long for their pilgrimage to end. *Ps.* 55: 6. 2 *Cor.* 5: 1–8.

Die in faith. *Heb.* 11: 13.

The world is not worthy of. *Heb.* 11: 38.

God is not ashamed to be called their God. *Heb.* 11: 16.

Typified. ISRAEL, *Exod.* 6: 4. *Exod.* 12: 11.

Exemplified. ABRAHAM, *Gen.* 23: 4. *Acts* 7: 4, 5. JACOB, *Gen.* 47: 9. SAINTS OF OLD, 1 *Chron.* 29: 15. *Heb.* 11: 13, 38. DAVID, *Ps.* 39: 12. THE APOSTLES, *Matt.* 19: 27.

POOR, THE

Made by God. *Job* 34: 19. *Prov.* 22: 2.

Are such by God's appointment. 1 *Sam.* 2: 7. *Job* 1: 21.

Condition of, often results from

Sloth. *Prov.* 20: 13.

Bad company. *Prov.* 28: 19.

Drunkenness and gluttony. *Prov.* 23: 21.

God

Regards, equally with the rich. *Job* 34: 19.

Forgets not. *Ps.* 9: 18.

Hears. *Ps.* 69: 33. *Isa.* 41: 17.

Maintains the right of. *Ps.* 140: 12.

Delivers. *Job* 36: 15. *Ps.* 35: 10.

Protects. *Ps.* 12: 5. *Ps.* 109: 31.

Exalts. 1 *Sam.* 2: 8. *Ps.* 107: 41.

Provides for. *Ps.* 68: 10. *Ps.* 146: 7.

Despises not the prayer of. *Ps.* 102: 17.

Is the refuge of. *Ps.* 14: 6.

Shall never cease out of the land. *Deut.* 15: 11. *Zeph.* 3: 12. *Matt.* 26: 11.

May be

Rich in faith. *Jas.* 2: 5.

Liberal. *Mark* 12: 42. 2 *Cor.* 8: 2.

Wise. *Prov.* 28: 11.

Upright.   *Prov*. 19: 1.

Christ lived as one of.   *Matt.* 8: 20.

Christ preached to.   *Luke* 4: 18.

Christ delivers.   *Ps*. 72: 12.

Offerings of, acceptable to God. *Mark* 12: 42: 44. 2 *Cor.* 8: 2, 12.

Should

Rejoice in God.   *Isa*. 29: 19.

Hope in God.   *Job* 5: 16.

Commit themselves to God. *Ps*. 10: 14.

When converted, rejoice in their exaltation.   *Jas*. 1: 9.

Provided for under the Law. *Exod*. 23: 11. *Lev*. 19: 9, 10.

Neglect towards, is

A neglect of Christ.   *Matt.* 25: 42–45.

Inconsistent with love to God. 1 *John* 3: 17.

A proof of unbelief.   *Jas*. 2: 15–17.

Rob not.   *Prov*. 22: 22.

Wrong not, in judgment.   *Exod.* 23: 6.

Take no usury from.   *Lev*. 25: 36.

Harden not the heart against. *Deut*. 15: 7.

Shut not the hand against. *Deut*. 15: 7.

Rule not, with rigour.   *Lev.* 25: 39, 43.

Oppress not.   *Deut*. 24: 14. *Zech*. 7: 10.

Despise not.   *Prov*. 14: 21. *Jas*. 2: 2–4.

Relieve.   *Lev*. 25: 35. *Matt.* 19: 21.

Defend.   *Ps*. 82: 3, 4.

Do justice to.   *Ps*. 82: 3. *Jer.* 22: 3, 16.

A care for,

Is characteristic of saints. *Ps*. 112: 9, with 2 *Cor*. 9: 9. *Prov*. 29: 7.

Is a fruit of repentance. *Luke* 3: 11.

Should be urged.   2 *Cor*. 8: 7, 8. *Gal*. 2: 10.

Give to,

Not grudgingly.   *Deut*. 15: 10. 2 *Cor*. 9: 7.

Liberally.   *Deut*.   14:   29. *Deut*. 15: 8, 11.

Cheerfully.   2 *Cor*. 8: 12. 2 *Cor*. 9: 7.

Without ostentation.   *Matt.* 6: 1.

Specially if saints.   *Rom*. 12: 13. *Gal*. 6: 10.

Pray for.   *Ps*. 74: 19, 21.

They who, in faith, relieve

Are happy.   *Prov*. 14: 21.

Are blessed.   *Deut*. 15: 10. *Ps*. 41: 1. *Prov*. 22: 9. *Acts* 20: 35.

Have the favour of God. *Heb*. 13: 16.

Have promises.   *Prov*. 28: 27. *Luke* 14: 13, 14.

By oppressing, God is reproached.   *Prov*. 14: 31.

By mocking, God is reproached. *Prov*. 17: 5.

The wicked

Care not for.   *John* 12: 6.

Oppress.   *Job*   24:   4–10. *Ezek*. 18: 12.

Vex.   *Ezek*. 22: 29.

Regard not the cause of. *Prov*. 29: 7.

Sell.   *Amos* 2: 6.

Crush.   *Amos* 4: 1.

Tread down.   *Amos* 5: 11.

Grind the faces of.   *Isa*. 3: 15.

Devour.   *Hab*. 3: 14.

Persecute.   *Ps*. 10: 2.

Defraud.   *Amos* 8: 5, 6.

Despise the counsel of. *Ps.* 14: 6.

Guilt of defrauding. *Jas.* 5: 4.

Punishment for

Oppressing. *Prov.* 22: 16. *Ezek.* 22: 29, 31.

Spoiling. *Isa.* 3: 13–15. *Ezek.* 18: 13.

Refusing to assist. *Job* 22: 7, 10. *Prov.* 21: 13.

Acting unjustly towards. *Job* 20: 19, 29. *Job* 22: 6, 10. *Isa.* 10: 1–3. *Amos* 5: 11, 12.

Oppression of—Illustrated. 2 *Sam.* 12: 1–6.

Care for—Illustrated. *Luke* 10: 33–35.

Exemplified. GIDEON, *Judges* 6: 15. RUTH, *Ruth* 2: 2. WIDOW OF ZAREPHATH, 1 *Kings* 17: 12. PROPHET'S WIDOW, 2 *Kings* 4: 2. SAINTS OF OLD, *Heb.* 11: 37.

Regard for—Exemplified. BOAZ, *Ruth* 2: 14. JOB, *Job* 29: 12–16. NEBUZARADAN, *Jer.* 39: 10. ZACCHEUS, *Luke* 19: 8. PETER AND JOHN, *Acts* 3: 6. DORCAS, *Acts* 9: 36, 39. CORNELIUS, *Acts* 10: 2. CHURCH AT ANTIOCH, *Acts* 11: 29, 30. PAUL, *Rom.* 15: 25. CHURCHES OF MACEDONIA AND ACHAIA, *Rom.* 15: 26. 2 *Cor.* 8: 1–5.

POWER OF GOD, THE

Is one of his attributes. *Ps.* 62: 11.

Expressed by the

Voice of God. *Ps.* 29: 3, 5. *Ps.* 68: 33.

Finger of God. *Exod.* 8: 19. *Ps.* 8: 3.

Hand of God. *Exod.* 9: 3, 15. *Isa.* 48: 13.

Arm of God. *Job* 40: 9. *Isa.* 52: 10.

Thunder of his power, etc *Job* 26: 14.

Described as

Great. *Ps.* 79: 11. *Nahum* 1: 3.

Strong. *Ps.* 89: 13. *Ps.* 136: 12.

Glorious. *Exod.* 15: 6. *Isa.* 63: 12.

Mighty. *Job* 9: 4. *Ps.* 89: 13.

Everlasting. *Isa.* 26: 4. *Rom.* 1: 20.

Sovereign. *Rom.* 9: 21.

Effectual. *Isa.* 43: 13. *Eph.* 3: 7.

Irresistible. *Deut.* 32: 39. *Dan.* 4: 35.

Incomparable. *Exod.* 15: 11, 12. *Deut.* 3: 24. *Job* 40: 9. *Ps.* 89: 8.

Unsearchable. *Job* 5: 9. *Job* 9: 10.

Incomprehensible. *Job* 26: 14. *Eccles.* 3: 11.

All things possible to. *Matt.* 19: 26.

Nothing too hard for. *Gen.* 18: 14. *Jer.* 32: 27.

Can save by many or by few 1 *Sam.* 14: 6.

Is the source of all strength 1 *Chron.* 29: 12. *Ps.* 68: 35.

Exhibited in

Creation. *Ps.* 102: 25. *Jer.* 10: 12.

Establishing and governing all things. *Ps.* 65: 6. *Ps.* 66: 7.

The miracles of Christ *Luke* 11: 20.

The resurrection of Christ 2 *Cor.* 13: 4. *Col.* 2: 12.

The resurrection of saints 1 *Cor.* 6: 14.

Making the gospel effectual *Rom.* 1: 16. 1 *Cor.* 1: 18, 24.

Delivering his people. *Ps.* 106: 8.

The destruction of the wicked. *Exod.* 9: 16. *Rom.* 9: 22.

Saints

Long for exhibitions of. *Ps.* 63: 1, 2.

Have confidence in. *Jer.* 20: 11.

Receive increase of grace by. 2 *Cor.* 9: 8.

Strengthened by. *Eph.* 6: 10. *Col.* 1: 11.

Upheld by. *Ps.* 37: 17. *Isa.* 41: 10.

Supported in affliction by. 2 *Cor.* 6: 7. 2 *Tim.* 1: 8.

Delivered by. *Neh.* 1: 10. *Dan.* 3: 17.

Exalted by. *Job* 36: 22.

Kept by, unto salvation. 1 *Pet.* 1: 5.

Exerted in behalf of saints. 2 *Chron.* 16: 9.

Works in, and for saints. 2 *Cor.* 13: 4. *Eph.* 1: 19. *Eph.* 3: 20.

The faith of saints stands in. 1 *Cor.* 2: 5.

Should be

Acknowledged. 1 *Chron.* 29: 11. *Isa.* 33: 13.

Pleaded in prayer. *Ps.* 79: 11. *Matt.* 6: 13.

Feared. *Jer.* 5: 22. *Matt.* 10: 28.

Magnified. *Ps.* 21: 13. *Jude* 25.

Efficiency of ministers is through. 1 *Cor.* 3: 6–8. *Gal.* 2: 8. *Eph.* 3: 7.

Is a ground of trust. *Isa.* 26: 4. *Rom.* 4: 21.

Is in the Name of Jesus. *Acts* 3: 16.

The wicked

Know not. *Matt.* 22: 29.

Have against them. *Ezra* 8: 22.

Shall be destroyed by. *Luke* 12: 5.

The heavenly host magnify. *Rev.* 4: 11. *Rev.* 5: 13. *Rev.* 11: 17.

POWER OF CHRIST, THE

As the Son of God, is the power of God. *John* 5: 11–19. *John* 10: 28–30.

As man, is from the Father. *Acts* 10: 38.

Described as

Supreme. *Eph.* 1: 20, 21. 1 *Pet.* 3: 22.

Unlimited. *Matt.* 28: 18.

Over all flesh. *John* 17: 2.

Over all things. *John* 3: 35. *Eph.* 1: 22.

Glorious. 2 *Thess.* 1: 9.

Everlasting. 1 *Tim.* 6: 16.

Is able to subdue all things *Phil.* 3: 21.

Exhibited in

Creation. *John* 1: 3, 10. *Col.* 1: 16.

Upholding all things. *Col.* 1: 17. *Heb.* 1: 3.

Salvation. *Isa.* 63: 1. *Heb.* 7: 25.

His teaching. *Matt.* 7: 28, 29. *Luke* 4: 32.

Working miracles. *Matt.* 8: 27. *Luke* 5: 17.

Enabling others to work miracles. *Matt.* 10: 1. *Mark* 16: 17, 18. *Luke* 10: 17.

Forgiving sins. *Matt.* 9: 6. *Acts* 5: 31.

Giving spiritual life. *John* 5: 21, 25, 26.

Giving eternal life. *John* 17: 2.

Raising the dead. *John* 5: 28, 29.

Raising himself from the dead. *John* 2: 19–21. *John* 10: 18.

Overcoming the world. *John* 16: 33.

Overcoming satan. *Col.* 2: 15. *Heb.* 2: 14.

Destroying the works of satan. 1 *John* 3: 8.

Ministers should make known. 2 *Pet.* 1: 16.

Saints

Made willing by. *Ps.* 110: 3.

Succoured by. *Heb.* 2: 18.

Strengthened by. *Phil.* 4: 13. 2 *Tim.* 4: 17.

Preserved by. 2 *Tim.* 1: 12. 2 *Tim.* 4: 18.

Bodies of, shall be changed by. *Phil.* 3: 21.

Rests upon saints. 2 *Cor.* 12: 9.

Present in the assembly of saints. 1 *Cor.* 5: 4.

Shall be specially manifested at his second coming. *Mark* 13: 26. 2 *Pet.* 1: 16.

Shall subdue all power. 1 *Cor.* 15: 24.

The wicked shall be destroyed by. *Ps.* 2: 9. *Isa.* 11: 4. *Isa.* 63: 3. 2 *Thess.* 1: 9.

POWER OF THE HOLY SPIRIT, THE

Is the power of God. *Matt.* 12: 28, with *Luke* 11: 20.

Christ commenced his ministry in. *Luke* 4: 14.

Christ wrought his miracles by. *Matt.* 12: 28.

Exhibited in

Creation. *Gen.* 1: 2. *Job* 26: 13. *Ps.* 104: 30.

The conception of Christ. *Luke* 1: 35.

Raising Christ from the dead. 1 *Pet.* 3: 18.

Giving spiritual life. *Ezek.* 37: 11–14, with *Rom.* 8: 11.

Working miracles. *Rom.* 15: 19.

Making the gospel efficacious. 1 *Cor.* 2: 4. 1 *Thess.* 1: 5.

Overcoming all difficulties. *Zech.* 4: 6, 7.

Promised by the Father. *Luke* 24: 49.

Promised by Christ. *Acts* 1: 8.

Saints

Upheld by. *Ps.* 51: 12.

Strengthened by. *Eph.* 3: 16.

Enabled to speak the truth boldly by. *Mic.* 3: 8. *Acts* 6: 5, 10. 2 *Tim.* 1: 7, 8.

Helped in prayer by. *Rom.* 8: 26.

Abound in hope by. *Rom.* 15: 13.

Qualifies ministers. *Luke* 4: 49. *Acts* 1: 8, 9.

God's word the instrument of. *Eph.* 6: 17.

PRAISE

God is worthy of. 2 *Sam.* 22: 4.

Christ is worthy of. *Rev.* 5: 12.

God is glorified by. *Ps.* 22: 23. *Ps.* 50: 23.

Offered to Christ. *John* 12: 13.

Acceptable through Christ. *Heb.* 13: 15.

Is due to God on account of

His majesty. *Ps.* 96: 1, 6. *Isa.* 24: 14.

His glory. *Ps.* 138: 5. *Ezek.* 3: 12.

His excellency. *Exod.* 15: 7. *Ps.* 148: 13.

His greatness. 1 *Chron.* 16: 25. *Ps.* 145: 3.

His holiness. *Exod.* 15: 11. *Isa.* 6: 3.

His wisdom. *Dan.* 2: 20. *Jude* 25.

His power. *Ps.* 21: 13.

His goodness. *Ps.* 107: 8. *Ps.* 118: 1. *Ps.* 136: 1. *Jer.* 33: 11.

His mercy. 2 *Chron.* 20: 21. *Ps.* 89: 1. *Ps.* 118: 1–4. *Ps.* 136.

His loving kindness and truth. *Ps.* 138: 2.

His faithfulness and truth. *Isa.* 25: 1.

His salvation. *Ps.* 18: 46. *Isa.* 35: 10. *Isa.* 61: 10. *Luke* 1: 68, 69.

His wonderful works. *Ps.* 89: 5. *Ps.* 150: 2. *Isa.* 25: 1.

His consolation. *Ps.* 42: 5. *Isa.* 12: 1.

His judgment. *Ps.* 101: 1.

His counsel. *Ps.* 16: 7. *Jer.* 32: 19.

Fulfilling of his promises. 1 *Kings* 8: 56.

Pardon of sin. *Ps.* 103: 1–3. *Hos.* 14: 2.

Spiritual health. *Ps.* 103: 3.

Constant preservation. *Ps.* 71: 6–8.

Deliverance. *Ps.* 40: 1–3. *Ps.* 124: 6.

Protection. *Ps.* 28: 7. *Ps.* 59: 17.

Answering prayer. *Ps.* 28: 6. *Ps.* 118: 21.

The hope of glory. 1 *Pet.* 1: 3, 4.

All spiritual blessings. *Ps.* 103: 2. *Eph.* 1: 3.

All temporal blessings. *Ps.* 104: 1, 14. *Ps.* 136: 25.

The continuance of blessings. *Ps.* 68: 19.

Is obligatory upon

Angels. *Ps.* 103: 20. *Ps.* 148: 2.

Saints. *Ps.* 30: 4. *Ps.* 149: 5.

Gentiles. *Ps.* 117: 1, with *Rom.* 15: 11.

Children. *Ps.* 8: 2, with *Matt.* 21: 16.

High and low. *Ps.* 148: 1, 11.

Young and old. *Ps.* 148: 1, 12.

Small and great. *Rev.* 19: 5.

All men. *Isa.* 107: 8. *Ps.* 145: 21.

All creation. *Ps.* 148: 1–10. *Ps.* 150: 6.

Is good and comely. *Ps.* 33: 1. *Ps.* 147: 1.

Should be offered

With the understanding. *Ps.* 47: 7, with 1 *Cor.* 14: 15.

With the soul. *Ps.* 103: 1. *Ps.* 104: 1, 35.

With the whole heart. *Ps.* 9: 1. *Ps.* 111: 1. *Ps.* 138: 1.

With uprightness of heart. *Ps.* 119: 7.

With the lips. *Ps.* 63: 3. *Ps.* 119: 171.

With the mouth. *Ps.* 51: 15. *Ps.* 63: 5.

With joy. *Ps.* 63: 5. *Ps.* 98: 4.

With gladness. 2 *Chron.* 29: 30. *Jer.* 33: 11.

With thankfulness. 1 *Chron.* 16: 4. *Neh.* 12: 24. *Ps.* 147: 7.

Continually. *Ps.* 35: 28. *Ps.* 71: 6.

During life. *Ps.* 104: 33.

More and more. *Ps.* 71: 14.

Day and night. *Rev.* 4: 8.

Day by day. 2 *Chron.* 30: 21.

For ever and ever. *Ps.* 145:
1, 2.

Throughout the world. *Ps.*
113: 3.

In psalms and hymns, etc.
Ps. 105: 2. *Eph.* 5: 19. *Col.*
3: 16.

Accompanied with musical instruments. 1 *Chron.* 16: 41,
42. *Ps.* 150: 3–5.

Is a part of public worship. *Ps.*
9: 14. *Ps.* 100: 4. *Ps.* 118: 19,
20. *Heb.* 2: 12.

Saints should

Show forth. *Isa.* 43: 21. 1
Pet. 2: 9.

Be endued with the spirit of.
Isa. 61: 3.

Render, under affliction.
Acts 16: 25.

Glory in. 1 *Chron.* 16: 35.

Triumph in. *Ps.* 106: 47.

Express their joy by. *Jas.* 5:
13.

Declare. *Isa.* 42: 12.

Invite others to. *Ps.* 34: 3.
Ps. 95: 1.

Pray for ability to offer. *Ps.*
51: 15. *Ps.* 119: 175.

Posture suited to. 2 *Sam.* 7:
18, 22. 1 *Chron.* 23: 30. *Neh.*
9: 5. *Dan.* 6: 10.

Called the

Fruit of the lips. *Heb.* 13:
15.

Voice of praise. *Ps.* 66: 8.

Voice of triumph. *Ps.* 47: 1.

Voice of melody. *Isa.* 51: 3.

Voice of a psalm. *Ps.* 98: 5.

Garment of praise. *Isa.* 61:
3.

Sacrifice of praise. *Heb.* 13:
15.

Sacrifices of joy. *Ps.* 27: 6.

Calves of the lips. *Hos.* 14:
2.

The heavenly host engage in.
Isa. 6: 3. *Luke* 2: 13. *Rev.* 4:
9–11. *Rev.* 5: 12.

Exemplified. MELCHIZEDEK,
Gen. 14: 20. MOSES, etc., *Exod.*
15: 1–21. JETHRO, *Exod.* 18:
10. ISRAELITES, 1 *Chron.* 16:
36. DAVID, 1 *Chron.* 29: 10–13.
Ps. 119: 164. PRIESTS AND LE-
VITES, *Ezra* 3: 10, 11. EZRA,
Neh. 8: 6. HEZEKIAH, *Isa.* 38:
19. ZACHARIAS, *Luke* 1: 64.
SHEPHERDS, *Luke* 2: 20. SIMEON,
Luke 2: 28. ANNA, *Luke* 2: 38.
MULTITUDES, *Luke* 18: 43. DIS-
CIPLES, *Luke* 19: 37, 38. THE
APOSTLES, *Luke* 24: 53. FIRST
CONVERTS, *Acts* 2: 47. LAME
MAN, *Acts* 3: 8. PAUL AND SILAS,
Acts 16: 25.

PRAYER

Commanded. *Isa.* 55: 6. *Matt.*
7: 7. *Phil.* 4: 6.

To be offered

To God. *Ps.* 5: 2. *Matt.* 4:
10.

To Christ. *Luke* 23: 32.
Acts 7: 59.

To the Holy Ghost. 2 *Thess.*
3: 5.

Through Christ. *Eph.* 2: 18.
Heb. 10: 19.

God hears. *Ps.* 10: 17. *Ps.* 65:
2.

God answers. *Ps.* 99: 6. *Isa.*
58: 9.

Is described as

Bowing the knees. *Eph.* 3:
14.

Looking up. *Ps.* 5: 3.

Lifting up the soul. *Ps.* 25:
1.

Lifting up the heart. *Lam.*
3: 41.

Pouring out the heart. *Ps.*
62: 8.

Pouring out the soul. 1 *Sam.* 1: 15.

Calling upon the name of the Lord. *Gen.* 12: 8. *Ps.* 116: 4. *Acts* 22: 16.

Crying unto God. *Ps.* 27: 7. *Ps.* 34: 6.

Drawing near to God. *Ps.* 73: 28. *Heb.* 10: 22.

Crying to heaven. 2 *Chron.* 32: 20.

Beseeching the Lord. *Exod.* 32: 11.

Seeking unto God. *Job* 8: 5.

Seeking the face of the Lord. *Ps.* 27: 8.

Making supplication. *Job* 8: 5. *Jer.* 36: 7.

Acceptable through Christ. *John* 14: 13, 14. *John* 15: 16. *John* 16: 23, 24.

Ascends to heaven. 2 *Chron.* 30: 27. *Rev.* 5: 8.

Quickening grace necessary to. *Ps.* 80: 18.

The Holy Ghost

Promised as a Spirit of. *Zech.* 12: 10.

As the Spirit of adoption, leads to. *Rom.* 8: 15. *Gal.* 4: 6.

Helps our infirmities in. *Rom.* 8: 26.

An evidence of conversion. *Acts* 9: 11.

Of the righteous, availeth much. *Jas.* 5: 16.

Of the upright, a delight to God. *Prov.* 15: 8.

Should be offered up

In the Holy Ghost. *Eph.* 6: 18. *Jude* 20.

In faith. *Matt.* 21: 22. *Jas.* 1: 6.

In full assurance of faith. *Heb.* 10: 22.

In a forgiving spirit. *Matt.* 6: 12.

With the heart. *Jer.* 29: 13. *Lam.* 3: 41.

With the whole heart. *Ps.* 119: 58, 145.

With preparation of heart. *Job* 11: 11.

With a true heart. *Heb.* 10: 22.

With the soul. *Ps.* 42: 4.

With the spirit and understanding. *John* 4: 22–24. 1 *Cor.* 14: 15.

With confidence in God. *Ps.* 56: 9. *Ps.* 86: 7. 1 *John* 5: 14.

With submission to God. *Luke* 22: 42.

With unfeigned lips. *Ps.* 17: 1.

With deliberation. *Eccles.* 5: 2.

With holiness. 1 *Tim.* 2: 8.

With humility. 2 *Chron.* 7: 14. 2 *Chron.* 33: 12.

With truth. *Ps.* 145: 18. *John* 4: 24.

With desire to be heard. *Neh.* 1: 6. *Ps.* 17: 1. *Ps.* 55: 1, 2. *Ps.* 61: 1.

With desire to be answered. *Ps.* 27: 7. *Ps.* 102: 2. *Ps.* 108: 6. *Ps.* 143: 1.

With boldness. *Heb.* 4: 16.

With earnestness. 1 *Thess.* 3: 10. *Jas.* 5: 17.

With importunity. *Gen.* 32: 26. *Luke* 11: 8, 9. *Luke* 18: 1–7.

Night and day. 1 *Tim.* 5: 5.

Without ceasing. 1 *Thess.* 5: 17.

Everywhere. 1 *Tim.* 2: 8.

In everything. *Phil.* 4: 6.

For temporal blessings. *Gen.* 28: 20. *Prov.* 30: 8. *Matt.* 6: 11.

For spiritual blessings. *Matt.* 6: 33. *Col.* 3: 1.

For mercy and grace to help in time of need. *Heb.* 4: 16.

Model for. *Matt.* 6: 9–13.

Vain repetitions in, forbidden. *Matt.* 6: 7.

Ostentation in, forbidden. *Matt.* 6: 5.

Accompanied with

Repentance. 1 *Kings* 8: 33. *Jer.* 36: 7.

Confession. *Neh.* 1: 4, 7. *Dan.* 9: 4–11.

Self-abasement. *Gen.* 18: 27.

Weeping. *Jer.* 31: 9. *Hos.* 12: 4.

Fasting. *Neh.* 1: 4. *Dan.* 9: 3. *Acts* 13: 3.

Watchfulness. *Luke* 21: 36. 1 *Pet.* 4: 7.

Praise. *Ps.* 66: 17.

Thanksgiving. *Phil.* 4: 6. *Col.* 4: 2.

Plead in, the

Promises of God. *Gen.* 32: 9–12. *Exod.* 32: 13. 1 *Kings* 8: 26. *Ps.* 119: 49.

Covenant of God. *Jer.* 14: 21.

Faithfulness of God. *Ps.* 143: 1.

Mercy of God. *Ps.* 51: 1. *Dan.* 9: 18.

Righteousness of God. *Dan.* 9: 16.

Rise early for. *Ps.* 5: 3. *Ps.* 119: 147.

Seek divine teaching for. *Luke* 11: 1.

Faint not in. *Luke* 18: 1.

Continue instant in. *Rom.* 12: 12.

Avoid hindrances in. 1 *Pet.* 3: 7.

Suitable in affliction. *Isa.* 26: 16. *Jas.* 5: 13.

Shortness of time a motive to. 1 *Pet.* 4: 7.

Postures in;

Standing. 1 *Kings* 8: 22. *Mark* 11: 25.

Bowing down. *Ps.* 95: 6.

Kneeling. 2 *Chron.* 6: 13. *Ps.* 95: 6. *Luke* 22: 41. *Acts* 20: 36.

Falling on the face. *Num.* 16: 22. *Joshua* 5: 14. 1 *Chron.* 21: 16. *Matt.* 26: 39.

Spreading forth the hands. *Isa.* 1: 15.

Lifting up the hands. *Ps.* 28: 2. *Lam.* 2: 19. 1 *Tim.* 2: 8.

The promises of God encourage to. *Isa.* 65: 24. *Amos* 5: 4. *Zech.* 13: 9.

The promises of Christ encourage to. *Luke* 11: 9, 10. *John* 14: 13, 14.

Experience of past mercies an incentive to. *Ps.* 4: 1. *Ps.* 116: 2.

PRAYER, PRIVATE

Christ was constant in. *Matt.* 14: 23. *Matt.* 26: 36, 39. *Mark* 1: 35. *Luke* 9: 18, 29.

Commanded. *Matt.* 6: 6.

Should be offered

At evening, morning, and noon. *Ps.* 55: 17.

Day and night. *Ps.* 88: 1.

Without ceasing. 1 *Thess.* 5: 17.

Shall be heard. *Job* 22: 27.

Rewarded openly. *Matt.* 6: 6.

An evidence of conversion. *Acts* 9: 11.

Nothing should hinder. *Dan.* 6: 10.

Exemplified. LOT, *Gen.* 19: 20. ELIEZER, *Gen.* 24: 12. JACOB, *Gen.* 32: 9–12. GIDEON, *Judges*

6: 22, 36, 39. HANNAH, 1 *Sam.*
1: 10. DAVID, 2 *Sam.* 7: 18–29.
HEZEKIAH, 2 *Kings* 20: 2.
ISAIAH, 2 *Kings* 20: 11. MANAS-
SEH, 2 *Chron.* 33: 18, 19. EZRA,
Ezra 9: 5, 6. NEHEMIAH, *Neh.*
2: 4. JEREMIAH, *Jer.* 32: 16–25.
DANIEL, *Dan.* 9: 3, 17. JONAH,
Jonah 2: 1. HABAKKUK, *Hab.*
1: 2. ANNA, *Luke* 2: 37. PAUL,
Acts 9: 11. PETER, *Acts* 9: 40.
Acts 10: 9. CORNELIUS, *Acts*
10: 30.

PRAYER, SOCIAL AND FAMILY

Promise of answers to. *Matt.*
18: 19.
Christ promises to be present
at. *Matt.* 18: 20.
Punishment for neglecting.
Jer. 10: 25.
Exemplified. ABRAM, *Gen.* 12:
5, 8. JACOB, *Gen.* 35: 2, 3, 7.
JOSHUA, *Joshua* 24: 15. DAVID,
2 *Sam.* 6: 20. JOB, *Job* 1: 5.
THE DISCIPLES, *Acts* 1: 13, 14.
CORNELIUS, *Acts* 10: 2. PAUL
AND SILAS, *Acts* 16: 25. PAUL,
etc., *Acts* 20: 36. *Acts* 21: 5.

PRAYER, PUBLIC

Acceptable to God. *Isa.* 56: 7.
God promises to hear. 2
Chron. 7: 14, 16.
God promises to bless in.
Exod. 20: 24.
Christ
Sanctifies by his presence.
Matt. 18: 20.
Attended. *Matt.* 12: 9. *Luke*
4: 16.
Promises answers to. *Matt.*
18: 19.
Instituted form of. *Luke* 11: 2.
Should not be made in an un-

known tongue. 1 *Cor.* 14: 14
–16.
Saints delight in. *Ps.* 42: 4. *Ps.*
122: 1.
Exhortation to. *Heb.* 10: 25.
Urge others to join in. *Ps.* 95:
6. *Zech.* 8: 21.
Exemplified. JOSHUA, etc.,
Joshua 7: 6–9. DAVID, 1 *Chron.*
29: 10–19. SOLOMON, 2 *Chron.*
6th chap. JEHOSHAPHAT, etc., 2
Chron. 20: 5–13. JESHUA, etc.,
Neh. 9th chap. JEWS, *Luke* 1:
10. PRIMITIVE CHRISTIANS, *Acts*
2: 46. *Acts* 4: 24. *Acts* 12: 5,
12. PETER, etc., *Acts* 3: 1.
TEACHERS AND PROPHETS AT
ANTIOCH, *Acts* 13: 3. PAUL, etc.,
Acts 16: 16.

PRAYER, INTERCESSORY

Christ set an example of. *Luke*
22: 32. *Luke* 23: 34. *John* 17:
9–24.
Commanded. 1 *Tim.* 2: 1. *Jas.*
5: 14, 16.
Should be offered up for
Kings. 1 *Tim.* 2: 2.
All in authority. 1 *Tim.* 2:
2.
Ministers. 2 *Cor.* 1: 11.
Phil. 1: 19.
The Church. *Ps.* 122: 6. *Isa.*
62: 6, 7.
All saints. *Eph.* 6: 18.
All men. 1 *Tim.* 2: 1.
Masters. *Gen.* 24: 12–14.
Servants. *Luke* 7: 2, 3.
Children. *Gen.* 17: 18. *Matt.*
15: 22.
Friends. *Job* 42: 8.
Fellow-countrymen. *Rom.*
10: 1.
The sick. *Jas.* 5: 14.
Persecutors. *Matt.* 5: 44.

Enemies among whom we dwell. *Jer.* 29: 7.

Those who envy us. *Num.* 12: 13.

Those who forsake us. 2 *Tim.* 4: 16.

Those who murmur against God. *Num.* 11: 1, 2. *Num.* 14: 13–19.

By ministers for their people. *Eph.* 1: 16. *Eph.* 3: 14–19. *Phil.* 1: 4.

Encouragement to. *Jas.* 5: 16. 1 *John* 5: 16.

Beneficial to the offerer. *Job* 42: 10.

Sin of neglecting. 1 *Sam.* 12: 23.

Seek an interest in. 1 *Sam.* 12: 19. *Heb.* 13: 18.

Unavailing for the obstinately-impenitent. *Jer.* 7: 13–16. *Jer.* 14: 10, 11.

Exemplified. ABRAHAM, *Gen.* 18: 23–32. ABRAHAM'S SERVANT, *Gen.* 24: 12–14. MOSES, *Exod.* 8: 12. *Exod.* 32: 11–13. SAMUEL, 1 *Sam.* 7: 5. SOLOMON, 1 *Kings* 8: 30–36. ELISHA, 2 *Kings* 4: 33. HEZEKIAH, 2 *Chron.* 30: 18. ISAIAH, 2 *Chron.* 32: 20. NEHEMIAH, *Neh.* 1: 4–11. DAVID, *Ps.* 25: 22. EZEKIEL, *Ezek.* 9: 8. DANIEL, *Dan.* 9: 3–19. STEPHEN, *Acts* 7: 60. PETER AND JOHN, *Acts* 8: 15. CHURCH OF JERUSALEM, *Acts* 12: 5. PAUL, *Col.* 1: 9–12. 2 *Thess.* 1: 11. EPAPHRAS, *Col.* 4: 12. PHILEMON, *Philem.* 22.

PRAYER, ANSWERS TO

God gives. *Ps.* 99: 6. *Ps.* 118: 5. *Ps.* 138: 3.

Christ gives. *John* 4: 10, 14. *John* 14: 14.

Christ received. *John* 11: 42. *Heb.* 5: 7.

Granted

Through the grace of God. *Isa.* 30: 19.

Sometimes immediately. *Isa.* 65: 24. *Dan.* 9: 21, 23. *Dan.* 10: 12.

Sometimes after delay. *Luke* 18: 7.

Sometimes differently from our desire. 2 *Cor.* 12: 8, 9.

Beyond expectation. *Jer.* 33: 3. *Eph.* 3: 20.

Promised. *Isa.* 58: 9. *Jer.* 29: 12. *Matt.* 7: 7.

Promised especially in times of trouble. *Ps.* 50: 15. *Ps.* 91: 15.

Received by those who

Seek God. *Ps.* 34: 4.

Seek God with all the heart. *Jer.* 29: 12, 13.

Wait upon God. *Ps.* 40: 1.

Return to God. 2 *Chron.* 7: 14. *Job* 22, 23, 27.

Ask in faith. *Matt.* 21: 22. *Jas.* 5: 15.

Ask in the name of Christ. *John* 14: 13.

Ask according to God's will. 1 *John* 5: 14.

Call upon God in truth. *Ps.* 145: 18.

Fear God. *Ps.* 145: 19.

Set their love upon God. *Ps.* 91: 14, 15.

Keep God's commandments. 1 *John* 3: 22.

Call upon God under oppression. *Isa.* 19: 20.

Call upon God under affliction. *Ps.* 18: 6. *Ps.* 106: 44. *Isa.* 30: 19, 20.

Abide in Christ. *John* 15: 7.

Humble themselves. 2 *Chron.* 7: 14, *Ps.* 9: 12.

Are righteous. *Ps.* 34: 15. *Jas.* 5: 16.

Are poor and needy. *Isa.* 41: 17.

Saints

Are assured of. 1 *John* 5: 15.

Love God for. *Ps.* 116: 1.

Bless God for. *Ps.* 66: 20.

Praise God for. *Ps.* 116: 17. *Ps.* 118: 21.

A motive for continued prayer. *Ps.* 116: 2.

Denied to those who

Ask amiss. *Jas.* 4: 3.

Regard iniquity in the heart. *Ps.* 66: 18.

Live in sin. *Isa.* 59: 2. *John* 9: 31.

Offer unworthy service to God. *Mal.* 1: 7–9.

Forsake God. *Jer.* 14: 10, 12.

Reject the call of God. *Prov.* 1: 24, 25, 28.

Hear not the law. *Prov.* 28: 9. *Zech.* 7: 11–13.

Are deaf to the cry of the poor. *Prov.* 21: 13.

Are blood-shedders. *Isa.* 1: 15. *Isa.* 59: 3.

Are idolaters. *Jer.* 11: 11–14. *Ezek.* 8: 15–18.

Are wavering. *Jas.* 1: 6, 7.

Are hypocrites. *Job* 27: 8, 9.

Are proud. *Job* 35: 12, 13.

Are self-righteous. *Luke* 18: 11, 12, 14.

Are the enemies of saints. *Ps.* 18: 40, 41.

Cruelly oppress saints. *Mic.* 3: 2–4.

Exemplified. ABRAHAM, *Gen.* 17: 20. LOT, *Gen.* 19: 19–21. ABRAHAM'S SERVANT, *Gen.* 24: 15–27. JACOB, *Gen.* 32: 24–30. ISRAELITES, *Exod.* 2: 23, 24. MOSES, *Exod.* 17: 4–6, 11–13. *Exod.* 32: 11–14. SAMSON, *Judges* 15: 18, 19, HANNAH, 1 *Sam.* 1: 27. SAMUEL, 1 *Sam.* 7: 9. SOLOMON, 1 *Kings* 3: 9, 12. MAN OF GOD, 1 *Kings* 13: 6. ELIJAH, 1 *Kings* 18: 36–38. *Jas.* 5: 17, 18. ELISHA, 2 *Kings* 4: 33–35. JEHOAHAZ, 2 *Kings* 13: 4. HEZEKIAH, 2 *Kings* 19: 20. JABEZ, 1 *Chron.* 4: 10. ASA, 2 *Chron.* 14: 11, 12. JEHOSHAPHAT, 2 *Chron.* 20: 6–17. MANASSEH, 2 *Chron.* 33: 13, 19. EZRA, etc., *Ezra* 8: 21–23. NEHEMIAH, *Neh.* 4: 9, 15. JOB, *Job* 42: 10. DAVID, *Ps.* 18: 6. JEREMIAH, *Lam.* 3: 55, 56. DANIEL, *Dan.* 9: 20–23. JONAH, *Jonah* 2: 2, 10. ZACHARIAS, *Luke* 1: 13. BLIND MAN, *Luke* 18: 38, 41–43. THIEF ON THE CROSS, *Luke* 23: 42, 43. APOSTLES, *Acts* 4: 29–31. CORNELIUS, *Acts* 10: 4, 31. PRIMITIVE CHRISTIANS, *Acts* 12: 5, 7. PAUL AND SILAS, *Acts* 16: 25, 26. PAUL, *Acts* 28: 8.

Refusal of, exemplified. SAUL, 1 *Sam.* 28: 15. ELDERS OF ISRAEL, *Ezek.* 20: 3. PHARISEES, *Matt.* 23: 14.

PRECIOUSNESS OF CHRIST

To God. *Matt.* 3: 17. 1 *Pet.* 2: 4.

To Saints. *Song of Sol.* 5: 10. *Phil.* 3: 8. 1 *Pet.* 2: 7.

On account of his

Goodness and beauty. *Zech.* 9: 17.

Excellence and grace. *Ps.* 45: 2.

Name. *Song of Sol.* 1: 3. *Heb.* 1: 4.

Atonement. 1 *Pet.* 1: 19, with *Heb.* 12: 24.

Words. *John* 6: 68.

Promises. 2 *Pet.* 1: 4.

Care and tenderness. *Isa.* 40: 11.

As the corner-stone of the Church. *Isa.* 28: 16, with 1 *Pet.* 2: 6.

As the source of all grace. *John* 1: 14. *Col.* 1: 19.

Unsearchable. *Eph.* 3: 8.

Illustrated. *Song of Sol.* 2: 3. *Song of Sol.* 5: 10–16. *Matt.* 13: 44–46.

PRESUMPTION

A characteristic of the wicked. 2 *Pet.* 2: 10.

A characteristic of Antichrist. 2 *Thess.* 2: 4.

Exhibited in

Opposing God. *Job* 15: 25, 26.

Wilful commission of sin. *Rom.* 1: 32.

Self-righteousness. *Hos.* 12: 8. *Rev.* 3: 17.

Spiritual pride. *Isa.* 65: 5. *Luke* 18: 11.

Esteeming our own ways right. *Prov.* 12: 15.

Seeking precedence. *Luke* 14: 7–11.

Planning for futurity. *Luke* 12: 18. *Jas.* 4: 13.

Pretending to prophesy. *Deut.* 18: 22.

Pray to be kept from sins of. *Ps.* 19: 13.

Saints avoid. *Ps.* 131: 1.

Punishment for. *Num.* 15: 30. *Rev.* 18: 7, 8.

Exemplified. BUILDERS OF BABEL, *Gen.* 11: 4. ISRAELITES, *Num.* 14: 44. KORAH, etc., *Num.* 16: 3, 7. MEN OF BETHSHEMESH, 1 *Sam.* 6: 19. UZZAH, 2 *Sam.* 6: 6. JEROBOAM, 1 *Kings* 13: 4. BEN-HADAD, 1 *Kings* 20: 10. UZZIAH, 2 *Chron.* 26: 16. SENNACHERIB, 2 *Chron.* 32: 13, 14. THEUDAS, *Acts* 5: 36. SONS OF SCEVA, *Acts* 19: 13, 14. DIOTREPHES, 3 *John* 9.

PRIDE

Is sin. *Prov.* 21: 4.

Hateful to God. *Prov.* 6: 16, 17. *Prov.* 16: 5.

Hateful to Christ. *Prov.* 8: 12, 13.

Often originates in

Self-righteousness. *Luke* 18: 11, 12.

Religious privileges. *Zeph.* 3: 11.

Unsanctified knowledge. 1 *Cor.* 8: 1.

Inexperience. 1 *Tim.* 3: 6.

Possession of power. *Lev.* 26: 19. *Ezek.* 30: 6.

Possession of wealth. 2 *Kings* 20: 13.

Forbidden. 1 *Sam.* 2: 3. *Rom.* 12: 3, 16.

Defiles a man. *Mark* 7: 20, 22.

Hardens the mind. *Dan.* 5: 20.

Saints

Give not way to. *Ps.* 131: 1.

Respect not, in others. *Ps.* 40: 4.

Mourn over, in others. *Jer.* 13: 17.

Hate, in others. *Ps.* 101: 5.

A hindrance to seeking God. *Ps.* 10: 4. *Hos.* 7: 10.

A hindrance to improvement. *Prov.* 26: 12.

A characteristic of

The devil. 1 *Tim.* 3: 6. *Ezek.* 28: 14–17.

The world. 1 *John* 2: 16.

False teachers. 1 *Tim.* 6: 3, 4.

The wicked. *Hab.* 2: 4, 5. *Rom.* 1: 30.

Comes from the heart. *Mark* 7: 21–23.

The wicked encompassed with. *Ps.* 73: 6.

Leads men to

Contempt and rejection of God's word and ministers. *Jer.* 43: 2.

A persecuting spirit. *Ps.* 10: 2.

Wrath. *Prov.* 21: 24.

Contention. *Prov.* 13: 10. *Prov.* 28: 25.

Self-deception. *Jer.* 49: 16. *Obad.* 3.

Exhortation against. *Jer.* 13: 15.

Is followed by

Shame. *Prov.* 11: 2.

Debasement. *Prov.* 29: 23. *Isa.* 28: 3.

Destruction. *Prov.* 16: 18. *Prov.* 18: 12.

Shall abound in the last days. *2 Tim.* 3: 2.

Woe-to. *Isa.* 28: 1, 3.

They who are guilty of, shall be

Resisted. *Jas.* 4: 6.

Brought into contempt. *Isa.* 23: 9.

Recompensed. *Ps.* 31: 23.

Marred. *Jer.* 13: 9.

Subdued. *Exod.* 18: 11. *Isa.* 13: 11.

Brought low. *Ps.* 18: 27. *Isa.* 2: 12.

Abased. *Dan.* 4: 37, with *Matt.* 23: 12.

Scattered. *Luke* 1: 51.

Punished. *Zeph.* 2: 10, 11. *Mal.* 4: 1.

Exemplified. AHITHOPHEL, *2 Sam.* 17: 23. HEZEKIAH, *2 Chron.* 32: 25. PHARAOH, *Neh.* 9: 10. HAMAN, *Esther* 3: 5. MOAB, *Isa.* 16: 6. TYRE, *Isa.* 23: 9. ISRAEL, *Isa.* 28: 1. HOS. 5: 5, 9. JUDAH, *Jer.* 13: 9. BABYLON, *Jer.* 50: 29, 32. ASSYRIA, *Ezek.* 31: 3, 10. TYRE, *Ezek.* 28. NEBUCHADNEZZAR, *Dan.* 4: 30. *Dan.* 5: 20. BELSHAZZAR, *Dan.* 5: 22, 23. EDOM, *Obad.* 3. SCRIBES, *Mark* 12: 38, 39. HEROD, *Acts* 12: 21–23. LAODICEANS, *Rev.* 3: 17.

PRIVILEGES OF SAINTS

Abiding in Christ. *John* 15: 4, 5.

Partaking of the Divine nature. *2 Pet.* 1: 4.

Access to God by Christ. *Eph.* 3: 12.

Being of the household of God. *Eph.* 2: 19.

Membership with the Church of the firstborn. *Heb.* 12: 23.

Having

Christ for their Shepherd. *Isa.* 40: 11, with *John* 10: 14, 16.

Christ for their Intercessor. *Rom.* 8: 34. *Heb.* 7: 25. 1 *John* 2: 1.

The promises of God. *2 Cor.* 7: 1. *2 Pet.* 1: 4.

The possession of all things. 1 *Cor.* 3: 21, 22.

All things working together for their good. *Rom.* 8: 28. *2 Cor.* 4: 15–17.

Their names written in the book of life. *Rev.* 13: 8. *Rev.* 20: 15.

Having God for their

King. *Ps.* 5: 2. *Ps.* 44: 4. *Isa.* 44: 6.

Glory. *Ps.* 3: 3. *Isa.* 60: 19.

Salvation. *Ps.* 18: 2. *Ps.* 27: 1.

Father. *Deut.* 32: 6. *Isa.* 64: 8.

Redeemer. *Ps.* 19: 14. *Isa.* 43: 14.

Friend. 2 *Chron.* 20: 7, with *Jas.* 2: 23.

Helper. *Ps.* 33: 20. *Heb.* 13: 6.

Keeper. *Ps.* 121: 4, 5.

Deliverer. 2 *Sam.* 22: 2. *Ps.* 18: 2.

Strength. *Ps.* 18: 2. *Ps.* 46: 1.

Refuge. *Ps.* 46: 1, 11. *Isa.* 25: 4.

Shield. *Gen.* 15: 1. *Ps.* 84: 11.

Tower. 2 *Sam.* 22: 3. *Ps.* 61: 3.

Light. *Ps.* 27: 1. *Isa.* 60: 19.

Guide. *Ps.* 48: 14. *Isa.* 58: 11.

Law-giver. *Neh.* 9: 13, 14. *Isa.* 33: 22.

Habitation. *Ps.* 90: 1. *Ps.* 91: 9.

Portion. *Ps.* 73: 26. *Lam.* 3: 24.

Union in God and Christ. *John* 17: 21.

Committing themselves to God. *Ps.* 31: 5. *Acts* 7: 59. 2 *Tim.* 1: 12.

Calling upon God in trouble. *Ps.* 50: 15.

Suffering for Christ. *Acts* 5: 41. *Phil.* 1: 29.

Profiting by chastisement. *Heb.* 12: 10, 11.

Pleading the covenant. *Jer.* 14: 21.

Being secure during public calamities. *Job* 5: 22, 23. *Ps.* 91: 5–7.

Interceding for others. *Gen.* 18: 23–33. *Isa.* 62: 7. *Jas.* 5: 16.

PROCRASTINATION

Condemned by Christ. *Luke* 9: 49–62.

Saints avoid. *Ps.* 27: 8. *Ps.* 119: 60.

To be avoided in

Hearkening to God. *Ps.* 95: 7, 8, with *Heb.* 3: 7, 8.

Seeking God. *Isa.* 55: 6.

Glorifying God. *Jer.* 13: 16.

Keeping God's commandments. *Ps.* 119: 60.

Making offerings to God. *Exod.* 22: 29.

Performance of vows. *Deut.* 23: 21. *Eccles.* 4: 4.

Motives for avoiding;

The present the accepted time. 2 *Cor.* 6: 2.

The present the best time. *Eccles.* 12: 1.

The uncertainty of life. *Prov.* 27: 1.

Danger of, illustrated. *Matt.* 5: 25. *Luke* 12: 25.

Exemplified. LOT, *Gen.* 19: 16. FELIX, *Acts* 24: 25. AGRIPPA, *Acts* 26: 28.

PROMISES OF GOD, THE

Contained in the scriptures. *Rom.* 1: 2.

Made in Christ. *Eph.* 3: 6. 2 *Tim.* 1: 1.

Made to

Christ. *Gal.* 3: 16, 19.

Abraham. *Gen.* 12: 3, 7, with *Gal.* 3: 16.

Isaac. *Gen.* 26: 3, 4.

Jacob. *Gen.* 28: 14.

David. 2 *Sam.* 7: 12. *Ps.* 89: 35, 36.

The Fathers. *Acts* 13: 32. *Acts* 26: 6, 7.

All who are called of God. *Acts* 2: 39.

Those who love him. *Jas.* 1: 12. *Jas.* 2: 5.

Confirmed by an oath. *Ps.* 89: 3, 4. *Heb.* 6: 17.

The covenant established upon. *Heb.* 8: 6.

God is faithful to. *Titus* 1: 2. *Heb.* 10: 23.

God remembers. *Ps.* 105: 42. *Luke* 1: 54, 55.

Are

Good. 1 *Kings* 8: 56.

Holy. *Ps.* 105: 42.

Exceeding great and precious. 2 *Pet.* 1: 4.

Confirmed in Christ. *Rom.* 15: 8.

Yea and amen in Christ. 2 *Cor.* 1: 20.

Fulfilled in Christ. 2 *Sam.* 7: 12, with ·*Acts* 13: 23. *Luke* 1: 69–73.

Through the righteousness of faith. *Rom.* 4: 13, 16.

Obtained through faith. *Heb.* 11: 33.

Given to those who believe. *Gal.* 3: 22.

Inherited through faith and patience. *Heb.* 6: 12, 15. *Heb.* 10: 36.

Performed in due season. *Jer.* 33: 14. *Acts* 7: 17. *Gal.* 4: 4.

Not one shall fail. *Joshua* 23: 41. 1 *Kings* 8: 56.

The law not against. *Gal.* 3: 21.

The law could not disannul. *Gal.* 3: 17.

Subjects of;

Christ. 2 *Sam.* 7: 12, 13, with *Acts* 13: 22, 23.

The Holy Ghost. *Acts* 2: 33. *Eph.* 1: 13.

The gospel. *Rom.* 1: 1, 2.

Life in Christ. 2 *Tim.* 1: 1.

A crown of life. *Jas.* 1: 12.

Eternal life. *Titus* 1: 2. 1 *John* 2: 25.

The life that now is. 1 *Tim.* 4: 8.

Adoption. 2 *Cor.* 6: 18, with 2 *Cor.* 7: 1.

Preservation in affliction. *Isa.* 43: 2.

Blessing. *Deut.* 1: 11.

Forgiveness of sins. *Isa.* 1: 18. *Heb.* 8: 12.

Putting the law into the heart. *Jer.* 31: 33, with *Heb.* 8: 10.

Second coming of Christ. 2 *Pet.* 3: 4.

New heavens and earth. 2 *Pet.* 3: 13.

Entering into rest. *Joshua* 22: 4, with *Heb.* 4: 1.

Should lead to perfecting holiness. 2 *Cor.* 7: 1.

The inheritance of the saints is of. *Rom.* 4: 13. *Gal.* 3: 18.

Saints

Children of. *Rom.* 9: 8. *Gal.* 4: 28.

Heirs of. *Gal.* 3: 29. *Heb.* 6: 17. *Heb.* 11: 9.

Stagger not at. *Rom.* 4: 20.

Have implicit confidence in. *Heb.* 11: 11.

Expect the performance of. *Luke* 1: 38, 45. 2 *Pet.* 3: 13.

Sometimes, through infirmity, tempted to doubt. *Ps.* 77: 8, 10.

Plead, in prayer. *Gen.* 32: 9, 12. 1 *Chron.* 17: 23, 26. *Isa.* 43: 26.

Should wait for the performance of. *Acts* 1: 4.

Gentiles shall be partakers of. *Eph.* 3: 6.

Man, by nature, has no interest in. *Eph.* 2: 12.

Scoffers despise. 2 *Pet.* 3: 3, 4.

Fear, lest ye come short of. *Heb.* 4: 1.

PROPHECIES RESPECTING CHRIST

As the Son of God. *Ps.* 2: 7. Fulfilled, *Luke* 1: 32, 35.

As the seed of the woman. *Gen.* 3: 15. Fulfilled, *Gal.* 4: 4.

As the seed of Abraham. *Gen.* 17: 7. *Gen.* 22: 18. Fulfilled, *Gal.* 3: 16.

As the seed of Isaac. *Gen.* 21: 12. Fulfilled *Heb.* 11: 17–19.

As the seed of David. *Ps.* 132: 11. *Jer.* 23: 5. Fulfilled, *Acts* 13: 23. *Rom.* 1: 3.

His coming at a set time. *Gen.* 49: 10. *Dan.* 9: 24, 25. Fulfilled, *Luke* 2: 1.

His being born of a virgin. *Isa.* 7: 14. Fulfilled, *Matt.* 1: 18. *Luke* 2: 7. *Gal.* 4: 4.

His being called Immanuel. *Isa.* 7: 14. Fulfilled, *Matt.* 1: 22, 23.

His being born in Bethlehem of Judea. *Mic.* 5: 2. Fulfilled, *Matt.* 2: 1. *Luke* 2: 4–6.

Great persons coming to adore him. *Ps.* 72: 10. Fulfilled, *Matt.* 2: 1–11.

The slaying of the children at Bethlehem. *Jer.* 31: 15. Fulfilled, *Matt.* 2: 16–18.

His being called out of Egypt. *Hos.* 11: 1. Fulfilled, *Matt.* 2: 15.

His being preceded by John the Baptist. *Isa.* 40: 3. *Mal.* 3: 1. Fulfilled, *Matt.* 3: 1, 3. *Luke* 1: 17.

His being anointed with the Spirit. *Ps.* 45: 7. *Isa.* 11: 2.

Isa. 61: 1. Fulfilled, *Matt.* 3: 16. *John* 3: 34. *Acts* 10: 38.

His being a Prophet like unto Moses. *Deut.* 18: 15–18. Fulfilled, *Acts* 3: 20–22.

His being a Priest after the order of Melchizedek. *Ps.* 110: 4. *Zech.* 6: 13. Fulfilled, *Heb.* 5: 5, 6.

His entering on his public ministry. *Isa.* 61: 1, 2. Fulfilled, *Luke* 4: 16–21, 43.

His ministry commencing in Galilee. *Isa.* 9: 1, 2. Fulfilled, *Matt.* 4: 12–16, 23.

His entering publicly into Jerusalem. *Zech.* 9: 9. Fulfilled, *Matt.* 21: 1–5.

His coming into the temple. *Hag.* 2: 7, 9. *Mal.* 3: 1. Fulfilled, *Matt.* 21: 12. *Luke* 2: 27–32. *John* 2: 13–16.

His poverty. *Isa.* 53: 2. Fulfilled, *Mark* 6: 3. *Luke* 9: 58.

His meekness and want of ostentation. *Isa.* 42: 2. Fulfilled, *Matt.* 12: 15, 16, 19.

His tenderness and compassion. *Isa.* 40: 11. *Isa.* 42: 3. Fulfilled, *Matt.* 12: 15, 20. *Heb.* 4: 15.

His being without guile. *Isa.* 53: 9. Fulfilled, 1 *Pet.* 2: 22.

His zeal. *Ps.* 69: 9. Fulfilled, *John* 2: 17.

His preaching by parables. *Ps.* 78: 2. Fulfilled, *Matt.* 13: 34, 35.

His working miracles. *Isa.* 35: 5, 6. Fulfilled, *Matt.* 11: 4–6. *John* 11: 47.

His bearing reproach. *Ps.* 22: 6. *Ps.* 69: 7, 9, 20. Fulfilled, *Rom.* 15: 3.

His being rejected by his brethren. *Ps.* 69: 8. *Isa.* 53: 3. Fulfilled, *John* 1: 11. *John* 7: 5.

His being a stone of stumbling to the Jews. *Isa.* 8: 14. Fulfilled, *Rom.* 9: 32. 1 *Pet.* 2: 8.

His being hated by the Jews. *Ps.* 69: 4. *Isa.* 49: 7. Fulfilled, *John* 15: 24, 25.

His being rejected by the Jewish rulers. *Ps.* 118: 22. Fulfilled, *Matt.* 21: 42. *John* 7: 48.

That Jews and Gentiles should combine against him. *Ps.* 2: 1, 2. Fulfilled, *Luke* 23: 12. *Acts* 4: 27.

His being betrayed by a friend. *Ps.* 41: 9. *Ps.* 55: 12–14. Fulfilled, *John* 13: 18, 21.

His disciples forsaking him. *Zech.* 13: 7. Fulfilled, *Matt.* 26: 31, 56.

His being sold for thirty pieces of silver. *Zech.* 11: 12. Fulfilled, *Matt.* 26: 15.

His price being given for the potter's field. *Zech.* 11: 13. Fulfilled, *Matt.* 27: 7.

The intensity of his sufferings. *Ps.* 22: 14, 15. Fulfilled, *Luke* 22: 42, 44.

His sufferings being for others. *Isa.* 53: 4–6, 12. *Dan.* 9: 26. Fulfilled, *Matt.* 20: 28.

His patience and silence under sufferings. *Isa.* 53: 7. Fulfilled, *Matt.* 26: 63. *Matt.* 27: 12–14.

His being smitten on the cheek. *Mic.* 5: 1. Fulfilled, *Matt.* 27: 30.

His visage being marred. *Isa.* 52: 14. *Isa.* 53: 3. Fulfilled, *John* 19: 5.

His being spitted on and scourged. *Isa.* 50: 6. Fulfilled, *Mark* 14: 65. *John* 19: 1.

His hands and feet being nailed to the cross. *Ps.* 22: 16. Fulfilled, *John* 19: 18. *John* 20: 25.

His being forsaken by God. *Ps.* 22: 1. Fulfilled, *Matt.* 27: 46.

His being mocked. *Ps.* 22: 7, 8. Fulfilled, *Matt.* 27: 39–44.

Gall and vinegar being given him to drink. *Ps.* 69: 21. Fulfilled, *Matt.* 27: 34.

His garments being parted and lots cast for his vesture. *Ps.* 22: 18. Fulfilled, *Matt.* 27: 35.

His being numbered with the transgressors. *Isa.* 53: 12. Fulfilled, *Mark* 15: 28.

His intercession for his murderers. *Isa.* 53: 12. Fulfilled, *Luke* 23: 34.

His death. *Isa.* 53: 12. Fulfilled, *Matt.* 27: 50.

That a bone of him should not be broken. *Exod.* 12: 46. *Ps.* 34: 20. Fulfilled, *John* 19: 33, 36.

His being pierced. *Zech.* 12: 10. Fulfilled, *John* 19: 34, 37.

His being buried with the rich. *Isa.* 53: 9. Fulfilled, *Matt.* 27: 57–60.

His flesh not seeing corruption. *Ps.* 16: 10. Fulfilled, *Acts* 2: 31.

His resurrection. *Ps.* 16: 10. *Isa.* 26: 19. Fulfilled, *Luke* 24: 6, 31, 34.

His ascension. *Ps.* 68: 18. Fulfilled, *Luke* 24: 51. *Acts* 1: 9.

His sitting on the right hand of God. *Ps.* 110: 1. Fulfilled, *Heb.* 1: 3.

His exercising the priestly office in heaven. *Zech.* 6: 13. Fulfilled, *Rom.* 8: 34.

His being the chief corner-stone of the Church. *Isa.* 28: 16. Fulfilled, 1 *Pet.* 2: 6, 7.

His being King in Zion. *Ps.* 2: 6. Fulfilled, *Luke* 1: 32. *John* 18: 33–37.

The conversion of the Gentiles to him. *Isa.* 10: 10. *Isa.* 42: 1. Fulfilled, *Matt.* 12: 17, 21. *John* 10: 16. *Acts* 10: 45, 47.

His righteous government. *Ps.* 45: 6, 7. Fulfilled, *John* 5: 30. *Rev.* 19: 11.

His universal dominion. *Ps.* 72: 8. *Dan.* 7: 14. Fulfilled, *Phil.* 2: 9, 11.

The perpetuity of his kingdom. *Isa.* 9: 7. *Dan.* 7: 14. Fulfilled, *Luke* 1: 32, 33.

PROPHECY

Is the foretelling of future events. *Gen.* 49: 1. *Num.* 24: 14.

God is the Author of. *Isa.* 44: 7. *Isa.* 45: 21.

God gives, through Christ. *Rev.* 1: 1.

A gift of Christ. *Eph.* 4: 11. *Rev.* 11: 3.

A gift of the Holy Ghost. 1 *Cor.* 12: 10.

Came not by the will of man. 2 *Pet.* 1: 21.

Given from the beginning. *Luke* 1: 70.

Is a sure word. 2 *Pet.* 1: 19.

They who uttered,

Raised up by God. *Amos* 2: 11.

Ordained by God. 1 *Sam.* 3: 20. *Jer.* 1: 5.

Sent by God. 2 *Chron.* 36: 15. *Jer.* 7: 25.

Sent by Christ. *Matt.* 23: 34.

Filled with the Holy Ghost. *Luke* 1: 67.

Moved by the Holy Ghost. 2 *Pet.* 1: 21.

Spake by the Holy Ghost. *Acts* 1: 16. *Acts* 11: 28. *Acts* 28: 25.

Spake in the name of the Lord. 2 *Chron.* 33: 18. *Jas.* 5: 10.

Spake with authority. 1 *Kings* 17: 1.

God accomplishes. *Isa.* 44: 26. *Acts* 3: 18.

Christ the great subject of. *Acts* 3: 22–24. *Acts* 10: 43. 1 *Pet.* 1: 10, 11.

Fulfilled respecting Christ. *Luke* 24: 44.

Gift of, promised. *Joel* 2: 28, with *Acts* 2: 16, 17.

Is for the benefit of after ages. 1 *Pet.* 1: 12.

Is as a light in a dark place. 2 *Pet.* 1: 19.

Is not of private interpretation. 2 *Pet.* 1: 20.

Despise not. 1 *Thess.* 5: 20.

Give heed to. 2 *Pet.* 1: 19.

Receive in faith. 2 *Chron.* 20: 20. *Luke* 24: 25.

Blessedness of reading, hearing, and keeping. *Rev.* 1: 3. *Rev.* 22: 7.

Guilt of pretending to the gift of. *Jer.* 14: 14. *Jer.* 23: 13, 14. *Ezek.* 13: 2, 3.

Punishment for

Not giving ear to. *Neh.* 9: 30.

Adding to, or taking from. *Rev.* 22: 18, 19.

Pretending to the gift of. *Deut.* 18: 20. *Jer.* 14: 15. *Jer.* 23: 15.

Gift of, sometimes possessed by unconverted men. *Num.* 24: 2–9. 1 *Sam.* 19: 20, 23. *Matt.* 7: 22. *John* 11: 49–51. 1 *Cor.* 13: 2.

How tested. *Deut.* 13: 1–3. *Deut.* 18: 22.

PROPHETS

God spake of old by. *Hos.* 12: 10. *Heb.* 1: 1.

The messengers of God. 2 *Chron.* 36: 15. *Isa.* 44: 26.

The servants of God. *Jer.* 35: 15.

The watchmen of Israel. *Ezek.* 3: 17.

Were called

Men of God. 1 *Sam.* 9: 6.

Prophets of God. *Ezra* 5: 2.

Holy prophets. *Luke* 1: 70. *Rev.* 18: 20. *Rev.* 22: 6.

Holy men of God. 2 *Pet.* 1: 21.

Seers. 1 *Sam.* 9: 9.

Were esteemed as holy men. 2 *Kings* 4: 9.

Women sometimes endowed as. *Joel* 2: 28.

God communicated to,

His secret things. *Amos* 3: 7.

At sundry times and in divers ways. *Heb.* 1: 1.

By an audible voice. *Num.* 12: 8. 1 *Sam.* 3: 4–14.

By angels. *Dan.* 8: 15–26. *Rev.* 22: 8, 9.

By dreams and visions. *Num.* 12: 6. *Joel* 2: 28.

Were under the influence of the Holy Ghost while prophesying. *Luke* 1: 67. 2 *Pet.* 1: 21.

Spake in the name of the Lord. 2 *Chron.* 33: 18. *Ezra* 3: 11. *Jas.* 5: 10.

Frequently spake in parables and riddles. 2 *Sam.* 12: 1–6. *Isa.* 5: 1–7. *Ezek.* 17: 2–10.

Frequently in their actions, etc., were made signs to the people. *Isa.* 20: 2–4. *Jer.* 19: 1, 10, 11. *Jer.* 27: 2, 3. *Jer.* 43: 9. *Jer.* 51: 63. *Ezek.* 4: 1–13. *Ezek.* 5: 1–4. *Ezek.* 7: 23. *Ezek.* 12: 3–7. *Ezek.* 21: 6, 7. *Ezek.* 24: 1–24. *Hos.* 1: 2–9.

Frequently left without divine communications on account of sins of the people. 1 *Sam.* 28: 9. *Ezek.* 7: 26.

Were required

To be bold and undaunted. *Ezek.* 2: 6. *Ezek.* 3: 8, 9.

To be vigilant and faithful. *Ezek.* 3: 17–21.

To receive with attention all God's communications. *Ezek.* 3: 10.

Not to speak anything but what they received from God. *Deut.* 18: 20.

To declare everything that the Lord commanded. *Jer.* 26: 2.

Sometimes received divine communications and uttered predictions under great bodily and mental excitement. *Jer.* 23: 9. *Ezek.* 3: 14, 15. *Dan.* 7: 28. *Dan.* 10: 8. *Hab.* 3: 2, 16.

Sometimes uttered their predictions in verse. *Deut.* 32: 44. *Isa.* 5: 1.

Often accompanied by music while predicting. 1 *Sam.* 10: 5. 2 *Kings* 3: 15.

Often committed their predictions to writing. 2 *Chron.* 21: 12. *Jer.* 36: 2.

Writings of, read in the synagogues every Sabbath. *Luke* 4: 17. *Acts* 13: 15.

Ordinary

Numerous in Israel. 1 *Sam.* 10: 5. 1 *Kings* 18: 4.

Trained up and instructed in schools. 2 *Kings* 2: 3, 5, with 1 *Sam.* 19: 20.

The sacred bards of the Jews.

Exod. 15: 20, 21. 1 *Sam.* 10: 5, 10. 1 *Chron.* 25: 1.

Extraordinary

Specially raised up on occasions of emergency. 1 *Sam.* 3: 19–21. *Isa.* 6: 8, 9. *Jer.* 1: 5.

Often endued with miraculous power. *Exod.* 4: 1–4. 1 *Kings* 17: 23. 2 *Kings* 5: 3–8.

Frequently married men. 2 *Kings* 4: 1. *Ezek.* 24: 18.

Wore a coarse dress of haircloth. 2 *Kings* 1: 8. *Zech.* 13: 4. *Matt.* 3: 4. *Rev.* 11: 3.

Often led a wandering unsettled life. 1 *Kings* 18: 10–12. 1 *Kings* 19: 3, 8, 15. 2 *Kings* 4: 10.

Simple in their manner of life. *Matt.* 3: 4.

The historiographers of the Jewish nation. 1 *Chron.* 29: 29. 2 *Chron.* 9: 29.

The interpreters of dreams, etc. *Dan.* 1: 17.

Were consulted in all difficulties. 1 *Sam.* 9: 6. 1 *Sam.* 28: 15. 1 *Kings* 14: 2–4. 1 *Kings* 22: 7.

Presented with gifts by those who consulted them. 1 *Sam.* 9: 7, 8. 1 *Kings* 14: 3.

Sometimes thought it right to reject presents. 2 *Kings* 5: 15, 16.

Were sent to

Reprove the wicked and exhort to repentance. 2 *Kings* 17: 13. 2 *Chron.* 24: 19. *Jer.* 25: 4, 5.

Denounce the wickedness of kings. 1 *Sam.* 15: 10, 16–19. 2 *Sam.* 12: 7–12. 1 *Kings* 18: 18. 1 *Kings* 21: 17–22.

Exhort to faithfulness and constancy in God's service. 2 *Chron.* 15: 1, 2, 7.

Predict the coming, etc., of Christ. *Luke* 24: 44. *John* 1: 45. *Acts* 3: 24. *Acts* 10: 43.

Predict the downfall of nations. *Isa.* 15: 1. *Isa.* 17: 1, etc. *Jer.* 47th chap. to *Jer.* 51st chap.

Felt deeply on account of the calamities which they predicted. *Isa.* 16: 9–11. *Jer.* 9: 1–7.

Predictions of,

Frequently proclaimed at the gate of the Lord's house. *Jer.* 7: 2.

Proclaimed in the cities and streets. *Jer.* 11: 6.

Written on tables and fixed up in some public place. *Hab.* 2: 2.

Written on rolls and read to the people. *Isa.* 8: 1. *Jer.* 36: 2.

Were all fulfilled. 2 *Kings* 10: 10. *Isa.* 44: 26. *Acts* 3: 18. *Rev.* 10: 7.

Assisted the Jews in their great national undertakings. *Ezra* 5: 2.

Mentioned in scripture;

Enoch. *Gen.* 5: 21–24, with *Jude* 14.

Noah. *Gen.* 9: 25–27.

Jacob. *Gen.* 49: 1.

Aaron. *Exod.* 7: 1.

Moses. *Deut.* 18: 18.

Miriam. *Exod.* 15: 20.

Deborah. *Judges* 4: 4.

Prophet sent to Israel. *Judges* 6: 8.

Prophet sent to Eli. 1 *Sam.* 2: 27.

Samuel. 1 *Sam.* 3: 20.

David. *Ps.* 16: 8–11, with
Acts 2: 25, 30.

Nathan. 2 *Sam.* 7: 2. 2
Sam. 12: 1. ! *Kings* 1: 10.

Zadok. 2 *Sam.* 15: 27.

Gad. 2 *Sam.* 24: 11. 1
Chron. 29: 29.

Ahijah. 1 *Kings* 11: 29. 1
Kings 12: 15. 2 *Chron.* 9:
29.

Prophet of Judah. 1 *Kings*
13: 1.

Iddo. 2 *Chron.* 9: 29. 2
Chron. 12: 15.

Shemaiah. 1 *Kings* 12: 22.
2 *Chron.* 12: 7, 15.

Azariah the son of Oded. 2
Chron. 15: 2, 8.

Hanani. 2 *Chron.* 16: 7.

Jehu the son of Hanani. 1
Kings 16: 1, 7, 12.

Elijah. 1 *Kings* 17: 1.

Elisha. 1 *Kings* 19: 16.

Micaiah the son of Imlah. 1
Kings 22: 7, 8.

Jonah. 2 *Kings* 14: 25.
Jonah 1: 1. *Matt.* 12: 39.

Isaiah. 2 *Kings* 19: 2. 2
Chron. 26: 22. *Isa.* 1: 1.

Hosea. *Hos.* 1: 1.

Amos. *Amos.* 1: 1. *Amos* 7:
14, 15.

Micah. *Mic.* 1: 1.

Oded. 2 *Chron.* 28: 9.

Nahum. *Nahum* 1: 1.

Joel. *Joel* 1: 1. *Acts* 2: 16.

Zephaniah. *Zeph.* 1: 1.

Huldah. 2 *Kings* 22: 14.

Jeduthun. 2 *Chron.* 35: 15.

Jeremiah. 2 *Chron.* 36: 12,
21. *Jer.* 1: 1, 2.

Habakkuk. *Hab.* 1: 1.

Obadiah. *Obad.* 1.

Ezekiel. *Ezek.* 1: 3.

Daniel. *Dan.* 12: 11, with
Matt. 24: 15.

Haggai. *Ezra* 5: 1. *Ezra* 6:
14. *Hag.* 1: 1.

Zechariah son of Iddo. *Ezra*
5: 1. *Zech.* 1: 1.

Malachi. *Mal.* 1: 1.

Zacharias the father of John.
Luke 1: 67.

Anna. *Luke* 2: 36.

Agabus. *Acts* 11: 28. *Acts*
21: 10.

Daughters of Philip. *Acts*
21: 9.

Paul. 1 *Tim.* 4: 1.

Peter. 2 *Pet.* 2: 1, 2.

John. *Rev.* 1: 1.

One generally attached to the
king's household. 2 *Sam.*
24: 11. 2 *Chron.* 29: 25. 2
Chron. 35: 15.

The Jews

Require to hear and believe.
Deut. 18: 15, with 2 *Chron.*
20: 20.

Often tried to make them
speak smooth things. 1
Kings 22: 13. *Isa.* 30: 10.
Amos 2: 12.

Persecuted them. 2 *Chron.*
36: 16. *Matt.* 5: 12.

Often imprisoned them. 1
Kings 22: 27. *Jer.* 32: 2. *Jer.*
37: 15, 16.

Often put them to death. 1
Kings 18: 13. 1 *Kings* 19:
10. *Matt.* 23: 34–37.

Often left without, on account of sin. 1 *Sam.* 3: 1.
Ps. 74: 9. *Amos* 8: 11, 12.

Were mighty through faith.
Heb. 11: 32–40.

Great patience of, under suffering. *Jas.* 5: 10.

God avenged all injuries
done to. 2 *Kings* 9: 7. 1
Chron. 16: 21, 22. *Matt.* 23:
35–38. *Luke* 11: 50.

Christ predicted to exercise
the office of. *Deut.* 18: 15,
with *Acts* 3: 22.

Christ exercised the office of. *Matt.* 24th chap. *Mark* 10: 32–34.

PROSELYTES

Described. *Esther* 8: 17. *Isa.* 56: 3.

Required

To give up all heathen practices. *Ezra* 6: 21.

To give up all heathen associates. *Ruth* 1: 16. *Ruth* 2: 11. *Ps.* 45: 10. *Luke* 14: 26.

To be circumcised. *Gen.* 17: 13, with *Exod.* 12: 48.

To enter into convenant to serve the Lord. *Deut.* 29: 10–13, with *Neh.* 10: 28, 29.

To observe the law of Moses as Jews. *Exod.* 12: 49.

Unfaithfulness in, punished. *Ezek.* 14: 7.

From the Ammonites and Moabites restricted for ever from holding office in the congregation. *Deut.* 23: 3.

From the Egyptians and Edomites restricted to the third generation from holding office in the congregation. *Deut.* 23: 7, 8.

Were entitled to all privileges. *Exod.* 12: 48. *Isa.* 56: 3–7.

Went up to the feasts. *Acts* 2: 10. *Acts* 8: 27.

Pharisees, etc., zealous in making. *Matt.* 23: 15.

Many, embraced the gospel. *Acts* 6: 5. *Acts* 13: 43.

Latterly called devout Greeks. *John* 12: 20, with *Acts* 17: 4.

PROTECTION

God is able to afford. 1 *Pet.* 1: 5. *Jude* 24.

God is faithful to afford. 1 *Thess.* 5: 23, 24. 2 *Thess.* 3: 3.

Of God, is

Indispensable. *Ps.* 127: 1.

Seasonable. *Ps.* 46: 1.

Unfailing. *Deut.* 31: 6. *John* 1: 5.

Effectual. *John* 10: 28–30. 2 *Cor.* 12: 9.

Uninterrupted. *Ps.* 121: 3.

Encouraging. *Isa.* 41: 10. *Isa.* 50: 7.

Perpetual. *Ps.* 121: 8.

Often afforded through means inadequate in themselves. *Judges* 7: 7. 1 *Sam.* 17: 45, 50. 2 *Chron.* 14: 11.

Is afforded to

Those who hearken to God. *Prov.* 1: 33.

Returning sinners. *Job* 22: 23, 25.

The perfect in heart. 2 *Chron.* 16: 9.

The poor. *Ps.* 14: 6. *Ps.* 72: 12–14.

The oppressed. *Ps.* 9: 9.

The Church. *Ps.* 48: 3. *Zech.* 2: 4, 5.

Is vouchsafed to saints, in

Preserving them. *Ps.* 145: 20.

Strengthening them. 2 *Tim.* 4: 17.

Upholding them. *Ps.* 37: 17, 24. *Ps.* 63: 8.

Keeping their feet. 1 *Sam.* 2: 9. *Prov.* 3: 26.

Keeping them from evil. 2 *Thess.* 3: 3.

Keeping them from falling. *Jude* 24.

Keeping them in the way. *Exod.* 23: 20.

Keeping them from temptation. *Rev.* 3: 10.

Providing a refuge for them. *Prov.* 14: 26. *Isa.* 4: 6. *Isa.* 32: 2.

Defending them against their enemies. *Deut.* 20: 1–4. *Deut.* 33: 27. *Isa.* 59: 19.

Defeating the counsels of enemies. *Isa.* 8: 10.

Temptation. 1 *Cor.* 10: 13. 2 *Pet.* 2: 9.

Persecution. *Luke* 21: 18.

Calamities. *Ps.* 57: 1. *Ps.* 59: 16.

All dangers. *Ps.* 91: 3–7.

All places. *Gen.* 28: 15. 2 *Chron.* 16: 9.

Sleep. *Ps.* 3: 5. *Ps.* 4: 8. *Prov.* 3: 24.

Death. *Ps.* 23: 4.

Saints

Acknowledge God as their. *Ps.* 18: 2. *Ps.* 62: 2. *Ps.* 89: 18.

Pray for. *Ps.* 17: 5, 8. *Isa.* 51: 9.

Praise God for. *Ps.* 5: 11.

Withdrawn from the

Disobedient. *Lev.* 26: 14–17.

Backsliding. *Joshua* 23: 12, 13. *Judges* 10: 13.

Presumptuous. *Num.* 14: 40–45.

Unbelieving. *Isa.* 7: 9.

Obstinately impenitent. *Matt.* 23: 38.

Not to be found in

Idols. *Deut.* 32: 37–39. *Isa.* 46: 7.

Man. *Ps.* 146: 3. *Isa.* 30: 7.

Riches. *Prov.* 11: 4, 28. *Zeph.* 1: 18.

Hosts. *Joshua* 11: 4–8, with *Ps.* 33: 16.

Horses. *Ps.* 33: 17. *Prov.* 21: 31.

Illustrated. *Deut.* 32: 11. *Ps.* 125: 1, 2. *Prov.* 18: 10. *Isa.* 25: 4. *Isa.* 31: 5. *Luke* 13: 14.

Exemplified. ABRAHAM, *Gen.* 15: 1. JACOB, *Gen.* 48: 16. JOSEPH, *Gen.* 49: 23–25. ISRAEL, *Joshua* 24: 17. DAVID, *Ps.* 18: 1, 2. ELISHA, 2 *Kings* 6: 17. SHADRACH, etc., *Dan.* 3: 28. DANIEL, *Dan.* 6: 22. PETER, *Acts* 12: 4–7. PAUL, *Acts* 18: 10. *Acts* 26: 17.

PROVIDENCE OF GOD, THE

Is his care over his works. *Ps.* 145: 9.

Is exercised in

Preserving his creatures. *Neh.* 9: 6. *Ps.* 36: 6. *Matt.* 10: 29.

Providing for his creatures. *Ps.* 104: 27, 28. *Ps.* 136: 25. *Ps.* 147: 9. *Matt.* 6: 26.

The special preservation of saints. *Ps.* 37: 28. *Ps.* 91: 11. *Matt.* 10: 30.

Prospering saints. *Gen.* 24: 48, 56.

Protecting saints. *Ps.* 91: 4. *Ps.* 140: 7.

Delivering saints. *Ps.* 91: 3. *Isa.* 31: 5.

Leading saints. *Deut.* 8: 2, 15. *Isa.* 63: 12.

Bringing his words to pass. *Num.* 26: 65. *Joshua* 21: 45. *Luke* 21: 32, 33.

Ordering the ways of men. *Prov.* 16: 9. *Prov.* 19: 21. *Prov.* 20: 24.

Ordaining the conditions and circumstances of men. 1 *Sam.* 2: 7, 8. *Ps.* 75: 6, 7.

Determining the period of human life. *Ps.* 31: 15. *Ps.* 30: 5. *Acts* 17: 26.

Defeating wicked designs.

Exod. 15: 9–11. 2 *Sam.* 17: 14, 15. *Ps.* 33: 10.

Overruling wicked designs for good. *Gen.* 45: 5–7. *Gen.* 50: 20. *Phil.* 1: 12.

Preserving the course of nature. *Gen.* 8: 22. *Job* 26: 10. *Ps.* 104: 5–9.

Directing all events. *Joshua* 7: 14. 1 *Sam.* 6: 7–10, 12. *Prov.* 16: 33. *Isa.* 44: 7. *Acts* 1: 26.

Ruling the elements. *Job* 37: 9–13. *Isa.* 50: 2. *Jonah* 1: 4, 15. *Nahum* 1: 4.

Ordering the minutest matters. *Matt.* 10: 29, 30. *Luke* 21: 18.

Is righteous. *Ps.* 145: 17. *Dan.* 4: 37.

Is ever watchful. *Ps.* 121: 4. *Isa.* 27: 3.

Is all-pervading. *Ps.* 139: 1–5.

Sometimes dark and mysterious. *Ps.* 36: 6. *Ps.* 73: 16. *Ps.* 77: 19. *Rom.* 11: 33.

All things are ordered by,

For his glory. *Isa.* 63: 14.

For good to saints. *Rom.* 8: 28.

The wicked made to promote the designs of. *Isa.* 10: 5–12. *Acts* 3: 17, 18.

To be acknowledged

In prosperity. *Deut.* 8: 18. 1 *Chron.* 29: 12.

In adversity. *Job* 1: 21. *Ps.* 119: 75.

In public calamities. *Amos* 3: 6.

In our daily support. *Gen.* 48: 15.

In all things. *Prov.* 3: 6.

Cannot be defeated. 1 *Kings* 22: 30, 34. *Prov.* 21: 30.

Man's efforts are vain without. *Ps.* 127: 1, 2. *Prov.* 21: 31.

Saints should

Trust in. *Matt.* 6: 33, 34. *Matt.* 10: 9, 29–31.

Have full confidence in. *Ps.* 16: 8. *Ps.* 139: 10.

Commit their works unto. *Prov.* 16: 3.

Encourage themselves in. 1 *Sam.* 30: 6.

Pray in dependance upon. *Acts* 12: 5.

Pray to be guided by. *Gen.* 24: 12–14. *Gen.* 28: 20, 21. *Acts* 1: 24.

Result of depending upon. *Luke* 22: 35.

Connected with the use of means. 1 *Kings* 21: 19, with 1 *Kings* 22: 37, 38. *Mic.* 5: 2 with *Luke* 2: 1–4. *Acts* 27: 22, 31, 32.

Danger of denying. *Isa.* 10: 13–17. *Ezek.* 28: 2–10. *Dan.* 4: 29–31. *Hos.* 2: 8, 9.

PRUDENCE

Exhibited in the manifestation of God's grace. *Eph.* 1: 8.

Exemplified by Christ. *Isa.* 52: 13. *Matt.* 21: 24–27. *Matt.* 22: 15–21.

Intimately connected with wisdom. *Prov.* 8: 12.

The wise celebrated for. *Prov.* 16: 21.

They who have

Get knowledge. *Prov.* 18: 15.

Deal with knowledge. *Prov.* 13: 16.

Look well to their goings. *Prov.* 14: 15.

Understand the ways of God. *Hos.* 14: 9.

Understand their own ways. *Prov.* 14: 8.

Crowned with knowledge. *Prov.* 14: 18.

Not ostentatious of knowledge. *Prov.* 12: 23.

Foresee and avoid evil. *Prov.* 22: 3.

Are preserved by it. *Prov.* 2: 11.

Suppress angry feelings, etc. *Prov.* 12: 16. *Prov.* 19: 11.

Regard reproof. *Prov.* 15: 5.

Keep silence in the evil time. *Amos* 5: 13.

Saints act with. *Ps.* 112: 5.

Saints should exercise, in their intercourse with unbelievers. *Col.* 4: 5.

Virtuous wives act with. *Prov.* 31: 16, 26.

The young should cultivate. *Prov.* 3: 21.

Of the wicked

Fails in times of perplexity. *Jer.* 49: 7.

Keeps them from the knowledge of the gospel. *Matt.* 11: 25.

Denounced by God. *Isa.* 5: 21. *Isa.* 29: 15.

Defeated by God. *Isa.* 29: 14. 1 *Cor.* 1: 19.

Necessity for—Illustrated. *Luke* 14: 28–32.

Exemplified. JACOB, *Gen.* 32: 3–23. JOSEPH, *Gen.* 41: 39. JETHRO, *Exod.* 18: 19, etc. GIDEON, *Judges* 8: 1–3. DAVID, 1 *Sam.* 16: 8. AGED COUNSELLORS OF REHOBOAM, 1 *Kings* 12: 7. SOLOMON, 2 *Chron.* 2: 12. NEHEMIAH, *Neh.* 2: 12–16. *Neh.* 4: 13–18. GAMALIEL, *Acts* 5: 34–39. SERGIUS PAULUS, *Acts* 13: 7. PAUL, *Acts* 23: 6.

PUNISHMENT OF THE WICKED, THE

Is from God. *Lev.* 26: 18. *Isa.* 13: 11.

On account of their

Sin. *Lam.* 3: 39.

Iniquity. *Jer.* 36: 31. *Amos* 3: 2.

Idolatry. *Lev.* 26: 30. *Isa.* 10: 10, 11.

Rejection of the law of God. *Hos.* 4: 6–9.

Ignorance of God. 2 *Thess.* 1: 8.

Evil ways and doings. *Jer.* 21: 14. *Hos.* 4: 9. *Hos.* 12: 2.

Pride. *Isa.* 10: 12. *Isa.* 24: 21.

Unbelief. *Rom.* 11: 20. *Heb.* 3: 18, 19.

Covetousness. *Isa.* 57: 17. *Jer.* 51: 13.

Oppressing. *Isa.* 49: 26. *Jer.* 30: 16, 20.

Persecuting. *Jer.* 11: 21, 22. *Matt.* 23: 34–36.

Disobeying God. *Neh.* 9: 26, 27. *Eph.* 5: 6.

Disobeying the gospel. 2 *Thess.* 1: 8.

Is the fruit of their sin. *Job* 4: 8. *Prov.* 22: 8. *Rom.* 6: 21. *Gal.* 6: 8.

Is the reward of their sin. *Ps.* 91: 8. *Isa.* 3: 11. *Jer.* 16: 18. *Rom.* 6: 23. *Heb.* 2: 2.

Often brought about by their evil designs. *Esther* 7: 10. *Ps.* 37: 15. *Ps.* 57: 6.

Often commences in this life. *Prov.* 11: 31.

In this life by

Sickness. *Lev.* 26: 16. *Ps.* 78: 50.

Famine. *Lev.* 26: 19, 20, 26, 29. *Ps.* 107: 34.

Noisome beasts. *Lev.* 26: 22.

War. *Lev.* 26: 25, 32, 33. *Jer.* 6: 4.

Deliverance unto enemies.
Neh. 9: 27.

Fear. *Lev.* 26: 36, 37. *Job*
18: 11.

Trouble and distress. *Isa.* 8:
22. *Zeph.* 1: 15.

Cutting off. *Ps.* 94: 23.

Bringing down their pride.
Isa. 13: 11.

Future, shall be awarded by
Christ. *Matt.* 16: 27. *Matt.*
25: 31, 41.

Future, described as

Hell. *Matt.* 5: 29. *Luke* 12:
5.

Darkness. *Matt.* 8: 12. 2
Pet. 2: 17.

Resurrection of damnation.
John 5: 29.

Rising to shame and ever-
lasting contempt. *Dan.* 12:
2.

Everlasting destruction. *Ps.*
52: 5. *Ps.* 92: 7. 2 *Thess.*
1: 9.

Everlasting fire. *Matt.* 25:
41. *Jude* 7.

Eternal death. *Rom.* 6: 23.
Rev. 21: 8.

Damnation of hell. *Matt.*
23: 33.

Eternal damnation. *Matt.*
3: 29.

Blackness of darkness. 2
Pet. 2: 17. *Jude* 13.

Everlasting burnings. *Isa.*
33: 14.

Wine of the wrath of God.
Rev. 14: 10.

Torment with fire. *Rev.* 14:
10.

Torment for ever and ever.
Rev. 14: 11.

The righteousness of God requires. 2 *Thess.* 1: 6.

Often sudden and unexpected.
Ps. 35: 8. *Ps.* 64: 7. *Prov.* 29: 1.
1 *Thess.* 5: 3.

Shall be

According to their deeds.
Matt. 16: 27. *Rom.* 2: 6, 9.
2 *Cor.* 5: 10.

According to the knowledge
possessed by them. *Luke*
12: 47, 48.

Increased by neglect of
privileges. *Matt.* 11: 21–24.
Luke 10: 13–15.

Without mitigation. *Luke*
16: 23–26.

Accompanied by remorse.
Isa. 66: 24, with *Mark* 9: 44.

No combination avails against.
Prov. 11: 21.

Deferred, emboldens them in
sin. *Eccles.* 8: 11.

Should be a warning to others.
Num. 26: 10. *Jude* 7.

Consummated at the day of
judgment. *Matt.* 25: 31, 46.
Rom. 2: 5, 16. 2 *Pet.* 2: 9.

REBELLION AGAINST GOD

Forbidden. *Num.* 14: 9.
Joshua 22: 19.

Provokes God. *Num.* 16: 30.
Neh. 9: 26.

Provokes Christ. *Exod.* 23:
20, 21, with 1 *Cor.* 10: 9.

Vexes the Holy Spirit. *Isa.* 63:
10.

Exhibited in

Unbelief. *Deut.* 9: 23. *Ps.*
106: 24, 25.

Rejecting his government. 1
Sam. 8: 7.

Revolting from him. *Isa.*
1: 5. *Isa.* 31: 6.

Despising his law. *Neh.* 9:
26.

Despising his counsels. *Ps.*
107: 11.

Distrusting his power. *Ezek.*
17: 15.

Murmuring against him. *Num.* 20: 3, 10.

Refusing to hearken to him. *Deut.* 9: 23. *Ezek.* 20: 8. *Zech.* 7: 11.

Departing from him. *Isa.* 59: 13.

Rebelling against governors appointed by him. *Joshua* 1: 18.

Departing from his precepts. *Dan.* 9: 5.

Departing from his instituted worship. *Exod.* 32: 8, 9. *Joshua* 22: 16–19.

Sinning against light. *Job* 24: 13.

Walking after our own thoughts. *Isa.* 65: 2.

Connected with

Stubbornness. *Deut.* 31: 27.

Injustice and corruption. *Isa.* 1: 23.

Contempt of God. *Ps.* 107: 11.

Man is prone to. *Deut.* 31: 27.

The heart is the seat of. *Jer.* 5: 23. *Heb.* 3: 12.

They who are guilty of,

Aggravate their sin by. *Job* 34: 37.

Practise hypocrisy to hide. *Hos.* 7: 14.

Persevere in. *Deut.* 9: 7, 24.

Increase in, though chastised. *Isa.* 1: 5.

Warned not to exalt themselves. *Ps.* 66: 7.

Denounced. *Isa.* 30: 1.

Have God as their enemy. *Isa.* 63: 10.

Have God's hand against them. 1 *Sam.* 12: 15, with *Ps.* 106: 26, 27.

Impoverished for. *Ps.* 68: 6.

Brought low for. *Ps.* 107: 11, 12.

Delivered into the hands of enemies on account of. *Neh.* 9: 26, 27.

Cast out in their sins for. *Ps.* 5: 10.

Cast out of the Church for. *Ezek.* 20: 38.

Restored through Christ alone. *Ps.* 68: 18.

Heinousness of. 1 *Sam.* 15: 23.

Guilt of,

Aggravated by God's fatherly care. *Isa.* 1: 2.

Aggravated by God's unceasing invitations to return to him. *Isa.* 65: 2.

To be deprecated. *Joshua* 22: 29.

To be confessed. *Lam.* 1: 18, 20. *Dan.* 9: 5.

God alone can forgive. *Dan.* 9: 9.

God is ready to forgive. *Neh.* 9: 17.

Religious instruction designed to prevent. *Ps.* 78: 5, 8.

Promises to those who avoid. *Deut.* 28: 1–13. 1 *Sam.* 12: 14.

Forgiven upon repentance. *Neh.* 9: 26, 27.

Ministers

Cautioned against. *Ezek.* 2: 8.

Sent to those guilty of. *Ezek.* 2: 3–7. *Ezek.* 3: 4–9. *Mark* 12: 4–8.

Should warn against. *Num.* 14: 9.

Should testify against. *Isa.* 30: 8, 9. *Ezek.* 17: 12. *Ezek.* 44: 6.

Should remind their people of past. *Deut.* 9: 7. *Deut.* 31: 27.

Punishment for. *Lev.* 26: 14–39. 1 *Sam.* 12: 15. *Isa.* 1: 20. *Jer.* 4: 16–18. *Ezek.* 20: 8, 38.

Punishment for teaching. *Jer.* 28: 16.

Ingratitude of—Illustrated. *Isa.* 1: 2, 3.

Exemplified. PHARAOH, *Exod.* 5: 1, 2. KORAH, etc., *Num.* 16: 11. MOSES AND AARON, *Num.* 20: 12, 24. ISRAELITES, *Deut.* 9: 23, 24. SAUL, 1 *Sam.* 15: 9, 23. JEROBOAM, 1 *Kings* 12: 28—33. ZEDEKIAH, 2 *Chron.* 36: 13. KINGDOM OF ISRAEL, *Hos.* 7: 14. *Hos.* 13: 16.

RECONCILIATION WITH GOD

Predicted. *Dan.* 9: 24, with *Isa.* 53: 5.

Proclaimed by angels at the birth of Christ. *Luke* 2: 14.

Blotting out the hand-writing of ordinances is necessary to. *Eph.* 2: 16. *Col.* 2: 14.

Effected for men

By God in Christ. *2 Cor.* 5: 19.

By Christ as High Priest. *Heb.* 2: 17.

By the death of Christ. *Rom.* 5: 10. *Eph.* 2: 16. *Col.* 1: 21, 22.

By the blood of Christ. *Eph.* 2: 13. *Col.* 1: 20.

While alienated from God. *Col.* 1: 21.

While enemies to God. *Rom.* 5: 10.

The ministry of, committed to ministers. *2 Cor.* 5: 18, 19.

Ministers, in Christ's stead, should beseech men to seek. *2 Cor.* 5: 20.

Effects of;

Peace with God. *Eph.* 2: 16, 17.

Access to God. *Eph.* 2: 18.

Union of Jews and Gentiles. *Eph.* 2: 14.

Union of things in heaven and earth. *Col.* 1: 20, with *Eph.* 1: 10.

A pledge of final salvation. *Rom.* 5: 10.

Necessity for—Illustrated. *Matt.* 5: 24—26.

Typified. *Lev.* 8: 15. *Lev.* 16: 20.

REDEMPTION

Defined. 1 *Cor.* 7: 23.

Is of God. *Isa.* 44: 21—23, with *Luke* 1: 68.

Is by Christ. *Matt.* 20: 28. *Gal.* 3: 13.

Is by the blood of Christ. *Acts* 20: 28. *Heb.* 9: 12. 1 *Pet.* 1: 19. *Rev.* 5: 9.

Christ sent to effect. *Gal.* 4: 4, 5.

Christ is made, unto us. 1 *Cor.* 1: 30.

Is from

The bondage of the law. *Gal.* 4: 5.

The curse of the law. *Gal.* 3: 13.

The power of sin. *Rom.* 6: 18, 22.

The power of the grave. *Ps.* 49: 15.

All troubles. *Ps.* 25: 22.

All iniquity. *Ps.* 130: 8. *Titus* 2: 14.

All evil. *Gen.* 48: 16.

This present evil world. *Gal.* 1: 4.

Vain conversation. 1 *Pet.* 1: 18.

Enemies. *Ps.* 106: 10, 11. *Jer.* 15: 21.

Death. *Hos.* 13: 14.

Destruction. *Ps.* 103: 4.

Man cannot effect. *Ps.* 49: 7.

Corruptible things cannot purchase. *1 Pet.* 1: 18.

Procures for us

Justification. *Rom.* 3: 24.

Forgiveness of sin. *Eph.* 1: 7. *Col.* 1: 14.

Adoption. *Gal.* 4: 4, 5.

Purification. *Titus* 2: 14.

The present life, the only season for. *Job* 36: 18, 19.

Described as

Precious. *Ps.* 49: 8.

Plenteous. *Ps.* 130: 7.

Eternal. *Heb.* 9: 12.

Subjects of,

The soul. *Ps.* 49: 15. *Ps.* 71: 23.

The body. *Rom.* 8: 23.

The life. *Ps.* 103: 4. *Lam.* 3: 58.

The inheritance. *Eph.* 1: 14.

Manifests the

Power of God. *Isa.* 50: 2.

Grace of God. *Isa.* 52: 3.

Love and pity of God. *Isa.* 63: 9.

A subject for praise. *Isa.* 44: 22, 23. *Isa.* 51: 11.

Old Testament saints partakers of. *Heb.* 9: 15.

They who partake of,

Are the property of God. *Isa.* 43: 1. 1 *Cor.* 6: 20.

Are first-fruits unto God. *Rev.* 14: 4.

Are a peculiar people. 2 *Sam.* 7: 23. *Titus* 2: 14, with 1 *Pet.* 2: 9.

Are assured of. *Job* 19: 25. *Ps.* 31: 5.

Are sealed unto the day of. *Eph.* 4: 30.

Are zealous of good works. *Titus* 2: 14.

Walk safely in holiness. *Isa.* 35: 8, 9.

Shall return to Zion with joy. *Isa.* 35: 10.

Alone can learn the songs of heaven. *Rev.* 14: 3, 4.

Commit themselves to God. *Ps.* 31: 5.

Have an earnest of the completion of. *Eph.* 1: 14, with 2 *Cor.* 1: 22.

Wait for the completion of. *Rom.* 8: 23.

Pray for the completion of. *Ps.* 26: 11. *Ps.* 44: 26.

Praise God for. *Ps.* 71: 23. *Rev.* 5: 9.

Should glorify God for. 1 *Cor.* 6: 20.

Should be without fear. *Isa.* 43: 1.

Typified. ISRAEL, *Exod.* 6: 6. FIRST-BORN, *Exod.* 13: 11–15. *Num.* 18: 15. ATONEMENT-MONEY, *Exod.* 30: 12–15. BOND-SERVANT, *Lev.* 25: 47–54.

REPENTANCE

Commanded to all by God. *Acts* 17: 30.

Commanded by Christ. *Rev.* 2: 5, 16. *Rev.* 3: 3.

Given by God. *Acts* 11: 18. 2 *Tim.* 2: 25.

Christ came to call sinners to. *Matt.* 9: 13.

Christ exalted to give. *Acts* 5: 31.

By the operation of the Holy Ghost. *Zech.* 12: 10.

Called repentance unto life. *Acts* 11: 18.

Called repentance unto salvation. 2 *Cor.* 7: 10.

We should be led to, by

The long-suffering of God. *Gen.* 6: 3, with 1 *Pet.* 3: 20. 2 *Pet.* 3: 9.

The goodness of God. *Rom.* 2: 4.

The chastisements of God. 1 *Kings* 8: 47. *Rev.* 3: 19.

Godly sorrow works. 2 *Cor.* 7: 10.

Necessary to the pardon of sin. *Acts* 2: 38. *Acts* 3: 19. *Acts* 8: 22.

Conviction of sin necessary to. 1 *Kings* 8: 38. *Acts* 2: 37, 38.

Preached

By Christ. *Matt.* 4: 17. *Mark* 1: 15.

By John the Baptist. *Matt.* 3: 2.

By the Apostles. *Mark* 6: 12. *Acts* 20: 21.

In the name of Christ. *Luke* 24: 47.

Not to be repented of. 2 *Cor.* 7: 10.

The present time the season for. *Ps.* 95: 7, 8, with *Heb.* 3: 7, 8. *Heb.* 4: 7.

There is joy in heaven over one sinner brought to. *Luke* 15: 7, 10.

Ministers should rejoice over their people on their. 2 *Cor.* 7: 9.

Should be evidenced by fruits. *Dan.* 4: 27. *Matt.* 3: 8. *Acts* 26: 20.

Should be accompanied by

Humility. 2 *Chron.* 7: 14. *Jas.* 4: 9, 10.

Shame and confusion. *Ezra* 9: 6–15. *Jer.* 31: 19. *Ezek.* 16: 61, 63. *Dan.* 9: 7, 8.

Self-abhorrence. *Job* 42: 6.

Confession. *Lev.* 26: 40. *Job* 33: 27.

Faith. *Matt.* 21: 32. *Mark* 1: 15. *Acts* 20: 21.

Prayer. 1 *Kings* 8: 33. *Acts* 8: 22.

Conversion. *Acts* 3: 19. *Acts* 26: 20.

Turning from sin. 2 *Chron.* 6: 26.

Turning from idolatry. *Ezek.* 14: 6. 1 *Thess.* 1: 9.

Greater zeal in the path of duty. 2 *Cor.* 7: 11.

Exhortations to. *Ezek.* 14: 6. *Ezek.* 18: 30. *Acts* 2: 38. *Acts* 3: 19.

The wicked

Averse to. *Jer.* 8: 6. *Matt.* 21: 32.

Not led to, by the judgments of God. *Rev.* 9: 20, 21. *Rev.* 16: 9.

Not led to, by miraculous interference. *Luke* 16: 30, 31.

Neglect the time given for. *Rev.* 2: 21.

Condemned for neglecting. *Matt.* 11: 20.

Danger of neglecting. *Matt.* 11: 20–24. *Luke* 13: 3, 5. *Rev.* 2: 22.

Neglect of, followed by swift judgment. *Rev.* 2: 5, 16.

Denied to Apostates. *Heb.* 6: 4–6.

Illustrated. *Luke* 15: 18–21. *Luke* 18: 13.

True—Exemplified. ISRAELITES, *Judges* 10: 15, 16. DAVID, 2 *Sam.* 12: 13. MANASSEH, 2 *Chron.* 33: 12, 13. JOB, *Job* 42: 6. NINEVEH, *Jonah* 3: 5–8. *Matt.* 12: 41. PETER, *Matt.* 26: 75. ZACCHEUS, *Luke* 19: 8. THIEF ON THE CROSS, *Luke* 23: 40, 41. CORINTHIANS, 2 *Cor.* 7: 9.

False—Exemplified. SAUL, 1 *Sam.* 15: 24–30. AHAB, 1 *Kings* 21: 27–29. JUDAS, *Matt.* 27: 3–5.

REPROOF

God gives, to the wicked. *Ps.* 50: 21. *Isa.* 51: 20.

Christ sent to give. *Isa.* 2: 4. *Isa.* 11: 3.

The Holy Spirit gives. *John* 16: 7, 8.

Christ gives, in love. *Rev.* 3: 19.

On account of

Impenitence. *Matt.* 11: 20–24.

Not understanding. *Matt.* 16: 9, 11. *Mark* 7: 18. *John* 8: 43.

Hardness of heart. *Mark* 8: 17. *Mark* 16: 14.

Fearfulness. *Mark* 4: 40. *Luke* 24: 37, 38.

Unbelief. *Matt.* 17: 17, 20. *Mark* 16: 14.

Hypocrisy. *Matt.* 15: 7. *Matt.* 23: 13, etc.

Reviling Christ. *Luke* 23: 40.

Unruly conduct. 1 *Thess.* 5: 14.

Oppressing our brethren. *Neh.* 5: 7.

Sinful practices. *Luke* 3: 19.

The scriptures are profitable for. *Eph.* 5: 13. 2 *Tim.* 3: 16.

When from God,

Is for correction. *Ps.* 39: 11.

Is despised by the wicked. *Prov.* 1: 30.

Should not discourage saints. *Heb.* 12: 5.

Pray that it be not in anger. *Ps.* 6: 1.

Should be accompanied by exhortation to repentance. 1 *Sam.* 12: 20–25.

Declared to be

Better than secret love. *Prov.* 27: 5.

Better than the praise of fools. *Eccles.* 7: 5.

An excellent oil. *Ps.* 141: 5.

More profitable to saints, than stripes to a fool. *Prov.* 17: 10.

A proof of faithful friendship. *Prov.* 27: 6.

Leads to

Understanding. *Prov.* 15: 32.

Knowledge. *Prov.* 19: 25.

Wisdom. *Prov.* 15: 31. *Prov.* 29: 15.

Honour. *Prov.* 13: 18.

Happiness. *Prov.* 6: 23.

Eventually brings more respect than flattery. *Prov.* 28: 23.

Of those who offend, a warning to others. 1 *Tim.* 5: 20.

Hypocrites not qualified to give. *Matt.* 7: 5.

Ministers are sent to give. *Jer.* 44: 4.

Ministers are empowered to give. *Mic.* 3: 8.

Ministers should give,

Openly. 1 *Tim.* 5: 20.

Fearlessly. *Ezek.* 2: 3–7.

With all authority. *Titus* 2: 15.

With long-suffering, etc. 2 *Tim.* 4: 2.

Unreservedly. *Isa.* 58: 1.

Sharply, if necessary. *Titus* 1: 13.

With Christian love. 2 *Thess.* 3: 15.

They who give, are hated by scorners. *Prov.* 9: 8. *Prov.* 15: 12.

Hatred of, a proof of brutishness. *Prov.* 12: 1.

Hatred of, leads to destruction. *Prov.* 15: 10. *Prov.* 29: 1.

Contempt of, leads to remorse. *Prov.* 5: 12.

Rejection of, leads to error. *Prov*. 10: 17.

Saints should

Give. *Lev*. 19: 17. *Eph*. 5: 11.

Give no occasion for. *Phil*. 2: 15.

Receive kindly. *Ps*. 141: 5.

Love those who give. *Prov*. 9: 8.

Delight in those who give. *Prov*. 24: 25.

Attention to, a proof of prudence. *Prov*. 15: 5.

Exemplified. SAMUEL, 1 *Sam*. 13: 13. NATHAN, 2 *Sam*. 12: 7–9. AHIJAH, 1 *Kings* 14: 7–11. ELIJAH, 1 *Kings* 21: 20. ELISHA, 2 *Kings* 5: 26. JOAB, 1 *Chron*. 21: 3. SHEMAIAH, 2 *Chron*. 12: 5. HANANI, 2 *Chron*. 16: 7. ZECHARIAH, 2 *Chron*. 24: 20. DANIEL, *Dan*. 5: 22, 23. JOHN THE BAPTIST, *Matt*. 3: 7. *Luke* 3: 19. STEPHEN, *Acts* 7: 51. PETER, *Acts* 8: 20. PAUL, *Gal*. 2: 11.

RESIGNATION

Christ set an example of. *Matt*. 26: 39, 42. *John* 12: 27. *John* 18: 11.

Commanded. *Ps*. 37: 7. *Ps*. 46: 10.

Should be exhibited in

Submission to the will of God. 2 *Sam*. 15: 26. *Matt*. 6: 10.

Submission to the sovereignty of God in his purposes. *Rom*. 9: 20, 21.

The prospect of death. *Acts* 21: 13.

Loss of goods. *Job* 1: 15, 16, 21.

Loss of children. *Job* 1: 18, 19, 21.

Chastisements. *Heb*. 12: 9.

Bodily suffering. *Job* 2: 8–10.

The wicked are devoid of. *Prov*. 19: 3.

Motives to;

God's greatness. *Ps*. 46: 10.

God's love. *Heb*. 12: 6.

God's justice. *Neh*. 9: 33.

God's wisdom. *Rom*. 11: 32, 33.

God's faithfulness. 1 *Pet*. 4: 19.

Our own sinfulness. *Lam*. 3: 39. *Mic*. 7: 9.

Exemplified. JACOB, *Gen*. 43: 14. AARON, *Lev*. 10: 3. ISRAELITES, *Judges* 10: 15. ELI, 1 *Sam*. 3: 18. DAVID, 2 *Sam*. 12: 23. HEZEKIAH, 2 *Kings* 20: 19. JOB, *Job* 2: 10. STEPHEN, *Acts* 7: 59. PAUL, *Acts* 21: 13. DISCIPLES, *Acts* 21: 14. PETER, 2 *Pet*. 1: 14.

RESURRECTION, THE

A doctrine of the Old Testament. *Job* 19: 26. *Ps*. 49: 15. *Isa*. 26: 19. *Dan*. 12: 2. *Gen*. 22: 5. *Heb*. 11: 19.

A first principle of the gospel. *Heb*. 6: 1, 2.

Expected by the Jews. *John* 11: 24. *Heb*. 11: 35.

Denied by the Sadducees. *Matt*. 22: 23. *Luke* 20: 27. *Acts* 23: 8.

Explained away by false teachers. 2 *Tim*. 2: 18.

Called in question by some in the primitive Church. 1 *Cor*. 15: 12.

Is not incredible. *Mark* 12: 24. *Acts* 26: 8.

Is not contrary to reason. *John* 12: 24. 1 *Cor*. 15: 35–44.

Assumed and proved by our

Lord. *Matt.* 22: 29–32.
Luke 14: 14. *John* 5: 28, 29.

Preached by the Apostles.
Acts 4: 2. *Acts* 17: 18. *Acts*
24: 15.

Credibility of, shown by resurrection of individuals. *Matt.*
9: 25. *Matt.* 27: 53. *Luke*
7: 14. *John* 11: 44. *Heb.* 11: 35.

Certainty of, proved by the resurrection of Christ. 1 *Cor.*
15: 12–20.

Effected by the power of

God. *Matt.* 22: 29.

Christ. *John* 5: 28, 29.
John 6: 39, 40, 44.

The Holy Ghost. *Rom.*
8: 11.

Shall be of all the dead. *John*
5: 28. *Acts* 24: 15. *Rev.* 20: 13.

Saints in, shall

Rise through Christ. *John*
11: 25. *Acts* 4: 2. 1 *Cor.*
15: 21, 22.

Rise first. 1 *Cor.* 15: 23.
1 *Thess.* 4: 16.

Rise to eternal life. *Dan.*
12: 2. *John* 5: 29.

Be glorified with Christ.
Col. 3: 4.

Be as the angels. *Matt.* 22:
30.

Have incorruptible bodies.
1 *Cor.* 15: 42.

Have glorious bodies. 1 *Cor.*
15: 43.

Have powerful bodies. 1
Cor. 15: 43.

Have spiritual bodies. 1
Cor. 15: 44.

Have bodies like Christ's.
Phil. 3: 21.

Be recompensed. *Luke* 14:
14.

Saints should look forward to.
Dan. 12: 13. *Phil.* 3: 11.

Of saints shall be followed by
the change of those then alive.
1 *Cor.* 15: 51, with 1 *Thess.* 4:
17.

The preaching of, caused

Mocking. *Acts* 17: 32.

Persecution. *Acts* 23: 6.
Acts 24: 11–15.

Blessedness of those who have
part in the first. *Rev.* 20: 6.

Of the wicked, shall be to

Shame and everlasting contempt. *Dan.* 12: 2.

Damnation. *John* 5: 29.

Illustrative of the new birth.
John 5: 25.

Illustrated. *Ezek.* 37: 1–10.
1 *Cor.* 15: 36, 37.

Associated with the Feast of
Tabernacles. *Lev.* 23. *Isa.*
25: 6–9. 1 *Cor.* 15: 54.

RESURRECTION OF CHRIST, THE

Foretold by the prophets. *Ps.*
16: 10, with *Acts* 13: 34, 35.
Isa. 26: 19.

Foretold by himself. *Matt.* 20:
19. *Mark* 9: 9. *Mark* 14: 28.
John 2: 19–22.

Was necessary to

The fulfilment of scripture.
Luke 24: 45, 46.

Forgiveness of sins. 1 *Cor.*
15: 17.

Justification. *Rom.* 4: 25.
Rom. 8: 34.

Hope. 1 *Cor.* 15: 19.

The efficacy of preaching.
1 *Cor.* 15: 14.

The efficacy of faith. 1 *Cor.*
15: 14, 17.

A proof of his being the Son of
God. *Ps.* 2: 7, with *Acts* 13:
33. *Rom.* 1: 4.

Effected by

The power of God. *Acts* 2:

24. *Acts* 3: 15. *Rom.* 8: 11.
Eph. 1: 20. *Col.* 2: 12.

His own power. *John* 2: 19.
John 10: 18.

The power of the Holy Ghost.
1 *Pet.* 3· 18.

On the first day of the week.
Mark 16: 9.

On the third day after his death.
Luke 24: 46. *Acts* 10: 40. 1
Cor. 15: 4. *Gen.* 1: 11–13.
Gen. 22: 4, 5. *Gen.* 40: 20.
Gen. 42: 18. *Exod.* 3: 18.
Exod. 15: 1. *Lev.* 23: 11. *Num.*
19: 12. *Esther* 4: 16. *Esther*
5: 1, 2.

The Apostles

At first did not understand
the predictions respecting.
Mark 9: 10. *John* 20: 9.

Very slow to believe. *Mark*
16: 13. *Luke* 24: 9, 11, 37, 38.

Reproved for their unbelief
of. *Mark* 16: 14.

He appeared after, to

Mary Magdalene. *Mark*
16: 9. *John* 20: 18.

The women. *Matt.* 28: 9.

Simon Peter. *Luke* 24: 34.

Two disciples. *Luke* 24: 13–
31.

Apostles, except Thomas.
John 20: 19, 24.

Apostles, Thomas being
present. *John* 20: 26.

Apostles at the sea of Tibe-
rias. *John* 21: 1.

Apostles in Galilee. *Matt.*
28: 16, 17.

Above five hundred brethren.
1 *Cor.* 15: 6.

James. 1 *Cor.* 15: 7.

All the Apostles. *Luke* 24:
51. *Acts* 1: 9. 1 *Cor.* 15: 7.

Paul. 1 *Cor.* 15: 8.

Fraud impossible in. *Matt.* 27:
63–66.

He gave many infallible proofs
of. *Luke* 24: 35, 39, 43.
John 20: 20, 27. *Acts* 1: 3.

Was attested by

Angels. *Matt.* 25: 5–7.
Luke 24: 4–7, 23.

Apostles. *Acts* 1: 22. *Acts*
2: 32. *Acts* 3: 15. *Acts* 4: 33.

His enemies. *Matt.* 28: 11–
15.

Asserted and preached by the
Apostles. *Acts* 25: 19. *Acts*
26: 23.

Saints

Begotten to a lively hope by.
1 *Pet.* 1: 3, 21.

Desire to know the power of.
Phil. 3: 10.

Should keep, in remem-
brance. 2 *Tim.* 2: 8.

Shall rise in the likeness of.
Rom. 6: 5. 1 *Cor.* 15: 49,
with *Phil.* 3: 21.

Is an emblem of the new birth.
Rom. 6: 4. *Col.* 2: 12.

The first-fruits of our resurrection. *Acts* 26: 23. 1 *Cor.* 15:
20, 23.

The truth of the gospel involved
in. 1 *Cor.* 15: 14, 15.

Followed by his exaltation.
Acts 4: 10, 11. *Rom.* 8: 34.
Eph. 1: 20. *Rev.* 1: 18.

An assurance of the judgment.
Acts 17: 31.

Typified. ISAAC, *Gen.* 22: 13,
with *Heb.* 11: 19. JONAH,
Jonah 2: 10, with *Matt.* 12:
40.

REVENGE

Forbidden. *Lev.* 19: 18. *Prov.*
24: 29. *Rom.* 12: 17, 19. 1
Thess. 5: 15. 1 *Pet.* 3: 9.

Christ an example of forbearing.
1 *Pet.* 2: 23.

Rebuked by Christ. *Luke* 9:
54, 55.

Inconsistent with Christian spirit. *Luke* 9: 55.

Proceeds from a spiteful heart. *Ezek.* 25: 15.

Instead of taking, we should

Trust in God. *Prov.* 20: 22. *Rom.* 12: 19.

Exhibit love. *Lev.* 19: 18. *Luke* 6: 35.

Give place unto wrath. *Rom.* 12: 19.

Exercise forbearance. *Matt.* 5: 38–41.

Bless. *Rom.* 12: 14.

Overcome others by kindness. *Prov.* 25: 21, with *Rom.* 12: 20.

Keep others from taking. 1 *Sam.* 24: 7. 1 *Sam.* 25: 24–31. 1 *Sam.* 26: 9.

Be thankful for being kept from taking. 1 *Sam.* 25: 32, 33.

The wicked are earnest after. *Jer.* 20: 10.

Punishment for. *Ezek.* 25: 15–17. *Amos* 1: 11, 12.

Exemplified. SIMEON AND LEVI, *Gen.* 34: 25. SAMSON, *Judges* 15: 7, 8. *Judges* 16: 28–30. JOAB, 2 *Sam.* 3: 27. ABSALOM, 2 *Sam.* 13: 23–29. JEZEBEL, 1 *Kings* 19: 2. AHAB, 1 *Kings* 22: 26. HAMAN, *Esther* 3: 8–15. EDOMITES, *Ezek.* 25: 12. PHILISTINES, *Ezek.* 25: 15. HERODIAS, *Mark* 6: 19–24. JAMES AND JOHN, *Luke* 9: 54. CHIEF PRIESTS, *Acts* 5: 33. JEWS, *Acts* 7: 54, 59. *Acts* 23: 12.

REVILING AND REPROACHING

Forbidden. 1 *Pet.* 3: 9.

Of rulers specially forbidden. *Exod.* 22: 28, with *Acts* 23: 4, 5.

The wicked utter, against

God. *Ps.* 74: 22. *Ps.* 79: 12.

Christ. *Matt.* 27: 39. *Luke* 7: 34.

Saints. *Ps.* 102: 8. *Zeph.* 2: 8.

Rulers. 2 *Pet.* 2: 10, 11. *Jude* 8, 9.

Of Christ, predicted. *Ps.* 69: 9, with *Rom.* 15: 3. *Ps.* 89: 51.

The conduct of Christ under. 1 *Pet.* 2: 23.

Saints

Endure. 1 *Tim.* 4: 10. *Heb.* 10: 33.

Endure for God's sake. *Ps.* 69: 7.

Endure for Christ's sake. *Luke* 6: 22.

Should expect. *Matt.* 10: 25.

Should not fear. *Isa.* 51: 7.

Sometimes depressed by. *Ps.* 42: 10, 11. *Ps.* 44: 16. *Ps.* 69: 20.

May take pleasure in. 2 *Cor.* 12: 10.

Supported under. 2 *Cor.* 12: 10.

Trust in God under. *Ps.* 57: 3. *Ps.* 119: 42.

Pray under. 2 *Kings* 19: 4, 16. *Ps.* 89: 50.

Return blessings for. 1 *Cor.* 4: 12. 1 *Pet.* 3: 9.

Ministers should not fear. *Ezek.* 2: 6.

Happiness of enduring, for Christ's sake. 1 *Pet.* 4: 14.

Blessedness of enduring, for Christ's sake. *Matt.* 5: 11. *Luke* 6: 22.

Excludes from heaven. 1 *Cor.* 6: 10.

Punishment for. *Zeph.* 2: 8, 9. *Matt.* 5: 22.

Exemplified. JOSEPH'S BROTHERS, *Gen.* 37: 19. GOLIATH,

1 *Sam.* 17: 43. MICHAL, 2 *Sam.* 6: 20. SHIMEI, 2 *Sam.* 16: 7, 8. SENNACHERIB, *Isa.* 37: 17, 23, 24. MOABITES AND AMMONITES, *Zeph.* 2: 8. PHARISEES, *Matt.* 12: 24. JEWS, *Matt.* 27: 39, 40. *John* 8: 48. MALEFACTOR, *Luke* 23: 39. ATHENIAN PHILOSOPHERS, *Acts* 17: 18.

REWARD OF SAINTS, THE

Is from God. *Col.* 3: 24. *Heb.* 11: 6.
Is of grace, through faith alone. *Rom.* 4: 4, 5, 16. *Rom.* 11: 6.
Is of God's good pleasure. *Luke* 12: 32.
Prepared by God. *Heb.* 11: 16.
Prepared by Christ. *John* 14: 2.
As servants of Christ. *Col.* 3: 24.
Not on account of their merits. *Rom.* 4: 4, 5.

Described as
Being with Christ. *John* 12: 26. *John* 14: 3. *Phil.* 1: 23. 1 *Thess.* 4: 17.
Beholding the face of God. *Ps.* 17: 15. *Matt.* 5: 8. *Rev.* 22: 4.
Beholding the glory of Christ. *John* 17: 24.
Being glorified with Christ. *Rom.* 8: 17, 18. *Col.* 3: 4.
Sitting in judgment with Christ. *Luke* 22: 30, with 1 *Cor.* 6: 2.
Reigning with Christ. 2 *Tim.* 2: 12. *Rev.* 5: 10. *Rev.* 20: 4.
Reigning for ever and ever. *Rev.* 22: 5.
A crown of righteousness. 2 *Tim.* 4: 8.
A crown of glory. 1 *Pet.* 5: 4.
A crown of life. *Jas.* 1: 12. *Rev.* 2: 10.
An incorruptible crown. 1 *Cor.* 9: 25.
Joint heirship with Christ. *Rom.* 8: 17.
Inheritance of all things. *Rev.* 21: 7.
Inheritance with saints in light. *Acts* 20: 32. *Acts* 26: 18. *Col.* 1: 12.
Inheritance eternal. *Heb.* 9: 15.
Inheritance incorruptible, etc. 1 *Pet.* 1: 4.
A kingdom. *Matt.* 25: 34. *Luke* 22: 29.
A kingdom immovable. *Heb.* 12: 28.
Shining as the stars. *Dan.* 12: 3.
Everlasting light. *Isa.* 60: 19.
Everlasting life. *Luke* 18: 30. *Rom.* 6: 23.
An enduring substance. *Heb.* 10: 34.
A house, eternal in the heavens. 2 *Cor.* 5: 1.
A city which hath foundations. *Heb.* 11: 10.
Entering into the joy of the Lord. *Matt.* 25: 21, with *Heb.* 12: 2.
Rest. *Heb.* 4: 9. *Rev.* 14: 13.
Fulness of joy. *Ps.* 16: 11.
The prize of the high calling of God in Christ. *Phil.* 3: 14.
Treasure in heaven. *Matt.* 19: 21. *Luke* 12: 33.
An eternal weight of glory. 2 *Cor.* 4: 17.
Is great. *Matt.* 5: 12. *Luke* 6: 35. *Heb.* 10: 35.
Is full. 2 *John* 8.

Is sure. *Prov.* 11: 18.

Is satisfying. *Ps.* 17: 15.

Is inestimable. *Isa.* 64: 4, with
1 *Cor.* 2: 9.

Saints may feel confident of.
Ps. 73: 24. 2 *Cor.* 5: 1. 2 *Tim.*
4: 8.

Hope of, a cause of rejoicing.
Rom. 5: 2.

Be careful not to lose. 2 *John*
8.

The prospect of, should lead to

Diligence. 2 *John* 8.

Pressing forward. *Phil.* 3:
14.

Enduring suffering for Christ.
2 *Cor.* 4: 16–18. *Heb.* 11:
26.

Faithfulness unto death.
Rev. 2: 10.

Present afflictions not to be
compared with. *Rom.* 8: 18.

Shall be given at the second
coming of Christ. *Matt.* 16:
27. *Rev.* 22: 12. 2 *Tim.* 4: 1, 8.

RICHES

God gives. 1 *Sam.* 2: 7. *Eccles.*
5: 19.

God gives power to obtain.
Deut. 8: 18.

The blessing of the Lord brings.
Prov. 10: 22.

Give worldly power. *Prov.*
22: 7.

Described as

Temporary. *Prov.* 27: 24.

Uncertain. 1 *Tim.* 6: 17.

Unsatisfying. *Eccles.* 4: 8.
Eccles. 5: 10.

Corruptible. *Jas.* 5: 2. 1 *Pet.*
1: 18.

Fleeting. *Prov.* 23: 5. *Rev.*
18: 16, 17.

Deceitful. *Matt.* 13: 22.

Liable to be stolen. *Matt.*
6: 19.

Perishable. *Jer.* 48: 36.

Thick clay. *Hab.* 2: 6.

Often an obstruction to the
reception of the gospel.
Mark 10: 23–25.

Deceitfulness of, chokes the
word. *Matt.* 13: 22.

The love of, the root of all evil.
1 *Tim.* 6: 10.

Often lead to

Pride. *Ezek.* 28: 5. *Hos.* 12:
8.

Forgetting God. *Deut.* 8:
13, 14.

Denying God. *Prov.* 30: 8,
9.

Forsaking God. *Deut.* 32:
15.

Rebelling against God.
Neh. 9: 25, 26.

Rejecting Christ. *Matt.*
19: 22. *Mark* 10: 22.

Self-sufficiency. *Prov.* 28:
11.

Anxiety. *Eccles.* 5: 12.

An overbearing spirit. *Prov.*
18: 23.

Violence. *Mic.* 6: 12.

Oppression. *Jas.* 2: 6.

Fraud. *Jas.* 5: 4.

Sensual indulgence. *Jas.*
5: 5.

Life consists not in abundance
of. *Luke* 12: 15.

Be not over-anxious for.
Prov. 30: 8.

Labour not for. *Prov.* 23: 4.

They who covet,

Fall into temptation and a
snare. 1 *Tim.* 6: 9.

Fall into hurtful lusts. 1
Tim. 6: 9.

Err from the faith. 1 *Tim.*
6: 10.

Use unlawful means to acquire. *Prov.* 28: 20.

Bring trouble on themselves. 1 *Tim.* 6: 10.

Bring trouble on their families. *Prov.* 15: 27.

Profit not in the day of wrath. *Prov.* 11: 4.

Cannot secure prosperity. *Jas.* 1: 11.

Cannot redeem the soul. *Ps.* 49: 6–9. 1 *Pet.* 1: 18.

Cannot deliver in the day of God's wrath. *Zeph.* 1: 18. *Rev.* 6: 15–17.

They who possess, should

Ascribe them to God. 1 *Chron.* 29: 12.

Not trust in them. *Job* 31: 24. 1 *Tim.* 6: 17.

Not set the heart on them. *Ps.* 62: 10.

Not boast of obtaining them. *Deut.* 8: 17.

Not glory in them. *Jer.* 9: 23.

Not hoard them up. *Matt.* 6: 19.

Devote them to God's service. 1 *Chron.* 29: 3.

Give of them to the poor. *Matt.* 19: 21. 1 *John* 3: 17.

Use them in promoting the salvation of others. *Luke* 16: 9.

Be liberal in all things. 1 *Tim.* 6: 18.

Esteem it a privilege to be allowed to give. 1 *Chron.* 29: 14.

Not be high-minded. 1 *Tim.* 6: 17.

When converted, rejoice in being humbled. *Jas.* 1: 9, 10.

Heavenly treasures superior to. *Matt.* 6: 19, 20.

Of the wicked laid up for the just. *Prov.* 13: 22.

The wicked

Often increase in. *Ps.* 73: 12.

Often spend their days in. *Job* 21: 13.

Swallow down. *Job* 20: 15.

Trust in the abundance of. *Ps.* 52: 7.

Heap up. *Job* 27: 16. *Eccles.* 2: 26.

Keep, to their hurt. *Eccles.* 5: 13.

Boast themselves in. *Ps.* 49: 6.

Profit not by. *Prov.* 13: 7. *Eccles.* 5: 11.

Have trouble with. *Prov.* 15: 6.

Must leave, to others. *Ps.* 49: 10.

Vanity of heaping up. *Ps.* 39: 6. *Eccles.* 5: 10, 11.

Guilt of trusting in. *Job* 31: 24, 28.

Guilt of rejoicing in. *Job* 31: 25, 28.

Denunciations against those who

Get, by vanity. *Prov.* 13: 11.

Get, unlawfully. *Jer.* 17: 11.

Increase, by oppression. *Prov.* 22: 16. *Hab.* 2: 6–8. *Mic.* 2: 2, 3.

Hoard up. *Eccles.* 5: 13, 14. *Jas.* 5: 3.

Trust in. *Prov.* 11: 28.

Receive their consolation from. *Luke* 6: 24.

Abuse. *Jas.* 5: 1, 5.

Spend, upon their appetite. *Job* 20: 15–17.

Folly and danger of trusting to—illustrated. *Luke* 12: 16–21.

Danger of misusing—Illustrated. *Luke* 16: 19–25.

Examples of saints possessing. ABRAM, *Gen.* 13: 2. LOT, *Gen.* 13: 5, 6. ISAAC, *Gen.* 26: 13, 14. JACOB, *Gen.* 32: 5, 10. JOSEPH, *Gen.* 45: 8, 13. BOAZ, *Ruth* 2: 1. BARZILLAI, 2 *Sam.* 19: 32. SHUNAMMITE, 2 *Kings* 4: 8. DAVID, 1 *Chron.* 29: 28. JEHOSHAPHAT, 2 *Chron.* 17: 5. HEZEKIAH, 2 *Chron.* 32: 27–29. JOB, *Job* 1: 3. JOSEPH OF ARIMATHEA, *Matt.* 27: 57. ZACCHEUS, *Luke* 19: 2. DORCAS, *Acts* 9: 36.

Examples of wicked men possessing. LABAN, *Gen.* 30: 30. ESAU, *Gen.* 36: 7. NABAL, 1 *Sam.* 25: 2. HAMAN, *Esther* 5: 11. AMMONITES, *Jer.* 49: 4. TYRIANS, *Ezek.* 28: 5. YOUNG MAN, *Matt.* 19: 22.

RIGHTEOUSNESS

Is obedience to God's law. *Deut.* 6: 25, with *Rom.* 10: 5.
God loves. *Ps.* 11: 7.
God looks for. *Isa.* 5: 7.

Christ

Is the Sun of. *Mal.* 4: 2.
Loves. *Ps.* 45: 7, with *Heb.* 1: 9.
Was girt with. *Isa.* 11: 5.
Put on, as a breast-plate. *Isa.* 59: 17.
Was sustained by. *Isa.* 59: 16.
Preached. *Ps.* 40: 9.
Fulfilled all. *Matt.* 3: 15.
Is made, unto his people. 1 *Cor.* 1: 30.
Is the end of the law for. *Rom.* 10: 4.
Has brought in everlasting. *Dan.* 9: 24.
Shall judge with. *Ps.* 72: 2. *Isa.* 11: 4. *Acts* 17: 31. *Rev.* 19: 11.

Shall reign in. *Ps.* 45: 6. *Isa.* 32: 1. *Heb.* 1: 8.
Shall execute. *Ps.* 99: 4. *Jer.* 23: 5.
None, by nature, have. *Job* 15: 14. *Ps.* 14: 3, with *Rom.* 3: 10.
Cannot come by the law. *Gal.* 2: 21. *Gal.* 3: 21.
No justification by works of. *Rom.* 3: 20. *Rom.* 9: 31, 32. *Gal.* 2: 16.
No salvation by works of. *Eph.* 2: 8, 9. 2 *Tim.* 1: 9. *Titus* 3: 5.
Unregenerate man seeks justification by works of. *Luke* 18: 9. *Rom.* 10: 3.
The blessing of God is not to be attributed to our works of. *Deut.* 9: 5.

Saints

Have, in Christ. *Isa.* 45: 24. *Isa.* 54: 17. 2 *Cor.* 5: 21.
Have, imputed. *Rom.* 4: 11, 22.
Are covered with the robe of. *Isa.* 61: 10.
Receive, from God. *Ps.* 24: 5.
Are renewed in. *Eph.* 4: 24.
Are led in the paths of. *Ps.* 23: 3.
Are servants of. *Rom.* 6: 16, 18.
Characterised by. *Gen.* 18: 25. *Ps.* 1: 5, 6.
Know. *Isa.* 51: 7.
Do. 1 *John* 2: 29. 1 *John* 3: 7.
Work, by faith. *Heb.* 11: 33.
Follow after. *Isa.* 51: 1.
Put on. *Job* 29: 14.
Wait for the hope of. *Gal.* 5: 5.
Pray for the spirit of. *Ps.* 51: 10.

Hunger and thirst after. *Matt.* 5: 6.

Walk before God in. 1 *Kings* 3: 6.

Offer the sacrifice of. *Ps.* 4: 5. *Ps.* 51: 19.

Put no trust in their own. *Phil.* 3: 6–8.

Count their own, as filthy rags. *Isa.* 64: 6.

Should seek. *Zeph.* 2: 3.

Should live in. *Titus* 2: 12. 1 *Pet.* 2: 24.

Should serve God in. *Luke* 1: 75.

Should yield their members as instruments of. *Rom.* 6: 13.

Should yield their members servants to. *Rom.* 6: 19.

Should have on the breastplate of. *Eph.* 6: 14.

Shall receive a crown of. 2 *Tim.* 4: 8.

Shall see God's face in. *Ps.* 17: 15.

Of saints endures for ever. *Ps.* 112: 3, 9, with 2 *Cor.* 9: 9.

An evidence of the new birth. 1 *John* 2: 29.

The kingdom of God is. *Rom.* 14: 17.

The fruit of the Spirit is in all. *Eph.* 5: 9.

The scriptures instruct in. 2 *Tim.* 3: 16.

Judgments designed to lead to. *Isa.* 26: 9.

Chastisements yield the fruit of. *Heb.* 12: 11.

Has no fellowship with unrighteousness. 2 *Cor.* 6: 14.

Ministers should

Be preachers of. 2 *Pet.* 2: 5.

Reason of. *Acts* 24: 25.

Follow after. 1 *Tim.* 6: 11. 2 *Tim.* 2: 22.

Be clothed with. *Ps.* 132: 9.

Be armed with. 2 *Cor.* 6: 7.

Pray for fruit of, in their people. 2 *Cor.* 9: 10. *Phil.* 1: 11.

Keeps saints in the right way. *Prov.* 11: 5. *Prov.* 13: 6.

Judgment should be executed in. *Lev.* 19: 15.

They who walk in, and follow,

Are righteous. 1 *John* 3: 7.

Are the excellent of the earth. *Ps.* 16: 3, with *Prov.* 12: 26.

Are accepted with God. *Acts* 10: 35.

Are loved by God. *Ps.* 146: 8. *Prov.* 15: 9.

Are blessed by God. *Ps.* 5: 12.

Are objects of God's watchful care. *Job* 36: 7. *Ps.* 34: 15. 1 *Pet.* 3: 12.

Are tried by God. *Ps.* 11: 5.

Are exalted by God. *Job* 36: 7.

Dwell in security. *Isa.* 33: 15, 16.

Are bold as a lion. *Prov.* 28: 1.

Are delivered out of all troubles. *Ps.* 34: 19. *Prov.* 11: 8.

Are never forsaken by God. *Ps.* 37: 25.

Are abundantly provided for. *Prov.* 13: 25.

Are enriched. *Ps.* 112: 3. *Prov.* 15: 6.

Think and desire good. *Prov.* 11: 23. *Prov.* 12: 5.

Know the secret of the Lord. *Prov.* 3: 32.

Have their prayers heard. *Ps.* 34: 17. *Prov.* 15: 29. 1 *Pet.* 3: 12.

Have their desires granted.
Prov. 10: 24.

Find it with life and honour.
Prov. 21: 21.

Shall hold on their way.
Job 17: 9.

Shall never be moved. *Ps.*
15: 2, 5. *Ps.* 55: 22. *Prov.*
10: 30. *Prov.* 12: 3.

Shall be ever remembered.
Ps. 112: 6.

Shall flourish as a branch.
Prov. 11: 28.

Shall be glad in the Lord.
Ps. 64: 10.

Brings its own reward.
Prov. 11: 18. *Isa.* 3: 10.

Tends to life. *Prov.* 11: 19.
Prov. 12: 28.

The work of, shall be peace.
Isa. 32: 17.

The effect of, shall be quiet-
ness and assurance for ever.
Isa. 32: 17.

Is a crown of glory to the
aged. *Prov.* 16: 31.

The wicked

Are far from. *Ps.* 119: 150.
Isa. 46: 12.

Are free from. *Rom.* 6: 20.

Are enemies of. *Acts* 13: 10.

Leave off. *Amos* 5: 7, with
Ps. 36: 3.

Follow not after. *Rom.* 9:
30.

Do not. 1 *John* 3: 10.

Do not obey. *Rom.* 2: 8,
with 2 *Thess.* 2: 12.

Love lying rather than. *Ps.*
52: 3.

Make mention of God, not
in. *Isa.* 48: 1.

Though favoured, will not
learn. *Isa.* 26: 10, with *Ps.*
106: 43.

Speak contemptuously against

those who follow. *Ps.* 31:
18.

Hate those who follow. *Ps.*
34: 21.

Slay those who follow. *Ps.*
37: 32. 1 *John* 3: 12, with
Matt. 23: 35.

Should break off their sins
by. *Dan.* 4: 27.

Should awake to. 1 *Cor.* 15:
34.

Should sow to themselves in.
Hos. 10: 12.

Vainly wish to die as those
who follow. *Num.* 23: 10.

The throne of kings established
by. *Prov.* 16: 12. *Prov.* 25: 5.

Nations exalted by. *Prov.* 14:
34.

Blessedness of

Having, imputed without
works. *Rom.* 4: 6.

Doing. *Ps.* 106: 3.

Hungering and thirsting after.
Matt. 5: 6.

Suffering for. 1 *Pet.* 3: 14.

Being persecuted for. *Matt.*
5: 10.

Turning others to. *Dan.* 12:
3.

Promised to the Church. *Isa.*
32: 16. *Isa.* 45: 8. *Isa.* 61: 11.
Isa. 62: 1.

Promised to saints. *Isa.* 60:
21. *Isa.* 61: 3.

Exemplified. JACOB, *Gen.* 30:
33. DAVID, 2 *Sam.* 22: 21. ZACH-
ARIAS, etc., *Luke* 1: 6. ABEL,
Heb. 11: 4. LOT, 2 *Pet.* 2: 8.

RIGHTEOUSNESS OF GOD, THE

Is part of his character. *Ps.* 7:
9. *Ps.* 116: 5. *Ps.* 119: 137.

Described as

Very high. *Ps.* 71: 19.

Abundant. *Ps.* 48: 10.

Beyond computation. *Ps.* 71: 15.

Everlasting. *Ps.* 119: 142.

Enduring for ever. *Ps.* 111: 3.

The habitation of his throne. *Ps.* 97: 2.

Christ acknowledged. *John* 17: 25.

Christ committed his cause to. 1 *Pet.* 2: 23.

Angels acknowledge. *Rev.* 16: 5.

Exhibited in

His testimonies. *Ps.* 119: 138, 144.

His commandments. *Deut.* 4: 8. *Ps.* 119: 172.

His judgments. *Ps.* 19: 9. *Ps.* 119: 7, 62.

His word. *Ps.* 119: 123.

His ways. *Ps.* 145: 17.

His acts. *Judges* 5: 11. 1 *Sam.* 12: 7.

His government. *Ps.* 96: 13. *Ps.* 98: 9.

The gospel. *Ps.* 85: 10, with *Rom.* 3: 25, 26.

The final judgment. *Acts* 17: 31.

The punishment of the wicked. *Rom.* 2: 5. 2 *Thess.* 1: 6. *Rev.* 16: 7. *Rev.* 19: 2.

Shown to the posterity of saints. *Ps.* 103: 17.

Shown openly before the heathen. *Ps.* 98: 2.

God delights in the exercise of. *Jer.* 9: 24.

The heavens shall declare. *Ps.* 50: 6. *Ps.* 97: 6.

Saints

Ascribe, to him. *Job* 36: 3. *Dan.* 9: 7.

Acknowledge, in his dealings. *Ezra* 9: 15.

Acknowledge, though the wicked prosper. *Jer.* 12: 1, with *Ps.* 73: 12–17.

Recognise, in the fulfilment of his promises. *Neh.* 9: 8.

Confident of beholding. *Mic.* 7: 9.

Upheld by. *Isa.* 41: 10.

Do not conceal. *Ps.* 40: 10.

Mention, only. *Ps.* 71: 16.

Talk of. *Ps.* 35: 28. *Ps.* 71: 15, 24.

Declare, to others. *Ps.* 22: 31.

Magnify. *Ps.* 7: 17. *Ps.* 51: 14. *Ps.* 145: 7.

Plead, in prayer. *Ps.* 143: 11. *Dan.* 9: 16.

Leads him to love righteousness. *Ps.* 11: 7.

We should pray

To be led in. *Ps.* 5: 8.

To be quickened in. *Ps.* 119: 40.

To be delivered in. *Ps.* 31: 1. *Ps.* 71: 2.

To be answered in. *Ps.* 143: 1.

To be judged according to. *Ps.* 35: 24.

For its continued manifestation. *Ps.* 36: 10.

His care and defence of his people designed to teach. *Mic.* 6: 4, 5.

The wicked have no interest in. *Ps.* 69: 27.

Illustrated. *Ps.* 36: 6.

RIGHTEOUSNESS IMPUTED

Predicted. *Isa.* 46: 13. *Isa.* 51: 5. *Isa.* 56: 1.

Revealed in the gospel. *Rom.* 1: 17.

Is of the Lord. *Isa.* 54: 17.

Described as

The righteousness of faith. *Rom.* 4: 13. *Rom.* 9: 30. *Rom.* 10: 6.

The righteousness of God, without the law. *Rom.* 3: 21.

The righteousness of God by faith in Christ. *Rom.* 3: 22.

Christ being made righteousness unto us. 1 *Cor.* 1: 30.

Our being made the righteousness of God, in Christ. 2 *Cor.* 5: 21.

Christ is the end of the law for. *Rom.* 10: 4.

Christ called THE LORD OUR RIGHTEOUSNESS by reason of. *Jer.* 23: 6.

Is an everlasting righteousness. *Dan.* 9: 24.

Is a free gift. *Rom.* 5: 17.

Never to be abolished. *Isa.* 51: 6.

The promises made through. *Rom.* 4: 13, 16.

Saints

Have, on believing. *Rom.* 4: 5, 11, 24.

Clothed with. *Isa.* 61: 10.

Made righteous by. *Rom.* 5: 19.

Justified by. *Rom.* 3: 26.

Exalted in. *Ps.* 89: 16.

Desire to be found in. *Phil.* 3: 9.

Glory in having. *Isa.* 45: 24, 25.

Exhortation to seek. *Matt.* 6: 33.

The Gentiles attained to. *Rom.* 9: 30.

Blessedness of those who have. *Rom.* 4: 6.

The wicked

Ignorant of. *Rom.* 10: 3.

Stumble at. *Rom.* 9: 32.

Submit not to. *Rom.* 10: 3.

Excluded from. *Ps.* 69: 27.

Exemplified. ABRAHAM, *Rom.* 4: 9, 22. *Gal.* 3: 6. PAUL, *Phil.* 3: 7–9.

SABBATH, THE

Instituted by God. *Gen.* 2: 3.

Grounds of its institution. *Gen.* 2: 2, 3. *Exod.* 20: 11.

The seventh day observed as. *Exod.* 20: 9, 10.

Made for man. *Mark* 2: 27.

God

Blessed. *Gen.* 2: 3. *Exod.* 20: 11.

Sanctified. *Gen.* 2: 3. *Exod.* 31: 15.

Hallowed. *Exod.* 20: 11.

Commanded, to be kept. *Lev.* 19: 3, 30.

Commanded, to be sanctified. *Exod.* 20: 8.

Will have his goodness commemorated in the observance of. *Deut.* 5: 15.

Shows favour in appointing. *Neh.* 9: 14.

Shows considerate kindness in appointing. *Exod.* 23: 12.

A sign of the covenant. *Exod.* 31: 13, 17.

A type of the heavenly rest. *Heb.* 4: 4, 9.

Christ

Is Lord of. *Mark* 2: 28.

Was accustomed to observe. *Luke* 4: 16.

Taught on. *Luke* 4: 31. *Luke* 6: 6.

Servants and cattle should be allowed to rest upon. *Exod.* 20: 10. *Deut.* 5: 14.

No manner of work to be done on. *Exod.* 20: 10. *Lev.* 23: 3.

No purchases to be made on. *Neh.* 10: 31. *Neh.* 13: 15–17.

No burdens to be carried on. *Neh.* 13: 19. *Jer.* 17: 21.

Divine worship to be celebrated on. *Ezek.* 46: 3. *Acts* 16: 13.

The scriptures to be read on. *Acts* 13: 27. *Acts* 15: 21.

The word of God to be preached on. *Acts* 13: 14, 15, 44. *Acts* 17: 2. *Acts* 18: 4.

Works connected with religious service lawful on. *Num.* 28: 9. *Matt.* 12: 5. *John* 7: 23.

Works of mercy lawful on. *Matt.* 12: 12. *Luke* 13: 16. *John* 9: 14.

Necessary wants may be supplied on. *Matt.* 12: 1. *Luke* 13: 5. *Luke* 14: 1.

Called

The sabbath of the Lord. *Exod.* 20: 10. *Lev.* 23: 3. *Deut.* 5: 14.

The sabbath of rest. *Exod.* 31: 15.

The rest of the holy sabbath. *Exod.* 16: 23.

God's holy day. *Isa.* 58: 13.

The Lord's Day. *Rev.* 1: 10.

First day of the week kept as, by primitive Church. *John* 20: 26. *Acts* 20: 7. 1 *Cor.* 16: 2.

Saints

Observe. *Neh.* 13: 22.

Honour God in observing. *Isa.* 58: 13.

Rejoice in. *Ps.* 118: 24. *Isa.* 58: 13.

Testify against those who desecrate. *Neh.* 13: 15, 20, 21.

Observance of, to be perpetual. *Exod.* 31: 16, 17, with *Matt.* 5: 17, 18.

Blessedness of honouring. *Isa.* 58: 13, 14.

Blessedness of keeping. *Isa.* 56: 2, 6.

Denunciations against those who profane. *Neh.* 13: 18. *Jer.* 17: 27.

Punishment of those who profane. *Exod.* 31: 14, 15. *Num.* 15: 32–36.

The wicked

Mock at. *Lam.* 1: 7.

Pollute. *Isa.* 56: 2. *Ezek.* 20: 13, 16.

Profane. *Neh.* 13: 17. *Ezek.* 22: 8.

Wearied by. *Amos* 8: 5.

Hide their eyes from. *Ezek.* 22: 26.

Do their own pleasure on. *Isa.* 58: 13.

Bear burdens on. *Neh.* 13: 15.

Work on. *Neh.* 13: 15.

Traffic on. *Neh.* 10: 31. *Neh.* 13: 15, 16.

Sometimes pretended to be zealous for. *Luke* 13: 14. *John* 9: 16.

May be judicially deprived of. *Lam.* 2: 6. *Hos.* 2: 11.

Honouring of—Exemplified. MOSES, etc., *Num.* 15: 32–34. NEHEMIAH, *Neh.* 13: 15, 21. THE WOMEN, *Luke* 23: 56. PAUL, *Acts* 13–14. DISCIPLES, *Acts* 16: 13. JOHN, *Rev.* 1: 10.

Dishonouring of—Exemplified. GATHERERS OF MANNA, *Exod.* 16: 27. GATHERER OF STICKS, *Num.* 15: 32. MEN OF TYRE, *Neh.* 13: 16. INHABITANTS OF JERUSALEM, *Jer.* 17: 21–23.

SAINTS, COMPARED TO

The sun. *Judges* 5: 31. *Matt.* 13: 43.

Stars. *Dan.* 12: 3.

Lights. *Matt.* 5: 14. *Phil.* 2: 15.

Mount Zion. *Ps.* 125: 1, 2.
Lebanon. *Hos.* 14: 5–7.
Treasure. *Exod.* 19: 5. *Ps.* 135: 4.
Jewels. *Mal.* 3: 17.
Gold. *Job* 23: 10. *Lam.* 4: 2.
Vessels of gold and silver. 2 *Tim.* 2: 20.
Stones of a crown. *Zech.* 9: 16.
Lively stones. 1 *Pet.* 2: 5.
Babes. *Matt.* 11: 25. 1 *Pet.* 2: 2.
Little children. *Matt.* 18: 3. 1 *Cor.* 14: 20.
Obedient children. 1 *Pet.* 1: 14.
Members of the body. 1 *Cor.* 12: 20, 27.
Soldiers. 2 *Tim.* 2: 3, 4.
Runners in a race. 1 *Cor.* 9: 24. *Heb.* 12: 1.
Wrestlers. 2 *Tim.* 2: 5.
Good servants. *Matt.* 25: 21.
Strangers and pilgrims. 1 *Pet.* 2: 11.
Sheep. *Ps.* 78: 52. *Matt.* 25: 33. *John* 10: 4.
Lambs. *Isa.* 40: 11. *John* 21: 15.
Calves of the stall. *Mal.* 4: 2.
Lions. *Prov.* 28: 1. *Mic.* 5: 8.
Eagles. *Ps.* 103: 5. *Isa.* 40: 31.
Doves. *Ps.* 68: 13. *Isa.* 60: 8.
Thirsting deer. *Ps.* 42: 1.
Good fishes. *Matt.* 13: 48.
Dew and showers. *Mic.* 5: 7.
Watered gardens. *Isa.* 58: 11.
Unfailing springs. *Isa.* 58: 11.
Vines. *Song of Sol.* 6: 11. *Hos.* 14: 7.
Branches of a vine. *John* 15: 2, 4, 5.
Pomegranates. *Song of Sol.* 4: 13.
Good figs. *Jer.* 24: 2–7.
Lilies. *Song of Sol.* 2: 2. *Hos.* 14: 5.

Willows by the water-courses. *Isa.* 44: 4.
Trees planted by rivers. *Ps.* 1: 3.
Cedars in Lebanon. *Ps.* 92: 12.
Palm trees. *Ps.* 92: 12.
Green olive trees. *Ps.* 52: 8. *Hos.* 14: 6.
Fruitful trees. *Ps.* 1: 3. *Jer.* 17: 8.
Corn. *Hos.* 14: 7.
Wheat. *Matt.* 3: 12. *Matt.* 13: 29, 30.
Salt. *Matt.* 5: 13.

SALVATION

Is of God. *Ps.* 3: 8. *Ps.* 37: 39. *Jer.* 3: 23.
Is of the purpose of God. 2 *Tim.* 1: 9.
Is of the appointment of God. 1 *Thess.* 5: 9.
God is willing to give. 1 *Tim.* 2: 4.
Is by Christ. *Isa.* 63: 9. *Eph.* 5: 23.
Is by Christ alone. *Isa.* 45: 21, 23. *Isa.* 59: 16. *Acts* 4: 12.
Announced after the fall. *Gen.* 3: 15.
Of Israel, predicted. *Isa.* 35: 4. *Isa.* 45: 17. *Zech.* 9: 16. *Rom.* 11: 26.
Of the Gentiles, predicted. *Isa.* 45: 22. *Isa.* 49: 6. *Isa.* 52: 10.
Revealed in the gospel. *Eph.* 1: 13. 2 *Tim.* 1: 10.
Came to the Gentiles through the fall of the Jews. *Rom.* 11: 11.

Christ
The Captain of. *Heb.* 2: 10.
The Author of. *Heb.* 5: 9.
Appointed for. *Isa.* 49: 6.
Raised up for. *Luke* 1: 69.
Has. *Zech.* 9: 9.
Brings, with him. *Isa.* 62: 11. *Luke* 19: 9.

Mighty to effect. *Isa.* 63: 1. *Heb.* 7: 25.

Came to effect. *Matt.* 18: 11. 1 *Tim.* 1: 15.

Died to effect. *John* 3: 14, 15. *Gal.* 1: 4.

Exalted to give. *Acts* 5: 31.

Is not by works. *Rom.* 11: 6. *Eph.* 2: 9. 2 *Tim.* 1: 9. *Titus* 3: 5.

Is of grace. *Eph.* 2: 5, 8. 2 *Tim.* 1: 9. *Titus* 2: 11.

Is of love. *Rom.* 5: 8. 1 *John* 4: 9, 10.

Is of mercy. *Ps.* 6: 4. *Titus* 3: 5.

Is of the long-suffering of God. 2 *Pet.* 3: 15.

Is through faith in Christ. *Mark* 16: 16. *Acts* 16: 31. *Rom.* 10: 9. *Eph.* 2: 8. 1 *Pet.* 1: 5.

Reconciliation to God, a pledge of. *Rom.* 5: 10.

Is deliverance from

Sin. *Matt.* 1: 21, with 1 *John* 3: 5.

Uncleanness. *Ezek.* 36: 29.

The devil. *Col.* 2: 15. *Heb.* 2: 14, 15.

Wrath. *Rom.* 5: 9. 1 *Thess.* 1: 10.

This present evil world. *Gal.* 1: 4.

Enemies. *Luke* 1: 71, 74.

Eternal death. *John* 3: 16, 17.

Confession of Christ necessary to. *Rom.* 10: 10.

Regeneration necessary to. 1 *Pet.* 3: 21.

Final perseverance necessary to. *Matt.* 10: 22.

Described as

Great. *Heb.* 2: 3.

Glorious. 2 *Tim.* 2:

Common. *Jude* 3.

From generation to generation. *Isa.* 51: 8.

To the uttermost. *Heb.* 7: 25.

Eternal. *Isa.* 45: 17. *Isa.* 51: 6. *Heb.* 5: 9.

Searched into and exhibited by the prophets. 1 *Pet.* 1: 10.

The gospel in the power of God unto. *Rom.* 1: 16. 1 *Cor.* 1: 18.

Preaching the word is the appointed means of. 1 *Cor.* 1: 21.

The scriptures are able to make wise unto. 2 *Tim.* 3: 15. *Jas.* 1: 21.

Now is the day of. *Isa.* 49: 8. 2 *Cor.* 6: 2.

From sin, to be worked out with fear and trembling. *Phil.* 2: 12.

Saints

Chosen to. 2 *Thess.* 2: 13. 2 *Tim.* 1: 9.

Appointed to obtain. 1 *Thess.* 5: 9.

Are heirs of. *Heb.* 1: 14.

Have, through grace. *Acts* 15: 11.

Have a token of, in their patient suffering for Christ. *Phil.* 1: 28, 29.

Kept by the power of God unto. 1 *Pet.* 1: 5.

Beautified with. *Ps.* 149: 4.

Clothed with. *Isa.* 61: 10.

Satisfied by. *Luke* 2: 30.

Love. *Ps.* 40: 16.

Hope for. *Lam.* 3: 26. *Rom.* 8: 24.

Wait for. *Gen.* 49: 18. *Lam.* 3: 26.

Long for. *Ps.* 119: 81, 174.

Earnestly look for. *Ps.* 119: 123.

Daily approach nearer to. *Rom.* 13: 11.

Receive, as the end of their faith. 1 *Pet.* 1: 9.

Welcome the tidings of. *Isa.* 52: 7, with *Rom.* 10: 15.

Pray to be visited with. *Ps.* 85: 7. *Ps.* 106: 4. *Ps.* 119: 41.

Pray for assurance of. *Ps.* 35: 3.

Pray for a joyful sense of. *Ps.* 51: 12.

Evidence, by works. *Heb.* 6: 9, 10.

Ascribe, to God. *Ps.* 25: 5. *Isa.* 12: 2.

Praise God for. 1 *Chron.* 16: 23. *Ps.* 96: 2.

Commemorate, with thanks. *Ps.* 116: 13.

Rejoice in. *Ps.* 9: 14. *Ps.* 21: 1. *Isa.* 25: 9.

Glory in. *Ps.* 21: 5.

Declare. *Ps.* 40: 10. *Ps.* 71: 15.

Godly sorrow worketh repentance unto. 2 *Cor.* 7: 10.

All the earth shall see. *Isa.* 52: 10. *Luke* 3: 6.

Ministers

Give the knowledge of. *Luke* 1: 77.

Show the way of. *Acts* 16: 17.

Should exhort to. *Ezek.* 3: 18. *Acts* 2: 40.

Should labour to lead others to. *Rom.* 11: 14.

Should be clothed with. 2 *Chron.* 6: 41. *Ps.* 132: 16.

Should use self-denial to lead others to. 1 *Cor.* 9: 22.

Should endure suffering that the elect may obtain. 2 *Tim.* 2: 10.

Are a sweet savour of Christ, unto God, in those who obtain. 2 *Cor.* 2: 15.

The heavenly host ascribe, to God. *Rev.* 7: 10. *Rev.* 19: 1.

Sought in vain from

Idols. *Isa.* 45: 20. *Jer.* 2: 28.

Earthly power. *Jer.* 3: 23.

No escape for those who neglect. *Heb.* 2: 3.

Is far off from the wicked. *Ps.* 119: 155. *Isa.* 59: 11.

Illustrated by

A rock. *Deut.* 32: 15. *Ps.* 95: 1.

A horn. *Ps.* 18: 2. *Luke* 1: 69.

A tower. 2 *Sam.* 22: 51.

A helmet. *Isa.* 59: 17. *Eph.* 6: 17.

A shield. 2 *Sam.* 22: 36.

A lamp. *Isa.* 62: 1.

A cup. *Ps.* 116: 13.

Clothing. 2 *Chron.* 6: 41. *Ps.* 132: 16. *Ps.* 149: 4. *Isa.* 61: 10.

Wells. *Isa.* 12: 3.

Walls and bulwarks. *Isa.* 26: 1. *Isa.* 60: 18.

Chariots. *Hab.* 3: 8.

A victory. 1 *Cor.* 15: 57.

Typified. *Num.* 21: 4–9, with *John* 3: 14, 15.

SANCTIFICATION

Is separation to the service of God. *Ps.* 4: 3. 2 *Cor.* 6: 17.

Effected by

God. *Ezek.* 37: 28. 1 *Thess.* 5: 23. *Jude* 1.

Christ. *Heb.* 2: 11. *Heb.* 13: 12.

The Holy Ghost. *Rom.* 15: 16. 1 *Cor.* 6: 11.

In Christ. 1 *Cor.* 1: 2.

Through the atonement of Christ. *Heb.* 10: 10. *Heb.* 13: 12.

Through the word of God. *John* 17: 17, 19. *Eph.* 5: 26.

Christ made, of God, unto us. 1 *Cor.* 1: 30.

Saints elected to salvation through. 2 *Thess.* 2: 13. 1 *Pet.* 1: 2.

All saints are in a state of. *Acts* 20: 32. *Acts* 26: 18. 1 *Cor.* 6: 11.

The Church made glorious by. *Eph.* 5: 26, 27.

Should lead to

Mortification of sin. 1 *Thess.* 4: 3, 4.

Holiness. *Rom.* 6: 22. *Eph.* 5: 7–9.

Offering up of saints acceptable through. *Rom.* 15: 16.

Saints fitted for the service of God by. 2 *Tim.* 2: 21.

God wills all saints to have. 1 *Thess.* 4: 3.

Ministers

Set apart to God's service by. *Jer.* 1: 5.

Should pray that their people may enjoy complete. 1 *Thess.* 5: 23.

Should exhort their people to walk in. 1 *Thess.* 4: 1, 3.

None can inherit the kingdom of God without. 1 *Cor.* 6: 9–11.

Typified. *Gen.* 2: 3. *Exod.* 13: 2. *Exod.* 19: 14. *Exod.* 40: 9–15. *Lev.* 27: 14–16.

SCORNING AND MOCKING

The sufferings of Christ by, predicted. *Ps.* 22: 6–8. *Isa.* 53: 3. *Luke* 18: 32.

Christ endured. *Matt.* 9: 24. *Matt.* 27: 29.

Saints endure, on account of

Being children of God. *Gen.* 21: 9, with *Gal.* 4: 29.

Their uprightness. *Job* 12: 4.

Their faith. *Heb.* 11: 36.

Their faithfulness in declaring the word of God. *Jer.* 30: 7, 8.

Their zeal for God's house. *Neh.* 2: 19.

The wicked indulge in, against

The second coming of Christ. 2 *Pet.* 3: 3, 4.

The gifts of the Spirit. *Acts* 2: 13.

God's threatenings. *Isa.* 5: 19. *Jer.* 17: 15.

God's ministers. 2 *Chron.* 36: 16.

God's ordinances. *Lam.* 1: 7.

Saints. *Ps.* 123: 4. *Lam.* 3: 14, 63.

The resurrection of the dead. *Acts* 17: 32.

All solemn admonitions. 2 *Chron.* 30: 6–10.

Idolaters addicted to. *Isa.* 57: 3–6.

Drunkards addicted to. *Ps.* 69: 12. *Hos.* 7: 5.

They who are addicted to,

Delight in. *Prov.* 1: 22.

Are contentious. *Prov.* 22: 10.

Are scorned by God. *Prov.* 3: 34.

Are hated by men. *Prov.* 24: 9.

Are avoided by saints. *Ps.* 1: 1. *Jer.* 15: 17.

Walk after their own lusts. 2 *Pet.* 3: 3.

Are proud and haughty. *Prov.* 21: 24.

Hear not rebuke. *Prov.* 13: 1.

Love not those who reprove. *Prov.* 15: 12.

Hate those who reprove. *Prov.* 9: 8.

Go not to the wise. *Prov.* 15: 12.

Bring others into danger. *Prov.* 29: 8.

Shall themselves endure. *Ezek.* 23: 32.

Characteristic of the latter days. 2 *Pet.* 3: 3. *Jude* 18.

Woe denounced against. *Isa.* 5: 18, 19.

Punishment for. 2 *Chron.* 36: 17. *Prov.* 19: 29. *Isa.* 29: 20. *Lam.* 3: 64–66.

Exemplified. ISHMAEL, *Gen.* 21: 9. YOUTHS AT BETHEL, 2 *Kings* 2: 23. EPHRAIM AND MANASSEH, 2 *Chron.* 30: 10. CHIEFS OF JUDAH, 2 *Chron.* 36: 16. SANBALLAT, *Neh.* 4: 1. ENEMIES OF JOB, *Job* 30: 1, 9. ENEMIES OF DAVID, *Ps.* 35: 15, 16. RULERS OF ISRAEL, *Isa.* 28: 14. AMMONITES, *Ezek.* 25: 3. TYRIANS, *Ezek.* 26: 2. HEATHEN, *Ezek.* 36: 2, 3. SOLDIERS, *Matt.* 27: 28–30. *Luke* 23: 36. CHIEF PRIESTS, etc., *Matt.* 27: 41. PHARISEES, *Luke* 16: 14. THE MEN WHO HELD JESUS, *Luke* 22: 63, 64. HEROD, etc., *Luke* 23: 11. PEOPLE AND RULERS, *Luke* 23: 35. SOME OF THE MULTI-TUDE, *Acts* 2: 13. ATHENIANS, *Acts* 17: 32.

SCRIPTURES, THE

Given by inspiration of God. 2 *Tim.* 3: 16.

Given by inspiration of the Holy Ghost. *Acts* 1: 16. *Heb.* 3: 7. 2 *Pet.* 1: 21.

Christ sanctioned, by appealing to them. *Matt.* 4: 4. *Mark* 12: 10. *John* 7: 42.

Christ taught out of. *Luke* 24: 27.

Are called the

Word. *Jas.* 1: 21–23. 1 *Pet.* 2: 2.

Word of God. *Luke* 11: 28. *Heb.* 4: 12.

Word of Christ. *Col.* 3: 16.

Word of truth. *Jas.* 1: 18.

Holy scriptures. *Rom.* 1: 2. 2 *Tim.* 3: 15.

Scripture of truth. *Dan.* 10: 21.

Book. *Ps.* 40: 7. *Rev.* 22: 19.

Book of the Lord. *Isa.* 34: 16.

Book of the law. *Neh.* 8: 3. *Gal.* 3: 10.

Law of the Lord. *Ps.* 1: 2. *Isa.* 30: 9.

Sword of the Spirit. *Eph.* 6: 17.

Oracles of God. *Rom.* 3: 2. 1 *Pet.* 4: 11.

Contain the promises of the gospel. *Rom.* 1: 2.

Reveal the laws, statutes, and judgments of God. *Deut.* 4: 5, 14, with *Exod.* 24: 3, 4.

Record divine prophecies. 2 *Pet.* 1: 19–21.

Testify of Christ. *John* 5: 39. *Acts* 10: 43. *Acts* 18: 28. 1 *Cor.* 15: 3.

Are full and sufficient. *Luke* 16: 29, 31.

Are an unerring guide. *Prov.* 6: 23. 2 *Pet.* 1: 19.

Are able to make wise unto salvation through faith in Christ Jesus. 2 *Tim.* 3: 15.

Are profitable both for doctrine and practice. *2 Tim.* 3: 16, 17.

Described as

Pure. *Ps.* 12: 6. *Ps.* 119: 140. *Prov.* 30: 5.

True. *Ps.* 119: 169. *John* 17: 17.

Perfect. *Ps.* 19: 7.

Precious. *Ps.* 19: 10.

Quick and powerful. *Heb.* 4: 12.

Written for our instruction. *Rom.* 15: 4.

Intended for the use of all men. *Rom.* 16: 26.

Nothing to be taken from, or added to. *Deut.* 4: 2. *Deut.* 12: 32. *Prov.* 30: 5, 6. *Rev.* 22: 18, 19.

One portion of, to be compared with another. *1 Cor.* 2: 13.

Designed for

Regenerating. *Jas.* 1: 18. *1 Pet.* 1: 23.

Quickening. *Ps.* 119: 50, 93.

Illuminating. *Ps.* 119: 130.

Converting the soul. *Ps.* 19: 7.

Making wise the simple. *Ps.* 19: 7.

Sanctifying. *John* 17: 17. *Eph.* 5: 26.

Producing faith. *John* 20: 31.

Producing hope. *Ps.* 119: 49. *Rom.* 15: 4.

Producing obedience. *Deut.* 17: 19, 20.

Cleansing the heart. *John* 15: 3. *Eph.* 5: 26.

Cleansing the ways. *Ps.* 119: 9.

Keeping from destructive paths. *Ps.* 17: 4.

Supporting life. *Deut.* 8: 3, with *Matt.* 4: 4.

Promoting growth in grace. *1 Pet.* 2: 2.

Building up in the faith. *Acts* 20: 32.

Admonishing. *Ps.* 19: 14. *1 Cor.* 10: 11.

Comforting. *Ps.* 119: 82. *Rom.* 15: 4.

Rejoicing the heart. *Ps.* 19: 8. *Ps.* 119: 111.

Work effectually in them that believe. *1 Thess.* 2: 13.

The letter of, without the spirit, killeth. *John* 6: 63, with *2 Cor.* 3: 6.

Ignorance of, a source of error. *Matt.* 22: 29. *Acts* 13: 27.

Christ enables us to understand. *Luke* 24: 45.

The Holy Ghost enables us to understand. *John* 16: 13. *1 Cor.* 2: 10–14.

No prophecy of, is of any private interpretation. *2 Pet.* 1: 20.

Everything should be tried by. *Isa.* 8: 20. *Acts* 17: 11.

Should be

The standard of teaching. *1 Pet.* 4: 11.

Believed. *John* 2: 22.

Appealed to. *1 Cor.* 1: 31. *1 Pet.* 1: 16.

Read. *Deut.* 17: 19. *Isa.* 34: 16.

Read publicly to ALL. *Deut.* 31: 11–13. *Neh.* 8: 3. *Jer.* 36: 6. *Acts* 13: 15.

Known. *2 Tim.* 3: 15.

Received, not as the word of men, but as the word of God. *1 Thess.* 2: 13.

Received with meekness. *Jas.* 1: 21.

Searched. *John* 5: 39. *John* 7: 52.

Searched daily. *Acts* 17: 11.

Laid up in the heart. *Deut.*
6: 6. *Deut.* 11: 18.

Taught to children. *Deut.*
6: 7. *Deut.* 11: 19. 2 *Tim.*
3: 15.

Taught to ALL. 2 *Chron.* 17:
7–9. *Neh.* 8: 7, 8.

Talked of continually. *Deut.*
6: 7.

Not handled deceitfully. 2
Cor. 4: 2.

Not only heard, but obeyed.
Matt. 7: 24, with *Luke* 11:
28. *Jas.* 1: 22.

Used against our spiritual
enemies. *Matt.* 4: 4, 7, 10,
with *Eph.* 6: 11, 17.

All should desire to hear. *Neh.*
8: 1.

Mere hearers of, deceive themselves. *Jas.* 1: 22.

Advantage of possessing. *Rom.*
3: 2.

Saints

Love exceedingly. *Ps.* 119:
97, 113, 159, 167.

Delight in. *Ps.* 1: 2.

Regard, as sweet. *Ps.* 119:
103.

Esteem, above all things.
Job 23: 12.

Long after. *Ps.* 119: 82.

Stand in awe of. *Ps.* 119:
161. *Isa.* 66: 2.

Keep, in remembrance. *Ps.*
119: 16.

Grieve when men disobey.
Ps. 119: 158.

Hide, in their heart. *Ps.*
119: 11.

Hope in. *Ps.* 119: 74, 81,
147.

Meditate in. *Ps.* 1: 2. *Ps.*
119: 99, 148.

Rejoice in. *Ps.* 119: 162.
Jer. 15: 16.

Trust in. *Ps.* 119: 42.

Obey. *Ps.* 119: 67. *Luke* 8:
21. *John* 17: 6.

Speak of. *Ps.* 119: 172.

Esteem, as a light. *Ps.* 119:
105.

Pray to be taught. *Ps.* 119:
12, 18, 33, 66.

Pray to be conformed to.
Ps. 119: 133.

Plead the promises of, in
prayer. *Ps.* 119: 25, 28, 41,
76, 169.

They who search, are truly
noble. *Acts* 17: 11.

Blessedness of hearing and obeying. *Luke* 11: 28. *Jas.* 1: 25.

Let them dwell richly in you.
Col. 3: 16.

The wicked

Corrupt. 2 *Cor.* 2: 17.

Make, of none effect through
their traditions. *Mark* 7:
9–13.

Reject. *Jer.* 8: 9.

Stumble at. 1 *Pet.* 2: 8.

Obey not. *Ps.* 119: 158.

Frequently wrest, to their
own destruction. 2 *Pet.* 3:
16.

Denunciations against those
who add to, or take from.
Rev. 22: 18, 19.

Destruction of, punished. *Jer.*
36: 29–31.

SEALING OF THE HOLY SPIRIT

Christ received. *John* 6: 27.

Saints receive. 2 *Cor.* 1: 22.
Eph. 1: 13.

Is unto the day of redemption.
Eph. 4: 30.

The wicked do not receive.
Rev. 9: 4.

Judgment suspended until all
saints receive. *Rev.* 7: 3.

Typified. *Rom.* 4: 11.

SECOND COMING OF CHRIST, THE

Time of, unknown. *Matt.* 24: 36. *Mark* 13: 32.

Called the

Times of refreshing from the presence of the Lord. *Acts* 3: 19.

Times of the restitution of all things. *Acts* 3: 21, with *Rom.* 8: 21.

Last time. 1 *Pet.* 1: 5.

Appearing of Jesus Christ. 1 *Pet.* 1: 7.

Revelation of Jesus Christ. 1 *Pet.* 1: 13. 1 *Cor.* 1: 7.

Glorious appearing of the great God and our Saviour. *Titus* 2: 13.

Coming of the day of God. 2 *Pet.* 3: 12.

Day of our Lord Jesus Christ. 1 *Cor.* 1: 8.

Foretold by

Prophets. *Dan.* 7: 13. *Jude* 14.

Himself. *Matt.* 25: 31. *John* 14: 3.

Apostles. *Acts* 3: 20. 1 *Tim.* 6: 14.

Angels. *Acts* 1: 10, 11.

Signs preceding. *Matt.* 24: 3, etc.

The manner of;

In clouds. *Matt.* 24: 30. *Matt.* 26: 24. *Rev.* 1: 7.

In the glory of his Father. *Matt.* 16: 17.

In his own glory. *Matt.* 25: 31.

In flaming fire. 2 *Thess.* 1: 8.

With power and great glory. *Matt.* 24: 30.

As He ascended. *Acts* 1: 9, 11.

With a shout and the voice of the Archangel, etc. 1 *Thess.* 4: 16.

Accompanied by Angels. *Matt.* 16: 27. *Matt.* 25: 31. *Mark* 8: 38. 2 *Thess.* 1: 7.

With his saints. 1 *Thess.* 3: 13. *Jude* 14.

Suddenly. *Mark* 13: 36.

Unexpectedly. *Matt.* 24: 44. *Luke* 12: 40.

As a thief in the night. 1 *Thess.* 5: 2. 2 *Pet.* 3: 10. *Rev.* 16: 15.

As the lightning. *Matt.* 24: 27.

The heavens and earth shall be dissolved, etc. 2 *Pet.* 3: 10, 12.

They who shall have died in Christ shall rise first at. 1 *Thess.* 4: 16.

The saints alive at, shall be caught up to meet him. 1 *Thess.* 4: 17.

Is not to make atonement. *Heb.* 9: 28, with *Rom.* 6: 9, 10, and *Heb.* 10: 14.

The purposes of, are to

Complete the salvation of saints. *Heb.* 9: 28. 1 *Pet.* 1: 5.

Be glorified in his saints. 2 *Thess.* 1: 10.

Be admired in them that believe. 2 *Thess.* 1: 10.

Bring to light the hidden things of darkness, etc. 1 *Cor.* 4: 5.

Judge. *Ps.* 50: 3, 4, with *John* 5: 22. 2 *Tim.* 4: 1. *Jude* 15. *Rev.* 20: 11–13.

Reign. *Isa.* 24: 23. *Dan.* 7: 14. *Rev.* 11: 15.

Destroy death. 1 *Cor.* 15: 23, 26.

Every eye shall see him at. *Rev.* 1: 7.

Should be always considered as at hand. *Rom.* 13: 12. *Phil.* 4: 5. 1 *Pet.* 4: 7.

Blessedness of being prepared for. *Matt.* 24: 46. *Luke* 12: 37, 38.

Saints

Assured of. *Job* 19: 25, 26.

Love. 2 *Tim.* 4: 8.

Look for. *Phil.* 3: 20. *Titus* 2: 13.

Wait for. 1 *Cor.* 1: 7. 1 *Thess.* 1: 10.

Haste unto. 2 *Pet.* 3: 12.

Pray for. *Rev.* 22: 20.

Should be ready for. *Matt.* 24: 44. *Luke* 12: 40.

Should watch for. *Matt.* 24: 42. *Mark* 13: 35–37. *Luke* 21: 36.

Should be patient unto. 2 *Thess.* 3: 5. *Jas.* 5: 7, 8.

Shall be preserved unto. *Phil.* 1: 6. 2 *Tim.* 4: 18. 1 *Pet.* 1: 5. *Jude* 24.

Shall not be ashamed at. 1 *John* 2: 28.

Shall be blameless at. 1 *Cor.* 1: 8. 1 *Thess.* 3: 13. 1 *Thess.* 5: 23. *Jude* 24.

Shall be like him at. *Phil.* 3: 21. 1 *John* 3: 2.

Shall see him as He is, at. 1 *John* 3: 2.

Shall appear with him in glory at. *Col.* 3: 4.

Shall receive a crown of glory at. 2 *Tim.* 4: 8. 1 *Pet.* 5: 4.

Shall reign with him at. *Dan.* 7: 27. 2 *Tim.* 2: 12. *Rev.* 5: 10. *Rev.* 20: 6. *Rev.* 22: 5.

Faith of, shall be found unto praise at. 1 *Pet.* 1: 7.

The wicked

Scoff at. 2 *Pet.* 3: 3, 4.

Presume upon the delay of. *Matt.* 24: 48.

Shall be surprised by. *Matt.* 24: 37–39. 1 *Thess.* 5: 3. 2 *Pet.* 3: 10.

Shall be punished at. 2 *Thess.* 1: 8, 9.

The man of sin to be destroyed at. 2 *Thess.* 2: 8.

Illustrated. *Matt.* 25: 6. *Luke* 12: 36, 39. *Luke* 19: 12, 15.

SEEKING GOD

Commanded. *Isa.* 55: 6. *Matt.* 7: 7.

Includes seeking

His name. *Ps.* 83: 16.

His word. *Amos* 8: 12.

His face. *Ps.* 27: 8. *Ps.* 105: 4.

His strength. 1 *Chron.* 16: 11. *Ps.* 105: 4.

His commandments. 1 *Chron.* 28: 8.

His precepts. *Ps.* 119: 45, 94.

His kingdom. *Matt.* 6: 33.

Christ. *Mal.* 3: 1. *Luke* 2: 15, 16.

Honour which comes from him. *John* 5: 44.

By prayer. *Job* 8: 5. *Dan.* 9: 3.

In his house. *Deut.* 12: 5. *Ps.* 27: 4.

Should be

Immediate. *Hos.* 10: 12.

Evermore. *Ps.* 105: 4.

While he may be found. *Isa.* 55: 6.

With diligence. *Heb.* 11: 6.

With the heart. *Deut.* 4: 29. 1 *Chron.* 22: 19.

In the day of trouble. *Ps.* 77: 2.

Ensures

His being found. *Deut.* 4: 29. *Chron.* 28: 9. *Prov.* 8: 17. *Jer.* 29: 13.

His favour. *Lam.* 3: 25.

His protection. *Ezra* 8: 22.

His not forsaking us. *Ps.* 9: 10.

Life. *Ps.* 69: 32. *Amos* 5: 4, 6.

Prosperity. *Job* 8: 5, 6. *Ps.* 34: 10.

Being heard of him. *Ps.* 34: 4.

Understanding all things. *Prov.* 28: 5.

Gifts of righteousness. *Hos.* 10: 12.

Imperative upon all. *Isa.* 8: 19.

Afflictions designed to lead to. *Ps.* 78: 33, 34. *Hos.* 5: 15.

None, by nature, are found to be engaged in. *Ps.* 14: 2, with *Rom.* 3: 11.

Saints

Specially exhorted to. *Zeph.* 2: 3.

Desirous of. *Job* 5: 8.

Purpose, in heart. *Ps.* 27: 8.

Prepare their hearts for. 2 *Chron.* 30: 19.

Set their hearts to. 2 *Chron.* 11: 16.

Engage in, with the whole heart. 2 *Chron.* 15: 12. *Ps.* 119: 10.

Early in. *Job* 8: 5. *Ps.* 63: 1. *Isa.* 26: 9.

Earnest in. *Song of Sol.* 3: 2.

Characterised by. *Ps.* 24: 6.

Is never in vain. *Isa.* 45: 19.

Blessedness of. *Ps.* 119: 2.

Leads to joy. *Ps.* 70: 4. *Ps.* 105: 3.

Ends in praise. *Ps.* 22: 26.

Promise connected with. *Ps.* 69: 32.

Shall be rewarded. *Heb.* 11: 6.

The wicked

Are gone out of the way of. *Ps.* 14: 2, 3, with *Rom.* 3: 11, 12.

Prepare not their hearts for. 2 *Chron.* 12: 14.

Refuse, through pride. *Ps.* 10: 4.

Not led to, by affliction. *Isa.* 9: 13.

Sometimes pretend to. *Ezra* 4: 2. *Isa.* 58: 2.

Rejected, when too late in. *Prov.* 1: 28.

They who neglect, denounced. *Isa.* 31: 1.

Punishment of those who neglect. *Zeph.* 1: 4–6.

Exemplified. ASA, 2 *Chron.* 14: 7. JEHOSHAPHAT, 2 *Chron.* 17: 3, 4. UZZIAH, 2 *Chron.* 26: 5. HEZEKIAH, 2 *Chron.* 31: 21. JOSIAH, 2 *Chron.* 34: 3. EZRA, *Ezra* 7: 10. DAVID, *Ps.* 34: 4. DANIEL, *Dan.* 9: 3, 4.

SELF-DELUSION

A characteristic of the wicked. *Ps.* 49: 18.

Prosperity frequently leads to. *Ps.* 30: 6. *Hos.* 12: 8. *Luke* 12: 17–19.

Obstinate sinners often given up to. *Ps.* 81: 11, 12. *Hos.* 4: 17. 2 *Thess.* 2: 10, 11.

Exhibited in thinking that

Our own ways are right. *Prov.* 14: 12.

We should adhere to established wicked practices. *Jer.* 44: 17.

We are pure. *Prov.* 30: 12.

We are better than others. *Luke* 18: 11.

We are rich in spiritual things. *Rev.* 3: 17.

We may have peace while in sin. *Deut.* 29: 19.

We are above adversity. *Ps.* 10: 6.

Gifts entitle us to heaven. *Matt.* 7: 21, 22.

Privileges entitle us to heaven. *Matt.* 3: 9. *Luke* 13: 25, 26.

God will not punish our sins. *Jer.* 5: 12.

Christ shall not come to judge. 2 *Pet.* 3: 4.

Our lives shall be prolonged. *Isa.* 56: 12. *Luke* 12: 19. *Jas.* 4: 13.

Frequently persevered in, to the last. *Matt.* 7: 22. *Matt.* 25: 11, 12. *Luke* 13: 24, 25.

Fatal consequences of. *Matt.* 7: 23. *Matt.* 24: 48–51. *Luke* 12: 20. 1 *Thess.* 5: 3.

Exemplified. AHAB, 1 *Kings* 20: 27, 34. ISRAELITES, *Hos.* 12: 8. JEWS, *John* 8: 33, 41. CHURCH OF LAODICEA, *Rev.* 3: 17.

SELF-DENIAL

Christ set an example of. *Matt.* 4: 8–10. *Matt.* 8: 20. *Rom.* 15: 3. *Phil.* 2: 6–8.

A test of devotedness to Christ. *Matt.* 10: 37, 38. *Luke* 14: 27, 33.

Necessary

In following Christ. *Luke* 9: 23, 24.

In the warfare of saints. 2 *Tim.* 2: 4.

To the triumph of saints. 1 *Cor.* 9: 25.

Ministers especially called to exercise. 2 *Cor.* 6: 4, 5.

Should be exercised in

Denying ungodliness and worldly lusts. *Rom.* 6: 12. *Titus* 2: 12.

Controlling the appetite. *Prov.* 23: 2.

Abstaining from fleshly lusts. 1 *Pet.* 2: 11.

No longer living to lusts of men. 1 *Pet.* 4: 2.

Mortifying sinful lusts. *Mark* 9: 43. *Col.* 3: 5.

Mortifying deeds of the body. *Rom.* 8: 13.

Not pleasing ourselves. *Rom.* 15: 1–3.

Not seeking our own profit. 1 *Cor.* 10: 24, 33. 1 *Cor.* 13: 5. *Phil.* 2: 4.

Preferring the profit of others. *Rom.* 14: 20, 21. 1 *Cor.* 10: 24, 33.

Assisting others. *Luke* 3: 11.

Even lawful things. 1 *Cor.* 10: 23.

Forsaking all. *Luke* 14: 33.

Taking up the cross and following Christ. *Matt.* 10: 38. *Matt.* 16: 24.

Crucifying the flesh. *Gal.* 5: 24.

Being crucified with Christ. *Rom.* 6: 6.

Being crucified unto the world. *Gal.* 6: 14.

Putting off the old man which is corrupt. *Eph.* 4: 22. *Col.* 3: 9.

Preferring Christ to all earthly relations. *Matt.* 8: 21, 22. *Luke* 14: 26.

Becomes strangers and pilgrims. *Heb.* 11: 13–15. 1 *Pet.* 2: 11.

Danger of neglecting. *Matt.* 16: 25, 26. 1 *Cor.* 9: 27.

Reward of. *Matt.* 19: 28, 29. *Rom.* 8: 13.

Happy result of. 2 *Pet.* 1: 4.

Exemplified. ABRAHAM, *Gen.* 13: 9. *Heb.* 11: 8, 9. WIDOW OF ZAREPHATH, 1 *Kings* 17: 12–15. ESTHER, *Esther* 4: 16. RECHABITES, *Jer.* 35: 6, 7. DANIEL, *Dan.* 5: 16, 17. APOSTLES, *Matt.* 19: 27. SIMON, ANDREW, JAMES AND JOHN, *Mark* 1: 16–20. POOR WIDOW, *Luke* 21: 4. PRIMITIVE CHRISTIANS, *Acts* 2: 45. *Acts* 4: 34. BARNABAS, *Acts* 4: 36, 37. PAUL, *Acts* 20: 24. 1 *Cor.* 9: 19, 27. MOSES, *Heb.* 11: 24, 25.

SELF-EXAMINATION

Enjoined. 2 *Cor.* 13: 5.

Necessary before the communion. 1 *Cor.* 11: 28.

Cause of difficulty in. *Jer.* 17: 9.

Should be engaged in

With holy awe. *Ps.* 4: 4.

With diligent search. *Ps.* 77: 6. *Lam.* 3: 40.

With prayer for divine searching. *Ps.* 26: 2. *Ps.* 139: 23, 24.

With purpose of amendment. *Ps.* 119: 59. *Lam.* 3: 40.

Advantages of. 1 *Cor.* 11: 31. *Gal.* 6: 4.

SELFISHNESS

Contrary to the law of God. *Jas.* 2: 8.

The example of Christ condemns. *John* 4: 34. *Rom.* 15: 3. 2 *Cor.* 8: 9.

God hates. *Mal.* 1: 10.

Exhibited in

Being lovers of ourselves. 2 *Tim.* 3: 2.

Pleasing ourselves. *Rom.* 15: 1.

Seeking our own. 1 *Cor.* 10: 33. *Phil.* 2: 21.

Seeking after gain. *Isa.* 56: 11.

Seeking undue precedence. *Matt.* 20: 21.

Living to ourselves. 2 *Cor.* 5: 15.

Neglect of the poor. 1 *John* 3: 17.

Serving God for reward. *Mal.* 1: 10.

Performing duty for reward. *Mic.* 3: 11.

Inconsistent with Christian love. 1 *Cor.* 13: 5.

Inconsistent with the communion of saints. *Rom.* 12: 4, 5, with 1 *Cor.* 12: 12–47.

Especially forbidden to saints. 1 *Cor.* 10: 24. *Phil.* 2: 4.

The love of Christ should constrain us to avoid. 2 *Cor.* 5: 14, 15.

Ministers should be devoid of. 1 *Cor.* 9: 19–23. 1 *Cor.* 10: 33.

All men addicted to. *Phil.* 2: 21.

Saints falsely accused of. *Job* 1: 9–11.

Characteristic of the last days. 2 *Tim.* 3: 1, 2.

Exemplified. CAIN, *Gen.* 4: 9. NABAL, 1 *Sam.* 25: 3, 11. HAMAN, *Esther* 6: 6. PRIESTS, *Isa.* 56: 11. JEWS, *Zech.* 7: 6. JAMES AND JOHN, *Mark* 10: 37. MULTITUDE, *John* 6: 26.

SELF-RIGHTEOUSNESS

Man is prone to. *Prov.* 20: 6. *Prov.* 30: 12.

Hateful to God. *Luke* 16: 15.

Is vain because our righteousness is

But external. *Matt.* 23: 25–28. *Luke* 11: 39–44.

But partial. *Matt.* 23: 25. *Luke* 11: 42.

No better than filthy rags. *Isa.* 64: 6.

Ineffectual for salvation. *Matt.* 5: 20, with *Rom.* 3: 20.

Unprofitable. *Isa.* 57: 12.

Is boastful. *Matt.* 23: 30.

They who are given to

Audaciously approach God. *Luke* 18: 11.

Seek to justify themselves. *Luke* 10: 29.

Seek to justify themselves before men. *Luke* 16: 15.

Reject the righteousness of God. *Rom.* 10: 3.

Condemn others. *Matt.* 9: 11–13. *Luke* 7: 39.

Consider their own way right. *Prov.* 21: 2.

Despise others. *Isa.* 65: 5. *Luke* 18: 9.

Proclaim their own goodness. *Prov.* 20: 6.

Are pure in their own eyes. *Prov.* 30: 12.

Are abominable before God. *Isa.* 65: 5.

Folly of. *Job* 9: 20.

Saints renounce. *Phil.* 3: 7–10.

Warning against. *Deut.* 9: 4.

Denunciation against. *Matt.* 23: 27, 28.

Illustrated. *Luke* 18: 10–12.

Exemplified. SAUL, 1 *Sam.* 15: 13. YOUNG MAN, *Matt.* 19: 20. LAWYER, *Luke* 10: 25, 29. PHARISEES, *Luke* 11: 39. *John* 8: 33. *John* 9: 28. ISRAEL, *Rom.* 10: 3. CHURCH OF LAODICEA, *Rev.* 3: 17.

SELF-WILL AND STUBBORNNESS

Forbidden. 2 *Chron.* 30: 8. *Ps.* 75: 5.

Proceed from

Unbelief. 2 *Kings* 17: 14.

Pride. *Neh.* 9: 16, 29.

An evil heart. *Jer.* 7: 24.

God knows. *Isa.* 48: 4.

Exhibited in

Refusing to hearken to God. *Prov.* 1: 24.

Refusing to hearken to the messengers of God. 1 *Sam.* 8: 19. *Jer.* 44: 16. *Zech.* 7: 11.

Refusing to walk in the ways of God. *Neh.* 9: 17. *Isa.* 42: 24. *Ps.* 78: 10.

Refusing to hearken to parents. *Deut.* 21: 18, 19.

Refusing to receive correction. *Deut.* 21: 18. *Jer.* 5: 3. *Jer.* 7: 28.

Rebelling against God. *Deut.* 31: 27. *Ps.* 78: 8.

Resisting the Holy Ghost. *Acts* 7: 51.

Walking in the counsels of an evil heart. *Jer.* 7: 24, with *Jer.* 23: 17.

Hardening the neck. *Neh.* 9: 16.

Hardening the heart. 2 *Chron.* 36: 13.

Going backward and not forward. *Jer.* 7: 24.

Heinousness of. 1 *Sam.* 15: 23.

Ministers should

Be without. *Titus* 1: 7.

Warn their people against. *Heb.* 3: 7–12.

Pray that their people may be forgiven for. *Exod.* 34: 9. *Deut.* 9: 27.

Characteristic of the wicked. *Prov.* 7: 11. 2 *Pet.* 2: 10.

The wicked cease not from. *Judges* 2: 10.

Punishment for. *Deut.* 21: 21. *Prov.* 29: 1.

Illustrated. *Ps.* 32: 9. *Jer.* 31: 18.

Exemplified. SIMEON AND LEVI, *Gen.* 49: 6. ISRAELITES, *Exod.* 32: 9. *Deut.* 9: 6, 13. SAUL, 1 *Sam.* 15: 19–23. DAVID, 2 *Sam.* 24: 4. JOSIAH, 2 *Chron.* 35: 22. ZEDEKIAH, 2 *Chron.* 36: 13.

SERVANTS

Christ condescended to the office of. *Luke* 22: 27. *John* 13: 5. *Phil.* 2: 7.

Are inferior to their masters. *Luke* 22: 27.

Should follow Christ's example. 1 *Pet.* 2: 21.

Duties of, to masters;

To pray for them. *Gen.* 24: 12.

To honour them. *Mal.* 1: 6. 1 *Tim.* 6: 1.

To revere them the more, when they are believers. 1 *Tim.* 6: 2.

To be subject to them. 1 *Pet.* 2: 18.

To obey them. *Eph.* 6: 5. *Titus* 2: 9.

To attend to their call. *Ps.* 123: 2.

To please them well in all things. *Titus* 2: 9.

To sympathise with them. 2 *Sam.* 12: 18.

To prefer their business to their own necessary food. *Gen.* 24: 33.

To bless God for mercies shown to them. *Gen.* 24: 27, 48.

To be faithful to them. *Luke* 16: 10–12. 1 *Cor.* 4: 2. *Titus* 2: 10.

To be profitable to them.

Luke 19: 15, 16, 18. *Philem.* 11.

To be anxious for their welfare. 1 *Sam.* 25: 14–17. 2 *Kings* 5: 2, 3.

To be earnest in transacting their business. *Gen.* 24: 54–56.

To be prudent in the management of their affairs. *Gen.* 24: 34–49.

To be industrious in labouring for them. *Neh.* 4: 16, 23.

To be kind and attentive to their guests. *Gen.* 43: 23, 24.

To be submissive even to the froward. *Gen.* 16: 6, 9. 1 *Pet.* 2: 18.

Not to answer them rudely. *Titus* 2: 9.

Not to serve them with eye-service, as men-pleasers. *Eph.* 6: 6. *Col.* 3: 22.

Not to defraud them. *Titus* 2: 10.

Should be contented in their situation. 1 *Cor.* 7: 20, 21.

Should be compassionate to their fellows. *Matt.* 18: 33.

Should serve

For conscience towards God. 1 *Pet.* 2: 19.

In the fear of God. *Eph.* 6: 5. *Col.* 3: 22.

As the servants of Christ. *Eph.* 6: 5, 6.

Heartily, as to the Lord, and not unto men. *Eph.* 6: 7. *Col.* 3: 23.

As doing the will of God from the heart. *Eph.* 6: 6.

In singleness of heart. *Eph.* 6: 5. *Col.* 3: 22.

With good will. *Eph.* 6: 7.

When patient under injury are

acceptable to God. 1 *Pet.* 2: 19, 20.

When good

Are the servants of Christ. *Col.* 3: 24.

Are brethren beloved in the Lord. *Philem.* 16.

Are the Lord's freemen. 1 *Cor.* 7: 22.

Are partakers of gospel privileges. 1 *Cor.* 12: 13. *Gal.* 3: 28. *Eph.* 6: 8. *Col.* 3: 11.

Deserve the confidence of their masters. *Gen.* 24: 2, 4, 10. *Gen.* 39: 4.

Often exalted. *Gen.* 41: 40. *Prov.* 17: 2.

Often advanced by masters. *Gen.* 39: 4, 5.

To be honoured. *Gen.* 24: 31. *Prov.* 27: 18.

Bring God's blessing upon their masters. *Gen.* 30: 27, 30. *Gen.* 39: 3.

Adorn the doctrine of God their Saviour in all things. *Titus* 2: 10.

Have God with them. *Gen.* 31: 42. *Gen.* 39: 21. *Acts* 7: 9, 10.

Are prospered by God. *Gen.* 39: 3.

Are protected by God. *Gen.* 31: 7.

Are guided by God. *Gen.* 24: 7, 27.

Are blessed by God. *Matt.* 24: 46.

Are mourned over after death. *Gen.* 35: 8. (*See marginal note*)

Shall be rewarded. *Eph.* 6: 8. *Col.* 3: 24.

The property of masters increased by faithful. *Gen.* 30: 29, 30.

When wicked

Are eye-servants. *Eph.* 6: 6. *Col.* 3: 22.

Are men-pleasers. *Eph.* 6: 6. *Col.* 3: 22.

Are deceitful. 2 *Sam.* 19: 26. *Ps.* 101: 6, 7.

Are quarrelsome. *Gen.* 13: 7. *Gen.* 26: 20.

Are covetous. 2 *Kings* 5: 20.

Are liars. 2 *Kings* 5: 22, 25.

Are thieves. *Titus* 2: 10.

Are gluttonous and drunken. *Matt.* 24: 49.

Are unmerciful to their fellows. *Matt.* 18: 30.

Will not submit to correction. *Prov.* 29: 19.

Do not bear to be exalted. *Prov.* 30: 21, 22, with *Isa.* 3: 5.

Shall be punished. *Matt.* 24: 50.

Good—Exemplified. ELIEZER, *Gen.* 24th chap. DEBORAH, *Gen.* 24: 59, with *Gen.* 35: 8. JACOB, *Gen.* 31: 36–40. JOSEPH, *Gen.* 39: 3. *Acts* 7: 10. SERVANTS OF BOAZ, *Ruth* 2: 4. JONATHAN'S ARMOUR-BEARER, 1 *Sam.* 14: 6, 7. DAVID'S SERVANTS, 2 *Sam.* 12: 18. CAPTIVE MAID, 2 *Kings* 5: 2–4. SERVANTS OF NAAMAN, 2 *Kings* 5: 13. SERVANTS OF CENTURION, *Matt.* 8: 9. SERVANTS OF CORNELIUS, *Acts* 10: 7. ONESIMUS AFTER HIS CONVERSION, *Philem.* 11.

Bad—Exemplified. SERVANTS OF ABRAHAM AND LOT, *Gen.* 13: 7. SERVANTS OF ABIMELECH, *Gen.* 21: 25. ABSALOM'S SERVANTS, 2 *Sam.* 13: 28, 29. 2 *Sam.* 14: 30. ZIBA, 2 *Sam.* 16: 1–4. SERVANTS OF SHIMEI, 1 *Kings* 2: 39. JEROBOAM, 1 *Kings* 11: 26. ZIMRI, 1 *Kings*

16: 9. GEHAZI, 2 *Kings* 5: 20.
SERVANTS OF AMON, 2 *Kings*
21: 23. JOB'S SERVANTS, *Job*
19: 16. SERVANTS OF THE HIGH
PRIEST, *Mark* 14: 65. ONESIMUS
BEFORE HIS CONVERSION,
Philem. 11.

SICKNESS

Sent by God. *Deut.* 32: 39. 2
Sam. 12: 15. *Acts* 12: 23.
The devil sometimes permitted
to inflict. *Job* 2: 6, 7. *Luke*
9: 39. *Luke* 13: 16.
Often brought on by intemperance. *Hos.* 7: 5.
Often sent as a punishment of
sin. *Lev.* 26: 14–16. 2 *Chron.*
21: 12–15. 1 *Cor.* 11: 30.

God
Promises to heal. *Exod.* 23:
25. 2 *Kings* 20: 5.
Heals. *Deut.* 32: 39. *Ps.*
103: 3. *Isa.* 38: 5, 9.
Exhibits his mercy in healing. *Phil.* 2: 27.
Exhibits his power in healing. *Luke* 5: 17.
Exhibits his love in healing.
Isa. 38: 17.
Often manifests saving grace
in sinners during. *Job* 33:
19–24.
Permits saints to be tried by.
Job 2: 5, 6.
Strengthens saints in. *Ps.*
41: 3.
Comforts saints in. *Ps.* 41:
3.
Hears the prayers of those in.
Ps. 30: 2. *Ps.* 107: 18–20.
Preserves saints in time of.
Ps. 91: 3–7.
Abandons the wicked to.
Jer. 34: 17.
Persecutes the wicked by.
Jer. 29: 18.

Healing of, lawful on the sabbath. *Luke* 13: 14–16.
Christ compassionated those in.
Isa. 53: 4, with *Matt.* 8: 16, 17.

Christ healed,
Being present. *Mark* 1: 31.
Matt. 4: 2, 3.
Not being present. *Matt.* 8:
13.
By imposition of hands.
Mark 6: 5. *Luke* 13: 13.
With a touch. *Matt.* 8: 3.
Through the touch of his garment. *Matt.* 14: 35, 36.
Mark 5: 27–34.
With a word. *Matt.* 8: 8,
13.
Faith required in those healed
of, by Christ. *Matt.* 9: 28,
29. *Mark* 5: 34. *Mark* 10: 52.
Often incurable by human
means. *Deut.* 28: 27. 2
Chron. 21: 18.
The Apostles were endued with
power to heal. *Matt.* 10: 1.
Mark 16: 18, 20.

Saints
Acknowledge that, comes
from God. *Ps.* 38: 1–8.
Isa. 38: 12, 15.
Are resigned under. *Job* 2:
10.
Mourn under, with prayer.
Isa. 38: 14.
Pray for recovery from. *Isa.*
38: 2, 3.
Ascribe recovery from, to
God. *Isa.* 38: 20.
Praise God for recovery from.
Ps. 103: 1–3. *Isa.* 38: 19.
Luke 17: 15.
Thank God publicly for recovery from. *Isa.* 38: 20.
Acts 3: 8.
Feel for others in. *Ps.* 35:
13.
Visit those in. *Matt.* 25: 36.

Visiting those in, an evidence of belonging to Christ. *Matt.* 25: 34, 36, 40.

Pray for those afflicted with. *Acts* 28: 8. *Jas.* 5: 14, 15.

The wicked

Have much sorrow, etc., with. *Eccles.* 5: 17.

Do not seek the aid of God in. 2 *Chron.* 16: 12.

Forsake those in. 1 *Sam.* 30: 13.

Visit not those in. *Matt.* 25: 43.

Not visiting those in, an evidence of not belonging to Christ. *Matt.* 25: 43, 45.

Illustrative of sin. *Isa.* 1: 5. *Jer.* 8: 22. *Matt.* 9: 12.

SIMPLICITY

Is opposed to fleshly wisdom. 2 *Cor.* 1: 12.

Necessity for. *Matt.* 18: 2, 3.

Should be exhibited

In preaching the gospel. 1 *Thess.* 2: 3–7.

In acts of benevolence. *Rom.* 12: 8.

In all our conduct. 2 *Cor.* 1: 12.

Concerning our own wisdom. 1 *Cor.* 3: 18.

Concerning evil. *Rom.* 16: 19.

Concerning malice. 1 *Cor.* 14: 20.

Exhortations to. *Rom.* 16: 19. 1 *Pet.* 2: 2.

They who have the grace of,

Are made wise by God. *Matt.* 11: 25.

Are made wise by the word of God. *Ps.* 19: 7. *Ps.* 119: 130.

Are preserved by God. *Ps.* 116: 6.

Made circumspect by instruction. *Prov.* 1: 4.

Profit by the correction of others. *Prov.* 19: 25. *Prov.* 21: 11.

Beware of being corrupted from that, which is in Christ. 2 *Cor.* 11: 3.

Illustrated. *Matt.* 6: 22.

Exemplified. DAVID, *Ps.* 131: 1, 2. JEREMIAH, *Jer.* 1: 6. PRIMITIVE CHRISTIANS, *Acts* 2: 46. *Acts* 4: 32. PAUL, 2 *Cor.* 1: 12.

SIN

Is the transgression of the law. 1 *John* 3: 4.

Is of the devil. 1 *John* 3: 8, with *John* 8: 44.

All unrighteousness is. 1 *John* 5: 17.

Omission of what we know to be good is. *Jas.* 4: 17.

Whatever is not of faith is. *Rom.* 14: 23.

The thought of foolishness is. *Prov.* 24: 9.

All the imaginations of the unrenewed heart are. *Gen.* 6: 5. *Gen.* 8: 21.

Described as

Coming from the heart. *Matt.* 15: 19.

The fruit of lust. *Jas.* 1: 15.

The sting of death. 1 *Cor* 15: 56.

Rebellion against God. 1 *Deut.* 9: 7. *Joshua* 1: 18.

Works of darkness. *Eph.* 5: 11.

Dead works. *Heb.* 6: 1. *Heb.* 9: 14.

The abominable thing that God hates. *Prov.* 15: 9. *Jer.* 44: 4, 11.

Defiling. *Prov.* 30: 12. *Isa.* 59: 3.

Deceitful. *Heb.* 3: 13.

Disgraceful. *Prov.* 14: 34.

Often very great. *Exod.* 32: 30. 1 *Sam.* 2: 17.

Often mighty. *Amos* 5: 12.

Often manifold. *Amos* 5: 12.

Often presumptuous. *Ps.* 19: 13.

Sometimes open and manifest. 1 *Tim.* 5: 24.

Sometimes secret. *Ps.* 90: 8. 1 *Tim.* 5: 24.

Besetting. *Heb.* 12: 1.

Like scarlet and crimson. *Isa.* 1: 18.

Reaching unto heaven. *Rev.* 48: 5.

Entered into the world by Adam. *Gen.* 3: 6, 7, with *Rom.* 5: 12.

All men are conceived and born in. *Gen.* 5: 3. *Job* 15: 14. *Job* 25: 4. *Ps.* 51: 5.

All men are shapen in. *Ps.* 51: 5.

Scripture concludes all under. *Gal.* 3: 22.

No man is without. 1 *Kings* 8: 46. *Eccles.* 7: 20.

Christ alone was without. 2 *Cor.* 5: 21. *Heb.* 4: 15. *Heb.* 7: 26. 1 *John* 3: 5.

God

Abominates. *Deut.* 25: 16. *Prov.* 6: 16–19.

Marks. *Job* 10: 14.

Remembers. *Rev.* 18: 5.

Is provoked to jealousy by. 1 *Kings* 14: 22.

Is provoked to anger by. 1 *Kings* 16: 2.

Alone can forgive. *Exod.* 34: 7. *Dan.* 9: 9. *Mic.* 7: 18. *Mark* 2: 7.

Recompenses. *Jer.* 16: 18. *Rev.* 18: 6.

Punishes. *Isa.* 13: 11. *Amos* 3: 2.

The law

Is transgressed by every. *Jas.* 2: 10, 11, with 1 *John* 3: 4.

Gives knowledge of. *Rom.* 3: 20. *Rom.* 7: 7.

Shews exceeding sinfulness of. *Rom.* 7: 13.

Made to restrain. 1 *Tim.* 1: 9, 10.

By its strictness stirs up. *Rom.* 7: 5, 8, 11.

Is the strength of. 1 *Cor.* 15: 56.

Curses those guilty of. *Gal.* 3: 10.

No man can cleanse himself from. *Job* 9: 30, 31. *Prov.* 20: 9. *Jer.* 2: 22.

No man can atone for. *Mic.* 6: 7.

God has opened a fountain for. *Zech.* 13: 1.

Christ was manifested to take away. *John* 1: 29. 1 *John* 3: 5.

Christ's blood redeems from. *Eph.* 1: 7.

Christ's blood cleanses from. 1 *John* 1: 7.

Saints

Made free from. *Rom.* 6: 18.

Dead to. *Rom.* 6: 2, 11. 1 *Pet.* 2: 24.

Profess to have ceased from. 1 *Pet.* 4: 1.

Cannot live in. 1 *John* 3: 9. 1 *John* 5: 18.

Resolve against. *Job* 34: 32.

Ashamed of having committed. *Rom.* 6: 21.

Abhor themselves on account of. *Job* 42: 6. *Ezek.* 20: 43.

Have yet the remains of, in them. *Rom.* 7: 17, 23, with *Gal.* 5: 17.

The fear of God restrains.

Exod, 20: 20. *Ps.* 4: 4. *Prov.* 16: 6.

The word of God keeps from. *Ps.* 119: 11.

The Holy Ghost convinces of. *John* 16: 8, 9.

If we say that we have no, we deceive ourselves, and the truth is not in us. 1 *John* 1: 8.

If we say that we have no, we make God a liar. 1 *John* 1: 10.

Confusion of face belongs to those guilty of. *Dan.* 9: 7, 8.

Should be

Confessed. *Job* 33: 27. *Prov.* 28: 13.

Mourned over. *Ps.* 38: 18. *Jer.* 3: 21.

Hated. *Ps.* 97: 10. *Prov.* 8: 13. *Amos* 5: 15.

Abhorred. *Rom.* 12: 9.

Put away. *Job* 11: 14.

Departed from. *Ps.* 34: 14. 2 *Tim.* 2: 19.

Avoided even in appearance. 1 *Thess.* 5: 22.

Guarded against. *Ps.* 4: 4. *Ps.* 39: 1.

Striven against. *Heb.* 12: 4.

Mortified. *Rom.* 8: 13. *Col.* 3: 5.

Wholly destroyed. *Rom.* 6: 6.

Specially strive against besetting. *Heb.* 12: 1.

Aggravated by neglected advantages. *Luke* 12: 47. *John* 15: 22.

Guilt of concealing. *Job* 31: 33. *Prov.* 28: 13.

We should pray to God

To search for, in our hearts. *Ps.* 139: 23, 24.

To make us know our. *Job* 13: 23.

To forgive our. *Exod.* 34: 9. *Luke* 11: 4.

To keep us from. *Ps.* 19: 13.

To deliver us from. *Matt.* 6: 13.

To cleanse us from. *Ps.* 51: 2.

Prayer hindered by. *Ps.* 66: 18. *Isa.* 59: 2.

Blessings withheld on account of. *Jer.* 5: 25.

The wicked

Servants to. *John* 8: 34. *Rom.* 6: 16.

Dead in. *Eph.* 2: 1.

Guilty of, in everything they do. *Prov.* 21: 4. *Ezek.* 21: 24.

Plead necessity for. 1 *Sam.* 13: 11, 12.

Excuse. *Gen.* 3: 12, 13. 1 *Sam.* 15: 13–15.

Encourage themselves in. *Ps.* 64: 5.

Defy God in committing. *Isa.* 5: 18, 19.

Boast of. *Isa.* 3: 9.

Make a mock at. *Prov.* 14: 9.

Expect impunity in. *Ps.* 50: 21. *Ps.* 94: 7.

Cannot cease from. 2 *Pet.* 2: 14.

Heap up. *Ps.* 78: 17. *Isa.* 30: 1.

Encouraged in, by prosperity. *Prov.* 10: 16.

Led by despair to continue in. *Jer.* 18: 12.

Try to conceal, from God. *Gen.* 3: 8, 10, with *Job* 31: 33.

Throw the blame of, on God. *Gen.* 3: 12. *Jer.* 7: 10.

Throw the blame of, on others. *Gen.* 3: 12, 13. *Exod.* 32: 22–24.

Tempt others to. *Gen.* 3: 6.
1 *Kings* 16: 2.

Delight in those who commit.
Rom. 1: 32.

Shall bear the shame of.
Ezek. 16: 52.

Shall find out the wicked.
Num. 32: 23.

Ministers should warn the
wicked to forsake. *Ezek.* 33:
9. *Dan.* 4: 27.

Leads to

Shame. *Rom.* 6: 21.

Disquiet. *Ps.* 38: 3.

Disease. *Job* 20: 11.

Death. *Rom.* 6: 23.

The ground was cursed on
account of. *Gen.* 3: 17, 18.

Toil and sorrow originated in.
Gen. 3: 16, 17, 19, with *Job*
14: 1.

Excludes from heaven. *Gal.*
5: 19–21. *Eph.* 5: 5. *Rev.* 21:
27.

When finished brings forth
death. *Jas.* 1: 15.

Death, the wages of. *Rom.* 6:
23.

Death, the punishment of.
Gen. 2: 17. *Ezek.* 18: 4.

SINS, NATIONAL

Often pervade all ranks. *Isa.*
1: 5. *Jer.* 5: 1–5. *Jer.* 6: 13.

Often caused and encouraged
by rulers. 1 *Kings* 12: 26–33.
2 *Chron.* 21: 11–13.

Often caused by prosperity.
Deut. 32: 15. *Ezek.* 28: 5.

Defile

The land. *Lev.* 18: 25. *Isa.*
24: 5.

The people. *Lev.* 18: 24.
Ezek. 14: 11.

National worship. *Hag.* 2:
14.

Aggravated by privileges. *Isa.*
5: 4–7. *Ezek.* 20: 11–13. *Matt.*
11: 21–24.

Lead the heathen to blaspheme.
Rom. 2: 24.

Are a reproach to a people.
Prov. 14: 34.

Should be

Repented of. *Jer.* 18: 8.
John 3: 5.

Mourned over. *Joel* 2: 12.

Confessed. *Judges* 10: 10.

Turned from. *Isa.* 1: 16.
Jonah 3: 10.

Saints especially mourn over.
Ps. 119: 136. *Ezek.* 9: 4.

Ministers should

Mourn over. *Ezra* 10: 6.
Ezek. 6: 11. *Joel* 2: 17.

Testify against. *Isa.* 30: 8, 9.
Ezek. 2: 3–5. *Ezek.* 22: 2.
Jonah 1: 2.

Try to turn the people from.
Jer. 23: 22.

Pray for forgiveness of.
Exod. 32: 31, 32. *Joel* 2: 17.

National prayer rejected on
account of. *Isa.* 1: 15. *Isa.*
59: 2.

National worship rejected on
account of. *Isa.* 1: 10–14.
Jer. 6: 19, 20.

Cause the withdrawal of privileges. *Lam.* 2: 9. *Amos* 8: 11.

Bring down national judgments.
Matt. 23: 35, 36. *Matt.* 27: 25.

Denunciations against. *Isa.*
1: 24. *Isa.* 30: 1. *Jer.* 5: 9.
Jer. 12: 17.

Punishment for. *Isa.* 3: 8.
Jer. 12: 17. *Jer.* 25: 12. *Ezek.*
28: 7–10.

Punishment for, averted on
repentance. *Judges* 10: 15,
16. 2 *Chron.* 12: 6, 7. *Jonah*
3: 10.

Exemplified. SODOM   AND
GOMORRAH, *Gen.* 18: 20. 2 *Pet.*

2: 6. CHILDREN OF ISRAEL,
Exod. 16: 8. *Exod.* 32: 31.
NATIONS OF CANAAN, *Deut.* 9: 4.
KINGDOM OF ISRAEL, 2 *Kings*
17: 8–12. Hos. 4: 1, 2. KING-
DOM OF JUDAH, 2 *Kings* 17: 19.
Isa. 1: 2–7. MOAB, *Jer.* 48: 29,
30. BABYLON, *Jer.* 51: 6, 13, 52.
TYRE, *Ezek.* 28: 2. NINEVEH,
Nahum 3: 1.

SINCERITY

Christ was an example of. 1
Pet. 2: 22.
Ministers should be examples
of. *Titus* 2: 7.
Opposed to fleshly wisdom.
2 *Cor.* 1: 12.

Should characterise

Our love to God. 2 *Cor.*
8: 8, 24.
Our love to Christ. *Eph.*
6: 24.
Our service to God. *Joshua*
24: 14.
Our faith. 1 *Tim.* 1: 5.
Our love to one another.
Rom. 12: 9. 1 *Pet.* 1: 22.
1 *John* 3: 18.
Our whole conduct. 2 *Cor.*
1: 12.
The preaching of the gospel.
2 *Cor.* 2: 17. 1 *Thess.* 2: 3–5.
A characteristic of the doctrines
of the gospel. 1 *Pet.* 2: 2.
The gospel sometimes preached
without. *Phil.* 1: 16.
The wicked devoid of. *Ps.*
5: 9. *Ps.* 55: 21.
Exhortations to. 1 *Cor.* 5: 8.
1 *Pet.* 2: 1.
Pray for, on behalf of others.
Phil. 1: 10.
Blessedness of. *Ps.* 32: 2.
Exemplified. MEN OF ZEBULUN,
1 *Chron.* 12: 33. HEZEKIAH,
Isa. 38: 3. NATHANAEL, *John* 1:
47. PAUL, 2 *Cor.* 1: 12. TIMO-
THY, 2 *Tim.* 1: 5. LOIS AND
EUNICE, 2 *Tim.* 1: 5.
Lord Jesus Christ. *Isa.* 53: 9.

SLANDER

An abomination unto God.
Prov. 6: 16, 19.
Forbidden. *Exod.* 23: 1. *Jas.*
4: 11.

Includes

Whispering. *Rom.* 1: 29.
2 *Cor.* 12: 20.
Backbiting. *Rom.* 1: 30.
2 *Cor.* 12: 20.
Evil surmising. 1 *Tim.* 6: 4.
Tale-bearing. *Lev.* 19: 16.
Babbling. *Eccles.* 10: 11.
Tattling. 1 *Tim.* 5: 13.
Evil speaking. *Ps.* 41: 5. *Ps.*
109: 20.
Defaming. *Jer.* 20: 10. 1
Cor. 4: 13.
Bearing false witness. *Exod.*
20: 16. *Deut.* 5: 20. *Luke* 3:
14.
Judging uncharitably. *Jas.*
4: 11, 12.
Raising false reports. *Exod.*
23: 1.
Repeating matters. *Prov.*
17: 9.
Is a deceitful work. *Ps.* 52: 2.
Comes from the evil heart.
Luke 6: 45.
Often arises from hatred. *Ps.*
41: 7. *Ps.* 109: 3.
Idleness leads to. 1 *Tim.* 5: 13.
The wicked addicted to. *Ps.*
50: 20. *Jer.* 6: 28. *Jer.* 9: 4.
Hypocrites addicted to. *Prov.*
11: 9.
A characteristic of the devil.
Rev. 12: 10.
The wicked love. *Ps.* 52: 4.
They who indulge in, are fools.
Prov. 10: 18.
They who indulge in, not to be
trusted. *Jer.* 9: 4.

Women warned against. *Titus* 2: 3.

Ministers' wives should avoid. 1 *Tim.* 3: 11.

Christ was exposed to. *Ps.* 35: 11. *Matt.* 26: 60.

Rulers exposed to. 2 *Pet.* 2: 10. *Jude* 8.

Ministers exposed to. *Rom.* 3: 8, 2. 2 *Cor.* 6: 8.

The nearest relations exposed-to. *Ps.* 50: 20.

Saints exposed to. *Ps.* 38: 12. *Ps.* 109: 2. 1 *Pet.* 4: 4.

Saints

Should keep their tongue from. *Ps.* 34: 13, with 1 *Pet.* 3: 10.

Should lay aside. *Eph.* 4: 31. 1 *Pet.* 2: 1.

Should be warned against. *Titus* 3: 1, 2.

Should give no occasion for. 1 *Pet.* 2: 12. 1 *Pet.* 3: 16.

Should return good for. 1 *Cor.* 4: 13.

Blessed in enduring. *Matt.* 5: 11.

Characterised as avoiding. *Ps.* 15: 1, 3.

Should not be listened to. 1 *Sam.* 24: 9.

Should be discountenanced with anger. *Prov.* 25: 23.

Effects of;

Separating friends. *Prov.* 16: 28. *Prov.* 17: 9.

Deadly wounds. *Prov.* 18: 8. *Prov.* 26: 22.

Strife. *Prov.* 26: 29.

Discord among brethren. *Prov.* 6: 19.

Murder. *Ps.* 31: 13. *Ezek.* 22: 9.

The tongue of, is a scourge. *Job.* 5: 21.

Is venomous. *Ps.* 140: 3. *Eccles.* 10: 11.

Is destructive. *Prov.* 11: 9.

End of, is mischievous madness. *Eccles.* 10: 13.

Men shall give account for. *Matt.* 12: 36.

Punishment for. *Deut.* 19: 16–21. *Ps.* 101: 5.

Illustrated. *Prov.* 12: 18. *Prov.* 25: 18.

Exemplified. LABAN'S SONS, *Gen.* 31: 1. DOEG, 1 *Sam.* 22: 9–11. PRINCES OF AMMON, 2 *Sam.* 10: 3. ZIBA, 2 *Sam.* 16: 3. CHILDREN OF BELIAL, 1 *Kings* 21: 13. ENEMIES OF THE JEWS, *Ezra* 4: 7–16. GASHMU, *Neh.* 6: 6. HAMAN, *Esther* 3: 8. DAVID'S ENEMIES, *Ps.* 31: 13. JEREMIAH'S ENEMIES, *Jer.* 38: 4. CHALDEANS, *Dan.* 3: 8. DANIEL'S ACCUSERS, *Dan.* 6: 13. JEWS, *Matt.* 11: 18, 19. WITNESSES AGAINST CHRIST, *Matt.* 26: 59–61. PRIESTS, *Mark* 15: 3. ENEMIES OF STEPHEN, *Acts* 6: 11. ENEMIES OF PAUL, etc., *Acts* 17: 7. TERTULLUS, *Acts* 24: 2, 5.

SOBRIETY

Commanded. 1 *Pet.* 1: 13. 1 *Pet.* 5: 8.

The gospel designed to teach. *Titus* 2: 11, 12.

With watchfulness. 1 *Thess.* 5: 6.

With prayer. 1 *Pet.* 4: 7.

Required in

Ministers. 1 *Tim.* 3: 2, 3. *Titus* 1: 8.

Wives of ministers. 1 *Tim.* 3: 11.

Aged men. *Titus* 2: 2.

Young men. *Titus* 2: 6.

Young women. *Titus* 2: 4.

All saints. *1 Thess.* 5: 6, 8.

Women should exhibit, in dress. *1 Tim.* 2: 9.

We should estimate our character and talents with. *Rom.* 12: 3.

We should live in. *Titus* 2: 12.

Motives to. *1 Pet.* 4: 7. *1 Pet.* 5: 8.

STEDFASTNESS

Exhibited by God in all his purposes and ways. *Dan.* 6: 26.

Commanded. *Phil.* 4: 1. *2 Thess.* 2: 15.

Godliness necessary to. *Job* 11: 13–15.

Secured by

The power of God. *Ps.* 55: 22. *Ps.* 62: 2.

The presence of God. *Ps.* 16: 8.

Trust in God. *Ps.* 26: 1.

The intercession of Christ. *Luke* 22: 31, 32.

A characteristic of saints. *Job* 17: 9. *John* 8: 31.

Should be manifested

In cleaving to God. *Deut.* 10: 20. *Acts* 11: 23.

In the work of the Lord. *1 Cor.* 15: 58.

In continuing in the Apostles' doctrine and fellowship. *Acts* 2: 42.

In holding fast our profession. *Heb.* 4: 14. *Heb.* 10: 23.

In holding fast the confidence and rejoicing of the hope. *Heb.* 3: 6, 14.

In keeping the faith. *Col.* 2: 5. *1 Pet.* 5: 9.

In standing fast in the faith. *1 Cor.* 16: 13.

In holding fast what is good. *1 Thess.* 5: 21.

In maintaining Christian liberty. *Gal.* 5: 1.

In striving for the faith of the gospel. *Phil.* 1: 27, with *Jude* 3.

Even under affliction. *Ps.* 44: 17–19. *1 Thess.* 3: 3.

Saints pray for. *Ps.* 17: 5.

Saints praise God for. *Ps.* 116: 8.

Ministers

Exhorted to. *2 Tim.* 1: 13, 14. *Titus* 1: 9.

Should exhort to. *Acts* 13: 43. *Acts* 14: 22.

Should pray for, in their people. *1 Thess.* 3: 13. *2 Thess.* 2: 17.

Encouraged by, in their people. *1 Thess.* 3: 8.

Rejoiced by, in their people. *Col.* 2: 5.

The wicked devoid of. *Ps.* 78: 8, 37.

Principle of—Illustrated. *Matt.* 7: 24, 25.

Want of—Illustrated. *Luke* 8: 6, 13. *2 Pet.* 2: 17. *Jude* 12.

Exemplified. CALEB, *Num.* 14: 24. JOSHUA, *Joshua* 24: 15. JOSIAH, 2 *Kings* 22: 2. JOB, *Job* 2: 3. DAVID, *Ps.* 18: 21, 22. SHADRACH, etc., *Dan.* 3: 18. DANIEL, *Dan.* 6: 10. PRIMITIVE CHRISTIANS, *Acts* 2: 42. CORINTHIANS, 1 *Cor.* 15: 1. COLOSSIANS, *Col.* 2: 5.

STRIFE

Christ, an example of avoiding. *Isa.* 42: 2, with *Matt.* 12: 15–19.

Forbidden. *Prov.* 3: 30. *Prov.* 25: 8.

A work of the flesh. *Gal.* 5: 20.

An evidence of a carnal spirit. *1 Cor.* 3: 3.

Existed in primitive Church.
1 *Cor*. 1: 11.

Excited by

Hatred. *Prov*. 10: 12.

Pride. *Prov*. 13: 10. *Prov*.
28: 25.

Wrath. *Prov*. 15: 18. *Prov*.
30: 33.

Frowardness. *Prov*. 16: 28.

A contentious disposition.
Prov. 26: 21.

Tale-bearing. *Prov*. 26: 20.

Drunkenness. *Prov*. 23:
29, 30.

Lusts. *Jas*. 4: 1.

Curious questions. 1 *Tim*.
6: 4. 2 *Tim*. 2: 23.

Scorning. *Prov*. 22: 10.

Difficulty of stopping, a reason
for avoiding it. *Prov*. 17: 14.

Shameful in saints. 2 *Cor*. 12:
20. *Jas*. 3: 14.

Saints should

Avoid. *Gen*. 13: 8.

Avoid questions that lead to.
2 *Tim*. 2: 14.

Not walk in. *Rom*. 13: 13.

Not act from. *Phil*. 2: 3.

Do all things without. *Phil*.
2: 14.

Submit to wrong rather than
engage in. *Matt*. 5: 39, 40.
1 *Cor*. 6: 7

Seek God's protection from.
Ps. 35: 1. *Jer*. 18: 19.

Praise God for protection
from. 2 *Sam*. 22: 44. *Ps*.
18: 43.

Saints kept from tongues of.
Ps. 31: 20.

Ministers should

Avoid. 1 *Tim*. 3. 3. 2 *Tim*.
2: 24.

Avoid questions that lead to.
2 *Tim*. 2: 23. *Titus* 3: 9.

Not preach through. *Phil*.
1: 15, 16.

Warn against. 1 *Cor*. 1: 10.
2 *Tim*. 2: 14.

Reprove. 1 *Cor*. 1: 11, 12.
1 *Cor*. 3: 3. 1 *Cor*. 11: 17, 18.

Appeased by slowness to anger.
Prov. 15: 18.

It is honourable to cease from.
Prov. 20: 3.

Hyprocrites make religion a
pretence for. *Isa*. 58: 4.

Fools engage in. *Prov*. 18: 6.

Evidences a love of transgression. *Prov*. 17: 19.

Leads to

Blasphemy. *Lev*. 24: 10, 11.

Injustice. *Hab*. 1: 3, 4.

Confusion and every evil
work. *Jas*. 3: 16.

Violence. *Exod*. 21: 18, 22.

Mutual destruction. *Gal*.
5: 15.

Temporal blessings embittered
by. *Prov*. 17: 1.

Excludes from heaven. *Gal*.
5: 20, 21.

Promoters of, should be ex-
pelled. *Prov*. 22: 10.

Punishment for. *Ps*. 55: 9.

Strength and violence of—
Illustrated. *Prov*. 17: 14.
Prov. 18: 19.

Danger of joining in—Illustrated. *Prov*. 26: 17.

Exemplified. HERDMEN OF
ABRAM AND OF LOT, *Gen*. 13: 7.
HERDMEN OF GERAR AND OF
ISAAC, *Gen*. 26: 20. LABAN AND
JACOB, *Gen*. 31: 36. TWO
HEBREWS, *Exod*. 2: 13. ISRAEL-
ITES, *Deut*. 1: 12. JEPHTHAH
AND AMMONITES, *Judges* 12: 2.
JUDAH AND ISRAEL, 2 *Sam*.
19: 41–43. DISCIPLES, *Luke* 22:
24. JEWS, *John* 6: 52. *John*
10: 19. JUDAISING TEACHERS,
Acts 15: 2. PAUL AND BARNA-
BAS, *Acts* 15: 39. PHARISEES

AND SADDUCEES, *Acts* 23: 7.
CORINTHIANS, 1 *Cor.* 1: 11.
1 *Cor.* 6: 6.

SWEARING FALSELY

Forbidden. *Lev.* 19: 12. *Num.* 30: 2. *Matt.* 5: 33.

Hateful to God. *Zech.* 8: 17.

We should not love. *Zech.* 8: 17.

Fraud often leads to. *Lev.* 6: 2, 3.

Saints abstain from. *Joshua* 9: 20. *Ps.* 15: 4.

Blessedness of abstaining from. *Ps.* 24: 4, 5.

The wicked
Addicted to. *Jer.* 5: 2. *Hos.* 10: 4.

Plead excuses for. *Jer.* 7: 9, 10.

Shall be judged on account of. *Mal.* 3: 5.

Shall be cut off for. *Zech.* 5: 3.

Shall have a curse upon their houses for. *Zech.* 5: 4.

False witnesses guilty of. *Deut.* 19: 16, 18.

Exemplified. SAUL, 1 *Sam.* 19: 6, 10. SHIMEI, 1 *Kings* 2: 41–43. JEWS, *Ezek.* 16: 59. ZEDEKIAH, *Ezek.* 17: 13–19. PETER, *Matt.* 26: 72, 74.

SWEARING, PROFANE

Of all kinds is desecration of God's name. *Matt.* 5: 34, 35. *Matt.* 23: 21, 22.

Forbidden. *Exod.* 20: 7. *Matt.* 5: 34–36. *Jas.* 5: 12.

Saints pray to be kept from. *Prov.* 30: 9.

The wicked
Addicted to. *Ps.* 10: 7. *Rom.* 3: 14.

Love. *Ps.* 109: 17.

Clothe themselves with. *Ps.* 109: 18.

Guilt of. *Exod.* 20: 7. *Deut.* 5: 11.

Woe denounced against. *Matt.* 23: 16.

Nations visited for. *Jer.* 23: 10. *Hos.* 4: 1–3.

Punishment for. *Lev.* 24: 16, 23. *Ps.* 59: 12. *Ps.* 109: 17, 18.

Exemplified. JOSEPH, *Gen.* 42: 15, 16. SON OF ISRAELITISH WOMAN, *Lev.* 24: 11. SAUL, 1 *Sam.* 28: 10. GEHAZI, 2 *Kings* 5: 20. JEHORAM, 2 *Kings* 6: 31. PETER, *Matt.* 26: 74. HEROD, *Mark* 6: 23, 26. ENEMIES OF PAUL, *Acts* 23: 21.

TEMPTATION

God cannot be the subject of. *Jas.* 1: 13.

Does not come from God. *Jas.* 1: 13.

Comes from
Lusts. *Jas.* 1: 14.

Covetousness. *Prov.* 28: 20. 1 *Tim.* 6: 9.

The devil is the author of. 1 *Chron.* 21: 1. *Matt.* 4: 1. 1 *Thess.* 3: 5.

Evil associates, the instruments of. *Prov.* 1: 10. *Prov.* 16: 29.

Often arises through
Poverty. *Prov.* 30: 9. *Matt.* 4: 2, 3.

Prosperity. *Prov.* 30: 9. *Matt.* 4: 8.

Worldly glory. *Num.* 22: 17. *Matt.* 4: 8.

To distrust of God's providence. *Matt.* 4: 3.

To presumption. *Matt.* 4: 6.

To worshipping the god of this world. *Matt.* 4: 9.

Often strengthened by the

perversion of God's word. *Matt.* 4: 6.

Permitted, as a trial of
Faith. 1 *Pet.* 1: 7.
Disinterestedness. *Job* 1: 9–12.
Always conformable to the nature of man. 1 *Cor.* 10: 13.
Often ends in sin and perdition. 1 *Tim.* 6: 9. *Jas.* 1: 15.

Christ
Endured, from the devil. *Mark* 1: 13.
Endured, from the wicked. *Matt.* 16: 1. *Matt.* 22: 18. *Luke* 10: 25.
Endured same kind of, as man. *Heb.* 4: 15.
Endured, yet without sin. *Heb.* 4: 15.
Resisted by the word of God. *Matt.* 4: 4, 7, 10.
Overcame. *Matt.* 4: 11. *John* 16: 33.
Sympathises with those under. *Heb.* 4: 15.
Is able to succour those under. *Heb.* 2: 18.
Intercedes for his people under. *Luke* 22: 31, 32. *John* 17: 15.
God will not suffer saints to be exposed to, beyond their power to bear. 1 *Cor.* 10: 13.
God will make a way for saints to escape out of. 1 *Cor.* 10: 13.
God enables saints to bear. 1 *Cor.* 10: 13.
God knows how to deliver saints out of. 2 *Pet.* 2: 9.
Christ keeps faithful saints from the hour of. *Rev.* 3: 10.
Saints may be in heaviness through. 1 *Pet.* 1: 6.

Saints should
Resist, in faith. *Eph.* 6: 16. 1 *Pet.* 5: 9.
Watch against. *Matt.* 26: 41. 1 *Pet.* 5: 8.
Pray to be kept from. *Matt.* 6: 13. *Matt.* 26: 41.
Not occasion, to others. *Rom.* 14: 13.
Restore those overcome by. *Gal.* 6: 1.
Avoid the way of. *Prov.* 4: 14, 15.
The devil will renew. *Luke* 4: 13.
Has strength through the weakness of the flesh. *Matt.* 26: 41.
Hypocrites fall away in time of. *Luke* 8: 13.
Blessedness of those who meet, and overcome. *Jas.* 1: 2–4, 12.
Exemplified. EVE, *Gen.* 3: 1, 4, 5. JOSEPH, *Gen.* 39: 7. BALAAM, *Num.* 22: 17. ACHAN, *Joshua* 7: 21. DAVID, 2 *Sam.* 11: 2. JEROBOAM, 1 *Kings* 15: 30. PETER, *Mark* 14: 67–71. PAUL, 2 *Cor.* 12: 7, with *Gal.* 4: 14.

THANKSGIVING
Christ set an example of. *Matt.* 11: 25. *Matt.* 26: 27. *John* 11: 41.
The heavenly host engage in. *Rev.* 4: 9. *Rev.* 7: 11, 12. *Rev.* 11: 16, 17.
Commanded. *Ps.* 50: 14.
Is a good thing. *Ps.* 92: 1.

Should be offered
To God. *Ps.* 50: 14.
To Christ. 1 *Tim.* 1: 12.
Through Christ. *Rom.* 1: 8. *Col.* 3: 17. *Heb.* 13: 15.
In the name of Christ. *Eph.* 5: 20.

In behalf of ministers. *2 Cor.* 1: 11.

In private worship. *Dan.* 6: 10.

In public worship. *Ps.* 35: 18.

In everything. *1 Thess.* 5: 18.

Upon the completion of great undertakings. *Neh.* 12: 31, 40.

Before taking food. *John* 6: 11. *Acts* 27: 35.

Always. *Eph.* 1: 16. *Eph.* 5: 20. *1 Thess.* 1: 2.

At the remembrance of God's holiness. *Ps.* 30: 4. *Ps.* 97: 12.

For the goodness and mercy of God. *Ps.* 106: 1, *Ps.* 107: 1. *Ps.* 136: 1–3.

For the gift of Christ. *2 Cor.* 9: 15.

For Christ's power and reign. *Rev.* 11: 17.

For the reception and effectual working of the word of God in others. *1 Thess.* 2: 13.

For deliverance through Christ, from in-dwelling sin. *Rom.* 7: 23–25.

For victory over death and the grave. *1 Cor.* 15: 47.

For wisdom and might. *Dan.* 2: 23.

For the triumph of the gospel. *2 Cor.* 2: 14.

For the conversion of others. *Rom.* 6: 17.

For faith exhibited by others. *Rom.* 1: 8. *2 Thess.* 1: 3.

For love exhibited by others. *2 Thess.* 1: 3.

For the grace bestowed on others. *1 Cor.* 1: 4. *Phil.* 1: 3–5. *Col.* 1: 3–6.

For the zeal exhibited by others. *2 Cor.* 8: 16.

For nearness of God's presence. *Ps.* 75: 1.

For appointment to the ministry. *1 Tim.* 1: 12.

For willingness to offer our property for God's service. *2 Chron.* 29: 6–14.

For the supply of our bodily wants. *Rom.* 14: 6, 7. *1 Tim.* 4: 3, 4.

For all men. *1 Tim.* 2: 1.

For all things. *1 Cor.* 9: 11. *Eph.* 5: 20.

Should be accompanied by intercession for others. *1 Tim.* 2: 1. *2 Tim.* 1: 3. *Philem.* 4.

Should always accompany prayer. *Neh.* 11: 17. *Phil.* 4: 6. *Col.* 4: 2.

Should always accompany praise. *Ps.* 92: 1. *Heb.* 13: 15.

Expressed in psalms. *1 Chron.* 16: 7.

Ministers appointed to offer, in public. *1 Chron.* 16: 4, 7. *1 Chron.* 23: 30. *2 Chron.* 31: 2.

Saints

Exhorted to. *Ps.* 105: 1. *Col.* 3: 15.

Resolve to offer. *Ps.* 18: 49. *Ps.* 30: 12.

Habitually offer. *Dan.* 6: 10.

Offer sacrifices of. *Ps.* 116: 17.

Abound in the faith with. *Col.* 2: 7.

Magnify God by. *Ps.* 69: 30.

Come before God with. *Ps.* 95: 2.

Should enter God's gates with. *Ps.* 104: 4.

Of hypocrites, full of boasting. *Luke* 18: 11.

The wicked averse to. *Rom.* 1: 21.

Exemplified. DAVID, 1 *Chron.* 29: 13. LEVITES, 2 *Chron.* 5: 12, 13. DANIEL, *Dan.* 2: 23. JONAH, *Jonah* 2: 9. SIMEON, *Luke* 2: 28. ANNA, *Luke* 2: 38. PAUL, *Acts* 28: 15.

THEFT

Is an abomination. *Jer.* 7: 9, 10.

Forbidden. *Exod.* 20: 15, with *Mark* 10: 19. *Rom.* 13: 9. 1 *Thess.* 4: 6.

From the poor specially forbidden. *Prov.* 22: 22.

Includes fraud in general. *Lev.* 19: 13.

Includes fraud concerning wages. *Lev.* 19: 13. *Mal.* 3: 5. *Jas.* 5: 4.

Proceeds from the heart. *Matt.* 15: 19.

Defiles a man. *Matt.* 15: 20.

The wicked

Addicted to. *Ps.* 119: 61. *Jer.* 7: 9.

Store up the fruits of. *Amos* 3: 10.

Lie in wait to commit. *Hos.* 6: 9.

Commit, under shelter of the night. *Job* 24: 14. *Obad.* 5.

Consent to those who commit. *Ps.* 50: 18.

Associate with those who commit. *Isa.* 1: 23.

May, for a season, prosper in. *Job* 12: 6.

Plead excuses for. *Jer.* 7: 9, 10.

Repent not of. *Rev.* 9: 21.

Destroy themselves by. *Prov.* 21: 7.

Connected with murder. *Jer.* 7: 9. *Hos.* 4: 2.

Shame follows the detection of. *Jer.* 2: 26.

Brings a curse on those who commit it. *Zech.* 5: 3. *Mal.* 3: 5.

Brings a curse on the family of those who commit it. *Zech.* 5: 4.

Brings the wrath of God upon those who commit it. *Ezek.* 22: 29, 31.

Brings down judgment on the land. *Hos.* 4: 2, 3.

Excludes from heaven. 1 *Cor.* 6: 10.

They who connive at,

Hate their own souls. *Prov.* 29: 24.

Shall be reproved of God. *Ps.* 50: 18, 21.

Mosaic law respecting. *Exod.* 22: 1–8.

Saints

Warned against. *Eph.* 4: 28. 1 *Pet.* 4: 15.

Pray to be kept from. *Prov.* 30: 7–9.

Repudiate the charge of. *Gen.* 31: 37.

All earthly treasure exposed to. *Job* 5: 5. *Matt.* 6: 19.

Heavenly treasure secure from. *Matt.* 6: 20. *Luke* 12: 33.

Woe denounced against. *Isa.* 10: 2. *Nahum* 3: 1.

Illustrates the guilt of false teachers. *Jer.* 23: 30. *John* 10: 1, 8, 10.

Exemplified. RACHEL, *Gen.* 31: 19. ACHAN, *Joshua* 7: 21. SHECHEMITES, *Judges* 9: 25. MICAH, *Judges* 17: 2. GEHAZI, 2 *Kings* 5: 20–24. TWO THIEVES, *Matt.* 27: 38. JUDAS, *John* 12: 6. BARABBAS, *John* 18: 40.

TITHE

The tenth of anything.   1 *Sam.* 8: 15, 17.

Antiquity of the custom of giving to God's ministers.   *Gen.* 14: 20. *Heb.* 7: 6.

Considered a just return to God for His blessings.   *Gen.* 28: 22.

Under the law belonged to God. *Lev.* 27: 30.

Consisted of a tenth

Of all the produce of the land. *Lev.* 27: 30.

Of all cattle.   *Lev.* 27: 32.

Of holy things dedicated. 2 *Chron.* 31: 6.

Given by God to the Levites for their services.   *Num.* 18: 21, 24. *Neh.* 10: 37.

The tenth of, offered by the Levites as an heave offering to God.   *Num.* 18: 26, 27.

The tenth of, given by the Levites to the priests as their portion.   *Num.* 18: 26, 28. *Neh.* 10: 38.

Reasonableness of appointing, for the Levites.   *Num.* 18: 20, 23, 24. *Joshua* 13: 33.

When redeemed to have a fifth part of the value added. *Lev.* 27: 31.

Punishment for changing. *Lev.* 27: 33.

The Jews slow in giving. *Neh.* 13: 10.

The Jews reproved for withholding.   *Mal.* 3: 8.

The pious governors of Israel caused the payment of. 2 *Chron.* 31: 5. *Neh.* 13: 11, 12.

Rulers appointed over, for distributing. 2 *Chron.* 31: 12. *Neh.* 13: 13.

The Pharisees scrupulous in

paying. *Luke* 11: 42. *Luke* 18: 12.

A second

Or its value yearly brought to the tabernacle and eaten before the Lord. *Deut.* 12: 6, 7, 17–19. *Deut.* 14: 22–27.

To be consumed at home every third year to promote hospitality and charity. *Deut.* 14: 28, 29. *Deut.* 26: 12–15.

TITLES AND NAMES OF CHRIST

Adam.   1 *Cor.* 15: 45.

Almighty.   *Rev.* 1: 8.

Amen.   *Rev.* 3: 14.

Alpha and Omega.   *Rev.* 1: 8. *Rev.* 22: 13.

Advocate.   1 *John* 2: 1.

Angel.   *Gen.* 48: 16. *Exod.* 23: 20, 21.

Angel of the Lord.   *Exod.* 3: 2. *Judges* 13: 15–18.

Angel of God's presence.   *Isa.* 63: 9.

Apostle.   *Heb.* 3: 1.

Arm of the Lord.   *Isa.* 51: 9. *Isa.* 53: 1.

Author and Finisher of our faith.   *Heb.* 12: 2.

Blessed and only Potentate.   1 *Tim.* 6: 15.

Beginning of the creation of God.   *Rev.* 3: 14. *Isa.* 4: 2.

Branch.   *Jer.* 23: 5. *Zech.* 3: 8. *Zech.* 6: 12.

Bread of life.   *John* 6: 35, 48.

Breaker.   *Mic.* 2: 13.

Captain of the Lord's host. *Joshua* 5: 14, 15.

Captain of salvation.   *Heb.* 2: 10.

Chief Shepherd.   1 *Pet.* 5: 4.

Christ of God.   *Luke* 9: 20.

Consolation of Israel. *Luke* 2: 25.

Chief Corner-stone. *Eph.* 2: 20. 1 *Pet.* 2: 6.

Commander. *Isa.* 55: 4.

Counsellor. *Isa.* 9: 6.

David. *Jer.* 30: 9. *Ezek.* 34: 23.

Day-spring. *Luke* 1: 78.

Deliverer. *Rom.* 11: 26.

Desire of all nations. *Hag.* 2: 7.

Door. *John* 10: 7.

Elect of God. *Isa.* 42: 1.

Emmanuel. *Isa.* 7: 14, with *Matt.* 1: 23.

Eternal life. 1 *John* 1: 2. 1 *John* 5: 20.

Everlasting Father. *Isa.* 9: 6.

Faithful witness. *Rev.* 1: 5. *Rev.* 3: 14.

First and last. *Rev.* 1: 17. *Rev.* 2: 8.

First-begotten of the dead. *Rev.* 1: 5.

Forerunner. *Heb.* 6: 20.

God. *Isa.* 40: 9. *John* 20: 28. *Heb.* 1: 8. *Ps.* 45: 6.

God blessed for ever. *Rom.* 9: 5.

God's fellow. *Zech.* 13: 7.

Glory of the Lord. *Isa.* 40: 5.

Good Shepherd. *John* 10: 14.

Great High Priest. *Heb.* 4: 14.

Governor. *Matt.* 2: 6.

Head of the Church. *Eph.* 5: 23. *Col.* 1: 18.

Heir of all things. *Heb.* 1: 2.

Holy Child Jesus. *Acts* 4: 30.

Holy One. *Ps.* 16: 10, with *Acts* 2: 27, 31.

Holy One of God. *Mark* 1: 24.

Holy One of Israel. *Isa.* 41: 14.

Horn of salvation. *Luke* 1: 69.

I AM. *Exod.* 3: 14, with *John* 8: 58.

JEHOVAH. *Isa.* 26: 4. *Isa.* 40: 3.

Jesus. *Matt.* 1: 21. 1 *Thess.* 1: 10.

Judge of Israel. *Mic.* 5: 1.

Just One. *Acts* 7: 52.

King. *Zech.* 9: 9, with *Matt.* 21: 5.

King of Israel. *John* 1: 49. *Matt.* 27: 42.

King of the Jews. *Matt.* 2: 2. *Matt.* 27: 37.

King of saints. *Rev.* 15: 3.

King of kings. 1 *Tim.* 6: 15. *Rev.* 17: 14.

Law-giver. *Isa.* 33: 22. *Jas.* 4: 12.

Lamb. *Rev.* 13: 8.

Lamb of God. *John* 1: 29, 36.

Leader. *Isa.* 55: 4.

Life. *John* 14: 6. *Col.* 3: 4. 1 *John* 1: 2.

Light of the world. *John* 8: 12.

Lion of the tribe of Judah. *Rev.* 5: 5.

Lord of glory. 1 *Cor.* 2: 8.

Lord of all. *Acts* 10: 36. *Rom.* 10: 12.

LORD OUR RIGHTEOUSNESS. *Jer.* 23: 6.

Lord God of the holy prophets. *Rev.* 22: 6, 16.

Lord God Almighty. *Rev.* 15: 3.

Mediator. 1 *Tim.* 2: 5.

Messenger of the covenant. *Mal.* 3: 1.

Messiah. *Dan.* 9: 25. *John* 1: 41.

Mighty God. *Isa.* 9: 6.

Mighty One of Jacob. *Isa.* 60: 16.

Morning-star. *Rev.* 22: 16.

Nazarene. *Matt.* 2: 23.

Offspring of David. *Rev.* 22: 16.

Only-begotten. *John* 1: 14.

Our Passover. 1 *Cor.* 5: 7.

Plant of renown. *Ezek.* 34: 29.

Prince of life. *Acts* 3: 15.

Prince of peace.   *Isa.* 9: 6.

Prince of the kings of the earth.
  Rev. 1: 5.

Prophet.   *Luke* 24: 19. *John*
  7: 40.

Ransom.   1 *Tim.* 2: 6.

Redeemer.   *Job* 19: 25. *Isa.*
  59: 20. *Isa.* 60: 16.

Resurrection and life.   *John*
  11: 25.

Rock.   1 *Cor.* 10: 4.

Root of David.   *Rev.* 22: 16.

Root of Jesse.   *Isa.* 11: 10.

Rose of Sharon.   *Song of Sol.*
  2: 1.

Ruler in Israel.   *Mic.* 5: 2.

Saviour.   2 *Pet.* 2: 20. 2 *Pet.*
  3: 18.

Servant.   *Isa.* 42: 1.

Shepherd and Bishop of souls.
  1 *Pet.* 2: 25.

Shiloh.   *Gen.* 49: 10.

Son of the Blessed.   *Mark* 14:
  61.

Son of God.   *Luke* 1: 35. *John*
  1: 49.

Son of the Highest.   *Luke* 1:
  32.

Son of David.   *Mal.* 9: 27.

Son of man.   *John* 5: 27. *John*
  6: 27.

Star.   *Num.* 24: 17.

Sun of righteousness.   *Mal.*
  4: 2.

Surety.   *Heb.* 7: 22.

True God.   1 *John* 5: 20.

True Light.   *John* 1: 9.

True Vine.   *John* 15: 1.

Truth.   *John* 14: 6.

Way.   *John* 14: 6.

Wisdom.   *Prov.* 8: 12.

Witness.   *Isa.* 55: 4.

Wonderful.   *Isa.* 9: 6.

Word.   *John* 1: 1. 1 *John* 5: 7.

Word of God.   *Rev.* 19: 13.

Word of life.   1 *John* 1: 1.

TITLES AND NAMES OF THE HOLY SPIRIT

Breath of the Almighty.   *Job*
33: 4. *Ezek.* 37: 9.

Comforter.   *John* 14: 16, 26.
John 15: 26.

Eternal Spirit.   *Heb.* 9: 14.

Free Spirit.   *Ps.* 51: 12.

God.   *Acts* 5: 3, 4.

Good Spirit.   *Neh.* 9: 20. *Ps.*
143: 10.

Holy Spirit.   *Ps.* 51: 11. *Luke*
11: 13.

Holy Spirit of God.   *Eph.* 4:
30.

Holy Spirit of promise.   *Eph.*
1: 13.

Lord, The.   2 *Thess.* 3: 5.

Power of the Highest.   *Luke*
1: 35.

Spirit, The.   *Matt.* 4: 1. *John*
3: 6. 1 *Tim.* 4: 1.

Spirit of the Lord God.   *Isa.*
61: 1.

Spirit of the Lord.   *Isa.* 11: 2.
Acts 5: 9.

Spirit of God.   *Gen.* 1: 2. 1
Cor. 2: 11.

Spirit of the Father.   *Matt.*
10: 20.

Spirit of Christ.   *Rom.* 8: 9.
1 *Pet.* 1: 11.

Spirit of the Son.   *Gal.* 4: 6.

Spirit of life.   *Rom.* 8: 2. *Rev.*
11: 11.

Spirit of grace.   *Zech.* 12: 10.
Heb. 10: 29.

Spirit of prophecy.   *Rev.* 19:
10.

Spirit of adoption.   *Rom.* 8: 15.

Spirit of wisdom.   *Isa.* 11: 2.
Eph. 1: 17.

Spirit of counsel.   *Isa.* 11: 2.

Spirit of might.   *Isa.* 11: 2.

Spirit of understanding.   *Isa.*
11: 2.

Spirit of knowledge. *Isa.* 11: 2.

Spirit of the fear of the Lord. *Isa.* 11: 2.

Spirit of truth. *John* 14: 17. *John* 15: 26.

Spirit of holiness. *Rom.* 1: 4.

Spirit of revelation. *Eph.* 1: 17.

Spirit of judgment. *Isa.* 4: 4. *Isa.* 28: 6.

Spirit of burning. *Isa.* 4: 4.

Spirit of glory. 1 *Pet.* 4: 14.

Seven Spirits of God. *Rev.* 1: 4.

Voice of the Lord. *Isa.* 6: 8.

TITLES AND NAMES OF THE CHURCH

Assembly of the saints. *Ps.* 89: 7.

Assembly of the upright. *Ps.* 111: 1.

Body of Christ. *Eph.* 1: 22, 23. *Col.* 1: 24.

Branch of God's planting. *Isa.* 60: 21.

Bride of Christ. *Rev.* 21: 9.

Church of God. *Acts* 20: 28.

Church of the Living God. 1 *Tim.* 3: 15.

Church of the first-born. *Heb.* 12: 23.

City of the Living God. *Heb.* 12: 22.

Congregation of saints. *Ps.* 149: 1.

Congregation of the Lord's poor. *Ps.* 74: 19.

Dove. *Song of Sol.* 2: 14. *Song of Sol.* 5: 2.

Family in heaven and earth. *Eph.* 3: 15.

Flock of God. *Ezek.* 34: 15. 1 *Pet.* 5: 2.

Fold of Christ. *John* 10: 16.

General assembly of the first-born. *Heb.* 12: 23.

Golden candlestick. *Rev.* 1: 20.

God's building. 1 *Cor.* 3: 9.

God's husbandry. 1 *Cor.* 3: 9.

God's heritage. *Joel* 3: 2. 1 *Pet.* 5: 3.

Habitation of God. *Eph.* 2: 22.

Heavenly Jerusalem. *Gal.* 4: 26. *Heb.* 12: 22.

Holy city. *Rev.* 21: 2.

Holy mountain. *Zech.* 8: 3.

Holy hill. *Ps.* 15: 1.

House of God. 1 *Tim.* 3: 15. *Heb.* 10: 21.

House of the God of Jacob. *Isa.* 2: 3.

House of Christ. *Heb.* 3: 6.

Household of God. *Eph.* 2: 19.

Inheritance. *Ps.* 28: 9. *Isa.* 19: 25.

Israel of God. *Gal.* 6: 16.

King's daughter. *Ps.* 45: 13.

Lamb's wife. *Rev.* 19: 7. *Rev.* 21: 9.

Lot of God's inheritance. *Deut.* 32: 9.

Mount Zion. *Ps.* 2: 6. *Heb.* 12: 22.

Mountain of the Lord of hosts. *Zech.* 8: 3.

Mountain of the Lord's house. *Isa.* 2: 2.

New Jerusalem. *Rev.* 21: 2.

Pillar and ground of the truth. 1 *Tim.* 3: 15.

Place of God's throne. *Ezek.* 43: 7.

Pleasant portion. *Jer.* 12: 10.

Sanctuary of God. *Ps.* 114: 2.

Sister of Christ *Song of Sol.* 4: 12. *Song of Sol.* 5: 2.

Spiritual house. 1 *Pet.* 2: 5.

Spouse of Christ. *Song of Sol.* 4: 12. *Song of Sol.* 5: 1.

Strength and glory of God. *Ps.* 78: 61.

Sought out, a city not forsaken. *Isa.* 62: 12.

Tabernacle. *Ps.* 15: 1.

The Lord's portion. *Deut.* 32: 9.

Temple of God. 1 *Cor.* 3: 16, 17.

Temple of the Living God. 2 *Cor.* 6: 16.

Vineyard. *Jer.* 12: 10. *Matt.* 21: 41.

TITLES AND NAMES OF MINISTERS

Ambassadors for Christ. 2 *Cor.* 5: 20.

Angels of the Church. *Rev.* 1: 20. *Rev.* 2: 1.

Apostles. *Luke* 6: 13. *Rev.* 18: 20.

Apostles of Jesus Christ. *Titus* 1: 1.

Elders. 1 *Tim.* 5: 17. 1 *Pet.* 5: 1.

Evangelists. *Eph.* 4: 11. 2 *Tim.* 4: 5.

Fishers of men. *Matt.* 4: 19. *Mark* 1: 17.

Labourers. *Matt.* 9: 38, with *Philem.* 1.

Labourers in the gospel of Christ. 1 *Thess.* 3: 2.

Lights. *John* 5: 35.

Men of God. *Deut.* 33: 1. 1 *Tim.* 6: 11.

Messengers of the Church. 2 *Cor.* 8: 23.

Messengers of the Lord of hosts. *Mal.* 2: 7.

Ministers of God. 2 *Cor.* 6: 4.

Ministers of the Lord. *Joel* 2: 17.

Ministers of Christ. *Rom.* 15: 16. 1 *Cor.* 4: 1.

Ministers of the sanctuary. *Ezek.* 45: 4.

Ministers of the gospel. *Eph.* 3: 7. *Col.* 1: 23.

Ministers of the word. *Luke* 1: 2.

Ministers of the New Testament. 2 *Cor.* 3: 6.

Ministers of the Church. *Col.* 1: 24, 25.

Ministers of righteousness. 2 *Cor.* 11: 15.

Overseers. *Acts* 20: 28.

Pastors. *Jer.* 3: 15. *Eph.* 4: 11.

Preachers. *Rom.* 10: 14. 1 *Tim.* 2: 7.

Preachers of righteousness. 2 *Pet.* 2: 5.

Servants of God. *Titus* 1: 1. *Jas.* 1: 1.

Servants of the Lord. 2 *Tim.* 2: 24.

Servants of Jesus Christ. *Phil.* 1: 1. *Jude* 1.

Servants of the Church. 2 *Cor.* 4: 5.

Shepherds. *Jer.* 23: 4.

Soldiers of Christ. *Phil.* 2: 25. 2 *Tim.* 2: 3, 4.

Stars. *Rev.* 1: 20. *Rev.* 2: 1.

Stewards of God. *Titus* 1: 7.

Stewards of the grace of God. 1 *Pet.* 4: 10.

Stewards of the mysteries of God. 1 *Cor.* 4: 1.

Teachers. *Isa.* 30: 20. *Eph.* 4: 11.

Watchmen. *Isa.* 62: 6. *Ezek.* 33: 7.

Witnesses. *Acts* 1: 8. *Acts* 5: 32. *Acts* 26: 16.

Workers together with God. 2 *Cor.* 6: 1.

TITLES AND NAMES OF SAINTS

Believers. *Acts* 5: 14. 1 *Tim.* 4: 12.

Beloved of God. *Rom.* 1: 7.

Beloved brethren. 1 *Cor.* 15: 58. *Jas.* 2: 5.

Blessed of the Lord. *Gen.* 24: 31. *Gen.* 26: 29.

Blessed of the Father. *Matt.* 25: 34.

Brethren. *Matt.* 23: 8. *Acts* 12: 17.

Brethren of Christ. *Luke* 8: 21. *John* 20: 17.

Called of Jesus Christ. *Rom.* 1: 6.

Children of the Lord. *Deut.* 14: 1.

Children of God. *John* 11: 52. 1 *John* 3: 10.

Children of the Living God. *Rom.* 9: 26.

Children of the Father. *Matt.* 5: 45.

Children of the Highest. *Luke* 6: 35.

Children of Abraham. *Gal.* 3: 7.

Children of Jacob. *Ps.* 105: 6.

Children of promise. *Rom.* 9: 8. *Gal.* 4: 28.

Children of the free-women. *Gal.* 4: 31.

Children of the kingdom. *Matt.* 13: 38.

Children of Zion. *Ps.* 149: 2. *Joel* 2: 23.

Children of the bride-chamber. *Matt.* 9: 15.

Children of light. *Luke* 16: 8. *Eph.* 5: 8.

Children of the day. 1 *Thess.* 5: 5.

Children of the resurrection. *Luke* 20: 36.

Chosen generation. 1 *Pet.* 2: 9.

Chosen ones. 1 *Chron.* 16: 13.

Chosen vessels. *Acts* 9: 15.

Christians. *Acts* 11: 26. *Acts* 26: 28.

Counsellors of peace. *Prov.* 12: 20.

Dear children. *Eph.* 5: 1.

Disciples of Christ. *John* 8: 31. *John* 15: 8.

Elect of God. *Col.* 3: 12. *Titus* 1: 1.

Epistles of Christ. 2 *Cor.* 3: 3.

Excellent, The. *Ps.* 16: 3.

Faithful brethren in Christ. *Col.* 1: 2.

Faithful, The. *Ps.* 12: 1.

Faithful of the land, The. *Ps.* 101: 6.

Fellow-citizens. *Eph.* 9: 19.

Fellow-heirs. *Eph.* 3: 6.

Fellow-servants. *Rev.* 6: 11.

Friends of God. 2 *Chron.* 20: 7. *Jas.* 2: 23.

Friends. *Song of Sol.* 5: 1. *John* 15: 15.

Godly, The. *Ps.* 4: 3. 2 *Pet.* 2: 9.

Heirs of God. *Rom.* 8: 17. *Gal.* 4: 7.

Heirs of the grace of life. 1 *Pet.* 3: 7.

Heirs of the kingdom. *Jas.* 2: 5.

Heirs of promise. *Heb.* 6: 17. *Gal.* 3: 29.

Heirs of salvation. *Heb.* 1: 14.

Hidden ones. *Ps.* 83: 3.

Holy brethren. 1 *Thess.* 5: 27. *Heb.* 3: 1.

Holy and mighty people. *Dan.* 8: 24.

Holy nation. *Exod.* 19: 6. 1 *Pet.* 2: 9.

Holy people. *Deut.* 26: 19. *Isa.* 62: 12.

Holy priesthood. 1 *Pet.* 2: 5.

Holy seed. *Isa.* 6: 13.

Joint-heirs with Christ. *Rom.* 8: 17.

Just, The. *Prov.* 20: 7. *Hab.* 2: 4.

Kings and priests unto God. *Rev.* 1: 6.

Kingdom of priests. *Exod.* 19: 6.

Lambs. *Isa.* 40: 11. *John* 21: 15.

Lights of the world. *Matt.* 5: 14.

Little children. *John* 13: 33. 1 *John* 2: 1.

Lively stones. 1 *Pet.* 2: 5.

Members of Christ. 1 *Cor.* 6: 15. *Eph.* 5: 30.

Men of God. *Deut.* 33: 1. 1 *Tim.* 6: 11.

Obedient children. 1 *Pet.* 1: 14.

Peculiar people. *Deut.* 14: 2. *Titus* 2: 14.

Peculiar treasure. *Exod.* 19: 5. *Ps.* 135: 4.

People of God. *Heb.* 4: 9. 1 *Pet.* 2: 10.

People of God's pasture. *Ps.* 95: 7.

People of inheritance. *Deut.* 4: 20.

People near unto God. *Ps.* 148: 14.

People prepared for the Lord. *Luke* 1: 17.

People saved by the Lord. *Deut.* 33: 29.

Pillars in the temple of God. *Rev.* 3: 12.

Ransomed of the Lord. *Isa.* 35: 10.

Redeemed of the Lord. *Isa.* 51: 11.

Righteous, The. *Ps.* 1: 6. *Mal.* 3: 18.

Royal priesthood. 1 *Pet.* 2: 9.

Salt of the earth. *Matt.* 5: 13.

Seed of Abraham. *Ps.* 105: 6.

Seed of the blessed of the Lord. *Isa.* 65: 23.

Servants of Christ. 1 *Cor.* 7: 22. *Eph.* 6: 6.

Servants of the Lord. *Deut.* 34: 5. *Isa.* 54: 17.

Servants of the Most High God. *Dan.* 3: 26.

Servants of righteousness. *Rom.* 6: 18.

Sheep of Christ. *John* 10: 1–16. *John* 21: 16.

Sheep of the flock. *Matt.* 26: 31.

Sheep of God's hand. *Ps.* 95: 7.

Sheep of God's pasture. *Ps.* 79: 13.

Sojourners with God. *Lev.* 25: 23. *Ps.* 39: 12.

Sons of God. *John* 1: 12. *Phil.* 2: 15.

Sons of the Living God. *Hos.* 1: 10.

Special people. *Deut.* 7: 6.

The Lord's freemen. 1 *Cor.* 7: 22.

The Lord's people. 1 *Sam.* 2: 24. 2 *Kings* 11: 17.

Trees of righteousness. *Isa.* 61: 3.

Vessels unto honour. 2 *Tim.* 2: 21.

Vessels of mercy. *Rom.* 9: 23.

Witnesses for God. *Isa.* 43: 10. *Isa.* 44: 8.

TITLES AND NAMES OF THE WICKED

Adversaries of the Lord. 1 *Sam.* 2: 10.

Children of Belial. *Deut.* 13: 13. 2 *Chron.* 13: 7.

Children of the devil. *Acts* 13: 10. 1 *John* 3: 10.

Children of the wicked-one. *Matt.* 13: 38.

Children of hell. *Matt.* 23: 15.

Children of the bond-woman. *Gal.* 4: 31.

Children of base men. *Job* 30: 8.

Children of fools. *Job* 30: 8.

Children of strangers. *Isa.* 2: 6.

Children of transgression. *Isa.* 57: 4.

Children of disobedience. *Eph.* 2: 2. *Col.* 3: 6.

Children in whom is no faith. *Deut.* 32: 20.

Children of the flesh. *Rom.* 9: 8.

Children of iniquity. *Hos.* 10: 9.

Children that will not hear the law of the Lord. *Isa.* 30: 9.

Children of pride. *Job* 41: 34.

Children of this world. *Luke* 16: 8.

Children of wickedness. *2 Sam.* 7: 10.

Children of wrath. *Eph.* 2: 3.

Children that are corrupters. *Isa.* 1: 4.

Cursed children. *2 Pet.* 2: 14.

Enemies of God. *Ps.* 37: 20. *Jas.* 4: 4.

Enemies of the cross of Christ. *Phil.* 3: 18.

Enemies of all righteousness. *Acts* 13: 10.

Evil doers. *Ps.* 37: 1. *1 Pet.* 2: 14.

Evil men. *Prov.* 4: 14. *2 Tim.* 3: 13.

Evil generation. *Deut.* 1: 35.

Evil and adulterous generation. *Matt.* 12: 39.

Fools. *Prov.* 1: 7. *Rom.* 1: 22.

Froward generation. *Deut.* 32: 20.

Generation of vipers. *Matt.* 3: 7. *Matt.* 12: 34.

Grievous revolters. *Jer.* 6: 28.

Haters of God. *Ps.* 81: 15. *Rom.* 1: 30.

Impudent children. *Ezek.* 2: 4.

Inventors of evil things. *Rom.* 1: 30.

Lying children. *Isa.* 30: 9.

Men of the world. *Ps.* 17: 14.

People laden with iniquity. *Isa.* 1: 4.

Perverse and crooked generation. *Deut.* 32: 5. *Matt.* 17: 17. *Phil.* 2: 15.

Rebellious children. *Isa.* 30: 1.

Rebellious people. *Isa.* 30: 9. *Isa.* 65: 2.

Rebellious nation. *Ezek.* 2: 3.

Rebellious house. *Ezek.* 2: 5, 8. *Ezek.* 12: 2.

Reprobates. *2 Cor.* 13: 5–7.

Scornful, The. *Ps.* 1: 1.

Seed of falsehood. *Isa.* 57: 4.

Seed of the wicked. *Ps.* 37: 28.

Seed of evil doers. *Isa.* 1: 4. *Isa.* 14: 20.

Serpents. *Matt.* 23: 33.

Servants of corruption. *2 Pet.* 2: 19.

Servants of sin. *John* 8: 34. *Rom.* 6: 20.

Sinful generation. *Mark* 8: 28.

Sinners. *Ps.* 26: 9. *Prov.* 1: 10.

Sons of Belial. *1 Sam.* 2: 12. *1 Kings* 21: 10.

Sottish children. *Jer.* 4: 22.

Strange children. *Ps.* 144: 7.

Stubborn and rebellious generation. *Ps.* 78: 8.

Transgressors. *Ps.* 37: 38. *Ps.* 51: 13.

Ungodly, The. *Ps.* 1: 1.

Ungodly men. *Jude* 4.

Unprofitable servants. *Matt.* 25: 30.

Untoward generation. *Acts* 2: 40.

Vessels of wrath. *Rom.* 9: 22.

Wicked of the earth. *Ps.* 75: 8.

Wicked transgressors. *Ps.* 59: 5.

Wicked servants. *Matt.* 25: 26.

Wicked generation. *Matt.* 12: 45. *Matt.* 16: 4.

Wicked-ones. *Jer.* 2: 33.

Wicked doers. *Ps.* 101: 8. *Prov.* 17: 4.

Workers of iniquity. *Ps.* 28: 3. *Ps.* 36: 12.

TITLES AND NAMES OF THE DEVIL

Abaddon. *Rev.* 9: 11.

Accuser of our brethren. *Rev.* 12: 10.

Adversary. 1 *Pet.* 5: 8.

Angel of the bottomless pit. *Rev.* 9: 11.

Apollyon. *Rev.* 9: 11.

Beelzebub. *Matt.* 12: 24.

Belial. 2 *Cor.* 6: 15.

Crooked serpent. *Isa.* 27: 1.

Dragon. *Isa.* 27: 1. *Rev.* 20: 2.

Enemy. *Matt.* 13: 39.

Evil spirit. 1 *Sam.* 16: 14.

Father of lies. *John* 8: 44.

Great red dragon. *Rev.* 12: 3.

Leviathan. *Isa.* 27: 1.

Liar. *John* 8: 44.

Lying spirit. 1 *Kings* 22: 22.

Murderer. *John* 8: 44.

Old serpent. *Rev.* 12: 9. *Rev.* 20: 2.

Piercing serpent. *Isa.* 27: 1.

Power of darkness. *Col.* 1: 13.

Prince of this world. *John* 14: 30.

Prince of the devils. *Matt.* 12: 24.

Prince of the power of the air. *Eph.* 2: 2.

Ruler of the darkness of this world. *Eph.* 6: 12.

Satan. 1 *Chron.* 21: 1. *Job* 1: 6.

Serpent. *Gen.* 3: 4, 14. 2 *Cor.* 11: 3.

Spirit that worketh in the children of disobedience. *Eph.* 2: 2.

Tempter. *Matt.* 4: 3. 1 *Thess.* 3: 5.

The god of this world. 2 *Cor.* 4: 4.

Unclean spirit. *Matt.* 12: 43.

Wicked-one. *Matt.* 13: 19, 38.

TRINITY, THE

Doctrine of, proved from Scripture. *Matt.* 3: 16, 17. *Rom.* 8: 9. 1 *Cor.* 12: 3–6. *Eph.* 4: 4–6. 1 *Pet.* 1: 2. 1 *John* 5: 7. *Jude* 20: 21.

Divine titles applied to the three Persons in. *Exod.* 20: 2, with *John* 20: 28, and *Acts* 5: 3, 4.

Each person in, described as

Eternal. *Rom.* 16: 26, with *Rev.* 22: 13, and *Heb.* 9: 14.

Holy. *Rev.* 4: 8. *Rev.* 15: 4, with *Acts* 3: 14, and 1 *John* 2: 20.

True. *John* 7: 28, with *Rev.* 3: 7, and 1 *John* 5: 6.

Omnipresent. *Jer.* 23: 24, with *Eph.* 1: 23, and *Ps.* 139: 7.

Omnipotent. *Gen.* 17: 1, with *Rev.* 1: 8, and *Rom.* 15: 19. *Jer.* 32: 17, with *Heb.* 1: 3, and *Luke* 1: 35.

Omniscient. *Acts* 15: 18, with *John* 22: 17, and 1 *Cor.* 2: 10, 11.

Creator. *Gen.* 1: 1, with *Col.* 1: 16, and *Job* 33: 4. *Ps.* 148: 5, with *John* 1: 3, and *Job* 26: 13.

Sanctifier. *Jude* 1, with *Heb.* 2: 11, and 1 *Pet.* 1: 2.

Author of all spiritual operations. *Heb.* 13: 21, with *Col.* 1: 29, and 1 *Cor.* 12: 11.

Source of eternal life. *Rom.* 6: 23, with *John* 10: 28, and *Gal.* 6: 8.

Teacher. *Isa.* 54: 13, with *Luke* 21: 15, and *John* 14:

26. *Isa.* 48: 17, with *Gal.* 1: 12, and 1 *John* 2: 20.

Raising Christ from the dead. 1 *Cor.* 6: 14, with *John* 2: 19, and 1 *Pet.* 3: 18.

Inspiring the prophets, etc. *Heb.* 1: 1, with 2 *Cor.* 13: 3, and *Mark* 13: 11.

Supplying ministers to the Church. *Jer.* 3: 15, with *Eph.* 4: 11, and *Acts* 20: 28. *Jer.* 26: 5, with *Matt.* 10: 5, and *Acts* 13: 2.

Salvation the work of. 2 *Thess.* 2: 13, 14. *Titus* 3: 4–6. 1 *Pet.* 1: 2.

Baptism administered in name of. *Matt.* 28: 19.

Benediction given in name of. 2 *Cor.* 13: 14.

Saints

Are the temple of. 2 *Cor.* 6: 16, with *Eph.* 3: 17, and 1 *Cor.* 3: 16. *Eph.* 2: 22, with *Col.* 1: 27, and 1 *Cor.* 6: 19.

Have fellowship with. 1 *John* 1: 3, with *Phil.* 2: 1.

Sin, a tempting of. *Deut.* 6: 16, with 1 *Cor.* 10: 9, and *Acts* 5: 9.

The Israelites in the wilderness tempted. *Exod.* 17: 7, with 1 *Cor.* 10: 9, and *Heb.* 3: 7, 9.

TRUST

God is the true object of. *Ps.* 65: 5.

The fear of God leads to. *Prov.* 14: 26.

Encouragements to;

The everlasting strength of God. *Isa.* 26: 4.

The goodness of God. *Nahum* 1: 7.

The loving-kindness of God. *Ps.* 36: 7.

The rich bounty of God. 1 *Tim.* 6: 17.

The care of God for us. 1 *Pet.* 5: 7.

Former deliverances. *Ps.* 9. 10. 2 *Cor.* 1: 10.

Should be with the whole heart. *Prov.* 3: 5.

Should be from youth up. *Ps.* 71: 5.

Of saints is

Not in the flesh. *Phil.* 3: 3, 4.

Not in themselves. 2 *Cor.* 1: 9.

Not in carnal weapons. 1 *Sam.* 17: 38, 39, 45. *Ps.* 44: 6. 2 *Cor.* 10: 4.

In God. *Ps.* 11: 1. *Ps.* 31: 14. 2 *Cor.* 1: 9.

In the word of God. *Ps.* 119: 42.

In the mercy of God. *Ps.* 13: 5. *Ps.* 52: 8.

In Christ. *Eph.* 3: 12.

Through Christ. 2 *Cor.* 3: 4.

Grounded on the covenant. 2 *Sam.* 23: 5.

Strong in the prospect of death. *Ps.* 23: 4.

Fixed. 2 *Sam.* 22: 3. *Ps.* 112: 7.

Unalterable. *Job* 13: 15.

Despised by the wicked. *Isa.* 36: 4, 7.

At all times. *Ps.* 62: 8.

For ever. *Ps.* 52: 8. *Isa.* 26: 4.

Saints plead, in prayer. *Ps.* 25: 20. *Ps.* 31: 1. *Ps.* 141: 8.

The Lord knows those who have. *Nahum* 1: 7.

Exhortations to. *Ps.* 4: 5. *Ps.* 115: 9–11.

Leads to

Being compassed with mercy.
Ps. 32: 10.

Enjoyment of perfect peace.
Isa. 26: 3.

Enjoyment of all temporal
and spiritual blessings. Isa.
57: 13.

Enjoyment of happiness.
Prov. 16: 20.

Rejoicing in God. Ps. 5: 11.
Ps. 33: 21.

Fulfilment of all holy desires.
Ps. 37: 5.

Deliverance from enemies.
Ps. 37: 40.

Safety in times of danger.
Prov. 29: 25.

Stability. Ps. 125: 1.

Prosperity. Prov. 28: 25.

Keeps from

Fear. Ps. 56: 11. Isa. 12: 2.
Heb. 13: 6.

Sliding. Ps. 26: 1.

Desolation. Ps. 34: 22.

To be accompanied by doing
good. Ps. 37: 3.

Blessedness of placing, in God.
Ps. 2: 12. Ps. 34: 8. Ps. 40: 4.
Jer. 17: 7.

Of the wicked

Is not in God. Ps. 78: 22.
Zeph. 3: 2.

Is in idols. Isa. 42: 17. Hab.
2: 18.

Is in man. Judges 9: 26. Ps.
118: 8, 9.

Is in their own heart. Prov.
28: 26.

Is in their own righteousness.
Luke 18: 9, 12.

Is in their religious privileges.
Jer. 7: 4, 8. Mic. 3: 11. John
8: 33.

Is in oppression. Ps. 62: 10.
Isa. 30: 12.

Is in wickedness. Isa. 47:
10.

Is in vanity. Job 15: 31.
Isa. 59: 4.

Is in falsehood. Isa. 28: 15.
Jer. 13: 25.

Is in earthly alliances. Isa.
30: 2. Ezek. 17: 15.

Is in fenced cities. Jer. 5:
17.

Is in chariots and horses.
Ps. 20: 7.

Is in wealth. Ps. 49: 6. Ps.
52: 7. Prov. 11: 28. Jer. 48:
7. Mark 10: 24.

Is vain and delusive. Isa.
30: 7. Jer. 2: 37.

Shall make them ashamed.
Isa. 20: 5. Isa. 30: 3, 5. Jer.
48: 13.

Shall be destroyed. Job 18:
14. Isa. 28: 18.

Woe and curse of false. Isa.
30: 1, 2. Isa. 31: 1–3. Jer. 17: 5.

Of saints—Illustrated. Ps. 91:
12. Prov. 18: 10.

Of the wicked—Illustrated. 2
Kings 18: 21. Job 8: 14. Job 18:
21.

Of saints—Exemplified. DAVID,
1 Sam. 17: 45. 1 Sam. 30: 6.
HEZEKIAH, 2 Kings 18: 5. JE-
HOSHAPHAT, 2 Chron. 20: 12.
SHADRACH, etc., Dan. 3: 28.
PAUL, 2 Tim. 1: 12.

Of the wicked—Exemplified.
GOLIATH, 1 Sam. 17: 43–45.
BENHADAD, 1 Kings 20: 10.
SENNACHERIB, 2 Chron. 32: 8.
ISRAELITES, Isa. 31: 1.

TRUTH

God is a God of. Deut. 32: 4.
Ps. 31: 5.

Christ is. John 14: 6, with
John 7: 18.

Christ was full of. John 1: 14.

Christ spake. John 8: 45.

The Holy Ghost is the Spirit of. *John* 14: 17.

The Holy Ghost guides into all. *John* 16: 13.

The word of God is. *Dan.* 10: 21. *John* 17: 17.

God regards, with favour. *Jer.* 5: 3.

The judgments of God are according to. *Ps.* 96: 13. *Rom.* 2: 2.

Saints should

Worship God in. *John* 4: 24, with *Ps.* 145: 18.

Serve God in. *Joshua* 24: 14. 1 *Sam.* 12: 24.

Walk before God in. 1 *Kings* 2: 4. 2 *Kings* 20: 3.

Keep religious feasts with. 1 *Cor.* 5: 8.

Esteem, as inestimable. *Prov.* 23: 23.

Love. *Zech.* 8: 19.

Rejoice in. 1 *Cor.* 13: 6.

Speak, to one another. *Zech.* 8: 16. *Eph.* 4: 25.

Execute judgment with. *Zech.* 8: 16.

Meditate upon. *Phil.* 4: 8.

Bind, about the neck. *Prov.* 3: 3.

Write, upon the tables of the heart. *Prov.* 3: 3.

God desires, in the heart. *Ps.* 51: 6.

The fruit of the Spirit is in. *Eph.* 5: 9.

Ministers should

Speak. 2 *Cor.* 12: 6. *Gal.* 4: 16.

Teach in. 1 *Tim.* 2: 7.

Approve themselves by. 2 *Cor.* 6: 7, 8.

Magistrates should be men of. *Exod.* 18: 21.

Kings are preserved by. *Prov.* 20: 28.

They who speak,

Shew forth righteousness. *Prov.* 12: 17.

Shall be established. *Prov.* 12: 19.

Are the delight of God. *Prov.* 12: 22.

The wicked

Destitute of. *Hos.* 4: 1.

Speak not. *Jer.* 9: 5.

Uphold not. *Isa.* 59: 14, 15.

Plead not for. *Isa.* 59: 4.

Are not valiant for. *Jer.* 9: 3.

Punished for want of. *Jer.* 9: 5, 9. *Hos.* 4: 1, 3.

The gospel as,

Came by Christ. *John* 1: 17.

Christ bare witness to. *John* 18: 37.

Is in Christ. 1 *Tim.* 2: 7.

John bare witness to. *John* 5: 33.

Is according to godliness. *Titus* 1: 1.

Is sanctifying. *John* 17: 17, 19.

Is purifying. 1 *Pet.* 1: 22.

Is part of the Christian armour. *Eph.* 6: 14.

Revealed abundantly to saints. *Jer.* 33: 6.

Abides continually with saints. 2 *John* 2.

Should be acknowledged. 2 *Tim.* 2: 25.

Should be believed. 2 *Thess.* 2: 12, 13. 1 *Tim.* 4: 3.

Should be obeyed. *Rom.* 2: 8. *Gal.* 3: 1.

Should be loved. 2 *Thess.* 2: 10.

Should be manifested. 2 *Cor.* 4: 2.

Should be rightly divided. 2 *Tim.* 2: 15.

The wicked turn away from. 2 *Tim.* 4: 4.

The wicked resist. 2 *Tim.* 3: 8.

The wicked destitute of. 1 *Tim.* 6: 5.

The Church is the pillar and ground of. 1 *Tim.* 3: 15.

The devil is devoid of. *John* 8: 44.

TRUTH OF GOD, THE

Is one of his attributes. *Deut.* 32: 4. *Isa.* 65: 16.

Always goes before his face. *Ps.* 89: 14.

He keeps, for ever. *Ps.* 146: 6.

Described as

Great. *Ps.* 57: 10.

Plenteous. *Ps.* 86: 15.

Abundant. *Exod.* 34: 6.

Inviolable. *Num.* 23: 19. *Titus* 1: 1, 2.

Reaching to the clouds. *Ps.* 57: 10.

Enduring to all generations. *Ps.* 100: 5.

United with mercy in redemption. *Ps.* 85: 10.

Exhibited in his

Counsels of old. *Isa.* 25: 1.

Ways. *Rev.* 15: 3.

Works. *Ps.* 33: 4. *Ps.* 111: 7. *Dan.* 4: 37.

Judicial statutes. *Ps.* 19: 9.

Administration of justice. *Ps.* 96: 13.

Word. *Ps.* 119: 160. *John* 17: 17.

Fulfilment of promises in Christ. 2 *Cor.* 1: 20.

Fulfilment of his covenant. *Mic.* 7: 20.

Dealings with saints. *Ps.* 25: 10.

Deliverance of saints. *Ps.* 57: 3.

Punishment of the wicked. *Rev.* 16: 7.

Remembered towards saints. *Ps.* 98: 3.

Is a shield and buckler to saints. *Ps.* 91: 4.

We should

Confide in. *Ps.* 31: 5. *Titus* 1: 2.

Plead, in prayer. *Ps.* 89: 49.

Pray for its manifestation to ourselves. 2 *Chron.* 6: 17.

Pray for its exhibition to others. 2 *Sam.* 2: 6.

Make known, to others. *Isa.* 38: 19.

Magnify. *Ps.* 71: 22. *Ps.* 138: 2.

Is denied by

The devil. *Gen.* 3: 4, 5.

The self-righteous. 1 *John* 1: 10.

Unbelievers. 1 *John* 5: 10.

Exemplified towards ABRAHAM, *Gen.* 24: 27. JACOB, *Gen.* 32: 10. ISRAEL, *Ps.* 98: 3.

TYPES OF CHRIST

Adam. *Rom.* 5: 14. 1 *Cor.* 15: 45.

Abel. *Gen.* 4: 8, 10, with *Acts* 2: 23. *Heb.* 12: 24.

Abraham. *Gen.* 17: 5, with *Eph.* 3: 15.

Aaron. *Exod.* 28: 1, with *Heb.* 5: 4, 5. *Lev.* 16: 15, with *Heb.* 9: 7, 24.

Ark. *Gen.* 7: 16, with 1 *Pet.* 3: 20, 21.

Ark of the covenant. *Exod.* 15: 16, with *Ps.* 40: 8. *Isa.* 42: 6.

Atonement, sacrifices offered on the day of. *Lev.* 16: 15, 16, with *Heb.* 9: 12, 24.

Brazen serpent. *Num.* 21: 9, with *John* 3: 14, 15.

Brazen altar. *Exod.* 27: 1, 2, with *Heb.* 13: 10.

Burnt-offering. *Lev.* 1: 2, 4, with *Heb.* 10: 10.

Cities of refuge. *Num.* 35: 6, with *Heb.* 6: 18.

David. 2 *Sam.* 8: 15, with *Ezek.* 37: 24. *Ps.* 89: 19, 20, with *Phil.* 2: 9.

Eliakim. *Isa.* 22: 20–22, with *Rev.* 3: 7.

First-fruits. *Exod.* 22: 29, with 1 *Cor.* 15: 20.

Golden candlestick. *Exod.* 25: 31, with *John* 8: 12.

Golden altar. *Exod.* 40: 5, 26, 27, with *Rev.* 8: 3, and *Heb.* 13: 15.

Isaac. *Gen.* 22: 1, 2, with *Heb.* 11: 17–19.

Jacob. *Gen.* 32: 28, with *John* 11: 42. *Heb.* 7: 25.

Jacob's ladder. *Gen.* 28: 12, with *John* 1: 51.

Joseph. *Gen.* 50: 19, 20, with *Heb.* 7: 25.

Joshua. *Joshua* 1: 5, 6, with *Heb.* 4: 8, 9. *Joshua* 11: 23, with *Acts* 20: 32.

Jonah. *Jonah* 1: 17, with *Matt.* 12: 40.

Laver of brass. *Exod.* 30: 18–20, with *Zech.* 13: 1. *Eph.* 5: 26, 27.

Leper's offering. *Lev.* 14: 4–7, with *Rom.* 4: 25.

Manna. *Exod.* 16: 11–15, with *John* 6: 32–35.

Melchizedek. *Gen.* 14: 18–20, with *Heb.* 7: 1–17.

Mercy-seat. *Exod.* 25: 17–22, with *Rom.* 3: 25. *Heb.* 4: 16.

Morning and evening sacrifices. *Exod.* 29: 38–41, with *John* 1: 29, 36.

Moses. *Num.* 12: 7, with *Heb.* 3: 2. *Deut.* 18: 15, with *Acts* 3: 20–22.

Noah. *Gen.* 5: 29. 2 *Cor.* 1: 5.

Paschal lamb. *Exod.* 12: 3–6, 46, with *John* 19: 36. 1 *Cor.* 5: 7.

Peace-offering. *Lev.* 3: 1, with *Eph.* 2: 14, 16.

Red heifer. *Num.* 19: 2–6, with *Heb.* 9: 13, 14.

Rock of Horeb. *Exod.* 17: 6, with 1 *Cor.* 10: 4.

Samson. *Judges* 16: 30, with *Col.* 2: 14, 15.

Scape-goat. *Lev.* 16: 20–22, with *Isa.* 53: 6, 12.

Sin-offering. *Lev.* 4: 2, 3, 12, with *Heb.* 13: 11, 12.

Solomon. 2 *Sam.* 7: 12, 13, with *Luke* 1: 32, 33. 1 *Pet.* 2: 5.

Tabernacle. *Exod.* 40: 2, 34, with *Heb.* 9: 11. *Col.* 2: 9.

Table and shew-bread. *Exod.* 25: 23–30, with *John* 1: 16, *John* 6: 48.

Temple. 1 *Kings* 6: 1, 38, with *John* 2: 19, 21.

Tree of life. *Gen.* 2: 9, with *John* 1: 4. *Rev.* 22: 2.

Trespass-offering. *Lev.* 6: 1–7, with *Isa.* 53: 10.

Veil of the tabernacle and temple. *Exod.* 40: 21. 2 *Chron.* 3: 14, with *Heb.* 10: 20.

Zerubbabel. *Zech.* 4: 7–9, with *Heb.* 12: 2, 3.

UNBELIEF

Is sin. *John* 16: 9.

Defilement inseparable from. *Titus* 1: 15.

All, by nature, concluded in. *Rom.* 11: 32.

Proceeds from

An evil heart. *Heb.* 3: 12.

Slowness of heart. *Luke* 24: 25.

Hardness of heart. *Mark* 16: 14. *Acts* 19: 9.

Disinclination to the truth. *John* 8: 45, 46.

Judicial blindness. *John* 12: 39, 40.

Not being Christ's sheep. *John* 10: 26.

The devil blinding the mind. 2 *Cor.* 4: 4.

The devil taking away the word out of the heart. *Luke* 8: 12.

Seeking honour from men. *John* 5: 44.

Impugns the veracity of God. 1 *John* 5: 10.

Exhibited in

Rejecting Christ. *John* 16: 9.

Rejecting the word of God. *Ps.* 106: 24.

Rejecting the gospel. *Isa.* 53: 1. *John* 12: 38.

Rejecting evidence of miracles. *John* 12: 37.

Departing from God. *Heb.* 3: 12.

Questioning the power of God. 2 *Kings* 7: 2. *Ps.* 78: 19, 20.

Not believing the works of God. *Ps.* 78: 32.

Staggering at the promise of God. *Rom.* 4: 20.

Rebuked by Christ. *Matt.* 17: 17. *John* 20: 27.

Was an impediment to the performance of miracles. *Matt.* 17: 20. *Mark* 6: 5.

Miracles designed to convince those in. *John* 10: 37, 38. 1 *Cor.* 14: 22.

The Jews rejected for. *Rom.* 11: 20.

Believers should hold no communion with those in. 2 *Cor.* 6: 14.

Those who are guilty of,

Have not the word of God in them. *John* 5: 38.

Cannot please God. *Heb.* 11: 6.

Malign the gospel. *Acts* 19: 9.

Persecute the ministers of God. *Rom.* 15: 31.

Excite others against saints. *Acts* 14: 2.

Persevere in it. *John* 12: 37.

Harden their necks. 2 *Kings* 17: 14.

Are condemned already. *John* 3: 18.

Have the wrath of God abiding upon them. *John* 3: 36.

Shall not be established. *Isa.* 7: 9.

Shall die in their sins. *John* 8: 24.

Shall not enter rest. *Heb.* 3: 19. *Heb.* 4: 11.

Shall be condemned. *Mark* 16: 16. 2 *Thess.* 2: 12.

Shall be destroyed. *Jude* 5.

Shall be cast into the lake of fire. *Rev.* 21: 8.

Warnings against. *Heb.* 3: 12. *Heb.* 4: 11.

Pray for help against. *Mark* 9: 24.

The portion of, award to all unfaithful servants. *Luke* 12: 46.

Exemplified. EVE, *Gen.* 3: 4—6. MOSES AND AARON, *Num.* 20: 12. ISRAELITES, *Deut.* 9: 23. NAAMAN, 2 *Kings* 5: 12. SAMARITAN LORD, 2 *Kings* 7: 2. DISCIPLES, *Matt.* 17: 17. *Luke* 24: 11, 25. ZACHARIAS, *Luke* 1: 20. CHIEF PRIESTS, *Luke* 22: 67. THE JEWS, *John* 5: 38. BRETHREN OF CHRIST, *John* 7: 5. THOMAS, *John* 20: 25. JEWS OF ICONIUM, *Acts* 14: 2. THESSALONIAN JEWS, *Acts* 17: 5.

EPHESIANS, *Acts* 19: 9. SAUL, 1 *Tim.* 1: 13. PEOPLE OF JERICHO, *Heb.* 11: 31.

UNION WITH CHRIST

As Head of the Church. *Eph.* 1: 22, 23. *Eph.* 4: 15, 16. *Col.* 1: 18.

Christ prayed that all saints might have. *John* 17: 21, 23.

Described as

Christ being in us. *Eph.* 3: 17. *Col.* 1: 27.

Our being in Christ. 2 *Cor.* 12: 2. 1 *John* 5: 20.

Includes union with the Father. *John* 17: 21. 1 *John* 2: 24.

Is of God. 1 *Cor.* 1: 30.

Maintained by

Faith. *Gal.* 2: 20. *Eph.* 3: 17.

Abiding in him. *John* 15: 4, 7.

His word abiding in us. *John* 15: 7. 1 *John* 2: 24. 2 *John* 9.

Feeding on him. *John* 6: 56.

Obeying him. 1 *John* 3: 24.

The Holy Ghost witnesses to. 1 *John* 3: 24.

The gift of the Holy Ghost is an evidence of. 1 *John* 4: 13.

Saints

Have, in mind. 1 *Cor.* 2: 16. *Phil.* 2: 5.

Have, in spirit. 1 *Cor.* 6: 17.

Have, in love. *Song of Sol.* 2: 16. *Song of Sol.* 7: 10.

Have, in sufferings. *Phil.* 3: 10. 2 *Tim.* 2: 12.

Have, in his death. *Rom.* 6: 3–8. *Gal.* 2: 20.

Have assurance of. *John* 14: 20.

Enjoy, in the Lord's Supper. 1 *Cor.* 10: 16, 17.

Identified with Christ by. *Matt.* 25: 40, 45. *Acts* 9: 4, with *Acts* 8: 1.

Are complete through. *Col.* 2: 10.

Exhorted to maintain. *John* 15: 4. *Acts* 11: 23. *Col.* 2: 7.

Necessary to growth in grace. *Eph.* 4: 15, 16. *Col.* 2: 19.

Necessary to fruitfulness. *John* 15: 4, 5.

Beneficial results of;

Righteousness imputed. 2 *Cor.* 5: 21. *Phil.* 3: 9.

Freedom from condemnation. *Rom.* 8: 1.

Freedom from dominion of sin. 1 *John* 3: 6.

Being created anew. 2 *Cor.* 5: 17.

The spirit alive to righteousness. *Rom.* 8: 10.

Confidence at his coming. 1 *John* 2: 28.

Abundant fruitfulness. *John* 15: 5.

Answers to prayer. *John* 15: 7.

They who have, ought to walk as He walked. 1 *John* 2: 6.

False teachers have not. *Col.* 2: 18, 19.

Is indissoluble. *Rom.* 8: 35.

Punishment of those who have not. *John* 15: 6.

Illustrated. VINE AND BRANCHES, *John* 15: 1, 5. FOUNDATION AND BUILDING, 1 *Cor.* 3: 10, 11. *Eph.* 2: 20, 21. 1 *Pet.* 2: 4–6. BODY AND MEMBERS, 1 *Cor.* 12: 12, 27. *Eph.* 5: 30. HUSBAND AND WIFE, *Eph.* 5: 25–32.

UNITY OF GOD

A ground for obeying him exclusively. *Deut.* 4: 39, 40.

A ground for loving him su-

premely. *Deut.* 6: 4, 5, with
Mark 12: 29, 30.

Asserted by

God himself. *Isa.* 44: 6, 8.
Isa. 45: 18, 21.

Christ. *Mark* 12: 29. *John*
17: 3.

Moses. *Deut.* 4: 39. *Deut.*
6: 4.

Apostles. 1 *Cor.* 8: 4, 6.
Eph. 4: 6. 1 *Tim.* 2: 5.

Consistent with the deity of
Christ and of the Holy Ghost.
John 10: 30, with 1 *John* 5: 7.
John 14: 9—11.

Exhibited in

His greatness and wonderful
works. 2 *Sam.* 7: 22. *Ps.*
86: 10.

His works of creation and
providence. *Isa.* 44: 24.
Isa. 45: 5—8.

His being alone possessed of
foreknowledge. *Isa.* 46: 9—
11.

His exercise of uncontrolled
sovereignty. *Deut.* 32: 39.

His being the sole object of
worship in heaven and earth.
Neh. 9: 6. *Matt.* 4: 10.

His being alone good. *Matt.*
19: 17.

His being the only Saviour.
Isa. 45: 21, 22.

His being the only source of
pardon. *Mic.* 7: 18, with
Mark 2: 7.

His unparalleled election and
care of his people. *Deut.* 4:
32—35.

The knowledge of, necessary to
eternal life. *John* 17: 3.

All saints acknowledge, in worshipping him. 2 *Sam.* 7: 22.
2 *Kings* 19: 15. 1 *Chron.* 17:
20.

All should know and acknowledge. *Deut.* 4: 35. *Ps.* 83: 18.

May be acknowledged without
saving faith. *Jas.* 2: 19, 20.

UPRIGHTNESS

God is perfect in. *Isa.* 26: 7.

God has pleasure in. 1 *Chron.*
29: 17.

God created man in. *Eccles.*
7: 29.

Man has deviated from.
Eccles. 7: 29.

Should be in

Heart. 2 *Chron.* 29: 34. *Ps.*
125: 4.

Speech. *Isa.* 33: 15.

Walk. *Prov.* 14: 2.

Judging. *Ps.* 58: 1. *Ps.* 75: 2.

Ruling. *Ps.* 78: 72.

The being kept from presumptuous sins is necessary to. *Ps.*
19: 13.

With poverty, is better than sin
with riches. *Prov.* 28: 6.

With poverty, is better than
folly. *Prov.* 19: 1.

They who walk in,

Fear God. *Prov.* 14: 2.

Love Christ. *Song of Sol.*
1: 4.

Countenanced by God. *Ps.*
11: 7.

Delighted in by God. *Prov.*
11: 20.

Their prayer delighted in by
God. *Prov.* 15: 8.

Prospered by God. *Job* 8: 6.
Prov. 14: 11.

Defended by God. *Prov.* 2:
7.

Upheld in it by God. *Ps.*
41: 12.

Recompensed by God. *Ps.*
18: 23, 24.

Find strength in God's way.
Prov. 10: 29.

Obtain good from God's word. *Mic.* 2: 7.

Obtain light in darkness. *Ps.* 112: 4.

Guided by integrity. *Prov.* 11: 3.

Walk surely. *Prov.* 10: 9.

Direct their way. *Prov.* 21: 29.

Kept by righteousness. *Prov.* 13: 6.

Scorned by the wicked. *Job* 12: 4.

Hated by the wicked. *Prov.* 29: 10. *Amos* 5: 10.

Abominated by the wicked. *Prov.* 29: 27.

Persecuted by the wicked. *Ps.* 37: 14.

Praise is comely for. *Ps.* 33: 1.

A blessing to others. *Prov.* 11: 11.

The truly wise walk in. *Prov.* 15: 21.

The way of, is to depart from evil. *Prov.* 16: 17.

They who walk in, shall

Possess good things. *Prov.* 28: 10.

Have nothing good withheld. *Ps.* 84: 11.

Dwell in the land. *Prov.* 2: 21.

Dwell on high and be provided for. *Isa.* 33: 16.

Dwell with God. *Ps.* 15: 2. *Ps.* 140: 13.

Be blessed. *Ps.* 112: 2.

Be delivered by righteousness. *Prov.* 11: 6.

Be delivered by their wisdom. *Prov.* 12: 6.

Be saved. *Prov.* 28: 18.

Enter into peace. *Ps.* 37: 37. *Isa.* 57: 2.

Have dominion over the wicked. *Ps.* 49: 14.

Have an inheritance for ever. *Ps.* 37: 18.

A characteristic of saints. *Ps.* 111: 1. *Isa.* 26: 7.

Saints should resolve to walk in. *Ps.* 26: 11.

The wicked

Have not, in heart. *Hab.* 2: 4.

Leave the path of. *Prov.* 2: 13.

Do not act with. *Mic.* 7: 2, 4.

Pray for those who walk in. *Ps.* 125: 4.

Reprove those who deviate from. *Gal.* 2: 14.

VANITY

A consequence of the fall. *Rom.* 8: 20.

Every man is. *Ps.* 39: 11.

Every state of man is. *Ps.* 62: 9.

Man at his best estate is. *Ps.* 35: 5.

Man is like to. *Ps.* 144: 4.

The thoughts of man are. *Ps.* 94: 11.

The days of man are. *Job* 7: 16. *Eccles.* 6: 12.

Childhood and youth are. *Eccles.* 11: 10.

The beauty of man is. *Ps.* 39: 11. *Prov.* 31: 30.

The help of man is. *Ps.* 60: 11. *Lam.* 4: 17.

Man's own righteousness is. *Isa.* 57: 12.

Worldly wisdom is. *Eccles.* 2: 15, 21. 1 *Cor.* 3: 20.

Worldly pleasure is. *Eccles.* 2: 1.

Worldly anxiety is. *Ps.* 39: 6. *Ps.* 127: 2.

Worldly labour is. *Eccles.* 2: 11. *Eccles.* 4: 4.

Worldly enjoyment is. *Eccles.* 2: 3, 10, 11.

Worldly possessions are. *Eccles.* 2: 4–11.

Treasures of wickedness are. *Prov.* 10: 2.

Heaping up riches is. *Eccles.* 2: 26. *Eccles.* 4: 8.

Love of riches is. *Eccles.* 5: 10.

Unblessed riches are. *Eccles.* 6: 2.

Riches gotten by falsehood are. *Prov.* 21: 6.

All earthly things are. *Eccles.* 1: 2.

Foolish questions, etc., are. 1 *Tim.* 1: 6, 7. 1 *Tim.* 6: 20. 2 *Tim.* 2: 14, 16. *Titus* 3: 9.

The conduct of the ungodly is. 1 *Pet.* 1: 18.

The religion of hypocrites is. *Jas.* 1: 26.

The worship of the wicked is. *Isa.* 1: 13. *Matt.* 6: 7.

Lying words are. *Jer.* 7: 8.

False teaching is but. *Jer.* 23: 32.

Mere external religion is. 1 *Tim.* 4: 8. *Heb.* 13: 9.

Almsgiving without charity is. 1 *Cor.* 13: 3.

Faith without works is. *Jas.* 2: 14.

Idolatry is. 2 *Kings* 17: 15. *Ps.* 31: 6. *Isa.* 44: 9, 10. *Jer.* 10: 8. *Jer.* 18: 15.

Wealth gotten by, diminishes. *Prov.* 13: 11.

Saints

Hate the thoughts of. *Ps.* 119: 113.

Pray to be kept from. *Ps.* 110: 37. *Prov.* 30: 8.

Avoid. *Ps.* 24: 4.

Avoid those given to. *Ps.* 26: 4.

The wicked

Especially characterised by. *Job* 11: 11.

Though full of, affect to be wise. *Job* 11: 12.

Love. *Ps.* 4: 2.

Imagine. *Ps.* 2: 1. *Acts* 4: 25. *Rom.* 1: 21.

Devise. *Ps.* 36: 4. *(See margin)*

Speak. *Ps.* 10: 7. *Ps.* 12: 2. *Ps.* 41: 6.

Count God's service as. *Job* 21: 15. *Mal.* 3: 14.

Allure others by words of. 2 *Pet.* 2: 18.

Walk after. *Jer.* 2: 5.

Walk in. *Ps.* 39: 6. *Eph.* 4: 17.

Inherit. *Jer.* 16: 19.

Reap. *Prov.* 22: 8. *Jer.* 12: 13.

Judicially given up to. *Ps.* 78: 33. *Isa.* 57: 13.

Fools follow those given to. *Prov.* 12: 11.

Following those given to, leads to poverty. *Prov.* 28: 19.

They who trust in, rewarded with. *Job* 15: 31.

VISIONS

God often made known His will by. *Ps.* 89: 19.

God especially made Himself known to prophets by. *Num.* 12: 6.

Often accompanied by

A representative of the divine person and glory. *Isa.* 6: 1.

An audible voice from heaven. *Gen.* 15: 1. 1 *Sam.* 3: 4, 5.

An appearance of angels.

Luke 1: 22, with 11. *Luke* 24: 23. *Acts* 10: 3.

An appearance of human beings. *Acts* 9: 12. *Acts* 16: 9.

Frequently difficult and perplexing to those who received them. *Dan.* 7: 15. *Dan.* 8: 15. *Acts* 10: 17.

Often communicated

In the night season. *Gen.* 46: 2. *Dan.* 2: 19.

In a trance. *Num.* 24: 16. *Acts* 11: 5.

Often recorded for the benefit of the people. *Hab.* 2: 2.

Often multiplied for the benefit of the people. *Hos.* 12: 10.

Mentioned in scripture;

To Abraham. *Gen.* 15: 1.

To Jacob. *Gen.* 46: 2.

To Moses. *Exod.* 3: 2, 3. *Acts* 7: 30–32.

To Samuel. *1 Sam.* 3: 2–15.

To Nathan. *2 Sam.* 7: 4, 17.

To Eliphaz. *Job* 4: 13–16.

To Isaiah. *Isa.* 6: 1–8.

To Ezekiel. *Ezek.* 1: 4–14. *Ezek.* 8: 2–14. *Ezek.* 10th chap. *Ezek.* 11: 24, 25. *Ezek.* 37: 1–10. *Ezek.* 40th chap. to *Ezek.* 48th chap.

To Nebuchadnezzar. *Dan.* 2: 28. *Dan.* 4: 5.

To Daniel. *Dan.* 2: 19. *Dan.* 7th chap. *Dan.* 8th chap. *Dan.* 10th chap.

To Amos. *Amos* 7: 1–9. *Amos* 8: 1–6. *Amos* 9: 1.

To Zechariah. *Zech.* 1: 8. *Zech.* 3: 1. *Zech.* 4: 2. *Zech.* 5: 2. *Zech.* 6: 1.

To Paul. *Acts* 9: 3, 6, 12. *Acts* 16: 9. *Acts* 18: 9. *Acts* 22: 18. *Acts* 27: 23. *2 Cor.* 12: 1–4.

To Ananias. *Acts* 9: 10, 11.

To Cornelius. *Acts* 10: 3.

To Peter. *Acts* 10: 9–17.

To John. *Rev.* 1: 12, etc. *Rev.* 4th chap. to *Rev.* 22nd chap.

Sometimes withheld for a long season. *1 Sam.* 3: 1.

The withholding of a great calamity. *Prov.* 29: 18. *Lam.* 2: 9.

False prophets pretended to have seen. *Jer.* 14: 14. *Jer.* 23: 16.

The prophets of God skilled in interpreting. *2 Chron.* 26: 5. *Dan.* 1: 17.

VOWS

Solemn promises to God. *Ps.* 76: 11.

Were made in reference to

Devoting the person to God. *Num.* 6: 2.

Dedicating children to God. *1 Sam.* 1: 11.

Devoting property to God. *Gen.* 28: 22.

Offering sacrifices. *Lev.* 7: 16. *Lev.* 22: 18, 22. *Num.* 15: 3.

Afflicting the soul. *Num.* 30: 13.

To be voluntary. *Deut.* 23: 21, 22.

To be performed faithfully. *Num.* 30: 2.

To be performed without delay. *Deut.* 23: 21, 23.

Danger of inconsiderately making. *Prov.* 20: 25.

Of children void without consent of parents. *Num.* 30: 3–5.

Of married women void without consent of husbands. *Num.* 30: 6–8, 10–13.

Of widows and women divorced from their husbands binding. *Num.* 30: 9.

Of wives, could only be objected to at the time of making. *Num.* 30: 14, 15.

Might be redeemed by paying a suitable compensation. *Lev.* 27: 1–8, 11–23.

Clean beasts the subjects of, not to be redeemed. *Lev.* 27: 9, 10.

Recorded in scripture;

Of Jacob. *Gen.* 28: 20–22. *Gen.* 31: 13.

Of Israelites. *Num.* 21: 2.

Of Jephthah. *Judges* 11: 30, 31.

Of Hannah. 1 *Sam.* 1: 11.

Of Elkanah. 1 *Sam.* 1: 24.

Of David. *Ps.* 132: 2, 5.

Of Mariners who cast out Jonah. *Jonah* 1: 16.

Of Jonah. *Jonah* 2: 9.

Of Lemuel's mother. *Prov.* 31: 1, 2.

Of Paul. *Acts* 18: 18.

Of certain Jews with Paul. *Acts* 21: 23, 24, 26.

All things dedicated by, to be brought to the tabernacle. *Deut.* 12: 6, 11, 17, 18, 26.

Of things corrupt or blemished an insult to God. *Lev.* 22: 23. *Mal.* 1: 14.

The hire of a prostitute or price of a dog could not be the subject of. *Deut.* 23: 18.

WAITING UPON GOD

As the God of providence. *Jer.* 14: 22.

As the God of salvation. *Ps.* 25: 5.

As the Giver of all temporal blessings. *Ps.* 104: 27, 28. *Ps.* 145: 15, 16.

For

Mercy. *Ps.* 123: 2.

Pardon. *Ps.* 39: 7, 8.

The consolation of Israel. *Luke* 2: 25.

Salvation. *Gen.* 49: 18. *Ps.* 62: 1, 2.

Guidance and teaching. *Ps.* 25: 5.

Protection. *Ps.* 33: 20. *Ps.* 59: 9, 10.

The fulfilment of his word. *Hab.* 2: 3.

The fulfilment of his promises. *Acts* 1: 4.

Hope of righteousness by faith. *Gal.* 5: 5.

Coming of Christ. 1 *Cor.* 1: 7. 1 *Thess.* 1: 10.

Is good. *Ps.* 52: 9.

God calls us to. *Zeph.* 3: 8.

Exhortations and encouragements to. *Ps.* 27: 14. *Ps.* 37: 7. *Hos.* 12: 6.

Should be

With the soul. *Ps.* 62: 1, 5.

With earnest desire. *Ps.* 130: 6.

With patience. *Ps.* 37: 7. *Ps.* 40: 1.

With resignation. *Lam.* 3: 26.

With hope in his word. *Ps.* 130: 5.

With full confidence. *Mic.* 7: 7.

Continually. *Hos.* 12: 6.

All the day. *Ps.* 25: 5.

Specially in adversity. *Ps.* 59: 1–9. *Isa.* 8: 17.

In the way of his judgments. *Isa.* 26: 8.

Saints resolve on. *Ps.* 52: 9. *Ps.* 59: 9.

Saints have expectation from. *Ps.* 62: 5.

Saints plead, in prayer. *Ps.* 25: 21. *Isa.* 33: 2.

The patience of saints often tried in. *Ps.* 69: 3.

They who engage in,

Wait upon him only. *Ps.* 62: 5.

Are heard. *Ps.* 40: 1.

Are blessed. *Isa.* 30: 18. *Dan.* 12: 12.

Experience his goodness. *Lam.* 3: 25.

Shall not be ashamed. *Ps.* 25: 3. *Isa.* 49: 23.

Shall renew their strength, etc. *Isa.* 40: 31.

Shall inherit the earth. *Ps.* 37: 9.

Shall be saved. *Prov.* 20: 22. *Isa.* 25: 9.

Shall rejoice in salvation. *Isa.* 25: 9.

Shall receive the glorious things prepared by God for them. *Isa.* 64: 4.

Predicted of the Gentiles. *Isa.* 42: 4. *Isa.* 60: 9.

Illustrated. *Ps.* 123: 2. *Luke* 12: 36. *Jas.* 5: 7.

Exemplified. JACOB, *Gen.* 49: 18. DAVID, *Ps.* 39: 7. ISAIAH, *Isa.* 8: 17. MICAH, *Mic.* 7: 7. JOSEPH OF ARIMATHAEA, *Mark* 15: 43.

WARFARE OF SAINTS

Is not after the flesh. 2 *Cor.* 10: 3.

Is a good warfare. 1 *Tim.* 1: 18, 19.

Called the good fight of faith. 1 *Tim.* 6: 12.

Is against

The devil. *Gen.* 3: 15. 2 *Cor.* 2: 11. *Eph.* 6: 12. *Jas.* 4: 7. 1 *Pet.* 5: 8. *Rev.* 12: 17.

The flesh. *Rom.* 7: 23. 1 *Cor.* 9: 25–27. 2 *Cor.* 12: 7. *Gal.* 5: 17. 1 *Pet.* 2: 11.

Enemies. *Ps.* 38: 19. *Ps.* 56: 2. *Ps.* 59: 3.

The world. *John* 16: 33. 1 *John* 5: 4, 5.

Death. 1 *Cor.* 15: 26, with *Heb.* 2: 14, 15.

Often arises from the opposition of friends or relatives. *Mic.* 7: 6, with *Matt.* 10: 35, 36.

To be carried on

Under Christ, as our Captain. *Heb.* 2: 10.

Under the Lord's banner. *Ps.* 60: 4.

With faith. 1 *Tim.* 1: 18, 19.

With a good conscience. 1 *Tim.* 1: 18, 19.

With stedfastness in the faith. 1 *Cor.* 16: 13. 1 *Pet.* 5: 9, with *Heb.* 10: 23.

With earnestness. *Jude* 3.

With watchfulness. 1 *Cor.* 16: 13. *Pet.* 5: 8.

With sobriety. 1 *Thess.* 5: 6. 1 *Pet.* 5: 8.

With endurance of hardness. 2 *Tim.* 2: 3, 10.

With self-denial. 1 *Cor.* 9: 25–27.

With confidence in God. *Ps.* 27: 1–3.

With prayer. *Ps.* 35: 1–3. *Eph.* 6: 18.

Without earthly entanglements. 2 *Tim.* 2: 4.

Mere professors do not maintain. *Jer.* 9: 3.

Saints

Are all engaged in. *Phil.* 1: 30.

Must stand firm in. *Eph.* 6: 13, 14.

Exhorted to diligence in. 1 *Tim.* 6: 12. *Jude* 3.

Encouraged in. *Isa.* 41: 11,

12. *Isa.* 51: 12. *Mic.* 7: 8. 1 *John* 4: 4.

Helped by God in. *Ps.* 118: 13. *Isa.* 41: 13, 14.

Helped by God in. *Ps.* 118: 13. *Isa.*

Protected by God in. *Ps.* 140: 7.

Comforted by God in. 2 *Cor.* 7: 5, 6.

Strengthened by God in. *Ps.* 20: 2. *Ps.* 27: 14. *Isa.* 41: 10.

Strengthened by Christ in. 2 *Cor.* 12: 9. 2 *Tim.* 4: 17.

Delivered by Christ in. 2 *Tim.* 4: 18.

Thank God for victory in. *Rom.* 7: 25. 1 *Cor.* 15: 57.

Armour for,

Girdle of truth. *Eph.* 6: 14.

Breastplate of righteousness. *Eph.* 6: 14.

Preparation of the gospel. *Eph.* 6: 15.

Shield of faith. *Eph.* 6: 16.

Helmet of salvation. *Eph.* 6: 17. 1 *Thess.* 5: 8.

Sword of the Spirit. *Eph.* 6: 17.

Called armour of God. *Eph.* 6: 11.

Called armour of righteousness. 2 *Cor.* 6: 7.

Called armour of light. *Rom.* 13: 12.

Not carnal. 2 *Cor.* 10: 4.

Mighty through God. 2 *Cor.* 10: 4, 5.

The whole, is required. *Eph.* 6: 13.

Must be put on. *Rom.* 13: 12. *Eph.* 6: 11.

To be on right hand and left. 2 *Cor.* 6: 7

Victory in, is

From God. 1 *Cor.* 15: 57. 2 *Cor.* 2: 14.

Through Christ. *Rom.* 7: 25. 1 *Cor.* 15: 27. 2 *Cor.* 12: 9. *Rev.* 12: 11.

By faith. *Heb.* 11: 33–37. 1 *John* 5: 4, 5.

Over the devil. *Rom.* 16: 20. 1 *John* 2: 14.

Over the flesh. *Rom.* 7: 24, 25. *Gal.* 5: 24.

Over the world. 1 *John* 5: 4, 5.

Over all that exalts itself. 2 *Cor.* 10: 5.

Over death and the grave. *Isa.* 25: 8. *Isa.* 26: 19. *Hos.* 13: 14. 1 *Cor.* 15: 54, 55.

Triumphant. *Rom.* 8: 37. 2 *Cor.* 10: 5.

They who overcome in, shall

Eat of the hidden manna. *Rev.* 2: 17.

Eat of the tree of life. *Rev.* 2: 7.

Be clothed in white raiment. *Rev.* 3: 5.

Be pillars in the temple of God. *Rev.* 3: 12.

Sit with Christ in his throne. *Rev.* 3: 21.

Have a white stone, and, in it a new name written. *Rev.* 2: 17.

Have power over the nations. *Rev.* 2: 26.

Have the name of God written upon them by Christ. *Rev.* 3: 12.

Have God as their God. *Rev.* 21: 7.

Have the morning-star. *Rev.* 2: 28.

Inherit all things. *Rev.* 21: 7.

Be confessed by Christ before God the Father. *Rev.* 3: 5.

Be sons of God. *Rev.* 21: 7.

Not be hurt by the second death. *Rev.* 2: 11.

Not have their names blotted out of the book of life. *Rev.* 3: 5.

Illustrated. *Isa.* 9: 5. *Zech.* 10: 5.

WATCHFULNESS

Christ an example of. *Matt.* 26: 38, 40. *Luke* 6: 12.

Commanded. *Mark* 13: 37. *Rev.* 3: 2.

Exhortations to. 1 *Thess.* 5: 6. 1 *Pet.* 4: 7.

God especially requires in ministers. *Ezek.* 3: 17, with *Isa.* 62: 6. *Mark* 13: 34.

Ministers exhorted to. *Acts* 20: 31. 2 *Tim.* 4: 5.

Faithful ministers exercise. *Heb.* 13: 17.

Faithful ministers approved by. *Matt.* 24: 45, 46. *Luke* 12: 41–44.

Should be

With prayer. *Luke* 21: 36. *Eph.* 6: 18.

With thanksgiving. *Col.* 4: 2.

With stedfastness in the faith. 1 *Cor.* 16: 13.

With heedfulness. *Mark* 13: 33.

With sobriety. 1 *Thess.* 5: 6. 1 *Pet.* 4: 7.

At all times. *Prov.* 8: 34.

In all things. 2 *Tim.* 4: 5.

Saints pray to be kept in a state of. *Ps.* 141: 3.

Motives to;

Expected direction from God. *Hab.* 2: 1.

Uncertain time of the coming of Christ. *Matt.* 24: 42. *Matt.* 25: 13. *Mark* 13: 35, 36.

Incessant assaults of the devil. 1 *Pet.* 5: 8.

Liability to temptation. *Matt.* 26: 41.

Blessedness of. *Luke* 12: 37. *Rev.* 16: 15.

Unfaithful ministers devoid of. *Isa.* 56: 10.

The wicked averse to. 1 *Thess.* 5: 7.

Danger of remissness in. *Matt.* 24: 48–51. *Matt.* 25: 5, 8, 12. *Rev.* 3: 3.

Illustrated. *Luke* 12: 35, 36.

Exemplified. DAVID, *Ps.* 102: 7. ANNA, *Luke* 2: 37. PAUL, 2 *Cor.* 11: 27.

WICKED, THE, ARE COMPARED TO

Abominable branches. *Isa.* 14: 19.

Ashes under the feet. *Mal.* 4: 3.

Bad fishes. *Matt.* 13: 48.

Beasts. *Ps.* 49: 12. 2 *Pet.* 2: 12.

Blind, The. *Zeph.* 1: 17. *Matt.* 15: 14.

Brass and iron, etc. *Jer.* 6: 28. *Ezek.* 22: 18.

Briars and thorns. *Isa.* 55: 13. *Ezek.* 2: 6.

Bulls of Bashan. *Ps.* 22: 12.

Carcasses trodden under feet. *Isa.* 14: 19.

Chaff. *Job* 21: 18. *Ps.* 1: 4. *Matt.* 3: 12.

Clouds without water. *Jude* 12.

Corn blasted. 2 *Kings* 19: 26.

Corrupt trees. *Luke* 6: 43.

Deaf adders. *Ps.* 58: 4.

Dogs. *Prov.* 26: 11. *Matt.* 7: 6. 2 *Pet.* 2: 22.

Dross. *Ps.* 119: 119. *Ezek.* 22: 18, 19.

Early dew that passeth away. *Hos.* 13: 3.

Evil figs. *Jer.* 24: 8.

Fading oaks. *Isa.* 1: 30.

Fiery oven. *Ps.* 21: 9. *Hos.* 7: 4.

Fire of thorns. *Ps.* 118: 12.

Fools building upon sand. *Matt.* 7: 26.

Fuel of fire. *Isa.* 9: 19.

Garden without water. *Isa.* 1: 30.

Goats. *Matt.* 25: 32.

Grass. *Ps.* 37: 2. *Ps.* 92: 7.

Grass on the house-top. 2 *Kings* 19: 26.

Green bay-trees. *Ps.* 37: 35.

Green herbs. *Ps.* 37: 2.

Heath in the desert. *Jer.* 17: 6.

Horses rushing into the battle. *Jer.* 8: 6.

Idols. *Ps.* 115: 8.

Lions greedy of prey. *Ps.* 17: 12.

Melting wax. *Ps.* 68: 2.

Morning-clouds. *Hos.* 13: 3.

Moth-eaten garments. *Isa.* 50: 9. *Isa.* 51: 8.

Passing whirlwinds. *Prov.* 10: 25.

Potsherds. *Prov.* 26: 23.

Raging waves of the sea. *Jude* 13.

Reprobate silver. *Jer.* 6: 30.

Scorpions. *Ezek.* 2: 6.

Serpents. *Ps.* 58: 4. *Matt.* 23: 33.

Smoke. *Hos.* 13: 3.

Stony ground. *Matt.* 13: 5.

Stubble. *Job* 21: 18. *Mal.* 4: 1.

Swine. *Matt.* 7: 6. 2 *Pet.* 2: 22.

Tares. *Matt.* 13: 38.

Troubled sea. *Isa.* 57: 20.

Visions of the night. *Job* 20: 8.

Wandering stars. *Jude* 13.

Wayward children. *Matt.* 11: 16.

Wells without water. 2 *Pet.* 2: 17.

Wheels. *Ps.* 83: 13.

Whited sepulchres. *Matt.* 23: 27.

Wild ass's colts. *Job* 11: 12.

WIDOWS

Character of true. *Luke* 2: 37. *Tim.* 5: 5, 10.

God

Surely hears the cry of. *Exod.* 22: 23.

Judges for. *Deut.* 10: 18. *Ps.* 68: 5.

Relieves. *Ps.* 146: 9.

Establishes the border of. *Prov.* 15: 25.

Will witness against oppressors of. *Mal.* 3: 5.

Exhorted to trust in God. *Jer.* 49: 11.

Should not be

Afflicted. *Exod.* 22: 22.

Oppressed. *Jer.* 7: 6. *Zech.* 7: 10.

Treated with violence. *Jer.* 22: 3.

Deprived of raiment in pledge. *Deut.* 24: 17.

Should be

Pleaded for. *Isa.* 1: 17.

Honoured, if widows indeed. 1 *Tim.* 5: 3.

Relieved by their friends. 1 *Tim.* 5: 4, 16.

Relieved by the Church. *Acts* 6: 1. 1 *Tim.* 5: 9.

Visited in affliction. *Jas.* 1: 27.

Allowed to share in our blessings. *Deut.* 14: 29. *Deut.* 16: 11, 14. *Deut.* 24: 19–21.

Though poor, may be liberal. *Mark* 12: 42, 43.

When young, exposed to many temptations. 1 *Tim.* 5: 11–14.

Saints

Relieve. *Acts* 9: 39.

Cause joy to. *Job* 29: 13.

Disappoint not. *Job* 31: 16.

The wicked

Do no good to. *Job* 24: 21.

Send away empty. *Job* 22: 9.

Take pledges from. *Job* 24: 3.

Reject the cause of. *Isa.* 1: 23.

Vex. *Ezek.* 22: 7.

Make a prey of. *Isa.* 10: 2. *Matt.* 23: 14.

Slay. *Ps.* 94: 6.

Curse for perverting judgment of. *Deut.* 27: 19.

Woe to those who oppress. *Isa.* 10: 1, 2.

Blessings on those who relieve. *Deut.* 14: 29.

A type of Zion in affliction. *Lam.* 5: 3.

WISDOM OF GOD, THE

Is one of his attributes. 1 *Sam.* 2: 3. *Job* 9: 4.

Described as

Perfect. *Job* 36: 4. *Job* 37: 16.

Mighty. *Job* 36: 5.

Universal. *Job* 28: 24. *Dan.* 2: 22. *Acts* 15: 18.

Infinite. *Ps.* 147: 5. *Rom.* 11: 33.

Unsearchable. *Isa.* 40: 28. *Rom.* 11: 33.

Wonderful. *Ps.* 139: 6.

Beyond human comprehension. *Ps.* 139: 6.

Incomparable. *Isa.* 44: 7. *Jer.* 10: 7.

Underived. *Job* 21: 22. *Isa.* 40: 44.

The gospel contains treasures of. 1 *Cor.* 2: 7.

Wisdom of saints is derived from. *Ezek.* 7: 25.

All human wisdom derived from. *Dan.* 2: 21.

Saints ascribe to him. *Dan.* 2: 20.

Exhibited in

His works. *Job* 37: 16. *Ps.* 104: 24. *Ps.* 136: 5. *Prov.* 3: 19. *Jer.* 10: 12.

His counsels. *Isa.* 28: 29. *Jer.* 32: 19.

His foreshowing events. *Isa.* 42: 9. *Isa.* 46: 10.

Redemption. 1 *Cor.* 1: 24. *Eph.* 1: 8. *Eph.* 3: 10.

Searching the heart. 1 *Chron.* 28: 9.

Understanding the thoughts. 1 *Chron.* 28: 9. *Ps.* 139: 2.

Exhibited in knowing

The heart. *Ps.* 44: 21. *Prov.* 15: 11. *Luke* 16: 15.

The actions. *Job* 34: 21. *Ps.* 139: 2, 3.

The words. *Ps.* 139: 4.

His saints. 2 *Sam.* 7: 20. 2 *Tim.* 2: 19.

The way of saints. *Job* 23: 10. *Ps.* 1: 6.

The wants of saints. *Deut.* 2: 7. *Matt.* 6: 8.

The afflictions of saints. *Exod.* 3: 7. *Ps.* 142: 3.

The infirmities of saints. *Ps.* 103: 14.

The minutest matters. *Matt.* 10: 29, 30.

The most secret things. *Matt.* 6: 18.

The time of judgment. *Matt.* 24: 36.

The wicked. *Neh.* 9: 10. *Job* 11: 11.

The works, etc., of the wicked. *Isa.* 66: 18.

Nothing is concealed from. *Ps.* 139: 12.

The wicked question. *Ps.* 73: 11. *Isa.* 47: 10.

Should be magnified. *Rom.* 16: 27. *Jude* 25.

WITNESS OF THE HOLY SPIRIT

Is truth. 1 *John* 5: 6.

To be implicitly received. 1 *John* 5: 6, 9.

Borne to Christ

As Messiah. *Luke* 3: 22, with *John* 1: 32, 33.

As coming to redeem and sanctify. 1 *John* 5: 6.

As exalted to be a Prince and Saviour to give repentance, etc. *Acts* 5: 31, 32.

As perfecting saints. *Heb.* 10: 14, 15.

As foretold by himself. *John* 15: 26.

In heaven. 1 *John* 5: 7, 11.

On earth. 1 *John* 5: 8.

The first preaching of the gospel confirmed by. *Acts* 14: 3, with *Heb.* 2: 4.

The faithful preaching of the Apostles accompanied by. 1 *Cor.* 2: 4. 1 *Thess.* 1: 5.

Given to saints

On believing. *Acts* 15: 8. 1 *John* 5: 10.

To testify to them of Christ. *John* 15: 26.

As an evidence of adoption. *Rom.* 8: 16.

As an evidence of Christ in them. 1 *John* 3: 24.

As an evidence of God in them. 1 *John* 4: 13.

Borne against all unbelievers. *Neh.* 9: 30. *Acts* 28: 25–27.

WIVES

Not to be selected from among the ungodly. *Gen.* 24: 3. *Gen.* 26: 34, 35. *Gen.* 28: 1.

Duties of, to their husbands;

To love them. *Titus* 2: 4.

To reverence them. *Eph.* 5: 33.

To be faithful to them. 1 *Cor.* 7: 3–5, 10.

To be subject to them. *Gen.* 3: 16. *Eph.* 5: 22, 24. 1 *Pet.* 3: 1.

To obey them. 1 *Cor.* 14: 34. *Titus* 2: 5.

To remain with them for life. *Rom.* 7: 2, 3.

Should be adorned

Not with ornaments. 1 *Tim.* 2: 9. 1 *Pet.* 3: 3.

With modesty and sobriety. 1 *Tim.* 2: 9.

With a meek and quiet spirits. 1 *Pet.* 3: 4, 5.

With a meek and quiet spirit. 2: 10. 1 *Tim.* 5: 10.

Good,

Are from the Lord. *Prov.* 19: 14.

Are a token of the favour of God. *Prov.* 18: 22.

Are a blessing to husbands. *Prov.* 12: 4. *Prov.* 31: 10, 12.

Bring honour on husbands. *Prov.* 31: 23.

Secure confidence of husbands. *Prov.* 31: 11.

Are praised by husbands. *Prov.* 31: 28.

Are diligent and prudent. *Prov.* 31: 13–27.

Are benevolent to the poor. *Prov.* 31: 20.

Duty of, to unbelieving husbands. 1 *Cor.* 7: 13, 14, 16. 1 *Pet.* 3: 1, 2.

Should be silent in the Churches. 1 *Cor.* 14: 34.

Should seek religious instruction from their husbands. 1 *Cor.* 14: 35.

Of ministers should be exemplary. 1 *Tim.* 3: 11.

Good—Exemplified. WIFE OF MANOAH, *Judges* 13: 10. ORPAH AND RUTH, *Ruth* 1: 4, 8. ABIGAIL, 1 *Sam.* 25: 3. ESTHER, *Esther* 2: 15–17. ELIZABETH, *Luke* 1: 6. PRISCILLA, *Acts* 18: 2, 26. SARAH, 1 *Pet.* 3: 6.

Bad—Exemplified. SAMSON'S WIFE, *Judges* 14: 15–17. MICHAL, 2 *Sam.* 6: 16. JEZEBEL, 1 *Kings* 21: 25. ZERESH, *Esther* 5: 14. JOB'S WIFE, *Job* 2: 9. HERODIAS, *Mark* 6: 17. SAPPHIRA, *Acts* 5: 1, 2.

WORKS, GOOD

Christ, an example of. *John* 10: 32. *Acts* 10: 38.

Called

Good fruits. *Jas.* 3: 17.

Fruits meet for repentance. *Matt.* 3: 8.

Fruits of righteousness. *Phil.* 1: 11.

Works and labours of love. *Heb.* 6: 10.

Are by Jesus Christ to the glory and praise of God. *Phil.* 1: 11.

They, alone, who abide in Christ can perform. *John* 15: 4, 5.

Wrought by God in us. *Isa.* 26: 12. *Phil.* 2: 13.

The scripture designed to lead us to. 2 *Tim.* 3: 16, 17. *Jas.* 1: 25.

To be performed in Christ's name. *Col.* 3: 17.

Heavenly wisdom is full of. *Jas.* 3: 17.

Justification unattainable by. *Rom.* 3: 20. *Gal.* 2: 16.

Salvation unattainable by. *Eph.* 2: 8, 9. 2 *Tim.* 1: 9. *Titus* 3: 5.

Saints

Created in Christ unto. *Eph.* 2: 10.

Preordained to walk in. *Eph.* 2: 10.

Exhorted to put on. *Col.* 3: 12–14.

Are full of. *Acts* 9: 36.

Are zealous of. *Titus* 2: 14.

Should be furnished unto all. 2 *Tim.* 3: 17.

Should be rich in. 1 *Tim.* 6: 18.

Should be careful to maintain. *Titus* 3: 8, 14.

Should be stablished in. 2 *Thess.* 2: 17.

Should be fruitful in. *Col.* 1: 10.

Should be perfect in. *Heb.* 13: 21.

Should be prepared unto all. 2 *Tim.* 2: 21.

Should abound to all. 2 *Cor.* 9: 8.

Should be ready to all. *Titus* 3: 1.

Should manifest, with meekness. *Jas.* 3: 13.

Should provoke each other to. *Heb.* 10: 24.

Should avoid ostentation in. *Matt.* 6: 1–18.

Bring to the light their. *John* 3: 21.

Followed into rest by their. *Rev.* 14: 13.

Holy women should manifest. 1 *Tim.* 2: 10. 1 *Tim.* 5: 10.

God remembers. *Neh.* 13: 14, with *Heb.* 6: 9, 10.

Shall be brought into the judgment. *Eccles.* 12: 14, with 2 *Cor.* 5: 10.

In the judgment, will be an evidence of faith. *Matt.* 25: 34—40, with *Jas.* 2: 14—20.

Ministers should

Be patterns of. *Titus* 2: 7.

Exhort to. 1 *Tim.* 6: 17, 18. *Titus* 3: 1, 8, 14.

God is glorified by. *John* 15: 8.

Designed to lead others to glorify God. *Matt.* 5: 16. 1 *Pet.* 2: 12.

A blessing attends. *Jas.* 1: 25.

The wicked reprobate unto. *Titus* 1: 16.

Illustrated. *John* 15: 5.

ZEAL

Christ an example of. *Ps.* 69: 9. *John* 2: 17.

Godly sorrow leads to. 2 *Cor.* 7: 10, 11.

Of saints, ardent. *Ps.* 119: 139.

Provokes others to do good. 2 *Cor.* 9: 2.

Should be exhibited

In spirit. *Rom.* 12: 11.

In well-doing. *Gal.* 4: 18. *Titus* 2: 14.

In desiring the salvation of others. *Acts* 26: 29. *Rom.* 10: 1.

In contending for the faith. *Jude* 3.

In missionary labours. *Rom.* 15: 19, 23.

For the glory of God. *Num.* 25: 11, 13.

For the welfare of saints. *Col.* 4: 13.

Against idolatry. 2 *Kings* 23: 4—14.

Sometimes wrongly directed. 2 *Sam.* 21: 2. *Acts* 22: 3, 4. *Phil.* 3: 6.

Sometimes not according to knowledge. *Rom.* 10: 2. *Gal.* 1: 14. *Acts* 21: 20.

Ungodly men sometimes pretend to. 2 *Kings* 10: 16. *Matt.* 23: 15.

Exhortation to. *Rom.* 12: 11. *Rev.* 3: 19.

Holy—Exemplified. PHINEHAS, *Num.* 25: 11, 13. JOSIAH, 2 *Kings* 23: 19—25. APOLLOS, *Acts* 18: 25. CORINTHIANS, 1 *Cor.* 14: 12. EPAPHRAS, *Col.* 4: 12, 13.